RENEWING
the
CHRISTIAN
MIND

ALSO BY DALLAS WILLARD

The Allure of Gentleness:
Defending the Faith in the Manner of Jesus

The Spirit of the Disciplines:
Understanding How God Changes Lives

The Divine Conspiracy:
Rediscovering Our Hidden Life in God

Hearing God:
Developing a Conversational Relationship with God

Renovation of the Heart:
Putting on the Character of Christ

The Great Omission:
Reclaiming Jesus's Essential Teachings on Discipleship

Knowing Christ Today:
Why We Can Trust Spiritual Knowledge

Living in Christ's Presence:
Final Words on Heaven and the Kingdom of God
(with John Ortberg)

The Divine Conspiracy Continued:
Fulfilling God's Kingdom on Earth
(coauthored by Gary Black Jr.)

RENEWING *the* CHRISTIAN MIND

Essays, Interviews, and Talks

DALLAS WILLARD

Edited by Gary Black Jr.

HarperOne
An Imprint of HarperCollins*Publishers*

FIRST EDITION

Designed by Beth Shagene

Library of Congress Cataloging-in-Publication Data

Names: Willard, Dallas, author.
Title: Renewing the Christian mind : essays, interviews, and talks / Dallas Willard.
Description: First edition. | New York, NY : HarperOne, [2016] | Includes bibliographical references and index.
Identifiers: LCCN 2016006044 (print) | LCCN 2016016686 (ebook) | ISBN 9780062296139 (pbk.) | ISBN 9780062472403 (audio) | ISBN 9780062296153 (ebook)
Subjects: LCSH: Theology, Doctrinal--United States. | Evangelicalism--United States.
Classification: LCC BX4827.W47 A25 2016 (print) | LCC BX4827.W47 (ebook) | DDC 230--dc23
LC record available at https://lccn.loc.gov/2016006044

18 19 20 21 LSC(H) 10 9 8 7 6 5 4 3 2

Contents

Introduction

The original kernel of an idea for publishing a Dallas Willard anthology surfaced in 2009. It came during the first of what would become several visits I made from the United Kingdom to Southern California to conduct research interviews with Dallas. We discussed his theological and philosophical work for my Ph.D. dissertation, which describes Dallas's influence on evangelical faith.[*] During a break in our conversations, Dallas took the opportunity to search for a reference in an article he'd written years prior. We walked from the living room to his office, and he opened a large drawer in a gray metal file cabinet full of manila file folders. The cabinet was a treasure chest of ideas. What you now hold in your hands are many of the articles that filled that fateful cabinet. Later that day we took a break for coffee, and he led me on a short walk around his property. He introduced me to the flora, including several fruit trees; fauna; and wildlife that nestled nearby. Eventually we came to the little white house adjacent to his property that held his extensive library. There he and I rummaged through several boxes of other writings—as well as audiocassette tapes of sermons, lectures, and speaking engagements—that spanned an enormously wide variety of subjects. At the time the vast array of topics I found was dizzying. I'm still overwhelmed by the scope of Dallas's thoughtfulness, how prolific his writing is, and the depth of his expertise on subjects ranging from epistemology to theology.

---

[*] This research can be found in Gary Black Jr., *The Theology of Dallas Willard: Discovering Protoevangelical Faith* (Eugene, OR: Pickwick Publications, 2013).

That afternoon, two very sobering realizations immediately consumed my thoughts. First, I realized that unless I was able to quickly narrow the research topics for my dissertation, I might never finish. Second, I became certain that the material he was showing me must be brought to light for the common good. We need and will benefit from continuing to hear Dallas's incisive voice of wisdom and grace engaging the essential realities of human existence and the eternal quality of life offered within the realm of Christ and his kingdom.

Many readers may be coming to Dallas's works for the first time. It's a privilege for me to provide them with at least some brief biographical details about this fascinating, humble, and erudite man.

Dallas Albert Willard was born in the impoverished, rural setting of Buffalo, Missouri, on September 4, 1935, during the height of the Great Depression. He began his studies at William Jewel College in Liberty, Missouri, and went on to earn his B.A. in psychology from Tennessee Temple College in Chattanooga, Tennessee, in 1956. It was at Tennessee Temple, at nineteen years of age, that he met and married his wife, Jane Lakes Willard, in 1955. Dallas earned another bachelor's degree in philosophy and religion from Baylor University in 1957 before moving to Madison, Wisconsin, and earning his Ph.D. in philosophy with a minor in the history of science from the University of Wisconsin.

Dallas accepted a teaching position at the University of Southern California in 1965, where he remained for forty-seven years. He was a decorated scholar and received Outstanding Faculty, Outstanding Contributions to Student Life, and Excellence in Teaching awards in recognition of his work. His dedication to his teaching, students, colleagues, and staff was legendary. USC colleague Donald Miller remembers Dallas as possessing "an encyclopedic mind" that left students awed by his wide range of knowledge.

But it wasn't just his teaching and intellect that drew people to Dallas. John Ortberg, a longtime friend and world-renowned pastor and writer, reflected that Dallas was not only the smartest man he'd ever met, but also a man from "another time zone." Dallas lived a quality of life that was so strongly enmeshed in the realities and blessings that flow from the kingdom of God that being in relationship with Dallas helped shape and form the character of those who knew him best. In fact, there is a common phrase bantered about in groups of Dallas's close friends. When a subject, idea, or action is on the table for discussion, someone will often ask, "WWDD?" (or, What Would Dallas Do?). John expressed what so many, including me, have experienced in relationship with Dallas. Dallas's presence and character represented "the unhurried, humble, selfless attention of a human being who lived deeply in the genuine awareness of the reality of the kingdom of God." In short, Dallas was one of the godliest people many had ever met. And he inspired others to be the same.

In a September 2006 article in *Christianity Today*, Dallas noted that his academic career began in the 1960s after he heard God tell him, "If you stay in the churches, the university will be closed to you, but if you stay in the university, the churches will be open to you." Willard's initial academic interest was focused on the influential twentieth-century German philosopher Edmund Husserl, who is understood by many as the principal founder of the field of phenomenology and a stalwart thinker who fought for epistemic realism. Husserl's work captivated Dallas because of his recognition of the necessity to understand that human beings must seek, and can attain, increasing levels of the knowledge of things as they are in and of themselves. And no search for knowledge was more intriguing to Dallas than that for the true knowledge of God, which is closely followed by the knowledge of the existential nature, formation, and transformation of the human soul. God, truth, and humanity, for Dallas, were the doorways that eventually led to every subject under the sun.

It was this quest that initially led Dallas to study psychology, then theology and religion, finally settling on the field of philosophy. In his opinion, the discipline of philosophy provided the best, albeit not a perfect, means through which propositions surrounding the nature of God, reality, and the root essence of human existence could be investigated. Dallas never saw theology and philosophy as competitors but rather as complements of a single search for wisdom and the knowledge of God regarding all of creation. As such, his philosophical interests took him into areas as diverse as metaphysics; contemporary European philosophy; ethics, with an emphasis on moral knowledge; politics; law; professionalism; the ontology of concepts; reasoning and logic; aesthetics; the history of philosophy; language and thought; phenomenology; and the history of the philosophy of religion. Yet Dallas understood each of these subdisciplines as a means through which he could engage philosophy's, humanity's, and scripture's four basic questions: What is real? What is the good life? Who is a good person? And, How does one become a good person?

Dallas taught that each of these questions has been thoroughly engaged—in some form or another—by the biblical writers, the gospel of Jesus, and church forebearers throughout the ages. Yet he gave his life to the belief that this search for increased understanding and awareness of God on the critical issues of our day must continue. In that way he could be understood as a "progressive," because he believed that as followers of Christ we should always seek wisdom and virtue as we conform our hearts and minds to the likeness of Christ. Thus, we must never stop seeking, asking for, progressing toward, and finding the truth about the nature of our creation and Creator.

But he was also a stalwart conservative. Dallas held that historic Christian knowledge represents the "knowledge of God" made available to us through tradition, scriptures, reason, and experience. As such, we must be willing to suffer the consequences of conserving the truth, speaking truth in love, and trusting God to care for us when the public tide turns away from what God has revealed as good and best. Dallas found purpose and meaning for himself and others in this search for knowledge and truth, and he spent his considerable talents spreading the Word of life, and the hope that comes from the fruit of repentance. Repentance for Dallas was captured in the Greek term *metanoia,* which he defined as reconsidering our considerations and rethinking our thinking. When this is done well, and truth is repentance's highest objective, the kingdom of God is close at hand.

What is key to understanding Dallas's contribution to American evangelical thought and Christian theology is the impact his world-class intellect made on leaders, teachers, and spokespersons within the church. Having lived and worked much of his life in the Bible belt and having remained a lifelong ordained Southern Baptist minister, Dallas was well aware of the crippling effects religious anti-intellectualism has on the sincere attempts innumerable Christians have made to understand and apply the knowledge of life and living that the gospel offers. Perhaps no other Christian thinker or writer in the past century has better deconstructed, and then fully reconstructed, a biblically valid, historically orthodox understanding of Christian theology and praxis than Dallas. Miller and others have compared the effect of Dallas's thoughtful yet incisive critique of and encouragement for the renewal of contemporary Evangelicalism to the work of C. S. Lewis, John Wesley, and even Martin Luther. My hope is that this volume continues that work.

The larger objective of this project is made up of two primary goals. First, this collection is designed as a tool to introduce a new generation of minds to Dallas's thought, allowing them to see and then come to a better appreciation of not only Dallas's depth and breadth of knowledge, but also his commitment to the inescapable veracity of philosophical and theological realism. These essays, interviews, and lectures will provide those coming to Dallas's work for the first time with a clear and easily understandable introduction to the wide horizon of his worldview.

Second, for those deeply familiar with Dallas's previously published work, this reader also provides a greater depth of understanding on a multitude of issues he believed Jesus was interested in and master over. Through the years I've had the privilege of meeting and discussing Dallas's works with many of his readers and students. I've often noticed a tendency that many, although certainly not all, seem to focus their interest primarily on the areas of his writing where they already agree, but remain largely unaware of the larger scope of his work. The reader may be aware of something he wrote about fasting, but not his understanding of the atonement. And too few are aware of his lifelong devotion to moral knowledge and the inescapable link he made between moral knowledge and the knowledge of Christ. I've often wondered whether this has resulted in too many readers missing the larger context and depth of vision he provided regarding the life and truth available to disciples of Jesus living within the kingdom of God. Dallas and I spoke about this phenomenon often over the years, and he would always shrug his shoulders, nod his head in agreement, and offer a somewhat perplexed but resolved response. He cared deeply about the impact of his work, but in the end he gave the results of his efforts up to God. Even still, I hope—as did Dallas—that this publication will provide more opportunities for readers to develop a more coherent bracket of understanding around his scope and depth of thought.

These two goals combine to become part and parcel of a much larger hope. Dallas understood better than most that the scriptures—specifically, the gospel Jesus preached—compared and contrasted all the features and effects of the kingdom of God against the actuality of human life in all its broken glory. In doing so, Dallas understood Jesus as the greatest master of life who unveils and then fulfills the promise of an unparalleled field of moral knowledge for those who desire to follow in his way, truth, and life. This Christocentric understanding of the nature of reality, the purpose of life, the essence of the kingdom of God, the qualities and characteristics of God's person, the eternal features of the good life, and the inescapability of truth all stem from and are served best through coming face to face with Jesus, the Christ, the power and wisdom of God (1 Cor. 1:24). Such an opportunity and the consequences of compliance with, rebellion against, or ignorance of the ineffable nature of God and God's ways will echo throughout all eternity. This is the ultimate goal of this work, for it is why Dallas spent his life and his unequaled talents describing, manifesting, teaching, and modeling the essential "goods" that Jesus reveals and demonstrates within his Good News.

Finally, one of the most poignant and enduring lessons I hope readers will receive from Dallas is the inescapable power of ideas. Ideas shape us. The potency of ideas carries the ability to not only influence but propel our actions, which then have a tendency, over time, to form our character. For Dallas the greatest and most crucial set of ideas for every human being, the one concept that carries the potential to shape and direct our lives more than any other, is what we think of, how we conceive of, what ideas we maintain or are bereft of regarding the existential nature and character of God. For Dallas, Jesus was the interpreter, the hermeneutic, the messenger, the revealer, the manifestation of the very "visible image of the invisible God" (Col. 1:15, NLT). Therefore, it is Jesus alone who best leads us into both the knowledge of God's personal character and God's knowledge regarding our world, our lives, and our destinies. These pages engage many of the crucial ideas that Dallas believed the scriptures address related to these eternal subjects, and how to best think about God's wisdom and then apply it to the activities and circumstances of everyday living. It was Dallas's prayer, and remains mine for this volume, that his writings will lead others into the wisdom, knowledge, love, grace, and truth of Christ that Dallas experienced and yearned to introduce to others.

Dallas's mother died when he was very young. But Dallas told me not long before his death that one of his mother's dying requests of his father was to "keep eternity ever before the children." This collection is but one more testament to that very legacy.

Grace and Peace.
Gary Black Jr.

PART I

Spiritual Transformation

CHAPTER 1

Transformation of the Mind

Though Dallas is best known for his Christian writings, his formal training was in the field of philosophy. The influence of Greek philosophy on his religious writings is apparent in several of his works. He often argued that Socrates's, Plato's, and Aristotle's brilliance was not only in their recognition of the need for moral reformation, but also in their revolutionary inductive method of leading people to moral knowledge. Dallas believed perhaps the ancient Greeks' greatest achievement was in recognizing the primacy of the human soul and the belief that knowledge of the good, at the level of the soul, would lead a person away from evil. By employing the Socratic method of teaching, Dallas helped many to better understand the specifics of why using a Christocentric lens is crucial for properly examining our lives. Therefore, I felt it appropriate that we start with this essay, which demonstrates the importance of the life of the mind and the transformational journey that is required in our pursuit of the knowledge of God.

First published in 2002 in *Renovation of the Heart*.

THE ULTIMATE FREEDOM WE HAVE AS HUMAN BEINGS IS THE power to select what we will allow our minds to dwell upon. It is in our thoughts that the first movements toward the renovation of the heart occur. Thoughts are the place where we can and must begin to change. There the light of God first begins to move upon us through the word of Christ, and there the divine Spirit begins to direct our will to God and his way. We are not totally free in this respect, but we do have great freedom here. We still have the ability and responsibility to try to retain God in our knowledge. And those who do so will surely make progress toward him; for if we truly do seek God as best we can, he, who always knows what is really in our hearts, will certainly make himself known to us.

Clearly our thoughts are one of the most basic sources of our life. By "thoughts" we mean all of the ways in which we are conscious of things—and it includes our memories, perceptions, and beliefs. Thoughts determine the orientation of everything we do and evoke the feelings that frame our world and motivate our actions. Interestingly, you can't evoke thoughts by feeling a certain way. However, we can evoke—and to some degree control—our feelings by directing our thoughts.

Our essential nature as active and creative beings depends upon our ability to envision what is not the case, as well as what is. Our ability to plan for the future must constantly run ahead of reality. And this we do in thought. A will that runs ahead depends, of course, upon our ability to think; and what we think, imagine, believe, or guess sets boundaries to what we can or will choose, and therefore to what we can create.

As our senses present a landscape for our body and its actions, so our thoughts present the "lifescape" for our will and our life as a whole. Within that "thought lifescape," which includes our perceptions, we make the decisions that determine what we will do and who we will become.

The realm of thought involves four main factors: ideas, images, information, and our ability to think. The two most powerful ones, of course, are ideas and images.

TRANSFORMING IDEAS

Ideas are very general models of our assumptions about reality. They are ways of thinking about and interpreting things. They are so pervasive and essential to how we think about and how we approach life that we often do not even know they are there or understand when and how they are at work. Examples of ideas may include freedom, education, the American dream, church, democracy, justice, family, God, and so on. And if you wish to see ideas in action, look closely at artistic endeavors in their various forms, such as movies and music—which encapsulate most of what is called pop culture—or efforts to persuade, such as in politics and commercials.

Christian spiritual formation is inescapably a matter of recognizing in ourselves the idea systems of evil that govern the present age and respective culture, as well as those that constitute life away from God. The needed transformation is largely a matter of replacing those idea systems of evil with the idea system that was embodied and taught by Jesus Christ. The apostle Paul, who also understood and taught about these things, warned us that "our struggle is not against flesh and blood, but against the rulers, against the powers, against the world forces of this darkness, against the spiritual forces of wickedness in the heavenly places" (Eph. 6:12). These higher-level powers and forces are spiritual agencies that work with the idea systems of evil. These systems are their main tool for dominating humanity.

By contrast, those who have been rescued "from the power of darkness and transferred into the kingdom of his beloved Son" (Col. 1:13) are to "let this mind be in you, which was also in Christ Jesus" (Phil. 2:5). This is what is intended when Christian colleges and universities speak about their unique commitment to Jesus Christ in their pursuit of all learning. It is an essential way of describing the substance—the underlying reality—of Christian spiritual formation. We are, in Paul's familiar language, transformed precisely by the "renewing of our mind" (Rom. 12:2).

SOUL EARTHQUAKES

To change governing ideas, whether in the individual or the group, is one of the most difficult and painful things in human life. Genuine conversion is a wrenching experience. It rarely happens to the individual or group except in the form of divine intervention, revolution, or a significant emotional event. At a group level, the 1960s illustrate this in the recent past of America. And in many parts of the world, Christians are persecuted and killed today because they threaten the dominant idea system of others in that country.

In fact, we are now undergoing an even more profound change than in the 1960s, though it is less noisy, with the emergence of generic spirituality. This change is the equivalent of a "soul earthquake" that leaves nothing unshaken and many individuals hurt or destroyed. From one essential perspective, of course, Jesus himself confronted and undermined an idea system and its culture, which in turn killed him. In the end, he proved himself greater than any idea system or culture, and is continuing the process of a worldwide idea shift that is crucial to his perpetual revolution, in which we each are assigned an essential part.

THE POWER OF IMAGES

Closely associated with governing ideas are the images that occupy our minds. Images are always concrete or specific, as opposed to the abstractness of ideas, and are heavily laden with feeling. They frequently present themselves with the force of perception and have a powerful emotional linkage to governing idea systems. They mediate the power of those idea systems into the real situations of ordinary life.

In many Christian churches today the worship services have been divided into "traditional" and "contemporary" primarily over imagery and the explosive feelings attached thereto. The guitar and organ are no longer just musical instruments; they are powerful symbols.

Jesus understood the great significance of images. He intentionally selected an image that would brilliantly convey himself and his message: the cross. The cross represents the lostness of man, as well as the sacrifice of God and the abandonment to God that brings redemption. No doubt it is the all-time most powerful image and symbol in human history. Need we say he knew what he was doing in selecting it? He planned it all, for he is also the master of images. For our own benefit, we as followers need to keep the image of the cross vividly present in our minds.

Accordingly, ideas and images are the primary focus of Satan's efforts to defeat God's purposes for humankind. This is the basic idea behind all temptation: God is presented as depriving us by his commands of what is good. As a result, we think we must take matters into our own hands and act contrary to what he has said. This image of God leads to our pushing him out of our thoughts and placing ourselves on the throne. The condition of both the ruined soul and world at large naturally results. The single most important thing in our mind is our idea of God and the associated images.

Thus A. W. Tozer did not exaggerate when he said:

> . . . Our idea of God [should] correspond as nearly as possible
> to the true being of God. . . . A right conception of God is to
> practical Christian living, what the foundation is to the temple;
> where it is inadequate or out of plumb the whole structure must
> sooner or later collapse. I believe there is scarcely an error in
> doctrine or a failure in applying Christian ethics that cannot be
> traced finally to imperfect and ignorant thoughts about God.[1]

The person and gospel of Jesus Christ—building on these simple lyrics, "Jesus loves me, this I know; for the Bible tells me so"—is the answer to the false and destructive images and ideas that control the life of those away from God. The process of spiritual formation in Christ is one of progressively replacing the destructive and inaccurate with the images and ideas that filled the mind of Jesus himself. With Jesus Christ as the guiding perspective behind our learning, our Christian educational institutions play an essential role in the development of healthy spiritual formation within the body of Christ. For Christ is the only one capable of communicating to and developing within the believer an accurate image and idea of God. To begin elsewhere is to build upon a defective foundation.

USING THE ABILITY TO THINK

To undermine the power of those ideas and images that structure life away from God, we must use our ability to think. What is thinking? It is the activity of searching out what must be true, or cannot be true, in light of given facts or assumptions. It extends the information we have and enables us to see the larger picture, both clearly and wholly. It reveals falseness, inaccuracy, and error to those who wish to know. It is a powerful gift of God to be used in the service of truth.

Martin Luther, thinking and standing in the power of God before his examiners at Worms, said, "Unless I am convicted by Scripture and plain reason . . . my conscience is captive to the Word of God. I cannot and will not recant anything, for to go against conscience is neither right nor safe. God help me. Amen."[2] The earliest printed version of his statement added the famous words: "Here I stand, I cannot do otherwise."

And so we must apply our thinking to the Word of God. We must thoughtfully take that Word in, dwell upon it, ponder its meaning, explore its implications—especially as it relates to our own lives. We must thoughtfully set it into practice. In doing so, we will be assisted by God's grace in ways far beyond anything we can understand on our own; and the ideas and images that governed the life of Christ through his thought life will possess us.

THINKING VS. FAITH

Perhaps we are in a time when thinking rightly is more important than ever. The prospering of God's cause on earth depends upon his people thinking well. Today we are apt to downplay or disregard the importance of good thinking as opposed to strong faith; and some, disastrously, regard good thinking as being opposed to faith. They do not realize that in so doing they are not honoring God. They do not realize that they are operating on the same satanic principle that produced the killing fields of Cambodia, where those with any sign of education—even the wearing of glasses—were killed on the spot or condemned to starvation and murderous labor.

Too easily we forget that it is great thinkers who have given direction to the people of Christ in their greatest moments: Paul, Augustine, Luther, and Wesley to name a few. At the head of the list is Jesus Christ, who was and is the most powerful thinker the world has ever known. Many Christians today will be surprised to learn that Isaac Watts—the composer of well-known hymns such as "Joy to the World," "When I Survey the Wondrous Cross," and "O God, Our Help in Ages Past," along with many others—also taught logic. He wrote a widely used textbook in his day, titled *Logic; Or the Right Use of Reason, in the Inquiry After Truth.*[3] Those hymns we enjoy so much owe their power to the depth of thought they contain. That is one reason we need to return to them constantly. Of logic itself, Watts writes in the dedication of his book,

> The great design of this noble science is to rescue our rea-
> soning powers from their unhappy slavery and darkness; and
> thus, with all due submission and deference, it offers a humble
> assistance to divine revelation. Its chief business . . . is to diffuse
> a light over the understanding in our inquiries after truth.[4]

Bluntly stated, to serve God well, we must think straight, as crooked thinking—intentional or not—always favors evil. By contrast, to take the "information" of scripture into a mind thinking straight, under the direction and empowerment of the Holy Spirit, is to place our feet solidly on the high road of spiritual formation under God.

DWELLING UPON GOD

To bring the mind to dwell intelligently upon God as he is presented in his Word will have the effect of causing us to love God passionately, and this love will in turn bring us to think of God steadily. Thus he will always be before our minds. As Thomas Watson beautifully wrote long ago,

> The first fruit of love is the musing of the mind upon God. He who is in love, his thoughts are ever upon the object. . . . By this we may test our love to God. What are our thoughts most upon? Can we say we are ravished with delight when we think on God? . . . Oh, how far are they from being lovers of God, who scarcely ever think of God![5]

As disciples engage in the practice of placing Jesus Christ at center stage in every branch of human knowledge, they are simultaneously being encouraged to train their thoughts ever upon God. In this way they enter not only a life of study, but also a life of worship.

To think of God rightly, as God is, one cannot help but lapse into worship; and worship is the single most powerful force in completing and sustaining the spiritual formation of the whole person. Worship naturally arises from thinking rightly of God on the basis of revealed truth confirmed in experience. We say flatly: worship is at once the overall character of the renovated thought life and the only safe place for any human being to stand.

CHAPTER 2

Living a Transformed Life

The core of Dallas's ministry and writing focused on our relationship with Jesus, which he argued ultimately allows us to establish a relationship with the kingdom of God. This relationship is one of discipleship in which we learn to live our lives as Jesus would through progressively embodying and manifesting a Christlike character, which is attained through establishing a discipling relationship to Jesus. What we do comes from who we are and what our hearts long to become. For Dallas, this is the nature and objective of Christian spiritual transformation. Like no other single work, the following essay condenses the bulk of his corpus on discipleship and spiritual transformation into a clear, concise summary.

Written for the Augustine Group in 2005
as "Living a Transformed Life Adequate to
Our Calling" (previously unpublished)

Walk in a manner worthy of the calling with which you have been called. (Eph. 4:1)

Since we stand before so great a cloud of witnesses, let us lay aside every encumbrance, and the sin which so easily entangles us, and let us run with endurance the race that is set before us, with our eyes set on Jesus, who initiated our faith and will bring it to perfection. (Heb. 12:1–2)

There is no good tree which produces bad fruit. . . . The good man
out of the good stored up in his heart, brings forth what is good.
(Luke 6:43–45)

To fulfill the high calling that God has placed upon us
in creating us and redeeming us, we must have the right inner
substance or character. We must come to grips with who we really
are, inside and out. For we will do what we are. So we will need
to become the kind of people who routinely and easily walk in the
goodness and power of Jesus our master. For this, a process of "spiritual formation"—really, transformation—is required.

Spiritual formation for the Christian is a Spirit-driven process of
forming the inner world of the human self—our "spiritual" or invisible aspects of human life—in such a way that it becomes like the
inner being of Christ himself. In the degree to which such a spiritual
transformation to inner Christlikeness is successful, the outer life
of the individual will become a natural expression or outflow of the
character and teachings of Jesus. We will simply "walk the walk," as
we say.

Christlikeness of the inner being is not a merely human attainment, of course. It is, finally, a gift of grace. Nevertheless,
well-informed human effort is indispensable. Spiritual formation
in Christ is not a passive process. Grace does not make us passive. Divine grace is God acting in our life to accomplish what
we cannot do on our own. It informs our being and actions and
makes them effective in the wisdom and power of God. Hence,
grace is not opposed to effort (our actions) but to earning (our
attitude).

Paul the apostle, who perhaps understood grace as none other,
remarks on his own efforts for Christ: "By the grace of God I am
what I am, and His grace toward me did not prove vain; but I labored even more than all of them, yet not I, but the grace of God
with me" (1 Cor. 15:10). The supernatural outcome that accompanies
grace-full action stands out.

Spiritual formation in Christ is the way of rest for the weary and overloaded, of the easy yoke and the light burden (Matt. 11:28–30), of cleaning the inside of the cup and the dish (Matt. 23:26), of the good tree that cannot bear bad fruit (Luke 6:43). It is the path along which God's commandments are found not to be "heavy" (1 John 5:3).

Before turning to some details of Christian spiritual transformation in the various dimensions of the human being, we need to be clear about the general pattern that all effective efforts toward personal transformation—not just Christian spiritual formation—must follow. Because we are active participants in the process, and because what we do or do not do makes a huge difference, our efforts must be based on understanding. The degree of success in such efforts will essentially depend upon the degree to which this general pattern is understood and intentionally followed. Jesus indeed said that without him we can do nothing (John 15:5). But we can also be sure that if we do nothing it will be without him. So he commands us to "abide in the Vine" (15:1–7). We must find a way to do that.

Let us begin with a couple of easy illustrations, and then spell out the pattern in its generality.

LEARNING TO SPEAK ARABIC

Suppose someone wishes to speak a language they do not presently know: say, Arabic or Japanese. In order to carry through with this simple case of (partial) personal transformation, they must have some idea of what it would be like to speak the language in question—of what their lives would then be like—and why this would be a desirable or valuable thing for them. They also need to have some idea of what must be done to learn to speak the language, and why the price in time, energy, and money that must be expended constitutes a "bargain," considering what they get in return. If they are to succeed, all of this needs to be clearly before them. They need to be gripped by the desirability of it. That would be their vision.

The general absence of such a vision explains why language

learning is generally so unsuccessful in educational programs in the United States. The presence of such a vision, on the other hand, explains why the English language is learned at a phenomenal rate all around the world. Multitudes clearly see the ways in which their life might be improved by knowledge of English. As the vision is clear and strong, it pulls everything else required along with it; and the language is learned, even in difficult and distracting circumstances.

Still, more than vision is required. There is also a necessity of an earnest intention. Projects of personal transformation do not succeed by accident, drift, or imposition. Effective action has to involve order, subordination, and progression, developing from the inside of the personality. It is, in other words, a spiritual matter, a matter of meaning and will, for we are spiritual beings. Conscious involvement with order, subordination, and progression, developing from the "inside" of the personality, is required.

Imagine, if you can, a person wondering day after day if he or she is going to learn Arabic, or if he or she is going to get married to a certain person—just waiting, to see whether it would "happen." That would be laughable. But many people actually seem to live in this way with respect to major issues involving them, including spiritual growth. That fact goes far to explain why lives often go as badly as they do. To learn a language, as for the many even more important concerns of life, we must resolutely intend the vision, if it is to be realized. That is, we must initiate, decide, bring into being, those factors that would turn the vision into reality.

And that brings us to the final element in the general pattern of personal transformation: that of means or instrumentalities. Carrying through with the pattern for the illustration at hand, one will sign up for language courses, listen to recordings, buy books, associate with people who speak Arabic, immerse oneself in the culture, possibly spend some intensive times in Jordan or Morocco, and practice, practice, practice. There are means known to be effective toward transforming people into speakers of Arabic or Russian and so forth. This is not mysterious. If the vision is clear and strong, and the employment of the means thoughtful and persistent, then the outcome will be ensured.

ANOTHER ILLUSTRATION: ALCOHOLICS ANONYMOUS

Another illustration of the "general pattern" of personal transformation is provided by Alcoholics Anonymous and similar "twelve step" programs. Here, of course, the significance of the transformation or change is perhaps far greater for the person involved than in the case of learning a language; and the outcome is a negative one—that is, a refraining from doing something very harmful, something that could possibly lead to untimely death. But the pattern is basically the same.

A desirable state of being is envisioned, and an intention to realize it is actuated in decision. Means are applied to fulfill the intention (and the corresponding decision) by producing the desirable state of being: in this case, abstinence from alcohol and a life of sobriety, with all the good that that entails. The familiar means of the traditional AA program—the famous "twelve steps" and the personal and social arrangements in which they are concretely embodied, including a conscious involvement of God in the individual's life—are highly effective in bringing about personal transformation.

VIM: THE GENERAL PATTERN

With these two illustrations before us (language learning and AA), the general pattern of personal transformation should now be clear. We emphasize that it also holds for those transformations that can occur only through grace: through the initiative and through the constant direction and upholding of God. To keep the general pattern in mind as we continue, we will use the little acronym "VIM," as in the phrase "vim and vigor":

Vision

Intention

Means

Vim is grammatically related to the Latin term *vis,* meaning direction, strength, force, vigor, power, energy, or virtue; and sometimes meaning sense, import, nature, or essence. Now, spiritual formation in Christlikeness is all of this to human existence. It is the path by which we can truly, as Paul told the Ephesians, "be empowered in the Lord and in the energy of his might" (Eph. 6:10) and "become mighty with his energy through his Spirit entering into the inward person" (3:16). It spells out the "life to the full" that Jesus, in his own person, brought into the life of humankind (John 10:10). Only by receiving this life do we become adequate to our calling. God never intended anything else.

So, if we are to be spiritually formed in Christ, we must implement the appropriate vision, intention, and means. Not just any path we take will do. If this VIM pattern is not properly put in place and resolutely adhered to, Christ simply will not be formed in us. We do not want to be "picky" about the details. That can sidetrack us into legalism. But apart from an overall VIM pattern of life, who we are inwardly will be left substantially as it was before we came to know Christ, and as it is in non-Christians. Our inner life—what makes up our inner being of will, thoughts, emotions, social connections, and even the dispositions of our body—will constantly entangle us and defeat us. Paul's penetrating description has never been improved on: "For the good that I wish, I do not do; but I practice the very evil that I do not wish" (Rom. 7:19). Paul, of course, did not stay there. He knew the bitter reality, but he also knew how to move on.

We will make a quick survey of VIM in spiritual formation, and then return to each part for a deeper look.

THE VISION OF LIFE IN THE KINGDOM

The vision of our life in the kingdom of God is the place we must start. This is the vision Jesus brought. It was the gospel he preached. He came announcing, manifesting, and teaching what the kingdom of the heavens was like, and that it was immediately available in himself. "I was sent for this purpose," he said (Luke 4:43). If we, from the heart, accept him and his kingdom, we will find our feet firmly planted on the path of Christian spiritual formation.

What is "the kingdom of God"? It is the range of God's effective will, where what God wants done is done. It is, like God himself, from everlasting to everlasting (Ps. 103:17; see also Ps. 93:1–2; Dan. 4:3; 7:14; etc.). The planet Earth and its immediate surroundings seem to be the only places in creation where God permits his will to not be done. Therefore, we pray and seek: "Thy kingdom come, Thy will be done, on earth as it is in heaven," and we hope for the time when that kingdom will be completely fulfilled even here on earth (Luke 21:31; 22:18)—where, in fact, it is already present (Luke 17:21; John 18:36–37), and is available to those who seek it with all their hearts (Matt. 6:13; 11:12; Luke 16:16). For those who do seek and find it in Christ, it is true even now that "all things work together for their good" (Rom. 8:28, PAR), and that nothing can cut them off from God's inseparable love and effective care (Rom. 8: 35–39). That is the nature of a life in the kingdom of the heavens now.

The vision that underlies spiritual (trans)formation into Christlikeness is, then, the vision of life now and forever in the range of God's effective will. This means we are partaking of the divine nature (2 Pet. 1:4; 1 John 3:1–2) through a birth "from above," and participating by our actions in what God is doing now in our lifetime on earth. Thus Paul tells us, "Whatever we do, speaking or acting, do all on behalf of the Lord Jesus, giving thanks through him to God the Father" (Col. 3:17, PAR). Being born into his kingdom, in everything we do we are permitted to do his work. That is what we are learning. That is the privilege extended to us in the gospel. What this vision calls us into is a life of abundance, available here and now, not just in the hereafter.

THE INTENTION TO BE A KINGDOM PERSON

The vision of life to the full in the kingdom through reliance upon Jesus makes it possible for us to intend to live in the kingdom as he did. We can actually decide to do it. Concretely, we intend to live in the kingdom of God by intending to obey the precise example and teachings of Jesus. This is the form taken by our confidence in him. Our confidence in him is not merely a matter of believing things about him, however true and important they may be. Indeed, no one can actually believe the truth about Jesus without trusting him by intending to obey him. It is a mental impossibility. To think otherwise is to indulge a widespread illusion that now smothers spiritual formation in Christlikeness among professing Christians and prevents Christlike transformation from naturally spreading worldwide.

Gandhi, who had closely observed Christianity as practiced around him in Great Britain and in Europe, remarked that if only Christians would live according to their belief in the teachings of Jesus, "we all would become Christians." We know what he meant, and he was right. But the dismaying truth is that the Christians *were* living according to their "belief" in the teachings of Jesus, when actually, they didn't believe them, nor did they really trust him!

Knowing the "right answers"—knowing which ones they are, being able to identify them and say them—does not mean we believe them. To believe them, like believing anything else, means that we are set to act as if they (the "right answers") are true, and that we will so act in appropriate circumstances. And acting as if the right answers are true means, in turn, that we intend to obey the example and teachings of Jesus our master. What else could we intend if we believed Jesus is who his people through the ages have declared him to be?

The idea that you can trust Christ and not intend to obey him is an illusion generated by the prevalence of an unbelieving "Christian culture." In fact, you can no more trust Jesus and not intend to obey him than you could trust your doctor or your auto mechanic and not intend to follow their advice. If you do not intend to follow their advice, you simply do not trust them.

INTENTION INVOLVES DECISION

Now, an intention is whole and real only if it includes a decision to fulfill or carry through with the intention. We commonly find people who say they intend (or intended) to do certain things that they do not do. To be fair, external circumstances may sometimes have prevented them from carrying out the action. And habits deeply rooted in our bodies and life contexts can, for a while, thwart even a sincere intention. But if something like that is not the case, we know that they never actually decided to do what they say they intended to do, and that they therefore did not really intend to do it. Accordingly, a lack of the power and order that intention brings into life processes is evident.

Of course the robust intention, with its inseparable decision, can be formed and sustained only upon the basis of a forceful vision. The elements of VIM are mutually reinforcing. Those whose word "is their bond," or "is as good as gold," are people with a vision of integrity. They see themselves standing in life and before God as those who do not say one thing and think or do another. They "mean what they say." This is greatly valued before God, who abominates "swearing falsely" and honors those "who stand by their oath even when it harms them" (Ps. 15:4, PAR). Similarly, it is the vision of life in God's kingdom and its goodness that provides an adequate basis for the steadfast intention to obey Christ. And that intention, carried through, will in turn enhance the vision by making it clearer and brighter.

MEANS

The clear vision and the solid intention to obey Christ will naturally lead to seeking out and applying the means to that end. That is the natural order in human life. Here the means in question are the means for spiritual transformation: for replacing the inner character of the "lost" person with the inner character of Jesus—his vision, understanding, feelings, decisions, and character. By finding such means we are not left to ourselves, but have rich resources available to us in the example and teachings of Jesus, in the scriptures generally, and in his people through the ages. They include such practices as solitude, memorization of and meditation upon scriptures, fellowship and accountability to others, and so forth. More on this will follow.

Suppose, for example, we are convinced that we should, as Jesus would, be generous to those who are in need, but who have already taken away some of our money or property through legal processes. Mere "will power," with gritted teeth, cannot be enough to enable us to do this. By what means, then, can we become the kind of person who would gladly do this, as Jesus himself would do it? If we have the vision of the goodness of it, and we intend (have decided) to do it, we can certainly find and implement the means.

For example, we might, in solitude, prayer, and scripture meditation, identify our resentment and our anger toward a person who needs our help as the cause of our not gladly helping him. And then there is justice. Ah, justice! Perhaps in the form of "I do not owe it to him. He has no claims on me." Or perhaps we feel that the legal case that went against us and in his favor was rigged or unfair. Or again, perhaps we think we must secure ourselves by holding onto whatever surplus items we have. After all, we may say, who knows what the future holds? Or perhaps we think giving to people what is unearned by them will harm them by corrupting their character, leading them to believe one can get something for nothing. Or perhaps it is just not our habit to give to people with no prior claim on us—without regard to whether they may also have injured or deprived us. Or perhaps our friends, including our religious friends, would think we are fools. And so forth, and so on, our rationalizations continue.

What a thicket of darkness and lostness stands in the way of doing a simple good thing: helping someone in need. These are some of the all-too-customary results of human thinking, feeling, and social practice that stand in the way. And, truthfully, it is very likely that little can be done on the spot to help one do the good thing that Jesus commands. But by a course of study, prayer, and practice we can become different inside, and then be able to do it with ease and joy.

This is characteristic of all Jesus's example and teaching. When my neighbor who has injured me or triumphed over me in the past now stands before me with a need I can remedy, I will not usually be able, "on the spot," to do the good thing, if my inner being is filled with all the thoughts, feelings, and habits that characterize the ruined soul and its world. On the other hand, if I intend to obey Jesus Christ, I must intend and decide to become the kind of person who would obey. That is, I must find the means of receiving his grace and changing my inner being until it is substantially like his, pervasively characterized by his thoughts, feelings, habits, and relationship to the Father. Overall, this will amount to a life organized around wise spiritual disciplines under grace. We learn that we cannot do what we should do just by trying, but that through training, in time, we can become the kind of person who would do the good with little thought or effort.

In the spiritual life it is actually true that "where there is a will there is a way." This is true because God is involved and makes his help available to those who seek it. On the other hand, where there is no will (firm intentions based on clear vision) there is no way. People who do not intend to be inwardly transformed, so that obedience to Christ "comes naturally," will not be transformed. God will not pick us up and throw us into transformed kingdom living, into "holiness," against our will.

In sum, the problem of spiritual transformation (and the normal lack thereof) among those who identify as Christians today is not that it is impossible, or that effectual means to spiritual transformation are not available. The problem is that spiritual transformation into Christlikeness is not intended. People do not see spiritual transformation and its value, and do not decide to carry through with it. They do not decide to do the things Jesus did and said. And this in turn is, today, largely due to the fact that they have not been given a vision of life in God's kingdom, within which such a decision and intention would make sense. The "gospel" they have heard did not provide a proper vision. As a result, the entire VIM of Christ's life and life in Christ is not the intentional substance and framework of their life.

Now, with this preliminary survey of how transformation into Christlikeness unfolds before us, let us go back and look into each division of VIM in greater depths.

> Therefore, brothers, be all the more diligent to make certain
> about His calling and choosing you; for as long as you practice
> these things, you will never stumble; for in this way the entrance
> into the eternal kingdom of our Lord and Savior Jesus Christ
> will be abundantly supplied to you. (2 Pet. 1:10–11)

THE VISION OF THE DISCIPLE OF JESUS

As a genuine disciple or apprentice of Jesus, I become caught up in his vision of the goodness and greatness of God and of life in his kingdom. On that basis I am with Jesus, by choice and by grace, learning from him how to live my life in the kingdom of God. To live in the kingdom means to live within the range of God's effective will with his life flowing through mine. Another good way of putting this is to say that as a disciple I am learning from Jesus to live my life as he would live my life if he were I. I am not necessarily learning to do everything he did, of course; but I am learning how to do everything *I do* in the manner and from the source from which he did all that *he did*.

It is in discipleship to Jesus that we become capable of walking in a manner "worthy of the calling with which we have been called" (Eph. 4:1). For the disciple, there are three main ways in which God comes to fill our vision. Through them the loveliness of God wins the steadfast love and confidence of the disciple. He comes to us (1) through his creation, (2) through his public acts on the scene of human history, and (3) through individual experiences of him by ourselves and others around us.

"GOD, THE FATHER ALMIGHTY, THE MAKER OF HEAVEN AND EARTH"

The apostle Paul explains that all human beings remain responsible before God, no matter how far away they may fall, precisely because of the clear way in which God stands forth in nature: "Since the creation of the world," he says, "God's invisible nature is clearly presented to their understanding through what has been made" (Rom. 1:19–20). In a later passage in Romans (10:18), Paul comes close to identifying the very "word of Christ," the gospel, with the word of God that goes out from nature to "the ends of the earth," according to Psalm 19. Through the ages and up to today, outstanding thinkers have continued to be convinced of the soundness of such thinking, and ordinary people usually grant that it is correct. But, though the rational processes involved in seeing the Creator through nature are important—and, I believe, they are conclusive when fairly examined—they are not all that is involved in our awareness of God in nature. It may be that for most people God is more sensed through nature than inferred—somewhat as I "sense" or "read" your thoughts, feelings, and presence when I am around you, and do not infer them.

The words of the poet Wordsworth express what many people find:

And I have felt
A presence that disturbs me with the joy
Of elevated thoughts; a sense sublime
Of something far more deeply interfused,
Whose dwelling is the light of setting suns,
And the round ocean and the living air,
And the blue sky, and in the mind of man;
A motion and a spirit, that impels
All thinking things, all objects of all thought,
And rolls through all things.[1]

However it may come, in the training that brings apprentices of Jesus to live on that solid rock of "hearing and doing" (Matt. 7:24–25), "God the Father almighty, maker of heaven and earth," must be made present to our minds in such a way that we can see his magnificent beauty and our love can be strongly and constantly drawn to him. This will make a huge and indispensable contribution to our ability to love him with all our heart, soul, mind, and strength, and to receive and follow our calling with ultimate confidence in Christ.

KNOWLEDGE OF THE GLORY OF GOD IN THE FACE OF CHRIST

We also bring the heart-wrenching goodness of God, his incomprehensible graciousness and generosity, before the mind of disciples by helping them to see and understand the person of Jesus. On a wearying, dreadful night, Jesus was saying a lot of things that were confusing and upsetting those in his little circle of friends. Philip blurted out, "You talk about the Father all the time. Just show us the Father and that will satisfy us" (John 14:8, PAR). Jesus patiently replied, "Haven't you yet understood who I am, Philip? Whoever has seen me has seen the Father" (v. 9). No doubt Philip and the others experienced this as just too good to be true. Could the character of God really be that of Jesus? The stunning answer is, Yes indeed. The key, then, to loving God is to see Jesus, to hold him before the mind with as much fullness and clarity as possible. It is to adore him.

For purposes of training others, and ourselves, we should divide this into four main aspects. First, we see his beauty, truth, and power while he lived among us as one human being among others. The content of the Gospels must come to life in such a way that the Gospels become a permanent presence in and possession of the mind of the disciple. The radiant person of Jesus shines forth from the gospel accounts up to the present day. The Gospels often introduce us to Jesus, and we can go through life with him "at our elbow," which is what the psalmist describes as "under the shadow of the Almighty" (Ps. 91:1).

Second, we see the way Jesus was executed as a common criminal among other criminals on our behalf. We don't have to understand exactly how it works. But this fact is something we must always have before our minds. That is a good reason to wear or display a cross. For all its mystery it still says: "I am delivered through the sufferings, death, and resurrection of Jesus and I belong to God. The divine mission of which I am a part shoots through human history in the form of a cross." Individual disciples must have indelibly imprinted upon our souls the reality of this wonderful person who walked among us and suffered a cruel death to enable each of us to have life in God. It should become something that is never beyond the margins of our consciousness. "God," Paul said, "makes clear the greatness of his love for us through the fact that Christ died for us while we were still rebelling against him" (Rom. 5:8). Upon this vision of God, transformation into Christlikeness is based.

The genuine exclusiveness of the Christian revelation of God lies here. No one can have an adequate view of the heart and purposes of the God of the universe who does not understand that he permitted his son to die on the cross to reach out to all people, even people who hated him. That is who God is. But this is not just a "right answer" to a theological question. It is God looking at me from the cross with compassion and providing for me, with never-failing readiness to take my hand to walk on through life, wherever I may find myself at the time.

Paul's sense of the meaning of the death of God's Son for individual human beings is spelled out in ecstatic detail in Romans 8:31–39:

> God is for us! Who is against us? Since he did not spare his own Son in reaching us, he obviously is ready to give us every good thing. Who will charge us with anything? God has cleared us of all his charges. Who condemns us? Jesus died for us. Yes, and he passed through death intact, and now stands in the place from which God acts, looking after our interests. Of all the terrible and frightening things the human mind discovers, not one can take us out of his loving hands. We don't just "manage" or cope. We thrive on it all! Nothing shall be able to separate us from the love of God which is in Jesus the Anointed, our Lord. (PAR)

With this radiant passage before us, the last two aspects of Jesus as a person to be imprinted on the disciple's soul in training are already in view.

Third, we see the reality of Jesus risen, his actual existence now as a person who is present among his people. We find him in his ecclesia, his sometimes motley but always glorious crew of called-out ones. We trace him from those uncomprehending encounters on the first Easter morning, and on through the amazingly different historical periods of the church. But we also find him now active among his disciples. Who he is, is revealed in an essential way in his people.

So the continuing incarnation of the divine Son in his scattered and his gathered people must fill our minds if we are to love him and his Father adequately and thus live on the rock of hearing and doing. And to see how he has been and is lived with and loved and served and presented and celebrated by all kinds of people across time and space adds to the force of our love for him and our vision of the Father.

Fourth, we see the Jesus who is the master of the created universe and of human history. He is the one in ultimate control of all the atoms, particles, quarks, "strings," and so forth upon which the physical cosmos depends. Human beings have long aspired to control the ultimate foundations of ordinary reality. We have made a little progress, and there remains an unwavering sense that this is the direction of our destiny. That is the theological meaning of the scientific and technological enterprise. It has always presented itself to "man on his own" as the instrument for solving human problems. But without a divine context it becomes idolatrous and veers wildly out of human control, threatening self-destruction.

But this Jesus is master of all reality through his word. Satan, in tempting him, claimed to be in possession of all the kingdoms of the earth. That is a lie. Lies are Satan's only hope. It is Jesus himself who is king of the kings of the earth, and who for good purposes allows Satan and evil to have some influence on humanity—for a while. And it is he, as the Logos, the cosmic Christ, who maintains and manipulates the ultimate laws of the physical universe. In him, the early Christians well understood, "are hidden all of the treasures of wisdom and of knowledge" (Col. 2:3).

Thoroughly presented in all these ways, the love of Jesus for us, and the magnificence of his person, brings the disciple to adore Jesus. His love and loveliness fill our lives. An older Franciscan brother said to Brennan Manning on the day he joined the order, "Once you come to know the love of Jesus Christ, nothing else in the world will seem as beautiful or desirable."

Jesus himself knew that this love was the key. The keeping of his commandments was the true sign of love for him, because that love is what made the commands possible and actual. In this love of Jesus everything comes together: "If anyone loves me, my word he will keep, and my Father will love him, and we will move in with him and live there" (John 14:23, PAR).

GOD'S HAND SEEN THROUGH THE EVENTS OF THE DISCIPLE'S LIFE

The last area of vision required to bring disciples to the place where they love the Lord with all their heart, soul, mind, and strength concerns the goodness of their own existence and of the life received through their natural birth and the following course of their life.

God, as our "faithful Creator" and as presented "in the face of Jesus Christ," is lovely and magnificent. But he will remain something to be admired, or even worshiped, at a distance if that is all we know of him. In order for disciples to be brought into a full and joyous love of God, we must see our very own life within the framework of unqualified goodness. Perhaps *see* is too strong a word, though it is certainly what we should hope for. But we should at least be sure in our heart of hearts that our life is a very good thing and that God has done well by us.

Saint Clare, won in her youth to a life of complete devotion to Jesus by Saint Francis of Assisi, had these for her last words, "Lord God, blessed be thou for having created me!" This can be the daily breath of a disciple of Jesus. Just previously, as she lay near death, Brother Rainaldo had exhorted her to bear her infirmities with patience. She replied, "Dearest brother, ever since I have known the grace of my Lord Jesus Christ through his servant Francis, no suffering has troubled me, no penance has been hard, no sickness too arduous."[2] Then, before her last words, she was heard to murmur to her soul, "Go forth, Christian soul, go forth without fear, for thou hast a good guide for thy journey. Go forth without fear for He hath created thee, hath sanctified thee, always hath He protected thee, and He loveth thee with the love of a mother."[3]

We will never have the easy, unhesitating love of God that makes obedience to Jesus our natural response, unless we are absolutely sure that it is good for us to exist, and to be who we are. This means we must have no doubt that the path appointed for us is good, and that nothing irredeemable has happened to us or could happen to us on our way to our destiny in God's world.

Most of our doubts about the goodness of our life concern very specific matters: our parents and family, our body, our marriage and children (or lack thereof), our opportunities in life, our work and calling (which are not the same thing), and our job. Careful study, teaching, training, and guidance must be received with reference to all the aspects of the disciple's life: parents, body, love and sexuality, marriage and children, and experience with work and jobs. The object in each case is to enable the disciple to be thankful for who we are and what we have. An often painful progression will be required: from honesty to acceptance to compassion and forgiveness and then on to thankfulness to God and the honoring of our lives in all of the aspects indicated. And when this training has been completed, Paul's words will make perfect sense: "Always giving thanks for all things on behalf of our Lord Jesus Christ to God, even the Father" (Eph. 5:20). And again: "I have learned how to be content whatever the circumstances. . . . I can do all things in him who gives me strength" (Phil. 4:11, 13). This is the vision of God that must undergird our calling.

It is being included in the eternal life of God that heals all wounds and allows us to stop demanding satisfaction for the hurts we have received. What really matters, of a personal nature, once it is clear that you are included in God's eternal life? You have been chosen. God chooses you. This is the message of the kingdom. A very touching passage occurs in the writings of Isaiah the prophet on this point. In his day, non-Israelites were always "on the outside looking in," as we say. And likewise eunuchs, who could never have a family of their own. But God says of them, "I will give them a place forever in my house, and a name better than sons and daughters; a name that will stand forever" (Isa. 56:3–5). The greatness and goodness of the great God who takes us up into his life—that is our peace and our joy.

30   Spiritual Transformation

INTENTION IN SPIRITUAL FORMATION

A clear vision of God and of the place he has made for us in him
enables us to form a strong and clear intention to live in that vision.
One of the most helpful things ever written on the centrality of intention and decision in the life of the disciple is chapter 2 of William
Law's book *A Serious Call to a Devout and Holy Life*.[4] The chapter
is titled "An Inquiry into the Reason, Why the Generality of Christians Fall So Far Short of the Holiness and Devotion of Christianity." In the previous chapter Law had discussed at length the failure
of the usual Christian, in his country at the time, to be different
from non-Christians. Then Law writes:

> It was [the] general intention [to please God in all things]
> that made the primitive Christians such eminent instances of
> piety, and made the goodly fellowship of the saints, and all
> the glorious army of martyrs and confessors. And if you will
> here stop, and ask yourselves, why you are not as pious as the
> primitive Christians were, your own heart will tell you that it
> is neither through ignorance, nor inability, but purely because
> you never thoroughly intended it. You observe the same Sunday
> worship that they did; and you are strict in it, because it is your
> full intention to be so. And when you as fully intend to be like
> them in their ordinary common life, when you intend to please
> God in all your actions, you will find it as possible, as to be
> strictly exact in the service of the Church. And when you have
> this intention to please God in all your actions, as the happiest
> and best thing in the world, you will find in you as great an aver-
> sion to every thing that is vain and impertinent in common life,
> whether of business or pleasure, as you now have to any thing
> that is profane. You will be as fearful of living in any foolish way,
> either of spending your time, or your fortune, as you are now
> fearful of neglecting the public worship.

Finally, Law concludes,

This doctrine does not suppose that we have no need of Divine grace, or that it is in our own power to make ourselves perfect. It only supposes, that through the want of a sincere intention of pleasing God in all our actions we fall into such irregularities of life as by the ordinary means of grace we should have power to avoid; and that we have not that perfection, which our present state of grace makes us capable of, because we do not so much as intend to have it. It only teaches us, that the reason why you see no real mortification or self-denial, no eminent charity, no profound humility, no heavenly affection, no true contempt of the world, no Christian meekness, no sincere zeal, no eminent piety in the common lives of Christians, is this, because they do not so much as intend to be exact and exemplary in these virtues.[5]

MEANS TO GROWTH IN GRACE

Law's words can seem shocking to contemporary Christians because of his presumption that the Christian would actually intend and choose to do what Jesus taught. Of course it was shocking in his own day as well, and in the day of a later writer, William Wilberforce, who in 1797 published his *A Practical View of the Prevailing Religious System of Professed Christians in the Higher and Middle Classes in This Country, Contrasted with Real Christianity.*[6] But we today are perhaps all the more shocked because we are almost totally out of touch with the practices, familiar to both Law and Wilberforce, through which transformation toward Christlikeness can reliably come to pass.

Those practices were understood as "means of grace," in the language of Law (see above) and, more famously, in that of John Wesley, one of his careful readers. That is, they are activities that open our lives to the action of God in our heart, mind, body, and soul, to progressively remake our whole personality. Another name for them—more ancient, and also more in use recently—is "spiritual disciplines," or "disciplines for the spiritual life." They train us for leading the life that

God intended for us: one that has the power and character to fulfill our calling. They are methods by which we obey the command to "put off" the old person and to "put on" the new person who is in the likeness of Christ (Col. 3:9–10; Eph. 4:22–24). They are "exercises unto godliness" (1 Tim. 4:7–8). Through them we become capable of doing, with God, all the wonderful things commanded in the Bible, which we know are impossible in our own strength and wisdom.

In general, a "discipline" is any activity within our power that we engage in to enable us to do what we cannot do by direct effort. Though we may not be aware of it, we experience "disciplines" every day. In these daily or "natural" disciplines we perform acts that result in a direct command of further abilities that we would not otherwise have. If I repeat the telephone number aloud after looking it up, I can remember it until I get it dialed. Otherwise, I probably couldn't. If I train rigorously, I can bench-press three hundred pounds; otherwise certainly not. Playing a musical instrument and carrying on a lively and interesting conversation are other illustrations of ordinary activities that require discipline in our physical or "natural" life. We have to "practice" them. Discipline, one can see, is an essential component of any worthwhile human existence.

Essentially the same thing happens with disciplines for our spiritual life. When through spiritual disciplines I become able to heartily bless those who curse me, to pray without ceasing, to be at peace when not given credit for good deeds I've done, or to master the evil that comes my way, it is because my disciplinary activities have inwardly poised me for more and more interaction with the powers of the living God and his kingdom. Such is the potential we tap into when we use the disciplines for the spiritual life.

SOME ACTIVITIES THAT SERVE AS DISCIPLINES

What, then, are some particular activities that can serve as disciplines for the spiritual life? And which should we choose for our individual strategy for spiritual growth? In answering these practical questions, we need not try to come up with a complete list of disciplines. Nor should we assume that our particular list will be right for others. Quite a few well-known practices will have a strong claim to be on everyone's list. On the other hand, there are a number of good activities that may not usually be thought of as disciplines, though they can be, and yet others that have served through the ages as spiritual disciplines but are now largely forgotten. For example, there is the *peregrinatio,* or voluntary exile, introduced by the Irish Saint Brendan (born 484) and widely practiced for some centuries thereafter.[7] There is the vigil or "watch," where one rejects sleep to concentrate on spiritual matters. The keeping of a journal or spiritual diary continues to be an activity that serves some individuals as a vital discipline, though it probably would not show up on any "standard" list. Sabbath keeping, as instituted in the Old Testament, can be a most productive discipline when adapted to modern life. Physical labor has proven to be a spiritual discipline, especially for those who are also deeply involved in solitude, fasting, study, and prayer (1 Thess. 4:11–12).

An activity that can be an especially effective spiritual discipline for those who are used to "the better things in life" is to do grocery shopping, banking, and other business in the poorer areas of the city. This has an immense effect on our understanding of and behavior toward our neighbors—both rich and poor—and upon our understanding of what it is to love and care for our fellow human beings.

In our modern society, which proceeds at such a frenetic pace, simple sleep and rest may be disciplines in the sense just described. They will, as we have said, enable us to do what we cannot do by direct effort, including staying in good emotional and physical health, and possibly being loving and sensitive to our family and coworkers. But usually when we rest we would not be practicing resting—though, in the current world, that too may sometimes be needed, for some people actually cannot even rest by simply doing it. Practice is discipline, but there are disciplines that do not amount to practicing.

Now, spiritual disciplines are not mere bodily behaviors. That is, they are disciplines designed to help us be active and effective in the spiritual realm of our own hearts, now spiritually alive by grace in relation to God and his kingdom. They are designed to help us withdraw from a total dependence on the merely human or natural; and, in that precise sense, they help us to mortify the "flesh," kill it off, let it die (Rom. 8:13; Col. 3:5), and to learn how to depend upon the ultimate reality, which is God and his kingdom.

Thus, for example, I fast from food to know that there is another food that sustains me. I memorize and meditate on scripture that the order of God's kingdom would become the order and power of my mind and my life.

In shaping our own list of spiritual disciplines, we should keep in mind that very few disciplines can be regarded as absolutely indispensable for a healthy spiritual life and work, though some are obviously more important than others. Also, some are more important than others at different stages of our spiritual life. Always practicing a range of activities that have proven track records across the centuries will keep us from erring. And, if other activities are needed, our progress won't be seriously hindered, and we'll probably be led into them.

So, to help us make our way into a life of planned disciplines, let us list some activities that have had a wide and profitable use among disciples of Christ, and discuss how to approach some of them in a prayerful, experimental way. The following list is divided into the disciplines of "abstinence" and the disciplines of "engagement." We cannot here discuss what each of these activities is and how each can make an especially important contribution to spiritual growth. But we will be illustrative and point the way to further study.

Disciplines of Abstinence

   solitude

   silence

fasting

frugality

chastity

secrecy

sacrifice

watching

Disciplines of Engagement

study

worship

celebration

service

prayer

fellowship

confession

submission

As we organize our plan for spiritual growth around some selection of these activities, and when we put that plan into practice, we will see a steady transformation of our thoughts, emotions, and will—even our body and social context—toward the character of Christlikeness. From the stages of early discipleship, where "the spirit is willing but the flesh is weak" (Mark 14:38), we increasingly pass to the stages where the flesh—think of that as what we more or less automatically feel, think, and do on our own strength alone—is increasingly aligned with the Spirit and supportive of God's deepest intentions in us. This is absolutely essential in order for our training to successfully bring us to do from the heart the things that Jesus knows to be best.

A further help in understanding what spiritual disciplines are for the disciples of Jesus is to recognize them as simply a matter of following him into his own practices, appropriately modified to suit our own condition. We find our way into a life where the power of inward hindrances to obedience/abundance are broken, by observing what Jesus and others who have followed him actually do, and learning to structure our lives around those same activities. Thus, although scripture does not tell us in formulaic terms what to do in order to build our life upon the rock, everyone who knows anything about Jesus's life, and the lives of his most effective followers, really does know what to do to that end. Or they can easily find out. It is not a secret. Or perhaps we could call it an "open secret."

TWO DISCIPLINES OF ABSTINENCE: SOLITUDE AND SILENCE

To put off the old person and put on the new we need only follow Jesus into the activities that he engaged in to nurture his own life in relation to the Father. Of course, his calling and mission were out of all proportion to ours, and he never had our weaknesses. Still, what he practiced is, roughly, what we must practice, in order to enter into his heart and character. For example, solitude had a huge place in his life, as the gospel records show.

By *solitude* we mean being out of human contact, being alone, and being so for lengthy periods of time. To get out of human contact is not something that can be done in a short while, for such contact lingers long after it is, in one sense, over. Silence, a gift of many dimensions, is a natural part of solitude and essential to its fullness. Most noise involves human contact. Silence means to escape from sounds and noises, other than perhaps the gentle sounds of nature. But it also means not talking, and the effects of not talking on our soul are different from those of simple quietness. Both dimensions of silence are crucial for the breaking of old habits and the formation of Christ's character in us. Silence well practiced is like the wind of eternity blowing upon us.

Now why, precisely, are these disciplines of abstinence so central to the curriculum for Christlikeness? A primary objective in training in Christlikeness is to break the power of our ready responses to do the opposite of what Jesus teaches: for example, scorn, anger, verbal manipulation, payback, silent collusion in the wrongdoing of others around us, and so forth. These responses mainly exist at what we might call the "epidermal" level of the self, the first point of contact with the world around us. They are almost totally "automatic," given the usual stimuli. The very language we use is laden with them, and of course they are the "buttons" by which our human surroundings more or less control us. They are not "deep"; they are just there, and constant. They lie in the areas where most of our life is lived, and in action they have the power to draw our whole being into the deepest of injuries and wrongs. ("Mob psychology" and "group think" are well-known testimonies to that.)

Solitude and silence allow us to escape the patterns of epidermal responses, with their consequences. They provide space to come to terms with these responses and to replace them, with God's help, by different immediate responses that are suitable to the kingdom environment—and, indeed, to the kind of life everyone in saner moments recognizes to be good. They break the pell-mell rush through life and create a kind of inner space that permits people to become aware of what they are doing and what they are about to do.

We hear the cries from our strife-torn streets, "Give peace a chance!" and "Can't we all just get along?" But you cannot give peace a chance if that is all you give a chance. You have to do the things that make peace possible and actual. When you listen to people talk about peace, you soon realize, in most cases, that they are unwilling to deal with the conditions of society and soul that make strife inevitable. They want to keep them and still have peace, but it is peace on their terms, which is impossible.

And we can't all just get along. Rather, we have to become the kinds of persons who can get along. As a major part of this, our epidermal responses have to be changed in such a way that the fire and the fight don't start immediately after we are "rubbed the wrong way." Solitude and silence give us a place to begin the necessary changes, though they are not a place to stop.

They also give us some space to reform our inmost attitudes toward people and events. They take the world off our shoulders for a time and interrupt our habit of constantly managing things, of being in control, or thinking we are. One of the greatest of spiritual attainments is the capacity to do nothing. Thus, the Christian philosopher Pascal insightfully remarks, "I have discovered that all the unhappiness of men arises from one single fact, that they cannot stay quietly in their own chamber."[8]

Now, this idea of doing nothing proves to be absolutely terrifying to most people, but at least the person who is capable of doing nothing proves capable of refraining from doing the wrong thing. Then he or she will be better able to do the right thing. Doing "nothing" has many other advantages. It may be a great blessing to others around us, who often hardly have a chance while we are in action. Possibly the gentle Father in the heavens would draw nigh if we would just be quiet and rest a bit. Generally speaking, he will not compete for our attention, and as long as we are "in charge" he is liable to keep a certain distance.

Every person should have regular periods in life when he or she has nothing to do. Periods of solitude and silence are excellent practices for helping us learn how to do that. The law that God has given for our benefit tells us that one-seventh of our time should be devoted to doing nothing—no work, not by ourselves or any of our family, employees, or animals. That includes, of course, religious work. This is Sabbath.

What do you do in solitude or silence? Well, so far as things to "get done," nothing at all. As long as you are doing "things to get done," you have not broken human contact. So don't go into solitude and silence with a list. Can we enjoy things in solitude and silence? Yes, but don't try to. Just be there. Don't try to get God to do anything. Just be there. He will find you.

Even lay aside your ideas as to what solitude and silence are supposed to accomplish in your spiritual growth. You will discover incredibly good things. One is that we have a soul. Another, that God is near and the universe is brimming with goodness. Another, that others aren't as bad as we often think. But don't try to discover these, or you won't. You'll just be busy and find more of your own doings.

The cure for too-much-to-do is solitude and silence, for there we find that we are safely more than what we do. Thus, the cure of loneliness is solitude and silence, for there we also discover in how many ways we are never alone. When we go into solitude and silence, we need to be relatively comfortable. Don't be a hero in this or in any spiritual discipline. You will need rest. Sleep until you wake up truly refreshed. And you will need to stay there long enough for the inner being to become different. Muddy water becomes clear only if we let it be still for a while.

You will know that this finding of soul and God is happening by an increased sense of who you are and a lessening of the feeling that you have to do this, that, and the other thing that befalls your lot in life. That harassing, hovering feeling of "have to" largely comes from the vacuum in our soul, where we ought to be at home with our Father in his kingdom. As the vacuum is rightly filled, we will increasingly know that we do not have to do many of those things— not even those we might want to do.

Liberation from our own desires is one of the greatest gifts of solitude and silence. When this all begins to happen, you will know you are arriving where you ought to be. Old bondages to wrongdoing will begin to drop off as they become seen for what they are. And the possibility of really loving people will dawn upon our hearts once again. Soon, the experience of what it is to live by grace, rather than just talking about it, will envelop the heart and mind in peace.

These are some of the fruits of solitude and silence. The apprentice will have to learn *how* to keep in solitude and silence, of course. For most of us, wise and loving practical arrangements must be made with those around us. And we should encourage and help family members and coworkers to enter such spiritual disciplines themselves.

Obviously the effects of these disciplines will greatly benefit our objective of loving God with a full heart. For the usual distractions of life greatly hinder our attention to God, and the habit of thinking about everything else is almost impossible to break in the bustle of life. Time away can help. People often complain that they cannot pray because their thoughts wander. Those thoughts are simply doing what they usually do. The grip of "the usual" is what must be broken. Appropriate solitude and silence are sure to do it.

TWO DISCIPLINES OF POSITIVE ENGAGEMENT: STUDY AND WORSHIP

It is a profound truth about human beings that our first area of freedom concerns where we will place our mind. Until solitude and silence have had their effects, our minds will very likely continue to be focused on the wrong things, or on good things in an anxious attitude of trying to dominate them. But as we, through relocating our bodies into solitude, escape and change the inputs that have constantly controlled our thoughts and feelings, we will have additional freedom to place our minds fully upon the great God, his kingdom, and its peace and strength.

This, in turn, will transform our emotional state, and thereby the very condition of our body. Most of those around us will sense that and begin to act differently themselves. The social context will change for the better, and what we have to respond to will be much more in the spirit of the kingdom. I have observed this on many occasions.

Once solitude has done its work, the key to progress in spiritual formation is study. It is in study that we place our minds fully upon God and his kingdom. And study is brought to its natural completion in the worship of God. When I study anything I take its order and nature into my thoughts, and even into my feelings and actions. At one time I did not know the alphabet, for example. But then I studied it. I brought it before my mind, with the help of my teacher, and related my body to it in ways well known to all. Before very long the order that is in the alphabet was in my mind and body. From there, that order enabled me to reproduce, recognize, and use the alphabet and its parts. The order that I took into myself by study gave me power to do many good things that I could not do until, by study, it had become mine.

What we learn about study from this simple example of the alphabet is true in all areas, from the most theoretical to the most practical. It is also true when we study what is evil, a very dangerous thing to do. Then we take on orders and powers of evil—or they take us. But, thankfully, most of what we naturally come to study is good. A student of plumbing or singing, for example, takes into his or her mind certain orders by purposely dwelling upon the relevant subject matter and activities in appropriate ways. That is how study works. And, of course, it always enables individuals "to do what they cannot do by direct effort"—the mark of a discipline.

The "blessed man" of Psalm 1 (and Josh. 1:8) is one whose "delight is in the law of the Lord, and in His law he meditates day and night. And he will be like a tree firmly planted by streams of water, which yields its fruit in its season, and its leaf does not wither; and in whatever he does, he prospers." You can't achieve that outcome on your own. You do it by indirection, absorbing your mind in the ways of God.

Now, disciples of Jesus are people who want to take into their being the order of the kingdom of God that is among us. They wish to live their life in that kingdom as Jesus himself would, and that requires internalization of its order. Study is the chief way in which they accomplish that. They devote their attention, their thoughtful inquiry, and their practical experimentation to the order of the kingdom as seen in Jesus, in the written word of scripture, in others who walk in the way, and, indeed, in every good thing in nature, history, and culture.

Thus Paul's practical advice from his jail cell to his friends at Philippi, "Whatever things are true, serious, right, pure, lovable, well regarded, any virtue and anything admirable, let your mind dwell on them. What you have learned, received, heard, and seen in me, do that. And the God of peace will be with you" (Phil. 4:8–9, PAR). For all such good things are of God and his reign.

Of course, in all our study the person of Jesus is the center of attention. But he is not really separable, for us, from the written revelatory word, including the law, the prophets, the history, and the wisdom of the Old Testament. One who would train disciples "to hear and do" will direct them to all these, still centered on the person of Jesus.

The twenty-third Psalm is also an exquisite summary of life in the kingdom. The mind of the disciple should have it internalized, to always foster the joy and peace of the kingdom as well as to orient all of his or her actions within it. The Ten Commandments, the Lord's Prayer, the Sermon on the Mount, Romans 8, Colossians 3, Philippians 2–4, and a few other passages of scripture should be frequently meditated on in depth, and much of them memorized. This is an essential part of any training for Christlikeness. Positive engagement with these scriptures will bring kingdom order into our entire personality. This is something you will strongly experience as you go through the process of such study.

I know many people who profess serious allegiance to Jesus, and claim him as their savior. But, unfortunately, they simply will not take essential scriptures into their soul and body and utilize them as here indicated. The result is that they continue to recycle their failures and make little or no real progress toward the abundance/ obedience essential to "walking worthily of the calling wherewith we are called" (Col. 1:10, PAR). Some of them even try to use other spiritual disciplines, but with little result. An essential ingredient is missing, and the order of their mind and life remains other than that of the kingdom.

Study is by no means simply a matter of gathering information to have on hand. Intensive internalization of the kingdom order through study of the written word and learning from the living

Word establishes good "epidermal responses" of thought, feeling, and action. And these in turn integrate us into the flow of God's eternal reign. We really come to think and believe differently, and that changes everything else: "Thy word have I hid in my heart, that I might not sin against Thee" (Ps. 119:11).

Now, we must not worship without study, for ignorant worship is of limited value and can be very dangerous. We may develop "a zeal for God, but not according to knowledge" (Rom. 10:2), and then do great harm to ourselves and others. But worship must be added to study to complete the renewal of our mind through a willing absorption in the radiant person who is worthy of all praise. Study without worship is also dangerous, and the people of Jesus constantly suffer from its effects, especially in academic settings. To handle the things of God without worship is always to falsify them.

In worship we are ascribing greatness, goodness, and glory to God. It is typical of worship that we put every possible aspect of our being into it, all of our sensuous, conceptual, active, and creative capacities. We embellish, elaborate, and magnify. Poetry and song, color and texture, food and incense, dance and procession are all used to exalt God. And sometimes it is in the quiet absorption of thought, the electric passion of encounter, or total surrender of the will. In worship we strive for adequate expression of God's greatness. But only for a moment, if ever, do we achieve what seems like adequacy. We cannot do justice to God or his Son or his kingdom or his goodness to us. So we must constantly return to worship.

Worship nevertheless imprints on our whole being the reality that we study. The effect is a radical disruption of the powers of evil in us and around us. Often an enduring and substantial change is brought about. The renewal of worship keeps the glow and power of our true homeland an active agent in all parts of our being. In the atmosphere of worship, to "hear and do" is the clearest, most obvious and natural thing imaginable.

Now we have very briefly touched upon four specific spiritual disciplines: solitude and silence, study and worship. Around these an individual and/or group "Curriculum for Christlikeness" can be framed. It should be clear how strongly such disciplines will nourish and be nourished by the principle objective of such a "curriculum"—that of bringing the disciple of Jesus to love God with heart, soul, mind, and strength. Other disciplines, such as fasting, service to others, fellowship, and so on, might be discussed as well, and, indeed, in a full treatment of a curriculum for Christlikeness they must be discussed. But if these four are pursued with intelligence and prayer, whatever else is needed will certainly come along.

The important insight to guide us at this point is that, to build our house upon the rock of obedience (Matt. 7:24–25)—putting off the old person and putting on the new—we must have a definite plan for doing so. Although this cannot be done without interaction with the grace of God, neither will it be imposed upon us. We must devise steps to the fullness of Christ's life that are biblical, time-tested, realistic, and experimental. Such steps, as seen in the disciplines for the spiritual life, are not laws of righteousness; they are wisdom, and our teacher will help us in every need as we live with him in the VIM pattern.

A COMPOSITE PICTURE OF
"CHILDREN OF LIGHT"

We can view the ideal outcome of the VIM process by sketching a composite picture of "the children of light," drawing on how they have changed in the various essential dimensions of their being. To call them children of light is, in biblical terminology, to say that they have the basic nature of light: that light is their parent and has passed on to them its nature, as any parent does. The apostle John summed up the message that he and his friends had heard from Jesus as this: "God is light, and in Him there is no darkness at all" (1 John 1:5).

Now, the people who have moved into the light of Christ are not perfect and do not live in a perfect world—yet. But they are remarkably different. The difference is not one of a pose they strike, either from time to time or constantly, or of things they do or don't do. They are not "performing"—though their behavior, too, is very different and distinctive. Where the children of light differ is primarily and most importantly on the "inside" of their life. It lies in what they are in their depths, in what they would do and could do.

A key distinction of a child of light is found in the condition of their thought life. Therefore, it is essential that our initial investigation of our inner life centers on what we think about, or what is on our mind. Simply stated, children of light think about God. He is never out of their mind. They love to dwell upon God and upon his greatness and loveliness, as brought to light in Jesus Christ. They adore him in nature, in history, in his Son, and in his saints. One could even say they are "God-intoxicated" (Acts 2:13; Eph. 5:18), though no one has a stronger sense of reality and practicality than they do. Their mind is filled with biblical expressions of God's nature, his actions, and his plans for them in his world. They do not dwell upon evil. It is not a big thing in their thoughts. They are sure of its defeat, but they still deal with it appropriately in specific situations.

Because their mind is centered upon God and oriented to all else with reference to him, all other good things are also welcome there. Again: "Whatever is true, whatever is honorable, whatever is right, whatever is pure, whatever is lovely, whatever is of good repute, if there is any excellence and if anything worthy of praise," their mind ponders those things (Phil. 4:8). They are positive, realistically so, based upon the nature of God as they understand it. "I have set the Lord continually before me," the psalmist says. "Because He is at my right hand, I will not be shaken" (16:8).

The second focus is directed to our feelings. Here we notice that the emotional life of the children of light is deeply characterized by love. That is how they invest the emotional side of their being. They love lots of good things, and they love people. They love their life and who they are. They are thankful for their life—even though it may contain many difficulties, even persecution and martyrdom

(Matt. 5:10–12). They receive all of it as God's gift, or at least as his allowance, where they will know his goodness and greatness and go on to live with him forever. And so joy and peace are with them even in the hardest of times—even when suffering unjustly. Because of what they have learned about God, they are confident and hopeful and do not indulge thoughts of rejection, failure, and hopelessness, because they know better.

The third priority surrounds the will/spirit/heart. As we look a little deeper we find that children of light are sincerely devoted to doing what is good and right. Their will is habitually attuned to it, just as their mind and emotions are habitually homing in on God. They are attentive to rightness, to kindness, to helpfulness, and they are purposefully knowledgeable about life—about what people need, and about how to do what is right and good in appropriate ways. They are not obsequious, but respectful of the rights and responsibilities of others.

These are people who do not think first of themselves and what they want, and they really care very little, if at all, about getting their own way: "Let each of you regard one another as more important than himself; do not look out for your own personal interests, but for the interests of others" (Phil. 2:3–4). These are easy and good words to them. They are abandoned to God's will and do not struggle and deliberate as to whether they will do what they know to be wrong. They do not hesitate to do what they know to be right. It is the obvious thing to do.

Next we focus on the physical body. Children of light learn to train their bodies to do the good they intend or will. The physical body is constantly poised to do what is right and good without thinking. And that also means that the body does not automatically move into what is wrong, even contrary to their resolves and intentions, before they can think not to do wrong. It is no longer true of them that their "spirit is willing, but the flesh is weak" (Matt. 26:41). They know by experience that those words of Jesus are not a declaration about the inevitable condition of humans, but a diagnosis of a condition to be corrected. The Spirit has substantially taken over their "members" (Rom. 6:13).

Consequently, we do not see them always being trapped by what their tongue, facial expressions, eyes, hands, and so on have already done before they can think. For their body and its parts are consecrated to serve God and are habituated to be his holy instruments. They instinctively avoid the paths of temptation. The bodies of these people even look different. There is a freshness about them, a kind of quiet strength, and a transparency. They are rested and playful in a bodily strength that is from God. He who raised up Christ Jesus from the dead has given life to their bodies through his Spirit that dwells in them (Rom. 8:10–12).

The next area involves human relationships. In their relations to others, children of light are able to be completely transparent because they walk in goodness, have no use for darkness, and thus achieve real contact or fellowship with others—especially other apprentices of Jesus: "If we walk in the light as He Himself is in the light, we have fellowship with one another, and the blood of Jesus His Son cleanses us from all sin" (1 John 1:7). And "The one who loves his brother abides in the light and there is no cause of offence in him" (1 John 2:10, PAR). There is no need to extend great effort to conceal their thoughts and feelings (nor do they impose them upon everyone). Because of their confidence in God, they do not try to manipulate and manage others. Needless to say, in their social contexts they do not go on the attack or on the hunt, intending to use or to hurt others.

Moreover, children of light are completely noncondemning, while at the same time they will not participate in evil. They pay evil only the attention absolutely required in any social setting, and beyond that, patient and joyful nonparticipation is the rule. They know how to really "be there" (wherever "there" is) without sharing in evil, as was true of Jesus himself. Of course, as with him, others may disapprove of their "being there," and there are always some occasions where one should just step away. But they do not reject or distance themselves from the people who may be involved in such situations. They know how to "love the sinner and hate the sin" gracefully and effectively.

Finally, as you come to know these people—though those who know only the human powers of the flesh will never be able to understand them (1 Cor. 2:14)—you see that all of the above is not just at the surface. It is deep, and in a certain obvious sense, it is effortless. It flows. That is, the things we have been describing are not things the children of light are constantly trying hard to do, gritting their teeth and carrying on. Instead, these are features of life that well up out of a soul that is at home in God.

This, then, is the outcome of spiritual formation in Christlikeness. Again, it doesn't mean perfection, but it does mean we have here a person whose entire life or soul is whole: a person who, through the internalized integrity of the law of God and the administrations of the gospel and the Spirit, has a restored soul. The law and the Lord have restored it (Ps. 19:7; 23:3). Such a soul effectively interfaces God with the full person and enables every aspect of the self to function as God intended.

THE SCRIPTURAL HIGH POINTS

Now, with this composite picture of the inner and outer person of the children of light before us, let us compare it with some of the New Testament descriptions of what the disciples/apprentices of Jesus are to be like. We are now in a position to understand them in a new and, I believe, very encouraging way. Certainly, that is just the opposite of their usual effect, even on very devout people. Usually, I think, these bright passages may inspire longing, but a longing that is tinged with hopelessness and guilt. Now we are in a position for that to change, for we know the realism and practicality of the VIM pattern.

The passages we have in mind are very well known. Of course

Matthew 5–7 heads the list, but properly understood it really goes no further than familiar passages in Paul's letters, or in those by Peter, James, and John. And there are similar, though on the whole somewhat less penetrating, passages in the Old Testament. We might cite in this connection Romans 12:1–21; 1 Corinthians 13; 2 Corinthians 3:12–7:1; Galatians 5:22–6:10; Ephesians 4:20–6:20; Philippians 2:3–16 and 4:4–9; Colossians 3:1–4:6; 1 Peter 2:1–3:16; 2 Peter 1:2–10; 1 John 4:7–21; and so on. Perhaps Micah 6:8 could serve well as an Old Testament point of reference. Deuteronomy 10:12–21 would also serve. It would be very worthwhile to plan a full day in silent retreat to read and reread these passages meditatively.

THE CONTRASTING PICTURE OF CHILDREN OF DARKNESS

These passages portraying the children of light are given additional force by contrasting passages on the "unfruitful works of darkness" (Eph. 5:11, NRSV). In Galatians 5 Paul described "the deeds of the flesh" where natural human impulses and abilities are allowed to be the rule of life. These "deeds" are acts of "[sexual] immorality, impurity, sensuality, idolatry, sorcery, enmities [or grudges], strife, jealously, outbursts of anger, disputes, dissensions, factions, envying, drunkenness, carousing, and things like these" (vv. 19–21).

Another of Paul's "dark" passages is 2 Timothy 3:2–5. Speaking of "the last days," apparently when evil on earth will have had time to "ripen," he says that "men will be lovers of self, lovers of money, boastful, arrogant, revilers, disobedient to parents, ungrateful, unholy, unloving, irreconcilable, malicious gossips, without self-control, brutal, [despisers] of good, treacherous, reckless, conceited, lovers of pleasure rather than lovers of God." They may be religious in outer form, but their words and acts belie all that is genuine in it.

"REDEEMING THE TIME"

Now, the life of faith in Jesus Christ, following the VIM pattern, leads us out of darkness evermore into the light. The time allotted to our life is redeemed by opening ourselves to God and his kingdom through nonlegalistic practices that break internal bondages and give us new habits and character. In his essay "On Method," Samuel Taylor Coleridge makes a remarkable statement on the power of ordering our time aright:

> If the idle are described as killing time, he [the methodical man] may be justly said to call it into life and moral being, while he makes it the distinct object not only of the consciousness, but of the conscience. He organizes the hours, and gives them a soul; and that, the very essence of which is to flee away, and evermore to have been, he takes up into his own permanence, and communicates to it the imperishableness of a spiritual nature. Of the good and faithful servant, whose energies, thus directed, are thus methodized, it is less truly affirmed, that he lives in time, than that time lives in him. His days, months, and years, as the stops and punctual marks in the records of duties performed, will survive the wreck of worlds, and remain extant when time itself shall be no more.[9]

Indeed, one of our greatest tests of faith—of our confidence in God—is how we plan to use our time. In particular, will we have faith to do the things that will secure us in goodness of God, in "his righteousness" (Matt. 6:33); or will we neglect them, and lose our lives in inefficient and futile struggles with powers that are too great for us? With his usual acuteness, William James, in his *Talks to Teachers,* gave this advice:

> Keep the faculty of effort alive in you by a little gratuitous exercise every day. That is, be systematically heroic in little unnecessary points; do every day or two something for no other reason than its difficulty, so that, when the hour of dire need

draws nigh, it may find you not unnerved and untrained to stand the test. Asceticism of this sort is like the insurance which a man pays on his house and goods. The tax does him no good at the time, and possibly may never bring him a return. But, if fire does come, his having paid it, it will be his salvation from ruin. So with the man who has daily inured himself to habits of concentrated attention, energetic volition, and self-denial in unnecessary things. He will stand like a tower when everything rocks around him, and when his softer fellow-mortals are winnowed like chaff in the blast.[10]

This may seem only a council of human wisdom. It is that, but it is more. For the same principle applies to us as embodied, social beings who have stepped into Christ's kingdom as his disciples. It speaks of that area of freedom and responsibility where our desire and choice for God determines what we will or will not do in pursuit of God. Because the way of the kingdom is open before us, it is our opportunity and responsibility to lead right where we are in the character and power of Christ. And in such a position "the fire" will certainly come.

CHRISTIAN LEADERS WHO ARE RESPONSIBLE FOR THE FUTURE OF THE WORLD

Because the resources of God's kingdom are available to them, the responsibility for the condition of the world in years or centuries to come rests upon Christian leaders and the teachers in the Christian church. They alone have at their disposal the means to bring their surroundings increasingly under the rule of God. On the one hand, they have the "all power" that is in the hands of the one who bade them go and teach all human groupings to do as he commanded, and promised to be with them always (Matt. 28:18–20). On the other hand, the teachers of the gospel have Christ's kingdom fellowship to live in and to offer to all. They have millions of people who regularly come to them, submitting to their leadership in the spiritual life even when unclear about what that means. And, further, they have knowledge of concrete practices of submission to righteousness within which, given adequate teaching and example, they and their hearers can make regular and remarkable progress into the character and power of Christ himself.

The disciplines for the spiritual life are available, concrete activities designed to render bodily beings such as we ever more sensitive and receptive to the kingdom of the heavens brought to us in Christ, even while living in a world set against God. Lovingly and intelligently practiced, they join with grace to enable us matter-of-factly to "come boldly to the very throne of God and stay there to receive his mercy and to find grace to help us in our times of need" (Heb. 4:16, TLB). Therefore, our calling to lead for God where we are is a realistic one, for it can be carried out from the resources of the kingdom.

Coventry Cathedral, in Coventry, England, was built in 1043, then destroyed by the German Luftwaffe in 1940. In the ruins of the old cathedral, which is now adjoined to a new cathedral, are several prayer panels mounted on the walls that bring the fullness of God into the fullness of human life. According to tradition, after reading the words on each plaque, one should repeat the refrain "Holy, holy, holy; Lord God of Hosts; Heaven and earth are full of Thy glory."

> Hallowed be Thy name in Industry:
> God be in my hands and in my making.
> Hallowed be Thy name in the Arts:
> God be in my sense and in my creating.
> Hallowed be Thy name in Commerce:
> God be at my desk and in my trading.
> Hallowed be Thy name in Government:
> God be in my plans and in my deciding.
> Hallowed be Thy name in Education:
> God be in my mind and in my growing.
> Hallowed be Thy name in the Home:

God be in my heart and in my loving.
Holy, holy, holy; Lord God of Hosts;
Heaven and earth are fully of Thy Glory.

Therefore we conclude, as Albert Schweitzer concluded his *Quest of the Historical Jesus,* with this wonderful picture of the personal call of Christ:

He comes to us as One unknown, without a name, as of old, by the lakeside, He came to those men who knew Him not. He speaks to us the same word: "Follow thou me!" and sets us to the tasks which He has to fulfil for our time. He commands. And to those who obey Him, whether they be wise or simple, He will reveal Himself in the toils, the conflicts, the sufferings which they shall pass through in His fellowship, and, as an ineffable mystery, they shall learn in their own experience Who He is.[11]

Flesh and Spirit

This article is one that Dallas was especially fond of. He continually strove to find better, more effective ways of communicating how crucial it was for our spiritual transformation to become an embodied reality. He believed in the essential requirement of moving beyond mere intellectual exercises in order to engage with and appreciate beauty.

As we reviewed this article while compiling materials for this reader, Dallas mentioned to me that in hindsight he wished he had used the word *lustful* to distinguish the type of desire he was describing. He believed the word would have more accurately portrayed the nature of the sensual cravings the scriptures intend to describe. Therefore, readers who compare this piece with the previously published version will notice a few differences.

First published in 2008 as "Spiritual Formation and the Warfare Between the Flesh and the Human Spirit" in the Talbot School of Theology's *Journal of Spiritual Formation and Soul Care*

Do not let sin reign in your mortal body that you should obey its lusts, and do not go on presenting the members of your body to sin as instruments of unrighteousness; but present yourselves to God as those alive from the dead, and your members as instruments of righteousness to God. For sin shall not be master over you, for you are not under law, but under grace." (Rom. 6:12–14)[1]

SPIRITUAL FORMATION IN CHRIST IS THE PROCESS THROUGH which disciples or apprentices of Jesus take on the qualities or characteristics of Christ himself, in every essential dimension of human personality. The overall orientation of their will, the kinds of thoughts and feelings that occupy them, the "automatic" inclinations and "readinesses" of their body in action, the prevailing posture of their relations toward others, and the harmonious wholeness of their soul—these all, through the formative processes undergone by his disciples, increasingly come to resemble the personal dimensions of their master. "A pupil is not above his teacher," Jesus said, "but everyone, after he has been fully trained, will be like his teacher" (Luke 6:40).

This holistic transformation is what Paul means by "Put on the Lord Jesus Christ" (Rom. 13:14) and by "Lay aside the old self . . . and put on the new self" (Eph. 4:22–24). His are not just pretty words, but the practical directions of an intelligent and divinely inspired man who knew by personal experience the reality and truth of what he was talking about. Routine, easy obedience to Christ with reference to specific actions, then, is the natural outcome of the transformation of the essential dimensions of our personality into Christlikeness. But such obedience is neither the direct aim nor the standard of discipleship. And any idea that we can achieve such obedience to perfection or that we can do it in our own strength alone is emphatically ruled out by the New Testament writers. Very well. But is such obedience then possible at all?

Today there is the widespread conviction—and corresponding levels of practice—that sin wins. Certain statements also made by Paul, or elsewhere in the Bible, are wrongly understood and misapplied to the life of the disciple when taken to mean that we must remain in perpetual spiritual and moral defeat. In short, spiritual formation in Christlikeness is considered impossible. The power of sin and its penetration into fallen human nature requires, it is thought, that the ideals of transformation and obedience clearly set forth in many parts of the Bible, and especially in the New Testament, cannot be realized. Good-bye to the Sermon on the Mount, 1 Corinthians 13, Ephesians 4 and 5, and so on, and so on. Good-bye even to "What does the Lord require of you but to do justice, to love kindness, and to walk humbly with your God?" (Mic. 6:8). We just can't have such a life, according to this view, but must live in constant moral failure and spiritual defeat.

It may seem like that is certainly the New Testament view, if you choose your verses carefully. Paul says that "the flesh sets its desire against the spirit, and the spirit against the flesh; for these are in opposition to one another, so that you may not do the things that you wish" (Gal. 5:17); that sounds so grim that we suddenly forget the previous verse, where he tells us, precisely, how to foil the flesh (more on this later). And then there is Paul's most famous statement on this point: "For the good that I would I do not: but the evil which I would not, that I do" (Rom. 7:19, KJV). This can easily be made to sound like a declaration of the perpetual human condition. And did not Jesus himself say, when confronted with a peculiarly poignant case of human failure, that "the human spirit is willing, but the flesh is weak" (Matt. 26:41)? And then there is Jeremiah: "The heart is more deceitful than all else and desperately sick; who can understand it?" (17:9).

The problem that confronts us here is not one that is peculiar to Christians. It is a severe difficulty at the heart of humanity. It is the problem of not doing the good that we would sincerely say we intend to do, that we clearly wish we would do, and that we grieve over and regret not having done. It is a fundamental problem for all who see life clearly and think deeply about it. Greek thought and civilization (such as it was) eventually failed in its attempts to solve the problem of how to do and bring others to do what they knew to be right. Socrates, famously, insisted that if we really knew what was good and right we would do it. Such "moral optimism" clearly puts too much weight on knowledge or on our cognitive faculties. Aristotle struggles with the problem at length under the heading "Weakness of Will," in book VII of his *Nicomachean Ethics*.[2] Although he regards Socrates's position as simplistic, he still locates the essential factors of failure at the level of cognition. But the apostle Paul had a deeper view of the dynamics of human action. He understood sin as a condition of the human self with which the Greek thinkers never came to grips. And he knew how to deal with it.

People today rarely do justice to Paul as a great thinker and one who, as a slave of Jesus Christ, laid the foundations of the millennia-long Western understanding of human life. Sir William Ramsay, of another day and with a clearer view, remarked that "in Paul, for the first time since Aristotle, Greek philosophy made a real step forward."[3] In his *A Man in Christ,* James S. Stewart remarked, "For sheer mental force, apart altogether from spiritual experience, Paul's place is with Plato and Socrates and the world's giants of thought."[4] To understand the battle between the flesh and the human spirit, according to Paul, and to learn how that battle can be won for Christ in the process of spiritual formation, we must take pains to use his words as he himself understood them.

"Flesh," in Paul's understanding, consists of the natural human abilities, considered in themselves and on their own, unaided by divine assistance and direction. Flesh is not necessarily bad, and it certainly is not "fallen or sinful human nature." For one thing, it is not human nature in sum, but only one part of it. For another it is not essentially sinful, fallen, or bad. It is a good creation of God, and needs only to keep or be kept to its proper function in life before God. Thus, "the son of the bondwoman [Hagar] was born according to the flesh" (Gal. 4:23)—that is, from normal human abilities. But "the son of the freewoman" [Sarah] was born through the promise and action of God, along with her and Abraham's normal human abilities. The mark of the action of the Holy Spirit with our action is always the incommensurability of the result with the outcome you could expect from normal human abilities and efforts alone. The "mind set on the flesh" is death (Rom. 8:6), because it draws upon natural human abilities alone, not upon the gracious actions of God in our life. Those who invest solely in their flesh get back only "corruption" (Gal. 6:8), for that is the only outcome of natural human abilities on their own, dominated by desires. To be corrupt means to be broken into pieces, to perish through internal disintegration.

Flesh naturally works by desire. Obsessive desire (ἐπιθυμία)—the kind of desire that can rule your whole life—is usually translated as "lust" in the New Testament. Lustful desire is the impulse toward possession or experience of its object. Lust "locks on" and cares for nothing else but its own satisfaction. "I want what I want when I want it," the song says.[5] Of course anyone caught in the grip of "lust" is already in real trouble. Those ruled by lust will sacrifice what is good, for themselves and others, to get what they want.

This overriding drive for gratification is the genuine root of "weakness of will," and Paul and the other New Testament writers saw it clearly. Desires taken by themselves are inherently chaotic (James 4:1–3), each clamoring for its own gratification. Lusts are deceitful (Eph. 4:22), because they each promise a fulfillment which they cannot deliver, and they drive us ever onward in the blindness of sensual futility (Eph. 4:17–19). Thus, "fleshly lusts wage war against the soul" (1 Pet. 2:11), against the inner principle of personal unity and integrity. We all have to be delivered from "the corruption [the disintegration of life] that is in the world by lust" (2 Pet. 1:4).

The terrible "deeds of the flesh"—"sexual immorality, impurity, sensuality, idolatry, sorcery, enmities, strife, jealousy, outbursts of anger, disputes, dissensions, factions, envying, drunkenness, carousing, and things like these"—that Paul enumerates as he continues his discussion in Galatians 5 are the natural and inevitable outcomes of "lusts" given free rein.[6] What is good and right is lost before the onslaught of untamed human desire. The will, the human spirit, cannot prevail going one-on-one with ungoverned desire. That is the situation described by Paul in Romans 7:19 and Galatians 5:17.

The human will or "spirit," by contrast, is very different from flesh actuated in unrestrained desire. It considers alternatives. That is its essential nature. It is our God-given ability by which we have an interest, not just in the present, but in what is better or best overall.

It takes a broad view of possibilities: not just of one lustful desire and its object, but of other desires and goods. That is where choice comes in. Choice involves deliberation between alternatives, with a view to what is best. It seeks light. It treasures the law. The conflict between "the flesh" and the (human) spirit is the conflict between desire—what I want—and the will for what is best. And hence it is also the conflict between desire and love, which is always directed toward what is good for its objects. Love is will-to-good. Lust and love are two utterly different kinds of things. You may say you love chocolate cake, but you don't—you don't will its good, nor perhaps your own—you just want to eat it.

Law also is directed toward what is good. That is why it often conflicts with desire. Desire says "Let's have sex" or "I wish you were dead." The law says: a greater good is at issue here—the purity of human love and faithfulness toward other human beings, or the preciousness of human life. So: "Thou shalt not." And beyond the explicit law is the general drive toward what is better and best. That is "the spirit of the law." That is love, which is committed to the well-being of its objects and so is the fulfillment of the law (Rom. 13:10). Hence in my will or spirit "I agree with the Law, confessing that it is good" (Rom. 7:16).

So the human will or spirit, the power of choice, always seeks a wider perspective than "what I want." But in the lives of people who are "without God in the world" (Eph. 2:12), lustful desires actually enslave the will, or even pose as the will. Many people lose any understanding that they have a will that is distinct from their desires, and they come to think that freedom is doing what they want, not what is good. We might even speak of a "vital" or "impulsive" will. That would be a will that is outwardly directed and moved by and moving toward things that simply are attractive.

You see this in a baby. A little baby very quickly begins to be attracted to things, to reach for them, and to move in relationship to them. That's all there really is to will in the baby. If the person does not develop beyond this stage of attraction alone, they will identify themselves with their will, and their will with what they want. They will never subordinate themselves to God and what is good, as a whole person living in God's world. Thus, "I want to" and "It pleases me" are now widely regarded as overriding reasons for doing something, when in fact they should never function by themselves as a final determiner for action. The meaning of the cross of Christ in human experience is that it stops any mere "I want to" from functioning as an adequate reason for action. The cross is therefore central to the moral life of humanity.

Impulsive will must give way to reflective will. The reflective will is oriented toward what is good for the person as a whole, in their communal setting, not merely to what is desired. So here arises the conflict that we all know too well, between the good and the bad, the good and the not so good, and the good and the better and the best. This conflict goes on constantly in human lives, and it trips up people at all levels of life in contemporary Christian circles. Moral and spiritual failure happens in cases where, for whatever precise reason, the reflective will has not effectively guided life. We then "do what we would not, and fail to do what we would."

By contrast, when we bring the reflective will to life in Christ (birth "from above"), and add the instruction of the law and the presence of the Holy Spirit, along with the fellowship of his body, we have the wherewithal to live in such a way that God is glorified in everything we do. The anticipation of this is seen in such great passages on the life in Christ as Colossians 3:17: "Whatsoever you do in word or deed, do all in the name of the Lord Jesus Christ, giving thanks to God and the Father through him." That becomes a real possibility, and progressive transformation toward inner likeness to Christ makes it increasingly actual. Vital or impulsive will is where you simply choose what you desire, and reflective will is where instead of just doing what you want, you choose what is good—and especially, as Christians, what is good under God, in the kingdom of God with Jesus.

A crucial third perspective on the will (human spirit) is to see it as embodied will. Embodied will is where impulsive will or reflective will has settled into your body to such an extent that you automatically, without prior deliberation, do what the will dictates. This is a sad—even a tragic—condition for those who have allowed their lustful desires to enslave their will, but that is the standard situation for most human beings on earth. Their body is running their life in terms of fleshly desires ("pleasures") that have enslaved their will and positioned their desire-enslaved will in their body. In this sense the body becomes the immediate, but not the ultimate, source of "the deeds of the flesh." This is perhaps what Jesus had in mind when he said that "everyone who commits sin is the slave of sin" (John 8:34).

Peter's denial of Christ perfectly illustrates this. It was an exercise of his embodied will. He did not reflect on the situation and then decide to deny Christ. When concretely faced with the accusation of association with Jesus he blurted out the denial. It was just sitting there on his tongue, ready to go. Such is embodied will for evil. After the fact, Peter discovered what he was really like "inside." He discovered what Jesus already knew about him.

To take another case, when people are verbally assaulted, what do they do without having to think about it? They assault back. When they are hurt, they hurt back. That is embodied will as it exists in a fallen world. When you are driving your car and don't do what someone thinks you should, they may honk at you, or make an obscene gesture, or other such things. The responses that then arise in the ordinary person are similar in kind. They are expressions of the embodied will. When someone "disses" another person, the other person (usually) does not say, "Huh, I have just been dissed. What shall I do?" No. Almost instantaneously with a WHOOSH the insult comes, "Right back at you!" Just like that. We can call that an "epidermal response," because it lies right at the surface of your "skin"—in your embodied thoughts and feelings.

It is the embodied will that must be captured by Christ through inner transformation. That will cannot be effectively controlled by "watchfulness" alone, by conscious monitoring, for it is always "out in front" of any conscious monitoring that we might do. Once Christ has captured the embodied will, watchfulness becomes very effective. But if we are living for fleshly desire, our embodied will will have already embroiled us in evil before we can reflectively take up a different direction. Our body must be spiritually developed to the point that what it is "ready" to do is what is good and right—what we "would" do. It then becomes a primary resource for living the life to which Christ calls us and for which he prepares us.

Therefore, Christian spiritual formation is the process through which the embodied/reflective will or "spirit" of the human being takes on the character of Christ's will. Think of Paul's magnificent statement: "The life which I live in the flesh I live by the faith of the Son of God who loved me and gave himself up for me" (Gal. 2:20). Not just faith *in* Christ, but the faith *of* Christ—the one by which he lived. I am to take his faith into me, becoming inwardly the person that Christ has called me to be, and this inward faith now spreads throughout my social, embodied self—more or less, and progressively more than less.

Let us be as clear as possible. When we speak of spiritual formation we are speaking of the formation of the human spirit. The spirit is the will or the heart, and, by extension, our character, which, in practice, lives mainly in our bodies. The main reason why merely preaching on the idea of spiritual transformation usually doesn't work is because it does not involve the body in the process of transformation. One of the ironies of spiritual formation is that every "spiritual" discipline requires or involves bodily behavior. We have to involve the body in spiritual formation because that is where we live and what we live from. Spiritual formation is formation of the "inner" dimensions of the human being, resulting in transformation of the whole person, including the body in its social context. Spiritual formation is never merely inward but is always manifested explosively outward.

In direct confrontation between human flesh and human spirit, between what is desired and what is good, sin wins. The futile human struggle with evil proves it. But fellowship with Jesus Christ in the new life from above brings new possibilities into play on the side of the human spirit in carrying out its intentions for good. Sin then loses as the desires of the flesh are ordered under the goodness and power of God in us. Thus, Paul tells us to "walk by the Spirit [the Holy Spirit], and you will not carry out the desire of the flesh" (Gal. 5:16). After listing the deeds of the flesh and outlining the fruit of the Spirit, he continues: "Now those who are of Christ Jesus have crucified the flesh with its passions and desires. If we live by the Spirit, let us also walk by [or follow] the Spirit" (vv. 24–25). In the other masterful passage in which he deals at length with the opposition between flesh and spirit, Romans 8:1–16, he states that "if you are living in terms of the flesh, you are about to die, but if by the Spirit you are putting to death the deeds of the body, you will live on" (v. 13).

Instead of engaging in futile, direct confrontation with the desires of flesh, organized by the evil one into a "world" set against God and what is good (Eph. 2:1–3; cf. 1 John 2:15–17), the wise and inspired apostle gives us a twofold counsel of indirection: (1) to crucify the flesh, and (2) to walk by or follow the Spirit. These are well summed up in his admonition to "put on the Lord Jesus Christ and make no provision for the flesh in regard to lusts" (Rom. 13:14)—that is, merely to achieve what the flesh wants. I believe that in following this counsel we should think of the two parts as being carried out simultaneously.

First, you will notice that crucifixion is not something you can do to yourself (you do not have enough hands). That is why Paul says, "If you through the Spirit do mortify the deeds of the body, you shall live" (Rom. 8:13, KJV). Endless grief has come to the people of Christ through efforts to use natural abilities and arrangements to restrain the flesh. Such efforts produce the many "circumcisions" that are found in "religious" life. Restraining the flesh is an essentially divine work, though we also must act. And what do we do? We simply refuse natural desires the right to direct our life. We decide that we shall not live for them to be satisfied. Living to satisfy natural desires is, as Jesus pointed out, how "Gentiles," those who don't know God, live (Matt. 6:32). We make a general surrender of the right to get what we want in favor of the call to do what is good under God. This is the right and healthy understanding of "death to self."

Following upon this general surrender is the practicing of specific disciplines (such as solitude, silence, fasting, study, worship, service, and so forth) to quell our desires that have been running our life and embed the will of Christ into our body in its social setting, making his will our embodied will. That is what Paul has in mind with "I bruise my body and make it my slave" (1 Cor. 9:27, PAR). The radical disciplines of abstinence, solitude, silence, and fasting are especially useful and necessary to retrain our body, along with the other active components of the self. "Surely I have composed and quieted my soul; like a weaned child rests against his mother, my soul is like a weaned child within me" (Ps. 131:2). That is our new reality. The chaos and turmoil of the self-life is now quieted, and I can stand firmly and effectively for what is good and right in the strength of the Lord. I am walking by the Spirit.

Secondly we must ask, What does that mean? It means, above all, to count on, to expect, that the Holy Spirit, God, Christ—the unbodily personal power that is the Trinitarian God—will act in my life to enable me to do the good and right in all things I am engaged with. I no longer "have to" do what is wrong in order to make things "turn out right." The ancient wisdom of the Proverbs says: "Trust in the Lord with all your heart, and do not lean on your own cleverness. In all your ways acknowledge Him, and He will smooth your paths" (3:5–6, PAR). To walk by the Spirit means to recognize him in everything you do and to expect his action. It means that you "set your mind on the things of the Spirit" (Rom. 8:5; 2 Cor. 4:16–18). It means, negatively, that you do not place your hopes in what natural abilities by themselves can accomplish (Jer. 17:5).

Jesus has arranged with the Father to give us a "Helper, the Holy Spirit, whom the Father will send in My name" (John 14:26). He will always be with us, and will direct and empower us, as we rely upon him and invite him into our activities. Now, obviously the experience of God in our affairs will strengthen our commitment to not having "our way," and the use of spiritual disciplines will train us away from trying to run things on our own. So (1) and (2) encourage and reinforce one another. They make for and fill out a life that is "from above," a "resurrection life that is already beyond death" (Col. 3:1–4), a life that is even now, before death, an eternal one (John 17:3; 1 John 2:17).

In such a life the desires of "the flesh" retreat to the very subordinate role for which they were created. Natural desires are good within the proper ordering of life. But they no longer control us, dictate our actions, and defeat the will for what is good: the love that fulfills the law and goes "beyond the righteousness of the scribes and Pharisees" (Matt. 5:20). Now, by intention, discipline and grace, I do the things I would and do not do the things I would not. Integrity is restored to my soul and spreads throughout my life. No doubt that is not yet perfectly so, but it is increasingly so as I grow in grace and knowledge toward a scene in which "that which is perfect has come and that which is in part is done away with" (1 Cor. 13:10). The peace of Christ and the joy of Christ and the love of Christ possess us, and, whatever battles remain to be fought, the outcome of the warfare between the flesh and the human spirit is no longer in doubt. Spiritual formation in Christlikeness conquers the flesh and makes it the servant of the spirit, both human and divine. That is the testimony of Paul, and the testimony of disciples through the ages.

CHAPTER 4

Beyond Pornography

This lecture conveys a central tenet of Dallas's thoughts on the nature of desire and willfulness. Here he uses the subject of pornography to address the broader subjects of addiction and compulsion and their predominant rise in contemporary culture. To address the issues of addiction, transformation, and wholeness, Dallas offers the "VIM" process and argues that applying this rather simple but powerful method can offer hope for lasting change.

Presented in 2008 as part of the Talbot School of Theology's Institute for Spiritual Formation lecture series and first published in 2016 as "Beyond Pornography: Spiritual Formation Studied in a Particular Case" in the *Journal of Spiritual Formation and Soul Care*

I HAVE DECIDED TO DISCUSS THE USE OF PORNOGRAPHY [(*porne* = prostitute) + (*graphy* = drawing)] because (1) it presents us with a peculiarly vivid case of spiritual formation and possible spiritual transformation, and (2) it is such a widespread problem for people today, including Christians and those in ministry. Indeed, it is a problem which generates a lot of hopelessness in those involved.

We need to make clear at the outset that everyone gets a spiritual formation. The most degraded person in the world has had a spiritual formation and that is why they are like what they are like. Hitler had a spiritual formation. A person who is engaged or involved with pornography is so because of their spiritual formation. Spiritual formation refers to how the basic elements of human life—the will, the thoughts, the feelings, the body, the social relationship, and the depths of the soul—have been shaped so that character and life come out of how they have been shaped. The fundamental distortion is in the human will, but the will quickly subordinates the mind. The will that is turned against God or turned against good hijacks the mind to justify what it is doing. The mind takes the emotions and feelings with it, and very soon you have a whole person who is wrapped up in something which perhaps others who are not in that position would look at and wonder, "How could that ever possibly happen? How could that be? How could someone do that sort of thing?"

So, I want to consider pornography as a peculiarly vivid case of spiritual formation and of possible transformation. Also, of course, since pornography is such a widespread problem, we need to discuss it with a view to helping people find their way out of it. A Promise Keepers survey found that 53 percent of its members consume pornography. A *Christianity Today* survey in 2000 found that 37 percent of pastors reported pornography as a current personal struggle and 57 percent of pastors listed pornography as the most sexually damaging issue in their congregations. A Barna research study released in February of 2007 found that 35 percent of men and 17 percent of women reported having used pornography within the last month. The pornography industry in the United States is large. *Adult Video News,* an industry publication, estimated 2006 revenues at 13.2 billion dollars. The United States is the world's largest producer and consumer of pornographic material, with pornographic websites drawing 72 million visitors every month and more than 13,000 pornographic video titles being produced yearly.[1]

NATURE OF PORNOGRAPHY

Pornography consists of writings, drawings, images, and pictures for use in arousing sexual desire and frequently in stimulating the body to achieve sexual discharge or release. The production of pornography and its use involves the degradation of human beings and cannot be an act of love, which wills the good of all involved. Pornography can vary somewhat in how it is presented and how it is consumed, but fundamentally it is an exercise in the excitation of desire. It is on a continuum with viewing actual people around one in order to stimulate, foster, and cultivate lust, which Jesus warned against in Matthew 5:28. In Matthew 5:28, Jesus responds to those who said, "I'm okay sexually because I don't do the deed," by stating, "That's not the full story." The person who uses others to excite their desires (i.e., sexual lust) is on a continuum and they are entering willingly into temptation. If someone says yes to temptation, they have already said yes to the wrong thing. Jesus is not talking about having a thought. Rather, He is talking about cultivating thoughts for the purpose of exciting desire.

It is important to remember that there is nothing inherently wrong with sexual desire and sexual thoughts. If we do not remember that, sexuality itself takes on a shady or wrong tone that actually makes it more powerful in that what is forbidden has in itself a way of calling for action and desire. Paul discusses how the law forbidding certain things actually excites the will and pulls people into it (Rom. 7:5–12). So, it is important to understand that sexuality, thoughts of sex, and sexual desire itself are good things and not bad things. That is true of desire in general.

THE ROLE OF DESIRE IN PORNOGRAPHY

The use of pornography is rooted in the fundamental role of desire in human life. Desire, on the biblical understanding, is not in itself bad, but it is dangerous because it has the tendency to take over a life. What happens with desire is that we lose sight of what is good; that is how desire takes over one's life. And if we relent to desire as the guide to our life, then we lose touch with what is good. Desire has the power to make us do that, which is partly because desire makes us focus on something. Desire gives us a very intense obsession with something. Desire, by its nature, obsesses. It is interesting that we rarely find anyone who is obsessed with what is good. We should be obsessed with what is good, but we are not. Instead, we regularly find people who are obsessed with something that is not good because they have come to desire it. Now, it may be something that is silly— for example, winning a game—but they are nevertheless obsessed with it. Obsession closes the horizon of the mind, and there is just that one thing that is there before the mind. The question, "Is it good?" is not allowed to arise.

So, desire must be subordinated to what is good, and it is the role of the will to see to it that it is subordinated to what is good. That is the difference between will and desire. Will always has a broader view. The will is looking at alternatives: "This may be good, but is it the best?" That is how the will functions in our life. The real danger is that desire will capture our will. There are many people who do not know they have a will distinct from their desires because their will has been captured by their desires. They think that if they desire something that is all that is needed. They have allowed their will to be obsessed by their desires, and when they do that their mind closes down. They learn that to hold on to their obsession, they must not open their mind to the truth. And, of course, when it comes to freeing someone up from obsession, we have to go to the mind and the will. The will can do what it is supposed to do only if it understands what is good and is strongly oriented toward it.

This is definitely not the case with those who are unaligned with God. In such persons, the will falls captive to desire: they live to do what they want. We can think here of the paradigmatic temptation in the Bible: Eve and the serpent. The serpent calls into question God's trustworthiness and then Eve desired the fruit. Since the teaching about what God had said was good disappears, Eve goes along with her desire and does the sinful thing. That is the general form of sin: to decide that I know better than God or better than good and that I will have what I desire.

In this sort of way, the world runs on desire and not on what is good. This general condition of fallen humanity is carefully laid out by Paul in Ephesians 4:17–19. We have to understand that Paul was a profoundly insightful person about the makeup of human life and why it goes the way it does. Here is what Paul says:

> Now this I say and testify in the Lord, that you must no longer walk as the Gentiles do, in the futility of their minds. They are darkened in their understanding, alienated from the life of God because of the ignorance that is in them, due to their hardness of heart. They have become callous [i.e., unfeeling] and have given themselves up to sensuality, greedy to practice every kind of impurity (ESV).

Paul is describing a progression. When persons have become calloused, they do not have normal feelings. They go to sensuality to feel something because it is very important to have feeling. Sensuality in the nature of the case does not satisfy and dulls quickly. And so, to get more and more feeling, they practice every kind of impurity with greediness. "But," Paul says, "that is not the way you learned in Christ" (v. 20). Christ has another way.

Or consider Romans 7:15–23. The heart of that passage is the saying: "the things I would, that I do not, and the things I would not, that I do" (ESV). That is the basic condition of humanity when it has been captivated by desire. It no longer thinks about what is good; it just thinks about desire. The will is, in the fallen personality, enslaved by desire, and so "I am doing the very thing I hate" (v. 15, NASB).

This is a precise picture of the person in some degree of bondage to pornography. In fact, this is why we need morals in human society. The task of morals is always to put people in a position where they can do what they do not want to do and not do what they want to do. If it were not for the overpowering and distorting or, to use Peter's words in 2 Peter 1:4, the "corrupting" role of desire in human life we would not need any ethics. The whole task of ethics is to find a reason or a basis on which to stand to enable you not to do what you want to do.

I often ask my students in class, "Do you think ethics is a good idea?" The most they say is that ethics is a necessary evil. You do not find people cheerleading for ethics or saying "Thank God for ethics." That is due to the corruption that is in the world through lust. And, of course, any individual who does not have the power to do what they do not want to do, and to not do what they do want to do, is in real trouble. We would not want to hire them. We want to hire someone who can do something they do not want to do—maybe even come to work on time. People need ethics if they are going to do that.

So, we really must pay attention to desire ("lust," "longing," επιθυμία) if we are to understand spiritual formation. We must understand that desire is not bad in itself, but if we allow it alone to control us, it will ruin us and ruin everyone around us because desire is not determined by what is good. And that leads us to one of our deepest cultural quandaries that reaches into the very heart of our churches. This cultural quandary is the idea that we can know what is good independently of what we want. The prevailing idea is that it is only desire that tells us what is good. And then love, which should be directed to what is good, is distorted to what you want.

One of the best illustrations on that point is when a person says he loves chocolate cake. But, of course, he does not love chocolate cake. He wants to eat chocolate cake and that is very different from love. If you were a chocolate cake and you heard someone standing by saying, "I love chocolate cake," you would not expect a knife coming next! That illustration helps show that there is a distinction between what is loved and what is desired. They are not the same thing. Love is always directed at what is good. You love something if you are set to advance what is good for it. So, if you love choco-late cake, you would be taking care of it, not eating it. Love seeks the good of what is loved. Desire seeks to have its way with what is desired. To love rightly is, of course, what redemption is about. The purpose of redemption is to bring us to love rightly. In relationship to pornography, the cure is love—treasuring what is good and what is right. But that is not something you can do just by telling yourself to do it.

The primary role of desire in human life is to impel us to action. If action were solely under the direction of thought, we would never survive infancy, and life would be an intolerable burden in which much that is good would not be realized. We have to have desire because we are not capable of thinking about all of the things that we need to do. Of course, that is just a part of the economy of the self. Habit is also involved, in that habit allows us to act without thinking, which is of course a good thing. For instance, the person you do not want to be driving the car is the one who has to think about what they are doing. You hope they think occasionally, but if they have to think about when to put on the breaks, how to do that, how to turn the wheel, and other aspects, then you are going to be lucky to get out alive.

So, desire moves us, and hence we speak of passion. Passion grabs us and that is the reason why people get addicted to things. Being grabbed, usually involving desire, involves them in life, keeps them moving, and that is essential to addiction. We have to keep that in mind, because when we address the causation involved in pornography, we are going to find things like boredom, alienation, and purposelessness are major factors in inducting people into pornography. We will rarely find anyone with a rich, full, exciting life who is engaged in pornography. There is a connection and it is very important in understanding why there is such a thing as pornography and what we can do about it. So God has arranged that we have desire and that it gives pleasure, and desire gives pleasure because it thrusts us in a direction and makes us feel alive.[2] Thus we get pleasure from desire itself, and so we desire to desire. Moreover, the gratification of desire gives us a sense of completeness and power—at least for a moment or so.[3] And yet, if people just did what they wanted all the time, there would be chaos. So, we have to understand the importance of desire and at the same time understand why it has to be limited. The primary problem is the contrast between what is desired and what is good, and the fact that desire brings feeling, excitement, and passion so that we wind up doing things just to get the feeling. And that is where serious trouble begins.

Thus, we do many things just to excite desire. Flirting (of various kinds) and titillation are major parts of life in fallen humanity. Temptation to sin is exciting because it plays with desire. This is a danger zone where people tell themselves, "Oh, this is innocent." And, in a sense it may be, but it leads into dynamics that can destroy persons. So, for instance, someone says, "I'll just try cocaine once." For some people that's enough, and they wind up addicted. That is the trouble with flirtation and titillation: it is exciting, it plays with desire, but when a person steps into it, they have no idea what is going to happen. Indeed, the adventure is part of what makes it exciting and interesting. A lot of troubles with faithfulness in marriage come from the excitement around flirtation and titillation.

Pornography, then, is only one of many ways in which the will can be enslaved by desire. In addition, the will can be enslaved to getting what one wants, looking good, dominating others, sex, violence, etc. These are all ways of exciting desire. In addition, many are enslaved to simple rebelliousness: the will enslaved by the will. Thus, John says that there are three things that are in the world: "the lust of the flesh, and the lust of the eyes, and the boastful pride of life" (1 John 2:16, NASB).

PORNOGRAPHY AND VISION, INTENTION, AND MEANS

With this understanding of desire before us, I would like to turn to my VIM formula for personal and spiritual growth.[4] The VIM formula is the idea that spiritual transformation into Christlikeness results from getting the right vision of reality and goodness, the right intention and decision (to actually become like Christ), and adequate means to carry out the intention. The same principle is involved whether one wants to lose weight, develop their muscles, save money, learn to speak French, or whatever. Personal change works through vision, intention, and means. If we have someone who is oriented toward something, has a vision of its goodness, has decided to do it, and gets the means, then we will see them be successful. However, everyone has had a spiritual formation—including those involved with pornography, or gluttony, or whatever—and it incorporates a VIM. Every condition of the sort—good or evil—incorporates a VIM that is in action and that VIM is the key to understanding whatever condition one is in. This applies equally to the spiritual life.

It is very important for Christians to understand this point if they are going to come to grips with the picture of the good life that the scriptures set forward to followers of Christ. Such a life will be accessible if we want it, if we have the vision, and if we implement the means. There is not a single thing that Jesus taught us to do that we cannot do, but we have to have the vision, we have to have made the intention, and we have to employ the means. We cannot do it merely by grunting it out. There is not a single thing Jesus taught us to do that we can do that way. But there is not a single thing he taught us to do that we cannot do if we appropriate this kind of pattern.

So, what is the VIM of the person engaging with pornography? Involvement with pornography is not an ultimate, indefinable fact that simply falls upon a person. That is also true of anger, resentment, contempt, and so on. These conditions do not just show up magically. They come from someone's vision, intention, and means. We just have to think of the lengths to which some people go to implement their resentment of others, or their resentment of certain types of people, or their resentment of their situation in life, and so on. So, if a person wants to get out of involvement with pornography, he works on replacing the VIM that put him there and holds him there with a godly VIM oriented to what is good to desire. That is something the person in question can do. God will help, but he will not do it for that person. Inevitably, at this point, we encounter issues in theology having to do with misunderstandings of grace. For example, the idea that grace eliminates effort or that effort eliminates grace. Such theological misunderstandings keep persons where they are because they cannot make the intelligent effort to change the conditions which result in situations like basing their happiness on food, pornography, or whatever else.

So, what is the vision of pornography users? It is a vision of women (for simplicity sake) as something to be used to stimulate and/or gratify sexual feeling and desire. Such a vision may be complicated by moments of repentance and thinking differently about things, but the vision of women as something to be used to stimulate and/or gratify sexual feeling and desire is the vision that governs the use of pornography. If someone does not have that vision, they will not engage in pornography because they will be thinking about the woman involved in a way that shuts down the whole enterprise. But, typically, a person engaged in pornography is thinking that women are for sexual gratification. Usually this is accompanied by contempt for women, which makes it easier to treat them as "sex objects." If one knows what pornography is and does not see that it is contempt for women, then that person is blind.

Pornography is also contempt for the one using it. I have never known a person who was engaged in pornography who thought it was something to be proud of and to talk about with others in a favorable way. Almost all are engaged in hiding because of how it makes them feel about themselves. They are actually using their own bodies and minds to gain pleasure and desire, and they know that that somehow is not right. Also, in most cases this will be accompanied by a vision of one's own body as a source of and means to pleasure. It may be that this view of one's body develops earlier in childhood than the pornographic view of women. But these foundations of pornographic involvement easily develop further into various forms of perversion, as one pursues sexual stimulation and satisfaction. This is because it is in general a rule of desire that if you satisfy desire, you do not *stay* satisfied. And, if your goal is simply satisfaction of desire, the satisfaction of desire will dull your gratification and you have to up the ante and go for something more stimulating. Of course that is why, in the end, pornography is so terribly destructive.

So, this prurient "vision" must be replaced by a vision of women and of oneself as creatures of God for his blessing, walking the hard path of life where they suffer afflictions and death but are headed for an eternity with God. This vision will allow us to look upon others with compassion and love as creatures of God. Such a vision—to see everything in the light of God—is what has to come back into place, and actually, in many cases that alone puts pornography away and one no longer has to deal with it. This is another illustration of how desire narrows your vision and how the will opens your vision, because the will is looking for alternatives. In general, the way to deal with any temptation is to broaden one's view. You put things in a larger context, and of course the context is God.

The pornographic "intention" is the intent and decision to use sexual sensuality as a major source of gratification. Often this is supported by the view of oneself as deprived or hopelessly burdened. One researcher, Mark Laaser, found that people who have high-demand but low-structured jobs and who spend a great deal of time at their computers are most likely to be in danger of pornography use.[5] Laaser points out three elements that foster sexual addiction: loneliness, anger, and boredom. In general, the focus of the pornographic "intention" is rooted in the view of oneself as deprived and hopelessly burdened, facing some sort of situation where there appears to be no way out and no way to cope.

For example, an unhappy marriage. For someone who thinks that they cannot get out of the marriage or deal with it in any other way, that person will say, "Well, this is my safety valve, this is how I deal with this situation." This intention is rooted in a vision of God and God's world as a place of bitter disappointment where humans must go after what is available and somehow endure the rest. Thus, the wrong vision of God lies at the foundation of pornographic practice. Ultimately, the picture of life as hopeless and a bitter disappointment is a picture of one who either is alienated from God or has a view of God according to which God does not care. Needless to say, a right view of God and God's world would of itself break the grip of a life of sexual sensuality.

The work to be done here should be obvious: the transforming of the mind by the truth about God and his world. But one also has to come to grips with the fact that they do intend and decide to use pornography (or food, violence, etc.). This is one of the things that people who feel hopeless find most difficult. Such persons are unable to deal honestly with the fact that they do choose or intend to use pornography. We will come to discuss some of the things we can do to help with that, but we must come to the point where we can say, "I don't have to overeat, I decide to overeat. I intend to overeat." Or, if that is too difficult, then at least "I do not intend *not* to overeat." The role of intention in all cases of addiction-like phenomena is difficult to come to accept because nearly all of them involve intense degrees of shame. But to deal honestly with the role of intention in pornography and other things of this sort is essential.

Once one's current intention has been owned, then the intention and decision not to use pornography must be formed. This will not be possible until the vision element is transformed along the lines suggested earlier. We simply cannot accomplish at the intention level what has to be accomplished at the vision level and we cannot accomplish at the means level what has to be accomplished at the intention and the vision level. One common problem is that we tend to accentuate the means and get all the means, but we do not have in place the vision or the intention.

One of the best illustrations of this is to look at how people learn languages in American universities, or rather, how they do not learn languages. For instance, one prominent American university has multimillion-dollar language-learning equipment, but the students generally do not learn languages. And yet in broad parts of the world there are people with no equipment, and they learn to speak English better than a lot of people in America. What is the difference? They have the vision and have made the intention. We have to do the work at the vision and intention level first, but once the vision element is there, then the correct intention can be formed. It is possible to deceive oneself about what one really does intend, so one must be very careful, searching, and honest in dealing with what one does and does not intend: what they have and have not decided to do. The fact is that people engaged with the use of pornography have decided to be there and have not decided *not* to be there. But "will power" alone will not solve the problem. It will not be solved without will power, but will power alone will not solve it. The vision and intention must be right and then the appropriate means will have to be employed to extricate oneself from pornographic use.

Now among the primary means to deliverance is taking care to see pornography in all of its dimensions for what it really is. For many people, to see the terrible degradation of others and oneself involved in pornography will strongly bolster their will to have no involvement with it. This is an application of the general truth that temptation of all kinds is defeated by "broadening the view" and looking at the solicitation in the larger context of life and of God. One has to have the intention to defeat that temptation or one has to broaden one's view. So vision and intention interact, and that is where the main problem is and where the main solution lies. Desire overpowers the will primarily by obsessing the mind.[6] What many think they experience as inevitability depends entirely upon their failure to see things as they really are. Will (i.e., the human "spirit") in its very nature seeks alternatives and the best of alternatives. But when the person has conceded desire the right to rule, desire blinds the mind and appears to give the will no alternatives (I have got to have that doughnut, see that picture, etc.).

So, desire shuts down alternatives that the will might contemplate. That is how desire works. So, if you want to loosen the grip of desire, you broaden your vision and you look deeper into what you are thinking. One of the things you do is you look at the people in the pictures as persons.[7] I can tell you from my personal experience that learning to see in this way changes everything. So you see that doughnut and you think, "Mmmmmm," and then you think, "blood sugar, diabetes, feet falling off . . ." All of a sudden that doughnut looks different, because now you put it in a broader context. I am really hoping that this basic point grips you, and that you go away with that burned into your mind.

But other means must be employed in most cases. Two of the most useful are: openness to others and resolute avoidance of situations in which pornography can be indulged. As for openness to others, this may involve confession (to appropriate persons in appropriate ways), sharing with others in the same difficulty, or an accountability system with a small group of others (not all necessarily in the same difficulty) that allows you to meet, to discuss regularly, and to call on others for prayer and support in the hard times. This functions somewhat like AA, which is an ingenious system for helping people break alcohol addiction. It would be a good idea for most churches to institute a similar program and not just for alcoholism (e.g., gossip).

Another measure that can be taken is to kneel down publically and pray out loud for deliverance from your temptation. Perhaps "in church." Saint Benedict threw himself into a briar patch upon the occasion of salacious thoughts, and it seems to have done wonders for him. Now, at this point one might say, "Are you serious?" My answer would be, "Are *you*?" Actually, a briar patch has a lot to recommend it against some other things you get into by avoiding the briar patch. I have seen many people who would have been much better off to have found the briar patch. To many these things will look outrageous, but they really are not. The real question is *Does the person intend to change?*

With respect to "resolute avoidance," make sure that pornography is not within your reach. You have to get rid of it and when tempted to replace it, resort to the helps mentioned in the previous paragraph. Someone will say: "I just can't do that." But anyone who says that has not decided to break the involvement or still has the poisonous vision or probably both. You cannot do the work at the "means" level that must be done at the "vision" and the "intention" level. And if you do not do the prior work, means will certainly fail to help you.

Of course you can get rid of pornography, and you can avoid

replacing it. It is not like fighting gravity. You are in a process of breaking habits that possess all dimensions of your being: will, thought, feeling, social context, and soul. It will impose some serious difficulties, but you can do it. You will be aided if you are practicing a sensible schedule of spiritual disciplines—solitude, silence, study, fasting, worship, etc.—that are not focused upon the avoidance of pornography, but upon the healthy fulfillment of your life under God in the dramatic goodness of God's world with others you love and serve. Pornography involvement is a sure indicator of the impoverishment of life. And here you need to remember Paul's advice in Philippians 4:8 to dwell on "whatever is true, whatever is honorable, whatever is right, whatever is pure, whatever is lovely, whatever is of good repute . . ." (NASB).

CONCLUSION

Jesus promised that "whoever drinks of the water that I will give him shall never thirst; but the water that I will give him will become in him a well of water springing up to eternal life" (John 4:14; cf. 6:35, NASB). By "thirst" I believe Jesus is referring to unsatisfied desire and its ravages upon people, such as the poor woman by the well to whom he spoke. The woman knew about unsatisfied desire. She was coming out in the heat of the day to get water because she did not want to have to deal with people around her who knew her. I do not mean to say it was her fault, because sometimes the unsatisfied desires you may suffer from are the unsatisfied desires of others. But the promise of Jesus is that if you drink of the water that he will give you, you will never thirst. What is the water that He will give you? It is the life of God. You participate in the life of God and that is how you escape the corruption that is in the world through lust. You become, as 2 Peter says, "partakers of the nature of God."

With reference to pornography or other enslaving fascinations, we are not talking about repressing desire or denying its reality. We are talking here about *not having* the desire. The person who would change must desire to not have the desires they now have, and be willing to do the things on the VIM pattern that will eliminate the desire or render it of no influence. Although there may well be cases where medical treatment, specialized counseling, or deliverance ministries are required, most people involved with the use of pornography have not come to the place where they desire not to desire it. For whatever reasons, they think it is too important to them and that they would be "missing out" if they did not have the desire for it. That concession traps them into continued use. It is like people who cannot imagine what it would be like not to be angry. It is so much a part of their life that they would not know who they were without it. Their identity is tied up with their desires. So, a person involved with pornography may wish they did not do what they do, but they have to go deeper. They have to be willing not to have the desires that they now have.

That is where looking to lust, as Jesus describes it, comes in. Why do people look to lust? In part it is just habit and their body is cued in so when something comes across their field of vision they think, "This is it." Actually, they can train themselves to where, when something comes across their field of vision, they will realize this is an occasion to do something else. This sounds terribly precious, but as a young man in high school I learned that I could deal with that by praying for the person who had come within my field of vision. One has to learn to do something else, and the very cues that clicked one into one response—in this case looking to lust—are cues now to do something else. That becomes a habit. But before we will do that, we have to think, "I'm not really going to be missing out on something if I don't do this." How can we think that if our desires are obsessed with looking to lust? We cannot. So we have to be willing to not desire the things we now desire. It is not enough to say, "I don't want to do it."

Anyone who follows the path of VIM outlined above will receive divine and other assistance to step out of involvement with pornography. What that means is that when something like the occasion to indulge in pornography presents itself to them, their first thought will be: Why would anyone want to be involved with that? Their vision will have to have changed. Their intentions will have to have changed. And they will have had to use some means before coming to that place. And then they will look at what had formally fascinated them as, "What?" That is why the progress of sanctification is a process in easy living. It does not get harder, instead, it actually gets easier. This is why Jesus said, "My yoke is easy and my burden is light" (Matt. 11:30, NASB). But you have to come to Him and learn (Matt. 11:29). And the learning process is what changes everything.

I often use the illustration of Jesus on the cross when He said, "Father, forgive them" (Luke 23:34, NASB). That was not hard for Him to do. It would have been hard for Jesus to say, "You blankety-blank-blokety-blokety-blank-blank, just wait until my Father gets His hands on you!" That would have been hard for Him to do because that was not in Him. We are talking about changing what is in us. That is what spiritual formation in Christlikeness does. So, it is not hard to bless rather than curse because blessing is in us. So, when Jesus says, "Bless those that curse you," He's not saying, "Get your will all whipped up, and be ready now, and regardless of how you feel about the matter, squeeze out a blessing." No, He is talking about becoming the kind of person for whom blessing is the natural response. That is changing the inside.

What we have said here in relation to pornography can be generalized, with appropriate modifications, to apply to all issues of spiritual transformation into Christlikeness, both negative and positive. The field of Christian spiritual formation is an area of reality that lends itself to knowledge and to practice governed by knowledge. One certainly understands this from reading the Bible, and especially passages such as Colossians 3, 2 Peter 1:2–11, and so forth. The field of spiritual formation is a field of play for grace, the actions of the Holy Spirit, and all of the instrumentalities of the kingdom of God. But, as we have seen here, it also requires well-directed effort on the part of human beings (cf. 2 Peter 1:5).

CHAPTER 5

Measuring Spiritual Formation

As a professional dedicated to higher education, Dallas was very aware of the growing trend within his field for collecting "hard" data related to assessing student learning and classroom instruction. Many educators in both Christian and secular spheres consider moral development and character formation as a "soft" (immeasurable or imprecise) area of student learning and therefore moral training is largely ignored. In this essay he argues otherwise and offers a rough outline of an assessment framework for Christian colleges and universities to consider.

Presented in 2006 at the Council for Christian Colleges and Universities' International Forum on Christian Higher Education as "Measuring Matters of the Heart: Spiritual Formation in the Age of Accountability" (previously unpublished)

ONE OF THE MOST COMMON QUESTIONS POSED TO ME HAS TO DO with whether or not—and how—we can measure—or accurately assess—moral and spiritual development. We are especially interested in "measuring" such development as a result of the context and training on Christian college and university campuses. Some fairly lavish promises are made by spokespeople for our various schools. How can we be held accountable—by ourselves and others—for the outcomes that we promise and hope for? How do we know which outcomes have occurred and why they have occurred?

When considering "matters of the heart" we are speaking of character. We are not just interested in actions and declared intentions, or even particular choices. We are, rather, looking at the nature and dynamics of the "hidden" aspects of the self or of the human being

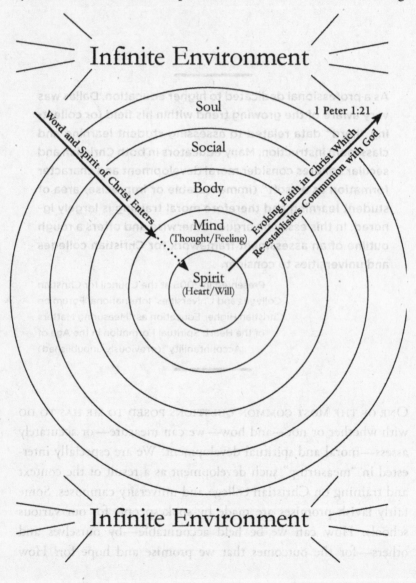

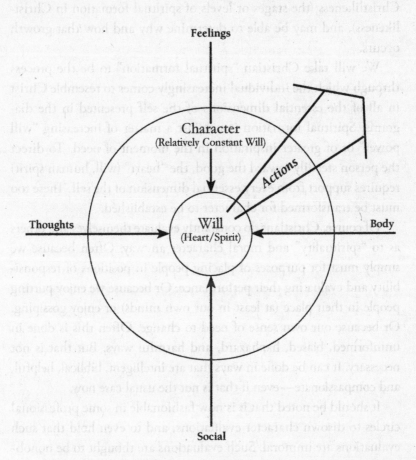

as a whole. We are looking at the reliable sources of actions. That is what character means. In order to bring this before us, see the two diagrams from *Renovation of the Heart* above.

Let us take as a plausible hypothesis at the outset that it is possible to know what the character of an individual is, and to know how it may have changed over a period of time, and why it changed in the way it did. Perhaps this is difficult to do and easy to get wrong. But it is fairly obvious in some cases—from reasons that can be given and verified—that some people are self-absorbed, hard-hearted, dominated by lust, have no regard for God, or are deceitful, and so forth. Or the moral and spiritual opposites. We can assess growth in

Christlikeness (the stages or levels of spiritual formation in Christ-likeness), and may be able to determine why and how that growth occurs.

We will take Christian "spiritual formation" to be the process through which the individual increasingly comes to resemble Christ in all of the essential dimensions of the self presented in the diagrams. Spiritual formation is not just a matter of increasing "will power" or of greater inspiration in the moment of need. To direct the person steadily toward the good, the "heart" (will, human spirit) requires support from every essential dimension of the self. These too must be transformed for character to be established.

Of course, Christians do constantly evaluate themselves and others as to "spirituality" and moral character anyway. Often because we simply must for purposes of placing people in positions of responsibility and evaluating their performance. Or because we enjoy putting people in their place (at least in our own minds) or enjoy gossiping. Or because our own sense of need to change. Often this is done in uninformed, biased, haphazard, and harmful ways. But that is not necessary. It can be done in ways that are intelligent, biblical, helpful, and compassionate—even if that is not the usual case now.

It should be noted that it is now fashionable in some professional circles to disown character evaluations, and to even hold that such evaluations are immoral. Such evaluations are thought to be nonobjective, arrogant, and hurtful to feelings—and feelings are sacred. But this just drives such evaluations underground, for they are unavoidable. We have to make responsible judgments about what people will be likely to do, and this cannot be done without assessments of character.

The setting of evaluation is absolutely crucial if it is to be effective, accurate, and helpful; and it must be done in a communal or at least nonindividualistic setting. Here we are very specifically going to be talking about the setting of an explicitly Christian community such as is represented by the public discourse of a Christian school. For such a setting there will need to be:

A. Public statements that substantial growth in Christlikeness is accepted as the norm by the community, and by those who enter the community. Everyone must understand this upon entry or upon considering entry. That this is a communal norm cannot be simply assumed, and the usual data (letters of recommendation, etc.) will not guarantee that people share this understanding. Church membership certainly does not guarantee it.

B. These public statements must not be vague, "public relations" talk. The entering student (faculty, staff) must understand that they are accepting the responsibility for their growth in Christlikeness, and that there will be thorough teaching of what this amounts to and fairly precise and realistic expectations that they will grow.

C. The expectation and teaching—and the accompanying evaluations—will be done in a spirit of love and acceptance. By taking individuals in, we have made a commitment to them that would mark expulsion as a very extreme measure. It must be understood that evaluation will be without condemnation, attack, withdrawal (distancing), isolation, stigmatization, or gossip. Complete privacy must be an iron-clad rule.

D. It is absolutely indispensable that the individual (student, faculty, staff) should own spiritual formation (growth in grace, putting on the character of Christ), as their project. The school is helping them with the project that they are committed to. It is not the school's project in which they must cooperate. It should be understood and explicitly said that procedures of evaluation are for the purpose of aiding the student or others to understand themselves and where they are on the spiritual path with Christ. It is to help them achieve the goals they have committed to as disciples of Jesus and members of your academic community under him. Intelligent and biblical evaluation procedures for spiritual formation simply cannot be done unless the subject desires that they be done. They cannot be done in an adversarial posture. (Here it is useful to rethink the entire matter of "grading.")

The school will find a great disadvantage in the fact that "Christians" are not automatically "disciples of Jesus" in any meaningful sense today. What it teaches and practices on this painful matter will have a direct and substantial bearing on what it can do by way of assessment of character growth.

It should be clear to all that faculty, staff, and administration are all involved in and subject to the same growth and evaluation process as the students. There will be differences in applications, but it is surely unthinkable that only students should be subject to the norms and evaluation procedures of a spiritual formation program. We cannot follow the saying "Do as I say, not as I do." It is also clear that such a program would have to be led from the top level of the school: the board of trustees, and the president and his or her staff must give it central priority. It cannot be left to designated under-lings. The idea that the work of the school is teaching and research in the standardly recognized disciplines, and that all else can be farmed out to Student Life, will require adjustment. Otherwise, the current presumption that spiritual growth is not what really matters will continue to prevail and have its effects.

It is crucial to say that if the statements above are not clearly un-derstood and heartily accepted and communicated by the campus leaders—those who determine policy and practice and preside over its execution—then we should not proceed with serious efforts at assessing matters of the heart. It would be ineffectual and do more harm than good. Of course A–D does not have to be totally worked out before you start some serious assessment. But the clear and clearly understood intent on the part of the school must be there.

What are we testing for? This is something we must be very clear about. And we must be very sure that we are not just testing for conformity to the particular "faith and practice" that distinguishes the school. We will be strongly tempted to do that. So here we will come up against tough theological issues.

We are not testing for behavior. Behavior/actions must be identi-fied, and in some cases must be dealt with. Behavior creates problems on its own that must be recognized, but actions are symptoms of what we are looking for in assessment. We are looking at "the inside of the cup," to borrow the language of Jesus. We are assessing or testing for the *sources* of behavior in the "hidden" dimensions of the self already referred to. The inclusive term for what we are assessing is *love*—love of God, and love of neighbor. Here again we take Jesus as our leader, as seen in Mark 12:29–31, drawing together the outcome of the Jewish experience of God. This love is seen through the fruit it produces in character and action, in Galatians 5:22–25 and 1 Corinthians 13 and elsewhere. Love is, as the song says, a "many-splendored thing," and we look for it in the many ways it displays itself in the character of individuals. Growth in love is a function of change in the essential dimensions of personality: what is in our mind and feelings, in our body and social relations, as well as in our dispositions of will.

Now, how do you test for the character of love thus understood? Remember, we are primarily helping the individual understand where they are and where they are going. Certainly actions are indicative of something, and must be noted, but it would never be appropriate to simply draw conclusions from an act that love is or is not the source (1 Cor. 13:1–3). Patterns of action over time and in diverse situations are much better indications of character, and tracking these can be illuminative of the state and of changes of the "heart." The individual can learn much by thoughtful and prayerful interpretations of their patterns of action.

On the assumption that the evaluation is going to be primarily self-assessment, carefully crafted questionnaires can be used to help the individual understand where they are and, possibly, what's going on in their trajectory through life. Such a questionnaire might be repeated at intervals (say, at the end of the spring semester or quarter), possibly revised in ways more aptly suited to show progress or lack thereof in specific dimensions of character. The results should be discussed with the subject in at least one interview conducted in the manner of a spiritual director, soon after the questionnaire's completion. Perhaps further personal interactions will seem advisable at that point, and could be suggested.

With respect to the questionnaire used, there are several available. The best one available, in my very nonexpert opinion, is the Christian Life Profile, developed in a local church context by Randy Frazee and some of his associates. On the basis of the questionnaire and interview, the subject can be directed on how to deal with specific issues: for example, fear (of various things), cheating, sexual issues, anger, and so forth. Assessment would have to go hand in hand with teaching. There should be good public teaching on campus that helps them understand why they fail, and what they can do to change the causes of the failure. Understanding and use of spiritual disciplines is vital for helping people change, and the keeping of a journal on problems and progress will be vital both to teaching and to assessment. It would itself indicate some growth. Intention to grow must be assisted by the willingness to implement means of change in all dimensions of the self, but especially in the thought life. What is constantly before the mind? A journal can be very useful in tracking this and leading to change.

Of course in progression toward Christlikeness the individual increasingly is holistically preoccupied by the good, and not only with the avoidance of evil. This comes through the transformation of each dimension of the self. Evil becomes less and less a thing of interest, less and less before the mind, and temptation therefore is more and more routinely and simply avoided. This can be helpfully tracked by journal keeping, which might then be a subject of discussion with the individual. Just tracking can have an immense effect on spiritual growth, and it lays a foundation for meaningful discussion, or even intervention with means of change.

The combination of (1) observation of patterns of actions, (2) questionnaires with (3) individual guidance/interaction, and (4) journaling can yield the data for reliable assessment of how things are (or are not) changing on the inside of the personal and social life, on campus and off. In particular, it can reveal the degree to which the individual is living in the great commandment in every dimension of their personality.

A major issue, now, will be what records are kept, if any, and how they might be used. For example, would a spiritual director write up something (per semester, per year, or at completion)? Would it be kept on file or given to the student, or made entirely optional to the student as to what would be done with it? Or would nothing at all be recorded? Or perhaps the individual him- or herself should write up something and decide what should be done with it. Needless to say, these matters would have to be handled very carefully, and policies and practices developed tentatively and slowly over the years. They would certainly have to be a part of the explicit understandings of those who enter the community at whatever level.

In a carefully handled program, the educational institution could check the validity of its own claims for students' spiritual growth and character development by keeping accurate, anonymous records using the above kinds of data, thereby gaining self-understanding as well as showing accountability. This would serve the school's need to direct policy wisely and know to what extent its claims about impacting character are true.

I maintain a strong belief that matters of the heart can be measured, or at least assessed with substantial accuracy, and, furthermore, that we should seriously undertake it. Certainly it can be done only on the basis of a profound understanding and teaching of the spiritual life in Christ.

CHAPTER 6

Spirituality for Smarties

As a longtime faculty member at a secular university, Dallas often engaged in robust discussion about the nature of intellectual discourse and the presuppositions, prejudices, and assumptions about religion in higher education. Upon the release of the book *Spirituality for Dummies,* Dallas found a surprising new platform to participate in these debates. Here, he discusses some of the intellectual biases that have surrounded the issue of spirituality versus materialism and naturalism, often couched in contemporary terms as the "faith versus science" debate.

Presented in 2007 at the University of Southern California for InterVarsity USA's "Spirituality and the Academy" conference (previously unpublished)

"SPIRITUALITY" IS NOW AN ACCEPTABLE AND EVEN A STYLISH PRESence in our cultural life, including the university or college. It can come in the form of religion, in some traditionally recognized sense. Religion can be, though it need not be, practiced as a form of spirituality, but much of spirituality's contemporary acceptance is due to its breaking free from religion in the public mind. A statement overheard in current interchanges is, "I'm not religious, but I am a very spiritual person." This says something quite deep, though I shall not try to go into it here.

"Diversity" has in recent years done a great deal to widen the doorway into university settings for both religion and spirituality.

Undoubtedly that is a good thing, so far as it goes. As you observe the phenomenon of spirituality broadly you see that spirituality meets two basic needs of human life: identity and empowerment. Spirituality tells you who you are, and it offers to give you some power over what goes on in your life. Many people today find these needs painfully unmet in their lives especially in a mass society organized almost totally around individualistic and passive consumption. Of course, such a painful condition is also found in other types of societies; but we have to deal with the condition before us, and [our society] is, for many people, one of paralyzing anonymity and passivity. Thus, anything that offers identity (turns me into a significant individual) and empowerment (brings important things under my control) becomes something to grab hold of. Spiritualties of all kinds, from vegetarianism to Satan worship, step in to fill the bill.

By a neat inversion, then, anything that gives me an identity and empowers me (or seems to) may be treated as a "spirituality." This accounts for the astonishingly broad application of the terms *spiritual* and *spirituality* today.[1] However, spirituality on the campus is not treated with intellectual seriousness. It is like a hobby or a sentimental attachment. Coming in under the flag of diversity entails that it shall not be treated with intellectual seriousness, nor, indeed, thought of in intellectual terms at all. Of course it could be studied in the manner of the social sciences—statistically and so forth. But no one would think of seriously examining Wiccan or Benedictine or Quaker spirituality for its truth or reasonableness, or of comparing them with respect to their moral qualities. One of the odd things about diversity is how it usually amounts to treating everything as "the same." But intellect comes to distinguish, to order, and to relate. So while "spiritualties" are welcomed back into the academy, they are not taken on in the central business of the university: the serious work of inquiry, the search for truth, in the hope of arriving at knowledge of "how things really are," as well as what is best.

So, in fact, things have not changed as much as one might be led to suspect from all the talk about spirituality. The title of the book

Spirituality for Dummies reaches deeper than just a snappy sales pitch.[2] In a sense spirituality is thought to be "for dummies." That you can be intelligent and spiritual at the same time, some people—not all—will allow. (You may actually know some people who are both.) Just don't treat your spirituality as an expression of your intelligence. Religion as a form of truth and knowledge was thrown out of the university a hundred or more years ago, and "spirituality" with it. Spiritualties and religions can be studied, intelligence can be applied to them in the social science manner (whatever that may be), but that is all. One cannot say, for example, that spirituality X is more intelligent than, more true to the "facts" than, or morally superior to spirituality Y. And this is the case, not merely to be polite or politically correct—though that may be in play too—but because the concepts of "smart," "intellectual," and especially "better" just do not apply to spiritualities or to religions, the way the language is now used. That, generally, is how things are now taken in the academy—or particularly at least in the "secular" academies. It is usually assumed that, if we don't approach spiritualties or religions in this way, they will not be fair, respectful, and generous to each other, nor we (academics) to them. "Tolerance," in this line of thinking, requires blindness, inattention, or refusal to see.

I believe that this way of looking at "spirituality" is a fundamental betrayal both of the spiritual dimension of life and of the intellectual mission of the university. I cannot address all of the difficult issues brought up by bringing spiritualities and religions under the fair scrutiny of intellect in the university setting, and, even if I could, I probably would not find a happy resolution to them. But I would like to try to make a start.

What are we to make of spirit and the spiritual, and hence of spirituality? What are these? What are we thinking of when we bring them before the mind? An old ethicist argues, "The word 'spirit,' even in its lowest uses, signifies something that acts; and when acting, is moved of itself and from within."[3] (For instance, we have alcoholic "spirits" as well as "team spirit" and "The Spirit of '76.")

The historical association of *spirit* with "wind" and "breath," in the Bible as elsewhere, occurs because spirit is thought of as an invisible power capable of producing visible effects. Wind is like that. But usually this invisible power, unlike wind, is thought of as more than, or perhaps totally other than, powers associated with the physical or the natural world and its objects—though all of that imposes serious tasks of clarification, to make any helpful sense. Because of this take on the "spiritual," it easily seems to blend over into the magical.[4] They are often confused.

Recently a book was published under the title *Employing Spirituality in the Workplace*.[5] Among other things it discusses how various symbols, incantations, or physical objects (pyramids, crystals, etc.) could be employed around computers, printers, copy machines, and other office devices to ward off the peculiar evils to which they are subject, and to infuse and sustain a proper order in them. Some would call that "spirituality," tapping into an extranatural order of causation, while others would treat it as magic. (Magic inclines toward disruption or suspension of causation—which is different from black magic.)

So, in a certain minimal sense, spirit is invisible power, and, most likely, a power other than those of the "physical"—whatever they may be. This, I think, will hold of all applications of "spirit," the "spiritual," and "spirituality." But further distinctions need to be drawn. Especially: (1) Is this "power" personal (the powers of a person), or impersonal, as in "The force be with you"? and (2) Is this power in some sense "in" human beings, or does it lie beyond, outside of them ("transcendental")—or both?

If the spiritual is impersonal, you can freely approach it with an engineering mentality. That is, you find out how to "work it," and then you use it for your purposes. It has an order to it, and it can be dangerous, as illustrated in Tahir Shah's book *Sorcerer's Apprentice*.[6] Yet, such concepts of spirituality suggest that if you come to learn how to deal with it you can make it do what you want and it has no choice in the matter. Such a position holds that spirituality is neither moral nor immoral. It just "works" or does not, like gravity and electricity, which are also invisible. If incantations, verbal commands, or spells are required to unlock or facilitate some action, it is not for the sake of a conversation. Therefore, one does not pray *to* their pyramid, even if they chant *at* it.

If the spiritual is deemed to be personal, however, whether it is a "familiar spirit," a fairy godmother, or Jehovah, you treat it as a person. It has choice and projects of its own; it can decide to do good or to do evil. It has moral personality, and you must come to terms with that. An engineering approach can be tried, as is common with most historical cases of the use of idols, but what comes of it is at the discretion of the spirit or spirits involved.

With reference to the second question, if the spirit and the spiritual are within you, there are, again, two ways this can be thought of. One is relatively tame. Here you simply discover among your images, thoughts, feelings, and choices some realities and powers you perhaps did not know you had or did not know how to draw upon. You learn how to engage them to discover who you really are, and how you can have results in your life that you desire but were previously unable to achieve. This is mainly what you find on the *Oprah* show and in Oprah's *O* magazine. It can be described as a milder form of "new age" thought, directed primarily at health, success, and good living.

In the second approach to the "in you" spirit, you actually turn out to be something very different from what you seemed to be. You turn out to be no less than God, the universe, everything. And everything is you. This is what is presented to us by Shirley MacLaine, by Alan Watts, and by Radakrishna, the Maharishi, and other "teachers from the East." Usually, what you turn out to be in this view is something "beyond personality," but the knowledge of this, and of how it works, brings identity and power into your daily life, however much of an "illusion" you and your daily life may be said to be.

Now, these descriptions and distinctions with reference to spirit and the spiritual can provide a kind of taxonomy for thinking about the different "spiritualties" that show up in our society and on our campuses. Any given spirituality will articulate, in general, a way of living that draws, in significant ways, upon invisible, nonphysical powers to bring about events and conditions in the course of daily existence. It will not be just an outward form of life—as religion sometimes is—but is primarily an inward and hidden source, no matter how it may be associated (or not) with outward forms and activities.

If what I have covered thus far is accurate and helpful, then I see no reason why intelligence should not be applied to the understanding of spirit and spiritualties, or why, in the abstract, one might not choose his or her spirituality on the basis of intellectual insight into what is true or false and what is good or bad. A spirituality is a definite sort of thing, with a nature of its own, with relations to other kinds of things, and it positions how one lives life, thinks, treats oneself and others, lives in the family and community, goes to work, and acts in the political and international arena.

In fact, I do not know if it is possible for a socialized human being to entirely escape spirituality, but in theory, at least, one might imagine someone living in total disregard of spirit and spirituality in the sense in which we have tried to explain it. Perhaps there is no such thing as spirit, and spirituality would then be based upon illusion. Perhaps that illusion is "necessary," as some argue, or not. But all of these are fair questions regarding truth or falsity. They are questions to which intellect is appropriately applied.

Clearly spiritualties are different, and often are different in very fundamental ways. Whatever "pluralism" is to mean, it cannot simply mean that "they're all the same"—at least not if one is to have a clear intellectual conscience. For spiritualties, cultures, and so forth are not the same. Just look at them, inspect them. If they were the same we would not have a problem to which pluralism is supposed to be an answer. If we do inspect the subject of spirituality wisely and fairly, putting our minds to the task, choosing not to be "dummies" on the matter, we will encounter a clear, fairly definable, and robust field of knowledge. We should never put our minds away, especially on the university campus, when we come to spiritualties.

Therefore, the only thing remaining to discuss is how we bring intelligence and spiritualties together in the academy. I suggest we need to start with developing our understanding of intelligence and what it is like to be genuinely intellectual in the approach that one takes to any area of life and thought. We need to understand what truth is, and how logical relations enter into the organization of knowledge. We need to understand logical relations and where they are present and where they are not. We need, as people of intellect, to be morally committed to adhering to truth and logical relations with careful attention and modesty. Our situation today is one where these commitments cannot be reliably counted on in our universities.

The intellectual life itself can be viewed as a kind of secular spirituality, and it often functions that way. Certainly truth and logic are forces, and are not physical forces. But that leads into a larger discussion that we cannot take up at present. In any case, academics are human too, and that means they can be governed by other than rational considerations: especially by how they want things to turn out. We need to be wary. Desire, as Plato told us long ago, is an unruly beast. It can twist and distort our thinking in any area of life. Our degrees and scholarly attainments and recognitions mean nothing to it.

With respect to spirituality, the practitioners on the campus should expect and welcome the most thorough intellectual scrutiny, and they should devote the same both to themselves and to others, as the occasion calls for. In addition, they should just be who they are, in terms of spirituality, wherever they are, within the boundaries of what is morally correct and sensible. Pluralism, insofar as it makes sense, is supposed to guarantee that, within those boundaries, one can be what one is without being socially isolated and mistreated for it, or deprived of economic or vocational opportunity. A practitioner of a given spirituality should assume that this ideal is respected (whether or not it is) by those around them in the academy, but they should at the same time understand that this does not mean exemption from intellectual scrutiny. As an English philosopher of some generations back, L. T. Hobhouse, used to say in sum that religion requires of philosophy only a fair field and no quarter given.

Such a "fair field" in intellectual terms is not always given. A couple of years ago there was a scientific conference at City College in New York City. A student arose to ask the distinguished panel—all of them Nobel laureates: "Can you be a good scientist and believe in God?" Reaction came quick and sharp from Herbert A. Hauptman, who shared the chemistry prize in 1985 for his work on the structure of crystals. He not only argued that belief in God is incompatible with good science, but also declared, "this kind of belief is damaging to the well-being of the human race."[7] One has only to think of all the great scientists who believed in God to see that this is an irresponsible statement, or perhaps a groundless redefinition of what "good science" is. What, after all, is the logical connection between believing in God and the ability to do "good science"? A "fair field" would require that Hauptman be faithful to sound reasoning and spell that connection out in a way that makes his claim at least plausible.

Perhaps somewhere he has done that. But I doubt it. People who make such claims, in my experience, have not seriously considered the evidence for their assertion. On occasion I have asked them for their data, and I have never found one who has taken seriously the provision of intellectual grounds for their claims. They are reasoning in terms of prejudice concerning what they believe must be the case.

A similar case of logical overreach is seen in a widely circulated statement by William Provine, professor of biological sciences at Cornell University.

> Let me summarize my views on what modern evolutionary biology tells us loud and clear. . . . There are no gods, no purposes, no goal-directed forces of any kind. There is no life

after death. When I die, I am absolutely certain that I am going to be dead. That's the end for me. There is no ultimate foundation for ethics, no ultimate meaning to life, and no free will for humans, either.[8]

Now, all the conclusions that Professor Provine has reached may be true. But his claim here is that they are dictated by "modern evolutionary biology." I think that neither he nor anyone else has shown us the path of logically sound reasoning by which established facts and theories in biology lead to the conclusion that "there are no gods," and so on. It would be very important to know of a professionally accredited textbook or peer-review journal in which this reasoning is laid out. Of course I am not qualified in this field, but I doubt there is a credible reference to such literature.

Often these kinds of grand conclusions are advanced upon the assumption that "nature" is all there is, and that what nature is, is exhaustively determined by the particular sciences. But none of the particular sciences, nor any combination thereof, includes in its subject matter any claims about all there is, or about all the sources of knowledge. Look and see. Such things are not a part of their competence.

Now, logical overreach is very common on the "spirituality" side as well. Trying to determine the age of the earth by reading the Bible is one example. But I have chosen these illustrations because of a tendency to credit antispirituality (I don't want to say "science") with a higher degree of intellectual responsibility than spirituality (especially religion). If this were ever justified, recent decades have removed that justification. Currently there is a remarkable upsurge of an older tendency, on the part of those who claim to speak for "science," toward "saving" the world from religion and from most of what would be called spirituality. Some want to keep spirituality, but help us understand it in strictly "naturalistic" terms by, for example, identifying spirituality with brain processes of certain kinds, or with human creativity.

Finally, there are some important insights available to us within the specifically Christian form of spirituality. Christian spirituality holds that the invisible and "unbodily" power that it involves is personal and transcendent, though much effort must be expended to explain exactly what that means. In a spirituality conceived in terms of transcendent personality, there are two sides to be observed: (1) On the human side, the individual takes action toward the spiritual realm by addressing it, invoking it, developing ways of understanding it, and finding ways of participating in its activities. One can fall into "spiritual engineering" in the process. But that need not be the case. In fact, one is usually warned against it. (2) On the transcendent side, the Holy Spirit is treated as a person who is in charge of the world, who works to bring about what is good, who is involved in human affairs for that purpose, but who leaves room for human beings to reject him, choose evil, and go their own way. Matthew Arnold's description of God as "a force working for righteousness in human history" does fairly well, if we understand the "force" in personalistic terms.

With some adjustments one can see the kinship of Christian spirituality with the other familiar theistic religions. Judaism and Islam are perhaps the most kindred, and, with even further adjustments, there is a similarity with Satanism, and some versions (at least) of Wicca or paganism. There are also some aspects of Confucianism and Hinduism, or of angel communion as now practiced in some quarters. But we will leave these lines of kinship and similarity unexplored areas for now.

In the Christian version of personalized spirit and spirituality, the spiritual life takes on the character of a personal relationship between individuals, with the attendant features of reciprocal attention, care, provision, assistance or service, emotional interaction, expectations, comfort, joy, and development or growth. In Western civilization as it has actually developed, the great record or testimony of spiritual life is the biblical book of Psalms. Just as an illustration, consider the twenty-third Psalm, with which most people are familiar, whether or not they self-identify as Christians. But the entire book of Psalms is a record, an enactment, a celebration of spirituality, of spiritual life, understood as an interactive relationship between persons in a personal as well as "natural" order. On one side there is a transcendental spiritual being—God, the LORD, the Shepherd—with his retinue and his realm or governance, and on the other side human beings, individually and in groups, all together constituting what is called "the kingdom of God."

This vision of life on a personal, spiritual basis in the kingdom of God is extended, for the Christian, in the person and teachings of Jesus (the Good Shepherd) in such a way as to include all of humanity, at their choice, without regard to any kind of personal, social, or cultural status, ethnic or otherwise, and to allow the individual participant to have the dignity and power to achieve a good life and become a good person. Devotion to Jesus Christ and to what he is doing in world history then and now is the center of a distinctively Christian version of spirituality.

Was Jesus a dummy? Or was he the smartest, most intelligent person who ever lived on earth? If he were a dummy, Christian spirituality would not rise above him. You might try to make a list of three people who you think were smarter than Jesus. Who in your field of specialization would those people be?

This extended vision of the spiritual life in the kingdom of God here and now is the vision that originated many universities, including the University of Southern California, and other great universities in the Western world, reaching back to Bologna, Paris, and Oxford. Although it did not always live up to its own ideals, Christian spirituality has been one that fostered the life of the intellect as an essential part of the spiritual life. The words of Jesus to his disciples, that they shall "know the truth, and the truth will make you free," is carved in the walls of more universities than any other saying. The ideology of truth and its discovery and dissemination is in fact a "spirituality" in the broadest sense explained above. The statuary around the central tower of the administration building on the USC campus is an eloquent if mute testimony to the underlying spirituality: Matthew Simpson and John Wesley (both Methodist ministers) facing the central quad, toward Doheny Library; Phillips Brooks and Borden Parker Bowne facing south; Plato and Cicero facing west; and Abraham Lincoln and Theodore Roosevelt facing north. What that says about spirituality and USC goes very deep into its history.

The relationship between Christian spirituality and the academy is written large in the past for anyone to read who will. Of course that history is just there—with many justifiable qualifications, no doubt, and large elements of non-Christian contributions, especially from Jewish participants. It doesn't particularly prove anything other than some *de facto* harmony and mutual support between spirituality and the academy. All the relevant questions about truth, reason, and value, with respect to a certain spirituality, have to be asked and answered by each generation as it goes by. Any spirituality, even a "secular" one, incorporates a set of claims about reality, truth, and value. The responsibility of people in the academy is to be intellectually thorough and honest with these questions, even if the officially recognized courses of study do not take them seriously (and they often don't).

The Christian in the academy has many useful models to look to. One of the most well-known, of course, is C. S. Lewis. His field of study, research, and teaching was medieval literature, in which he was, to say the least, a recognized scholar with many published contributions to his credit. After he became Christian, he was, simply, a Christian, wherever he was—"warts and all," as we say. His field of expertise naturally spilled over into a wide range of literary productions in which the truths and values he upheld as a Christian were, as a matter of course, artistically presented; and because of who he was all around he found many occasions to address the general public, including the academy and its varied inhabitants, concerning his beliefs and values as a Christian, with no holds barred and no question ducked.

Another individual actually came to be a Christian from reading one of Lewis's books, *Mere Christianity*. He is Francis Collins, well known for his work on the human genome and for identifying genetic defects that predispose one to cystic fibrosis and other diseases. He simply is who he is and overtly practices his brand of Christian spirituality wherever he is, as appropriate. In his case, his special expertise put him in position to write the book *The Language of God: A Scientist Presents Evidence for Belief.* Like Lewis, he is not dogmatic. His work simply tries to be thorough and honest about the facts and the logic, about what we know and what we don't know, and to leave matters open for discussion where the weight of evidence does not incline in any particular direction.

In thinking about spirituality and the academy, it should be understood that the work of intellect and of the researcher or teacher is not to get people to believe things or do things. It is to bring understanding, awareness, truth, and evidence to light. In a 1918 paper titled "Science as a Vocation," Max Weber says that "it is not the role of a professor in the execution of his duties to sell the student a Weltanschauung or a code of conduct. . . . And if he feels called upon to intervene in the struggle of worldviews and party opinions, he may do so outside, in the market place, in the press, in meetings, in associations, wherever he wishes."[9] But this is still true when we move beyond the range of worldviews and codes of conduct. If I am teaching geometry, as I once did, it is not my job to get the student to believe the Pythagorean theorem, or to act upon it—though at some point I will want to know if they can act upon it. As a researcher and teacher I am not "selling" anything. My task is to bring understanding of what is true, and of what means what, and of what is (or is not) evidence for what. If the intellectual or valuational content of my spirituality, of whatever kind it may be, is relevant to that task, then I have a duty to discuss it, so far as it is relevant. Otherwise it remains in the domain of who I am, where it is open to all to scrutinize and interpret or misinterpret as they see fit. My task with reference to it is simply to be who I am, in openness, humility, and benevolence to all. Its reality will speak for itself to all fair-minded persons. And if it is a spirituality that is also intelligent—a spirituality for "smarties," shall we say—that, too, will be clear upon inquiry. It must gladly stand the tests.

CHAPTER 7

When God Moves In

My Experience with *Deeper Experiences of Famous Christians*

This essay is unique in that it reveals a significant aspect of Dallas's personal spiritual transformation, part of the means he applied, and his thoughts on the outcome. In many ways he walks the reader through the application of his VIM methodology through the unique lens of his own life. The result is one of the most autobiographical reflections we have to date. Dallas believed in the benefits of anecdotal learning and here articulates the power of personal narratives that testify to the faithfully unique ways in which God teaches and guides his children to grow in the knowledge and grace of Christ.

First published in 2003 as chapter six of
*Indelible Ink: 22 Prominent Christian Leaders
Discuss the Books That Shape Their Faith*

THE ONE BOOK OTHER THAN THE BIBLE THAT HAS MOST INFLU-enced me is a little-known book by James Gilchrist Lawson, called *Deeper Experiences of Famous Christians.*[1] It was first published in 1911, and was most recently republished in 1999 by Barbour Publishing of Uhrichsville, Ohio.[2]

From a literary or scholarly point of view the book is of little distinction, which perhaps explains why it is not widely known and seems never to have been widely read or influential. But, given to me in 1954 by a college classmate, Billy Glenn Dudley, it entered my life at a very appropriate time, and, perhaps even more important, it opened to me inexhaustible riches of Christ and his people through the ages. This brought before me, in turn, a world of profound Christian literature of much greater significance for the understanding and practice of life in Christ than that book itself.

The peculiar doctrinal slant of the author led him to interpret "deeper experiences" almost entirely in terms of the filling with, or baptism in, the Holy Spirit. That is an unfortunate grid to place upon the "deeper experiences" of famous or not-so-famous Christians, as becomes quite clear from the "experiences" of the individuals described in the book. But, fortunately, that particular slant did not hinder the author from going, in considerable detail, into what actually happened in the lives of a wide range of outstanding followers of Christ—few of whom would have shared anything close to his view of the relationship between filling or baptism and deeper experiences of God.

The book begins with discussions of biblical characters, from Enoch to the apostle Paul. Then, interestingly, it takes up certain "Gentile Sages" (Greek, Persian, and Roman) that are also described as under the influence of God's Holy Spirit. Then a section is devoted to outstanding Christians of the early centuries of the church, and, finally, a section (very brief) to "Reformed Churches" and the Reformation period.

The first individual selected by Lawson for a separate chapter was Girolamo Savonarola (born 1452), a major precursor of the Protestant Reformation. What most struck me about Savonarola—and I truly was smitten—was his drive toward holiness, toward a different and a supernatural kind of life—a life "from above"—and his readiness to sacrifice all to achieve such a life. Indeed this is what stood out in all of the people Lawson dealt with in his book. And the deeper experiences that brought them forward on their way clearly were not all fillings, or baptisms, with the Holy Spirit, though no doubt the Spirit was always involved and genuine fillings and baptisms occurred. But more often than not they were moments of realization, of extreme clarity of insight into profound truth, joined together with floods of feeling arising therefrom. These experiences often were what George Fox called "openings," and they went right to the bone and changed the life forever.

Thus, of John Bunyan, Lawson writes,

> Bunyan's complete deliverance from his dreadful doubts and despair came one day while he was passing through a field. Suddenly the sentence fell upon his soul, "Thy righteousness is in heaven." By the eye of faith he seemed to see Jesus, his righteousness, at God's right hand. He says, "Now did my chains fall off my legs indeed; I was loosed from my afflictions and irons; my temptations also fled away; so that, from that time, those dreadful Scriptures of God left off to trouble me! Now went I also home rejoicing, for the grace and love of God."[3]

I think the book's effect on me will be better understood if we indicate the individuals singled out for chapter-length treatment. After Savonarola came Madame Guyon, François Fenelon, George Fox, John Bunyan, John Wesley, George Whitefield, John Fletcher, Christmas Evans, Lorenzo Dow, Peter Cartwright, Charles G. Finney, Billy Bray, Elder Jacob Knapp, George Müller, A. B. Earle, Frances Ridley Havergal, A. J. Gordon, D. L. Moody, General William Booth, and, in the final chapter, "Other Famous Christians" (Thomas à Kempis, William Penn, Dr. Adam Clarke, William Bramwell, William Carvosso, David Brainerd, Edward Payson, Dorothea Trudel, Pastor John Christoph Blumhardt, Phoebe Palmer, and P. P. Bliss).

Now, clearly this is a very selective and not well-balanced list of "famous Christians." But that was not something that bothered me as I took up the book and studied it. In fact, that these were, by and large, quite ordinary people only impressed me all the more that the amazing life into which they were manifestly led could be mine. I had been raised in religious circles of very fine people where the emphasis had been exclusively on faithfulness to right beliefs, and upon bringing others to profess those beliefs. Now, that, of course, is of central importance. But when that alone is emphasized, the result is a dry and powerless religious life, no matter how sincere, and one constantly vulnerable to temptations of all kinds.

Therefore, to see actual invasions of human life by the presence and action of God, right up into the twentieth century, greatly encouraged me to believe that the life and promises given in the person of Christ and in scripture were meant for us today. I saw that ordinary individuals who sought the Lord would find him real—actually, that he would come to them and convey his reality.

It was clear that these "famous Christians" were not seeking specific experiences, not even the experience of the filling or baptism of the Holy Spirit. They were seeking the Lord, his kingdom, and his holiness (Matt. 6:33). Seeking was clearly, from the lives portrayed, a major part of life in Christ. The "doctrinal correctness alone" view of Christianity was, in practice, one of nonseeking. It was basically one of "having arrived," not of continuous pursuit, and the next essential stop on its path was heaven after death. But in the light of these "famous Christians" it became clear to me that the path of constant seeking, as portrayed in the Bible (e.g., Phil. 3:7–15, Col. 3:1–17, 2 Pet. 1:2–11, etc.), was the life of faith intended for us by God. Salvation by grace through faith was a life, not just an outcome; and the earnest and unrelenting pursuit of God was not "works salvation" but the natural expression of the faith in Christ which saves. Constant discipleship, with its constant seeking for more grace and life, was the only sensible response to confidence in Jesus as the Messiah. The natural (supernatural) accompaniment of that response would of course be intermittent but not infrequent experiences of God, some deeper and some not so deep.

Now, "deeper" also meant "broader." Lawson was remarkably unbiased in his selection of the "famous Christians," and this taught me a lot. The individuals selected for presentation ranged very broadly as to cultural and denominational connections. There were a lot of Baptists in the group, which was my own denominational background. That helped me. But there were also Catholics, Anglicans, Methodists, Salvation Army, and others. Seeing that the experience of God in the calling to holiness and power did not respect sectarian boundaries taught me that I should disregard a lot of things that make for doctrinal and practical insularity in others, and place no weight upon them for myself. It taught me, in Paul's lovely image, to distinguish the treasure from the vessel (2 Cor. 4:7), to attend to the treasure—which is Christ living in the individual life, and the individual living into obedience to Christ. The blessing of God has a natural tendency among men to create denominations, but denominations have no tendency to uniquely foster the blessing of God on anyone. We can and often should honor a denomination or tradition because God has blessed those within it. But denominations, after all, are a vessel and not the treasure, and we humbly acknowledge this to be true of our individual denominational vessel as well.

The hunger for holiness, and for power to stand in holiness, to the blessing of multitudes of people, also knows no social or economic boundaries. This too was very important to me and was made brilliantly clear in the lives of the "famous Christians," many of whom were of no standing among humanity, or who disowned their standing. Not only did that give me hope personally, but it opened afresh the events of scripture for me, and showed for modern times how "unlearned and ignorant men" (Acts 4:13) could also bring the knowledge and reality of God to the world. It showed how God, through one individual, no matter how insignificant in the eyes of human beings, could make a great difference for good. I resolved that should anything come of my life and ministry it would not be because of my efforts to make that happen.

I moved on from Lawson's book to study the works of these and many other "famous Christians." The first was *The Imitation of Christ,* by Thomas à Kempis.[4] That work became my constant companion. Then it was the works of John Wesley, and especially his "Journal" and the standard set of his "Sermons."[5] Then William Law, *A Serious Call to a Devout and Holy Life,*[6] along with Jeremy Taylor's *Holy Living and Holy Dying.*[7] Then the various writings of Charles Finney, especially his *Autobiography* and *Revival Lectures.*[8] Later, as my reading and study broadened, the writings of Luther and Calvin, along with the later Puritan writers, meant much to me, especially in filling out a theology that could support the spiritual life as one of discipleship and the quest for holiness and power in Christ, without the least touch of perfectionism or meritorious works. (Book 3 of Calvin's *Institutes* has been especially helpful in this regard.)[9] I also learned that the follies of "discipleshipless Christianity," what Dietrich Bonhoeffer called "cheap grace," could never be derived from Luther or Calvin's vision of Christian life.[10]

These great Christian writings meshed closely with my continuous reading of philosophers, from Plato on, which I began upon graduation from high school and continued through two years of life as a migrant agricultural worker. (I carried a volume of Plato in my duffel bag.) The effect of all my reading has been to constantly bring me back to the Bible, and especially the Gospels, in an attempt to find in Jesus and his teachings what Paul rightly called "the unsearchable riches of Christ" (Eph. 3:8), which is the wisdom and reality that humanity vainly strives to discover on our own.

Jesus answers the four great questions of life: What is real? (God and his kingdom.) Who is well off or "blessed"? (Anyone alive in the kingdom of God.) Who is a genuinely good person? (Anyone possessed and permeated with agape, God's kind of love.) And how can I become a genuinely good person? (By being a faithful apprentice of Jesus in kingdom living, learning from him how to live my life as he would live my life if he were I.) These are the questions that every human being must answer, because of the very nature of life, and that every great teacher must address. Jesus Christ answers them in the Gospels and, then, in his people, in a way that becomes increasingly understandable and experimentally verifiable, and as no other person on earth has ever answered them. He evades no question and ducks no issues. The present age is waiting for his disciples to do the same today.

I never cease to be thankful for James Gilchrist Lawson and his little book. It came to me at the right time and helped me to see the actual presence of Jesus Christ and his kingdom and Spirit in the real life of real people. Thus it helped me to know something of "what is the hope of His calling, what are the riches of the glory of His inheritance in the saints, and what is the surpassing greatness of His power toward us who believe, in accordance with the working of the strength of His might which He brought about in Christ, when He raised Him from the dead and seated Him at His right hand in the heavenlies" (Eph. 1:18–20). Any reader should take from reading Lawson the simple but profound truth that they too can know by experience the truths of Christ and his kingdom that are set forth in the Bible: that if with all their heart they truly seek God, they will be found and claimed by him (Jer. 29:13). This is what human life is for.

CHAPTER 8

Apologetics in the Manner of Jesus

In this short essay, Dallas offers an incisive and powerful reflection on the means and ends of Christian apologetics. Though he lived in an era in which many apologists seemed to gauge success based on the level of contention they created, Dallas suggests here that following the lead of Christ requires an altogether different approach.

First published in 1999 in Reasons
to Believe's *Facts for Faith*

WHEN WE DO THE WORK OF APOLOGETICS WE DO IT AS DISCIPLES of Jesus, and therefore in the manner in which he would do it. This means, first of all, that we do it to help people, and especially those who want to be helped. Apologetics is a helping ministry.

The picture presented in the context of 1 Peter 3:15 is that of disciples who are devoted to promoting what is good, but are being persecuted for it. Their response, as Jesus had taught them, was to "rejoice and be glad." This led those looking on to inquire how the disciples could be joyous and hopeful in such circumstances. This question would, of course, be inevitable in an angry, hopeless, and joyless world. So the disciples were charged by the author of 1 Peter to "be ready to help people understand the hope that is in them, but with gentleness and fear" (v. 15), and always with a clear conscience that one has done what is right (v. 16).

So we give our explanation, our apologetic, as an act of neighborly love. As we do so we are to be as shrewd as serpents and as innocent as doves (Matt. 10:16). The serpent's wisdom is timeliness based on watchful observation. And doves are incapable of guile or of misleading anyone. So are we to be. Love of those we deal with will help us to observe them accurately and to stay entirely away from manipulating them—meanwhile intensely longing and praying for them to recognize that Jesus Christ is master of the cosmos in which they live.

Love will also purge us of any desire merely to win, as well as of intellectual self-righteousness and contempt for the opinions and abilities of others. The apologist for Christ is a person characterized as having "humbleness of mind" (translation of the Greek *tapeino-phrosúnē*[1] in Col. 3:12, Acts 20:19, and 1 Pet. 5:5)—which is a vital New Testament concept that cannot be captured by our word *humility* alone.[2]

So the call to "give an account" is, first, not a call to beat unwilling people into intellectual submission, but to be the servant of those in need: often, indeed, the servant of those who are in the grip of their own intellectual self-righteousness and pride, usually reinforced by their social surroundings.

Second, we do the work of apologetics as relentless servants of truth. Jesus said that he "came into the world to testify to the truth" (John 18:37), and he is called "the faithful and true witness" (Rev. 3:14). This is why we "fear" as we give our account. Truth reveals reality, and reality can be described as what we humans run into when we are wrong. In the collision we always lose.

Being mistaken about life, about the things of God and the human soul, is a deadly serious matter. That is why the work of apologetics is so important. So we speak the truth in love (Eph. 5:14). And we speak with all the clarity and reasonableness we can muster, simultaneously counting on the Spirit of truth (John 16:13) to accomplish with what we do an effect that lies far beyond our natural abilities.

Truth is the point of reference that we share with all human
beings. No one can live without truth. Though we may disagree
about which particular things are true or false, allegiance to truth—
whatever the truth may be—permits us to stand alongside every
person as honest fellow inquirers. Our attitude is therefore not one
of "us and them," but of "we." And we are forever here to learn and
not only to teach.

So, if at all possible—sometimes it is not, due to others—we
"give our account" in an atmosphere of mutual inquiry animated
by generous love. However firm we may be in our convictions, we
do not become overbearing, contemptuous, hostile, or defensive.
For we know that Jesus himself would not do so because we cannot
help people in that way. He had no need of it, nor do we. And in
apologetics as everywhere, he is our model and our master. Our
confidence is totally in him. That is the "special place" we give him
in our hearts—how we "sanctify Christ in our hearts as Lord"—in
the crucial service of apologetics.

CHAPTER 9

A History of Asceticism and the Formation of a Christlike Character

---

Many of Dallas's more well-known publications introduced readers to the enduring benefits of engaging the spiritual disciplines of Christian living. Here he provides a thorough argument for asceticism (self-denial) as an essential but neglected element in the Christian theory of a moral life. He also explores the robust ideological history behind the ascetic life and the ways in which it is a model for achieving a more Christlike character.

Written for the 1985 meeting of the Society of Christian
Philosophers in San Francisco, CA, as "Asceticism:
An Essential but Neglected Element in the Christian
Theory of the Moral Life" (previously unpublished)

It is well said, then, that it is by doing just acts that the just man is produced, and by doing temperate acts the temperate man; without doing these no one would have even a prospect of becoming good.

We are inquiring, not in order to know what virtue is, but in order to become good, since otherwise our inquiry would have been of no use.
—Aristotle, *Nicomachean Ethics*[1]

The barbarians are not waiting beyond the frontiers; they have already been governing us for quite some time. And it is our lack

of consciousness of this that constitutes part of our predicament.
We are waiting not for a Godot, but for another—doubtless very
different—St. Benedict."

—Alasdair C. MacIntyre, *After Virtue*[2]

I WOULD LIKE TO BEGIN BY STATING THE PARTICULAR ISSUE IN THE
moral life to which asceticism has, historically, provided one response. That is, namely, of how to bring one's actions into conformity with one's moral ideals, and further, how to become a good
person. Of course there has been much more to asceticism as a cultural phenomenon than simply a response to this one issue, especially
where ascetic practices have served as punishment or as a means to
merit, or where they have been expressions of abhorrence or hatred of
the body or of physical existence generally. But there is in the Western world, at least from Philo on, the tradition that finds in ascetic
practices the exertions of the "spiritual athlete," intended to train
the individual's personality toward the point of spiritual and moral
fulfillment, and then to maintain life on a high moral and spiritual
plane by continuation in systematic, routine practices.

In Philo's expositions, Jacob—who wrestled with the angel all
night and would not let him go until the spiritual blessing was
imparted—stood as the model of the spiritual athlete. According
to the article on ἀσκέω in Kittel's *Theological Dictionary of the New
Testament,* the early church fathers, from the time of Clement of
Alexandria and Origen on, followed Philo's interpretations.[3] Thus
they laid a foundation for a range of ascetic practices, which was,
with modifications, to characterize Western Christianity for a
millennium.

The specific practices that we shall be referring to as "ascetic"
include solitude, silence, fasting and deprivations of various kinds,
certain types of prayer, frugality, simplicity or plainness, certain acts
of service or submission to others, pilgrimage, "watching" (going
without sleep), submission to a director, and meditation. However,
they may also include poverty and celibacy, and have on occasion

involved more extreme practices such as wearing uncomfortable clothing or painful harnesses, living for years on a small platform on top of a pole (Simon Stylites et al.), living in a cubicle no bigger than a small closet, flagellation (inflicted by oneself or by others), refusing to protect oneself from the elements or even from insects, and avoiding the sight of a woman (even one's relatives) for decades.

Of course not all of these practices that have historically passed either as an ascetic practice or as a discipline for the spiritual life need be regarded as "legitimate." Here we are not so much concerned with which particular practices are "legitimate" or not, but rather are focusing on the idea of engaging in a particular discipline for the sake of its contribution to the realization of moral ideals.

Modern Western civilization, drawing largely upon Protestant concepts of religion and morality, generally assumes that such practices make no essential contribution at all, and are possibly even harmful to developing our cultural, moral, or spiritual life. In his fine (though now outdated) study *Askese und Mönchtum* (Asceticism and Monasticism) Otto Zöckler entitles the chapter on Protestantism simply "Anti-asketismus" (Anti-Ascetics).[4] And this is, on the whole, certainly justified, though the many sects originating from the Reformation were not without ascetical practices, some of which have even carried on into the present century. For instance, we still witness regular fasting days (Wednesday, Friday, or both) observed in some Methodist faiths, or the frugality and plainness intended by Quakers and Mennonites.

Generally speaking, however, Lutheran and Reformed teaching on the essentials of religious practice (see the Augsburg Confession, for example) come down to the preaching of the (correct) gospel and the (correct) administration of baptism and communion. Increasingly in American Protestantism even these have come to be regarded as more or less optional, since intellectual enlightenment in the more Liberal wing, and "salvation by grace through faith alone" in the more Conservative, have come to be regarded as the essential and sufficient substance of the religious life.

Thus the age-old practices associated with the spiritual life cannot, from the modern point of view, be regarded as desirable "where men judge of things by their natural, unprejudiced reason, without the delusive glosses of superstition and false religion."[5] These, as you may recall, are the words of David Hume, who here, as in so many other respects, gave precise expression to the modern worldview underlying the current version of "the good life." How nicely he puts it:

> Celibacy, fasting, penance, mortification, self-denial, humility, silence, solitude, and the whole train of monkish virtues:—
> for what reason are they everywhere rejected by men of sense, but because they serve to no manner of purpose; neither advance a man's fortune in the world, nor render him a more valuable member of society; neither qualify him for the entertainment of company, nor increase his power of self-enjoyment? We observe, on the contrary, that they cross all these desirable ends; stupefy the understanding and harden the heart, obscure the fancy and sour the temper. . . . A gloomy, hair-brained enthusiast, after his death, may have a place in the Calendar; but will scarcely ever be admitted, when alive, into intimacy and society, except by those who are as delirious and dismal as himself.[6]

Yet we must ask if this outlook, so much a part of the contemporary world, is compatible with an adequate theory of the moral life, much less an adequate Christian theory of the moral life. I think Hume's view is most inadequate. In particular, if I am right, his proposal cannot deal with the problem of how individuals become good, consistently acting and feeling as they know they ought. Hume's theory sustains itself only by means of a naive hope in the power of enlightenment over life.

Henry Sidgwick and others have pointed out that there is a natural desire in man to do that which is right and reasonable. But, as George F. Thomas responded some decades ago:

. . . that desire, by itself, is not strong enough in most men to overcome the natural passions and social forces which are opposed to the right and the reasonable. It is not enough to appeal to the reason; the will and the affections must somehow be brought into line with the dictates of reason. Plato realized the importance of moral education through associating pleasure with the good and pain with evil, and Aristotle emphasized the necessity of forming right habits. But philosophers have seldom probed this problem very deeply. They have tended to assume that if we know our true good we will seek it and if we know our duty we will do it. Therefore, they have thought that when they have defined the good and the right, their task is over. But man's will is divided and he cannot love his true good with all his heart. Again and again, he finds himself in the tragic situation of St. Paul: he knows what is good but he chooses the evil. He is powerless by himself to acquire the virtues or perform the duties which are required of him by moral philosophy. If he is to attain true goodness, he must be radically transformed. His desires must be redirected and his affections fixed firmly upon the good."[7]

It seems to me those who adopt Hume's view on ascetic practices cannot deal with this problem of moral formation. I maintain they cannot do so precisely because that view does not take seriously the bodily nature of human personality and the foundation of the effective will for good and right in the ingrained behavioral tendencies of the body and its parts. It is because the effective moral will is so founded that I refer to asceticism as an essential element in the Christian theory of the moral life.

To be an adequate theory of moral phenomena, any account of the moral life must provide plausible answers to questions of the following four types:

Intentional: What is (the nature, analysis, definition of) goodness, rightness, worth, obligation, virtue, and so forth, and their opposites?

Extensional: Which particular person, or type of persons, acts, character traits, institutions, and so forth are good, right, obligatory, praiseworthy, blameworthy, and so forth?

Criteriological: How does one identify, discern, or know which things or acts or persons and so forth are good, right, obligatory, and so forth? That is: What are the marks, criteria, or evidence used to determine goodness and rightness in a particular object?

Technological: How are good persons and institutions, or right and praiseworthy actions and behavioral traits, *produced* and *maintained*? What are their *conditions* in reality that are open to human control? Education? Training? Social structure? Law? Sanctions? Something else (such as drugs, genetic engineering, evolution, psychotherapy, divine grace)?

These conditions of adequacy in theory seem to me to be much the same for moral phenomena as for any other in the domain of concrete things and events—for example, the chemical or economic.

Now, when we turn to what is to be said about moral phenomena from the Christian point of view, there can be little doubt concerning the general outlines, at least, of the ideal of human goodness and virtue that is set before us in the writings of the New Testament and in the history of the church. We are to follow Jesus Christ. We ought to be like him in the moral as well as in the spiritual dimensions of our lives. That means that we ought to be dominated in our inner motivations (thus going "beyond the kind of righteousness found in the scribes and Pharisees" that lie at the level of overt action alone) by love of God and of our fellows. That is to say, we are to hold precious, to delight in and care for, persons, finite and infinite, guiding our actions accordingly. This is the characterizing feature of those generally regarded as approximating to the ideal type, such as Saint Francis of Assisi or Mother Teresa of Calcutta.

In order that the Christian imperative to love not dissipate into formless abstractions at the level of feeling or concept, we have illustrations of what the morally ideal person may do in the very concrete images of going the second mile, turning the other cheek, and not using others as the object of disdain or lust. We are directed to: "love your enemies, bless them that curse you, do good to them that hate you, and pray for them which despitefully use you and persecute you, that you may be the children of your Father which is in heaven. . . . Be ye therefore perfect, even as your Father which is in heaven is perfect" (Matt. 5:44–48, KJV).

The Pauline interpretation of the Love Principle takes its place alongside the Sermon on the Mount as an expression of what the human being ought to be and can be within the economy of the kingdom of God, which is his proper habitat: "Love is patient and kind: love is not jealous or boastful; it is not arrogant or rude. Love does not insist on its own way; it is not irritable or resentful: it does not rejoice at wrong, but rejoices in the right. Love bears all things, believes all things, hopes all things, endures all things. Love never ends" (1 Cor. 13:4–8, RSV). In the classical formulations of Christian ethics, love, with its necessary companions faith and hope, was to provide the foundation upon which the cardinal virtues of temperance, courage, wisdom (or prudence), and justice could pervasively and harmoniously operate within society and the individual personality.

So much for the Christian moral ideal. How is it to be realized in or by particular persons? What precise steps can bring us to actual participation in this ideal, against which the ordinary course of human existence seems so steadily to offend? I think that Christian ethical thinking in the modern period has not done well with this question because of its (often knee-jerk) rejection of ascetic practices as a possible means of Christ-realization in the individual self. This is associated with a usual failure to understand the body's positive contribution to moral transformation and the realization of ethical ideals.

If we but allow ourselves to think of the New Testament as containing the reflections of some rather observant and intelligent people who were heirs of centuries (if not millennia) of sophisticated or "high" culture concerned with human behavior and character, we may be permitted to find in it an incipient philosophy of the body and some significant contribution to the theory of moral enablement and formation. It is almost proverbial in Christian circles, and very commonly accepted beyond, that the primary hindrance to doing what we admittedly ought lies in the "flesh," and thereby in the body. "The spirit is willing but the flesh is weak" (Matt. 26:41) can be regarded not as a scolding, but as an analysis; "In me [that is, in my flesh] dwelleth no good thing" (Rom. 7:18) can be taken not as a complaint or a condemnation, but as a description, stating a useful truth about a fundamental component of human personality.

It is the active tendencies to feel and act that are present in the substance and the parts of the human body that foil the conscious and sincere intent to realize Christlike character—or, more generally, the ordinary human intent to do what is acknowledged to be right and good. The general human condition is then characterized by the words of Saint Paul: "The good that I would I do not: but the evil which I would not, that I do" (Rom. 7:19).

This need not be taken as saying that the body or the bodily is, as such, opposed to moral behavior, or even to the higher reaches of the spiritual life. It is no part of the position taken here that the flesh or the physical is inherently evil. It is enough that the body as we normally find it functioning in developed human personality has very much of a life of its own, which in various ways opposes—but equally well might assist—conscious intent, whether prudential, moral, or spiritual.

Two elements in what I am calling the "incipient philosophy of the body" found in the New Testament have been given considerable philosophical elaboration during the last century or so: (1) the body as a locus of (not necessarily self-conscious) intentionalities; and (2) the "plasticity" of the substance of the body.

1. Schopenhauer's doctrine of the body as "will" carries a conception of the body as a complex of selective tendencies that, so far from being exhausted or guided by "representation," actually serves as the

condition and guide of all our representations. A similar such view of
the body is revived and given extensive elaboration in the twentieth-
century French Existentialist thinkers Marcel, Sartre, and, above all,
Merleau-Ponty.[8] For Merleau-Ponty, there are intentional orienta-
tions implicit in the living organism of each type, which determine
a priori what will be experienced and undergone in the course of its
life. To these *a priori* intentionalities or tendencies are then added,
under the contingencies of existence, *a posteriori* ones that they make
possible, such as the "acquired" tendencies and abilities that make
up actual mastery of the English language, ice-skating, or solfeggio.[9]

The important thing to say in the present context is that, in his
view of the body, these intentionalities are "in our members." They
occupy, in the manner peculiar to them, certain vaguely defined areas
of the body, whether the brain tissue or the musculature of the legs,
the hand, or tongue, for example. These bodily meanings, both *a priori*
and acquired, serve to make possible our field of conscious representation and choice—but then also, of course, to determine what and how
we represent things and what choices effectively present themselves to
us. We are always poised to think, feel, and act in certain definite ways
in virtue of them, and will so act, for the most part, independently
of—and possibly contrary to—any conscious intent and effort.

2. The second theory suggests the human body is highly mallea-
ble before the meanings that may inhabit it, and is thus "plastic" in
the sense made familiar by William James's famous statement:

> Plasticity . . . means the possession of a structure weak
> enough to yield to an influence, but strong enough not to yield
> all at once. Each relatively stable phase of equilibrium in such
> a structure is marked by what we may call a new set of habits.
> Organic matter, especially nervous tissue, seems endowed with
> a very extraordinary degree of plasticity of this sort; so that we
> may without hesitation lay down . . . that the phenomena of
> habit in living beings, are due to the plasticity of the organic
> materials of which their bodies are composed.[10]

While we cannot by direct effort just *will* selective tendencies of feeling, thought, and action into or out of our bodies and minds, we *can,* within limits, choose to enter courses of action and experience that result in those tendencies being changed.

The phenomena here in question are, of course, not essentially religious or moral. Demosthenes, the great Attic orator and statesman of the fourth century BC, is said to have made himself into a tolerable public speaker, in spite of some difficulty of speech, by placing pebbles in his mouth and speaking over the sound of the waves by the seashore. To strengthen his lungs for speaking to large groups in a day without benefit of Edison's inventions, he orated as he ran uphill. He also shut himself up in a cell, having first guarded himself against a longing for human company by shaving one side of his head, and copied out Thucydides eight times over in order to provide an abundant store of material from which to speak. There can be little doubt that such self-selected activities would make a considerable difference in the active tendencies and abilities ready to be displayed at the appropriate time. There can also be little doubt that such an asceticism as this, painstaking training to make possible what cannot be realized by direct effort of will, remains just as crucial when we come to moral or spiritual accomplishment.

The human body is, then, the plastic bearer of massive intentionalities of will, feeling, and perception, which do not depend for their functioning upon self-conscious awareness or direct effort, but rather provide the essential foundation of such awareness and effort. The body thus understood is not transformed by religious conversion or ritual alone, much less by mere intellectual enlightenment, but by intense, large-scale, and long-run experience, and especially by ascetic practices or spiritual "disciplines." Such a transformation is essential to bring us to the point where we effectively do what we would (or ought) do and do not do what we would (or ought) not do.

That the way to transformation is hard is something that has been long recognized. In Hesiod's *Works and Days,* section 287, it is said: "Unto wickedness men attain easily and in multitudes; smooth is the way and her dwelling is very near at hand. But the gods have ordained much sweat upon the path to virtue." The ingrained tendencies that Saint Paul refers to as "the motions of sin which work in our members to bring forth fruit unto death" (Rom. 7:5), or "the law of sin which is in my members" (7:23), defeats the moral intent in two main ways: (1) through the speed of its reaction it leads to action before reflection can bring the moral intent into play; (2) through persistence of feelings and cognitive tendencies associated with contra-moral activity it wears down the will to good and right. With these two ways working together, the self remains entangled in patterns of feeling, action, and social interaction that overwhelm the moral intent and direct efforts to perform and be as one ought. But the automatic and persistent active tendencies toward evil or wrongdoing are diminished, redirected, or even replaced through appropriate ascetic practices in such a way that "the flesh" becomes the ally of "the spirit," and the individual becomes free and able to do the good that he or she would and to avoid the evil that is in fact not intended.

To refer back once more to the New Testament writings, it is clear that ascetic practices were seriously engaged in by Jesus as well as by Saint Paul. Both were upon occasion intensely involved, for long periods of time, with solitude, fasting, prayer, poverty, and sacrificial service, and not because those conditions were unavoidable. It would seem, then, that those who would follow Christ, and follow Paul as he followed Christ (1 Cor. 11:1), must find in those practices an important part of what they should undertake as his disciples.

Certainly this was so in the early centuries of the Christian era. For some reason, however, it is rarely done now; and outstanding Christian writers of the present time do not normally suggest that the practices of Jesus and Paul should be adopted by us. We are to be like them, but without following techniques that they seem to have found essential.

In *An Interpretation of Christian Ethics,* for example, Reinhold Niebuhr acknowledges that humanity "cannot, by taking thought, strengthen their will. . . . The strength of the will depends upon the strength of the factors which enter into its organization." But the necessary supplement as indicated by Niebuhr is a combination of "the socio-spiritual inheritance of the individual and . . . the result of concatenations of circumstance." Also, "The church is the body of Christ and . . . the noble living and noble dead in her communion help to build up in her the living Christ, a dimension of life which transcends the inclinations of the natural man."[11] Further, Niebuhr states, "Deeds of love are not the consequence of specific acts of will. They are the consequence of a religio-moral tension in life which is possible only if the individual consciously lives in the total dimension of life."[12] Finally, "The law of love is not obeyed simply by being known. Whenever it is obeyed at all, it is because life in its beauty and terror has been more fully revealed to man."[13]

How characteristic these pretty words are of writings by Christian moralists in the twentieth century! A fine discussion could be mounted of what, if anything, they really mean for practice. But they do not seem to address with any realism and practicality the problem of moral and spiritual enablement; and they seem to be in some wholly different vein from the rigorous advice on life handed out on the pages of the New Testament and by the church throughout most of its history. They are, I believe, a form of the Protestant delusion that the fellowship of the church or of Christ infuses in us the power to do as we ought to do without our undertaking a rigorous, individualized program of "exercise unto godliness" (1 Tim. 4:7).

Current philosophical ethics has even less to say about the technological questions in ethical theory, though it provides a few discussions under the heading of "moral education." I suspect that this is largely due to a feeling that to deal with these questions is to descend to the level of moralizing, or to enter the arena of mere psychology (Kohlberg and the like). Perhaps there is some justification for this feeling. However, it seems to me that no ethical theory that fails to deal with the technological questions can be complete. In particular, it must deal with the question, What kinds of persons must we endeavor to be, what kind of life must we lead, in order to be in a position to fulfill our moral obligations and realize our moral ideals? As Samuel Clarke observed over two centuries ago:

> Great intemperance and ungoverned passions, not only incapacitate a man to perform his duty; but also expose him to run headlong into the commission of the greatest enormities: there being no violence or injustice whatsoever, which a man who has deprived himself of his reason by intemperance or passion, is not capable of being tempted to commit. So that all the additional obligations which a man is in any way under, to forbear committing the most flagrant crimes, lie equally upon him to govern his passions and restrain his appetites: without doing which, he can never secure himself effectually from being betrayed into the commission of all iniquity. This is indeed the great difficulty of life, to subdue and conquer our unreasonable appetites and passions. But it is absolutely necessary to be done: and it is moreover the bravest and most glorious conquest in the world.[14]

It *is* a question of moral theory regarding how we must aim in order to do our duty, as it is a problem in ballistics *how* we must aim the gun in order to hit the target, calculating on all the forces that bear upon our action. As we will miss the distant target if we aim our rifle directly at it, so we shall not be able to do our duty if all we aim at is to do our duty. The rifle must be aimed appropriately above or away from the target if the bullet is to find it, and we can come into position to reliably fulfill our moral ideals for action only if we aim higher, aim at being a certain kind of person.

This is true without regard to whether or not we are religious. Ascetic practices are relevant to the kinds of persons we become. Without them we can only drift, subject to whatever influences come our way. With them, on the other hand, we have the possibility of some significant control over our moral future. This is also especially true for the Christian, who can also count upon an assistance beyond him- or herself—though not an assistance that replaces our own initiative toward moral realization through planned disciplinary exercises. A philosophically clarified understanding of ascetic practices that are psychologically and theologically sound is needed if we are to understand the meaning and process of the redemption of human personality. The Saint Benedict for whom we wait must not come with a bundle of switches.

CHAPTER 10

How to Love Your Neighbor as Yourself

One of the primary focal points of Dallas's ministry rested on the essential requirement that every professing Christian enter into a discipling relationship to Christ. He would often implore pastors and leaders to gather intimate groups of willing apprentices to Christ in order to intentionally learn to do the things that Jesus commanded. This essay comes out of that exhortation, and was initially created for a small group setting.

Presented in 2010 to a group of church leaders who were developing a neighborhood outreach program (previously unpublished)

SUMMARY: WE WANT TO FIND A REALISTIC UNDERSTANDING THAT loving our neighbor is something we can do in our actual world, and in our real circumstances. We must see why it is the "second commandment" and not the "first." That is because loving others as well as ourselves is something that can flow only from a life grounded and surrounded in the kingdom of the heavens. We must see what that means in practice and why we are not to love everyone as we love ourselves, but are instead to love them as neighbors. The Pharisee in the parable of the Good Samaritan asks an important question: Who are our neighbors? (Luke 10:29) I suggest we need to think *small* here with humility and boundaries based on humility. How many "neighbors" could you have? We are to invest in a few key relationships with openness, intentionality, and planning the how, when, and why we are attempting to love those close to us—those "nigh" to us. We will certainly learn as we go. We also discover the role of practicing the spiritual disciplines in all of this.

Here are a few first steps to consider.

First, we need to understand the scriptural basis for loving our neighbors. We can see this in Leviticus 19:18 and 34; Micah 6:8; Matthew 7:12; and Luke 10:25–37. Primarily what these scriptures reveal is the fact that all of us, including our neighbors, are "under God." Second, there is a higher opportunity and standard among disciples of Jesus to love our neighbors (John 13:34–35). The higher standard is the healing standard from which broken human relations are restored. We can see this demonstrated in the Good Samaritan story of Luke 10:29–37. Jesus designed this parable to make certain points:

1. That religiosity can tend to displace the two great commandments (loving God and our neighbor) and especially, in the parable of the Good Samaritan, the second commandment.

2. To illuminate the "quibble-question" (v. 29) of Who is my neighbor?

3. To emphasize this question as a very serious practical question.

This is especially important for us today because we can become overwhelmed with people and their significant problems and trials. We need to understand what really distinguished the Samaritan. Not what he did, but who he was. He was a person who had compassion for the injured man. The other two characters did not demonstrate compassion for the wounds and trials of others. However, the Samaritan, "when he saw him, he felt compassion" (v. 33), which reveals the nature of the compassionate "Lord" and his forgiveness (Matt. 18:27). This helps us understand the nature of what love is: we love something when we are devoted to its good or well-being.

This applies to God, our "neighbor," our flower garden, or our bank account. Love is will-to-good and therefore involves compassion. Love is not the same as desire, which is not always directed rightly or ordered rightly. Love involves compassion.

A person of compassion is one who feels the needs of others and whose compassion is not something that can be turned on and off like a water faucet. It is always on. It is a constant burden of life. This is why so many reject the commandment to love others: because love and compassion require resources of personal strength and wisdom in action. Loving your neighbor as yourself is a matter of who you are, not, primarily, of what you decide to do.

We can "afford" to be compassionate only if we know there is abundant compassion for us, toward us, by persons who have appropriate means. This is primarily God: "We love because he first loved us" (1 John 4:19). The perfect love of God toward us casts out fear (v. 18). Think of the role of fear in the Good Samaritan story! So, our experience of God's love is what allows us, empowers us, to set aside anger, selfishness, lusting, and so on in our relationships to others.

The first major step in becoming one of those who love their neighbors as themselves is to decide to live in compassion. Now let us be clear: this is a decision to receive the abundance of the kingdom of the heavens as the basis for your life. Matthew 6:33 describes what we are to be and do. We must understand this practically in order to be free of self-concern, and our self-kingdom or-queendom. This explains why neighbor-love is not the first but the second commandment. They are not two separate commandments, but one with two aspects. (Compare the closely associated teaching about forgiving others and having God's forgiveness [Mark 11:25–26 etc.].) They are not wholly separate things.

Now, suppose you are a person who has received compassion and can, therefore, afford to be compassionate. Your next major step is to decide on who your neighbors are. We said this is a serious question, though it can be used to justify not loving. The word *neighbor* comes out of older English, where it referred to "the boor that is nigh thee."

Here I want you to think of your neighbors as simply those we are intimately engaged with in life. The Samaritan found himself in intimate engagement with a victim of violence, and he responded accordingly. While the priest and the Levite rejected the engagement, after it occurred, they did not love their neighbor and did not "prove to be a neighbor to the man" (Luke 10:36).

A common usage of the word *neighbor* today locates the neighbor as one who lives "next door" or close by. A "next-door" neighbor is one with a special degree of intimacy, in this understanding, and there is something to that. But in this understanding my most important neighbor is overlooked: the one who lives with me—my family, or others taken in by us. They are the ones I am most intimately engaged with in my life. They are the ones who first and foremost I am to love as I love myself. If only this were done, nearly every problem in families would be resolved, and the love would spread to others.

But our closest intimates frequently are also the ones we have hurt most and been hurt by. Here is where the fellowship of disciples comes in, and where the higher standard of "as I have loved you" can/should/would create a context of restoration of compassion and love for those near us in life. The local assembly or congregation would, realistically, act like a hospital, with various people at various states of treatment and recovery. Then we move outward in love to those around us in the natural connections of life.

The second step is actually rather complicated, but it can be described as the decision to have compassion upon those closest to us wherever we are—at home, work, school, neighborhood, and so forth. Here it is very important to understand that the command is not to love everyone. God does but we can't even begin to achieve such a task. Love can only be specific, and love cannot exceed our resources. Suppose the next day the Samaritan came upon a similar case. And the next day. And the day after. At what point does the "as yourself" come into effect? There is no general rule here. Yet, we must respect our limitations and prayerfully seek the presence of

God in action with us. We also have the responsibility to care for ourselves under God, though in the rare case that may mean we are called to radical sacrifice, even death. Though this is not the normal case, still we must face and make such judgments in faith.

As a third step, we could experiment with a little exercise. Start by creating a list of the few people you are most "intimately engaged with in life." This should be a pretty small number, though obviously not in the case of those living in a large "family." Then make a list of those in the "next" circle of degree of engagement. These are close, intimate friends. This list should probably contain no more than eight or ten names. Finally, a third list might include coworkers, next-door neighbors, and so on. The purpose of these lists is to recognize that beginning to love your neighbor as yourself requires us to start thinking small, not big.

Humility is always crucial to love. The range of our love can grow as we grow. But if we start by wanting to love all orphans suffering from HIV/AIDS in Africa, for example, we are likely to get lost in sentimental abstraction. If one's circumstances, calling, and neighborly context are such that one can really do something for AIDS orphans, that is a different matter. Yet few of us can start there, and if we try, it is easy to lose both our way and our hope in trying to tackle such an enormous undertaking.

Finally, the fourth step is to begin as best we can with that first list of those in our "inner circle" and devote serious attention, thought, prayer, and service specifically to those two or three people. Allow time for this to develop, probably several months at least, until your ability to demonstrate love becomes a grace-sustained habit. Then you can bring more people into the range of your effective neighborly love.

As we go about these exercises it will become increasingly clear how necessary it is to practice a range of what we think of as the standard disciplines for the spiritual life (silence, solitude, fasting, prayer, study, and so forth) in order to receive the compassion, grace, and growth required to live a life of neighborly love. We may never feel adequate to such a life, in view of the depth of need that surrounds us. But it is right and good to understand that we aren't adequate to love as we should and could! Instead we are to stand with others in the fellowship of disciples of Jesus Christ and under the presence and resources of the kingdom of God.

In summary, here are the steps in effectual loving of our neighbor as ourselves:

Decide to receive compassion as a way of life.

Decide to be the embodiment of love and compassion to the particular people around you.

List those people in terms of degree of closeness.

Begin to practice loving those closest to you, paying special attention to your sincere concern, assistance, and compassion for their lives through your words and actions directed to those individuals.

Slowly work your way to your larger spheres of influence.

Engage in the spiritual disciplines that enable you to operate from a constant fullness of grace.

PART II

Interviews

These interviews were selected primarily for the scope of topics covered and the unique ways they reflect Dallas's refreshing in-person conversational candor and charisma. In addition, some entries were chosen based on how they reveal his unique personality and the remarkable way he embodied a Christlike character.

CHAPTER 11

Reflections on
Renovation of the Heart

This interview discusses Dallas's book *Renovation of the Heart* and investigates both the individual and communal aspects of the work. Founded by Richard J. Foster in 1988, Renovaré USA is a Christian nonprofit organization that seeks to "model, resource, and advocate for the fullness of life with God experienced, by grace, through the spiritual practices of Jesus and of the historical Church."[1] Dallas was part of a team of early leaders at Renovaré that taught at conferences and seminars around the world.

Interview conducted by Lyle SmithGraybeal
in 2002 and first published in Renovaré's
Perspectives as "A Conversation with Dallas
Willard About *Renovation of the Heart*"

What makes *Renovation of the Heart* different from *The Divine Conspiracy* and your other books on spiritual formation?

There is a great deal of difference. In none of the other books do I go into the details of how the essential parts of the human personality must change in the process of spiritual formation in Christ. That's what is distinctive about *Renovation of the Heart*. There are a number of other concerns, but the heart of the matter is saying we know we can't be spiritually transformed by just focusing on the will.

In one way or another, it is a common mistake to think transformation is all in the will. And it isn't! It's in the mind—how we think, what occupies our minds, and so forth. It's in our feelings. It's in our body. What is distinctive about *Renovation of the Heart* is the idea that we renovate the heart by, of course, changing it, but we can't do that, really, without changing the other essential parts of the human personality.

Now, there are two other really big concerns that go along with this. One concern is the many alternative forms of spiritual formation that are now coming forward. In the first chapter I set the project in the field of general human concerns that have been here forever and, therefore, concern any culture and any person. I recognize that there are alternative answers to the same question, and that these are very big now and growing; everything from Oprah to Deepak Chopra to the really inadequate ideas of education that dominate the secular world.

In the last two chapters I deal with another concern in the church by stating, "You really can't justify anything else but giving your whole attention to spiritual formation in Christ." If that is done, most of the rest of the stuff that churches are generally about will not matter or will come along. But if we do not make formation in Christ the priority, then we're just going to keep on producing Christians that are indistinguishable in their character from many non-Christians.

Like Renovaré, all of my books focus on specific kinds of questions. *The Divine Conspiracy* is really about the gospel: What is the Good News? What does it mean for human life? *The Spirit of the Disciplines* is the biblical and theoretical framework of the disciplines starting out with the idea, "What are we trying to do? What is salvation?" with the answer, "It is a life, and this life is not something that is imposed upon us; we receive it and work with it." One chapter focuses on the means, the specific disciplines. *Hearing God* is about the very specific issue of what it means to live with guidance in our life.

It seems in one way or another all of your books have tried to interact with contemporary culture, but *Renovation of the Heart*

may be the most intentional in its very structure in doing so. Is that a fair statement?

Oh, yes, I think that's true. It's so important to urge this point, you know. If we reject the Christian answer, we still have the problem. We're going to adopt some alternative, because the questions will not go away, the questions of "What kind of person am I becoming?" and "What is my role in that?" and so on. We have a whole range of extremely inadequate answers to these questions, and what we need to push as Christians is to say, "Look, we're not here to prove we're right; we're here to help people." If they can do as well going anywhere else, then God bless them. That's the issue.

What do you feel a person misses if they do not read *Renovation of the Heart*?

What they're going to miss is a picture of the dimensions of their own life and how they fit together and how they can be made to work toward the end of glory to God and human fulfillment.

All of the [new age] spiritualities that are now clamoring for attention, from explicit Satanism to what we hear on *Oprah,* are concerned with the two issues of identity and empowerment.[2] Who am I? How can I have the power to live? Those are the questions everyone has to deal with. If we don't come to terms with these, we lapse into some form of human decadence and failure. *Renovation of the Heart* is simply an attempt to say, "Here's the Christian picture. It's all true. It works. It's accessible to everybody. And there's nothing that compares with it on earth."

Also I emphasize at the beginning and end of the book that it doesn't take a budget, we don't have to be brilliant, it's very simple. Anyone—any church or any individual—can do this because God is in favor of it and he will meet us and help us.

From a practical point of view, *Renovation* centers around chapter 5, which is the VIM formula. We have to have the Vision. And we have to form the Intention. And we have to adopt the Means. Vision. Intention. Means. And if we do that, then it works! Every individual, every church, every organization . . . that's all we need to do. We don't need to do fancy stuff and create megaprograms. This, that, and the other. Just simple, straightforward practice.

Why did you write *Renovation of the Heart*? Was there an experience in your life or some similar motivation that created the need in you to write it?

The motivation was seeing all of these other forms of spirituality and formation blundering down the road, and the church sitting there with really nothing to say on the subject, and the members of the church getting more out of *Oprah* than they get out of their church. For example, there are large evangelical churches that have large contingents of the people who come on Sunday that are really big into *A Course in Miracles* and *Conversations with God*.[3]

Oh, yes. Kind of stream-of-consciousness stuff?

Well, guides in these kinds of books profess to be writing under the guidance of the spirit world. That's "automatic writing." It is stream-of-consciousness stuff, and you just attribute it to God, and who knows who else is in there pulling the strings and pushing the buttons. But you're just writing it out. And it seems to me superficial, and it's been done over and over and over again before.

There are multitudes of people in the evangelical and mainstream churches who are living off of this stuff, and they don't even know what the Bible says concerning these issues. Their churches don't tell them or give them practical guidance. They don't teach them about spiritual formation and how to do it. Many people get what they need from church attendance because the word is preached, and the rituals are carried on, and God works. But it's drift more than anything else. And that's why the churches keep reaching for some programmatic formula that will make people come and give money. It's just really very sad. I don't want to get off the point here. The thing that drove me to write *Renovation* was addressing the issue of spiritual formation and the need to do this in the contemporary context.

Can you talk a little bit about the biblical teaching on the soul?

Well, yes, I can talk a little bit about that. The Bible, of course, is not a theology book. It is certainly not a philosophy book. So we have to derive the meaning of terms from the context in use. And that is what we see in the scripture. It's a wonderful thing to do an inductive study with our concordance. We see that the soul is the deepest and the most vital part of the person as a whole. It is often treated as the person, and we actually do this when we talk about "saving our soul." Well, you know, we don't save our soul and leave our emotions and our feelings and our body and all the rest of it out. That's just a way of talking that emphasizes the soul as so fundamental that we can, in some cases, treat it as the whole person because it actually is the thing that integrates all of these aspects of the self and makes them work together. Now, I don't think we can find a passage in the Bible that says that. We have to read and study how it addresses the soul, and we then see that it is the deepest, most vital part of the human self.

It's important to distinguish the soul from the spirit, or will, because the will or the heart or the spirit is the executive center of the self. In other words, the spirit is the part that is supposed to consciously direct everything in the person, including the soul.

Generally speaking, we don't want to hear from the soul. We want it to just do its job. Unfortunately, in a broken world, it also is broken, and we're going to hear from it because many of the ordinary miseries and extraordinary glories of human life are expressions of the state of the soul.

There is talk in the scripture like, "The law of the Lord is perfect, restoring the soul." See, the "law of the Lord" draws the soul into the ways of God at a deep level that heals it. The soul's order is re-established in God through the law. Or the twenty-third Psalm: "He restoreth my soul." These are extremely crucial passages.

I do emphasize that we cannot just get out of the Bible a definition of the soul. The Bible defines almost nothing because it isn't a book for scholars and philosophers or free thinkers. It's a book for people who want help. It's primarily a book for pastors. They're the ones that can use it in such a way that it actually achieves its purpose.

Going back to the example you gave of the spirit being the executive center, if you use the analogy of an automobile, might the spirit be the steering wheel and the soul be the engine?

Well, I would say the soul would be more than the engine. The soul would be like the computer system that coordinates everything, from the smog device to the fuel-injection system to the brakes. Now, of course, you have guidance devices and all sorts of things. The soul would be more like the way this is all hooked together, a system of coordination.

The engine might be more like the body. In ourselves that is the source of our strength. As we reach out to God, we get another source of strength. But no matter how lost a person is, they still draw on their body. So the body would be more like the motor. Suppose we have a motor and our transmission doesn't work or our clutch or whatever. Then our body, our motor, just takes us down the road. Or our brakes don't work! We must have a coordination system.

The different parts of the automobile like the ignition switch, the various buttons, the steering wheel—the interfaces between the driver and the machine—are our spirit or heart. The different controls are the spirit.

Then we have the issue of what's in control of the driver. And the driver had better be under some control! Hopefully, that will be God. And so the relation of redemption and sanctification would be the ongoing relationship between the driver and God who is directing him. Now, if God isn't directing him, he may go wild and do all sorts of things criminal and crazy.

Think of the soul as the computer system that runs the whole thing. And then the spirit is the executive center. It's the faculty of choice. And then you want that faculty governed by the truth of God and the Spirit of God. We really do need analogies for all of this, because the only alternative is to write a long book of philosophy that no one would understand.

What does a church committed to the spiritual formation of its members look like? What are its priorities? What does it emphasize? How does it spend its time?

The crucial thing would be that it would have as its aim the formation of all the people in the congregation internally in such a way that the deeds and words of Christ would just naturally flow from them wherever they are. That is really the picture of the people of Christ in the Bible and through the ages. That's the intent.

Now, what would it look like? Well, everything they do would be, as best as possible, sensibly directed toward the end of formation. That would mean, among other things, that we would have teaching and programs of instruction and practice in doing the things that Jesus said.

I always like to illustrate this with "blessing those who curse you" because that is obviously difficult. So, for example, we would actually be teaching people how to bless those who curse them. This would be true of all the other things that Jesus taught. This is precisely what the Great Commission tells us to do. The Great Commission is still the mission statement of the church. It's just stunning to watch churches struggle to get mission statements when there it is, the Great Commission, and they should simply do what it says. Make disciples. Surround them in the reality of the Trinity in a fellowship of disciples. Teach them to do everything Jesus says. We're not going to improve on that. That was the church-growth program that conquered the world.

I was in a fascinating meeting where one man had been in China recently. A Chinese professor has found evidence that Christians reached western China before AD 90. Before AD 90! The idea isn't all that astonishing when we think about it. That's what the disciples thought they were supposed to do! And, I'm sure, the disciples just said, "That's it. Let's go!" And they all wound up dead. But everyone else did too!

If you wouldn't mind, please elaborate a little bit on the chapter in *Renovation* on the social impact of spiritual formation. You

mention that if people are formed inwardly, then the outer issues between us become much more manageable.

I think I learned more writing that chapter than any other. When we are formed inwardly, outer issues do become much more manageable. But we also have to say our relations with others are not external. They enter into our very identity. And that's why people struggle with them so. Relations between parents and children and siblings and mates. This is not external. We can't separate them.

I know [pastor/author and founder of Renovaré] Richard Foster has undoubtedly met this same thing, the illusion that spiritual formation or spiritual disciplines is privatization, that it's something that doesn't have anything to do with the social world or the real world. That's just a total misunderstanding of what it's all about. The transformation of our relationships to others is part of it and, particularly, the two points that I emphasize inherent in the fallen world of "withdrawal" and "attack," getting to where that isn't how we relate to others no matter who they are, no matter how worthy we think they are of being attacked. We just don't do it.

That's the secret of Jesus. You watch Jesus, and you see he never did "withdraw" and then "attack." All of the time people wanted him to do it and in many ways, but he would not. Then to the body of believers he said, "This will show everyone that you are my disciples, if you love one another," but he had already said, "Love one another as I have loved you." So that's the model. In that sense the transformation of the social world is at its heart the transformation of personal relations. That's the key to transforming society in the larger arena. There is no cure for the social battles that we fight in our culture—and there's so much grief around race, gender, and so forth—until you eliminate "withdrawal" and "attack" and replace them with "acceptance" and "help." Once you do that and not just talk about it, these other issues will fall into place quickly. They will not fall into place at all unless it is done this way.

We may do some things, march and shout and so on, because it's not happening, but that isn't the solution. And if we have to do other things, from demonstrating to passing laws and so forth, that will not get us where we want to go. These things may be necessary and good—I'm not questioning that—but they will not get us where we want to go.

Those are really temporary fixes.

They are, and they're very important. But we now have a nation that is sick and angry, with battles over justice, and in that respect we have to find a different basis. We cannot handle injustice by finding more ways to impose what is in fact "right" on people. It has to come from the inside. And that's where the church should be working.

When you say "withdrawal" and "attack" being replaced by "acceptance" and "help," that's really talking about an inner posture of the self.

Oh, yes. But again, you can't separate that from the action. That's the illusion—the idea that you can be all right on the inside and not act it out—and it has affected us in many ways. That's a part of the idea that professing is enough.

We have churches full of people who profess all kinds of stuff that they don't believe. They think that by professing it they're doing something good. Really, they're just deluding themselves. In the area of social righteousness, we cannot be right on the inside and not do it. We cannot! Of course we have people who pretend that they can, but it simply isn't true. If we are right on the inside, we will address these issues straightforwardly and take a stand on them, and, if necessary, die for them. We will be that committed.

CHAPTER 12

A New Age of Ancient Christian Spirituality

Dallas surprised a small band of theology students who were studying his book *Renovation of the Heart* one afternoon at the Talbot School of Theology in La Mirada, CA. This is the transcribed conversation he had with the students.

First published in 2002 in Talbot School of Theology's *Steadfast* newsletter

What led you into your investigation of spiritual formation?

The conviction that Jesus is the center of all things and that what he is doing is good. I became convicted that I did not know enough about the human soul to be a preacher. At the time, the people who talked more about [the human soul] were philosophers. I was ministering to people who were in a tremendous amount of trouble, and did not know what to do about it. These were people who were already saved and, from their theological perspective, there wasn't really anything else for them to do about their condition. It became clear to me that I just wasn't saying much that was really helpful to people. I was becoming uneasy about a lot of the theology regarding salvation and, especially, it was becoming clearer to me that what was being presented as the essence of the matter involving salvation just wasn't congruent with what the New Testament (or, for that matter, the Old Testament) teaches.

What I would like to do for people is to present the life in Christ as something that is accessible and something that works. So that all of the wonderful phraseology (like you find in Ephesians 4, Galatians 5, Colossians 3, 1 Corinthians 13, or Matthew 5) doesn't just sit over there like a Platonic form, out of reach, where you're just able to see enough of it to feel guilty. [Life with Christ] doesn't just have to do with forgiveness, but more than anything it has to do with a relationship to real life.

When I began to study philosophy, I saw from the very beginning that Plato's *Republic* is essentially a book on spiritual formation. Its real question was, How can you get leaders who can be trusted?—which is a lively topic today. We have the same problem with both ministers and elected officials. That problem . . . has come all the way down through history and remains unsolved from the secular point of view. What really grips me is the realization that there is really no solution to that problem apart from the life in the kingdom of God lived as discipleship, where questions like, "How am I going to get ahead?" "How am I going to secure myself?" "How am I going to get what I want?"—are adequately dealt with in a framework of real life. I've just been responding to what I've seen to be the needs of the person who has good sense and is devoted to Christ. And I've been trying to minister what is found in the Bible and in the history of God's people. How do you make that available? How do you claim it for yourself, first of all, and how do you give it to others? My intention in studying philosophy was to become less harmful in the pulpit. I really just wanted to not make [the present situation] worse.

To live and minister in light of these truths [of the gospel], you really do have to have a lot of peace in your heart. That comes from the realization that you don't have to make it happen. You just be truthful, follow your studies, stay with your fellowship and the few who are close to you, and just keep going. Because, truthfully, what we need is a revolution, but revolution is always very dangerous. And human revolutions always devour their children. So what we need is a revolution that is actually conducted by Christ. And that means that we have to be content not to make things happen.

Discuss spiritual formation and the gospel.

We need to have Vision, Intention, and Means in order to achieve spiritual formation. That's the basic issue regarding the teaching of Jesus. There isn't a single thing that Jesus taught that a person cannot come to do by engaging his grace. Not a single thing. But you have to want to. And you have to decide to. And that's what is lacking. Why? It goes back to the [nature of the] gospel that is preached today.

The gospel that is preached today doesn't touch on [formation in Christ]. The gospel that is preached is only about forgiveness. Why should I bother to do what Jesus taught? That's what you teach! That the gospel is all about forgiveness! It turns out that what [we] really think about Jesus is revealed by what [we] do after [we] find out that [we] don't have to do anything. That's what really tells what you think about Jesus. If you think that Jesus is working in the world, then you're going to want to be part of it. But if you think that all Jesus did was to die for us, pay for our sins, and that's it, then there's no reason to try to do what [Jesus] said. There's no justification for it based on [such a message].

How can we keep spiritual formation from becoming merely a fad?

The important thing is to tie spiritual formation to obedience to Christ. Spiritual formation is pointless in itself. It is obedience to Christ that is everything. This is especially possible for a biblically oriented group. Our problem is that we're so biblical that we defend obedience against the Bible. We're so used to reading [the Bible] without putting it into practice, and yet we [claim to have] such high views of scripture. This is a real problem because it creates a culture in which we are close to God with our lips, but our hearts are far from him. We think that we're all right just because we've heard the words. That's the hardest part to break through.

Suppose you're going to actually do it . . . you're going to begin putting spiritual formation into practice in the church. That's where the block comes in, because our churches are set up to say, "No, we don't really need to do that. . . . That's inessential." As long as [spiritual formation] is inessential, spiritual formation will never be more than a fad. As long as it is not conceptually connected with the gospel that is preached, then we will cycle [through] one fad after another one, and spiritual formation will just be one among many. So we cannot approach spiritual formation without the appropriate understanding of the gospel, the appropriate ontology of the universe and the human self. So unless we get back to the theology that deals with it, then, at most, some people will see the point of it, and the rest will not and move on to the next thing. Now, what is preached as the gospel by most evangelicals is [only] one theory of the atonement—that's presented as *the* gospel. But the gospel is not just about forgiveness. The gospel is about life!

Discuss the kingdom of God.

The kingdom of God is what God is doing. Both testaments use the word *reign* in this respect. The reign of God is the kingdom of God. So what is the kingdom of God? You need to know that or else you cannot "seek first the kingdom of God," can you? So how do you seek first the kingdom of God? Well, you would try to find out what God is doing and get involved with it. You can't find out what God is doing without identifying his righteousness. Therefore, you need to have a vision of God. Everything that exists outside of the human realm automatically expresses the kingdom of God. And some things within the human realm, if they are surrendered to God, also express the kingdom of God (e.g., the teachings of Jesus, the Ten Commandments, etc.). So if you wanted to seek the kingdom of God, the first thing you need to do is to step into those teachings. Now, if you try to do that by [strictly applying] the teachings, you'll become a legalist. We have to become not someone who [merely] does the law, but the kind of person who naturally does what the law says. That is the process of spiritual growth.

We want to seek to be this kind of person in all areas of our life. That means we have to be prepared. So we need various kinds of disciplines to help us. I can't simply resist anger in the moment when I'm confronted with a frustrating incident. I must be prepared for it. If we want to exhibit the fundamental aspects of the soul (e.g., peace, love, and joy) on various occasions, we have to be prepared. We are either peaceful, joyful, and loving, or not. We have to attend to these deep conditions of the soul. That is where spiritual formation comes in. And if you don't have that you'll just become a guilt-ridden legalist, and you'll find yourself trying to act in a way that you're really not.

What role does desire play in American culture? How is it activated, and how can we avoid being mastered by it?

You know, I've been thinking much more about that since I wrote [*Renovation of the Heart*]. We live in a sensualist culture, and that's where the problems come from. And the church has bought into that, has accepted that. Everything from the degradation of sports, to obesity, to the horrible things that are done to little children, to the CEO scandals—all of this fundamentally derives from people pursuing feelings. Desire itself (and among religions, this is truly distinctive to Christianity) is not bad. But desire is not meant to master our lives, and that is what we're seeing. Take addiction for example. The reason why drugs are [such a problem] in the Western world is because the Western world is a sensuous world. Addiction only exists where people have conceded to feeling. And it isn't really that feelings are overwhelming, but they are overwhelming if you concede to them. What you see in an addict, whether its coffee or nicotine or marijuana or whatever, is a person who has said, "If I don't get what I want, something is wrong. I am justified in having whatever I want." And it's that mentality that is the trip wire for the addict—that inner concession. No matter how tough your addiction is, you can stop the addictive behavior if you have decided that is what you want to do. You can do that. There are ways you can do that. We have conceded [to] the right of desire.

Now, that is what the teaching of the cross is directed at. Jesus takes up the image of the cross before anyone believes he is going to die because he understands the power of it, and what the cross means is the ultimate frustration of desire. And if you don't have that settled, then desire will veto you until it gets its way.

Whenever you hear of a minister of whom we say, "He has fallen,"—no, no. He had fallen long before that. It wasn't that he was some fine person sailing along and then one day something just hit him. What often comes out is that desire had been eating at him for a time. Perhaps he's been behaving rightly for a long time because he has believed that would get him what he wanted. However, at a certain point, he came to realize that he's not going to get what he wanted. Or, maybe, he does get what he wanted. It's fascinating to see how many people fall apart when they succeed. What has actually been holding their life together has been their commitment to succeed. Well, it's a long story to what actually does it. If you don't know Pitirim Sorokin's book *The Crisis of Our Age,* I would plead with you to read it. Sorokin analyzes the ruling forces that entered the modern age. He very rightly sees that it's what people, en masse, take to be real and valuable that determines the quality of an age. It's good to read that book in tandem with Ortega y Gasset's book *The Revolt of the Masses.* What people have, en masse, taken to be reality in our culture is that our desires should be met.

One of the fundamental problems today is that Christian spokespeople have, by and large, accepted this—that they do not question it. And so, for example, Christian ministers try to get people [in their congregations] to do things by making them feel things. We first approach people on the basis of feeling and try to get them to profess faith, and then we spend the rest of the time trying to get them to do things. We just need to get out of the business of trying to get people to do things, and get into the business of actually changing their beliefs. It is a great moment in one's life when one comes to the realization that people always live up to their beliefs.

Now, we have the illusion that they don't, that they have all of these wonderful beliefs that they just don't live up to. The problem is not that people have these accurate beliefs that they can't live up to; it's that they actually don't believe that, but they believe a bunch of other stuff. This is not a conscious thing. Most of it is buried in our bodies. Take this as a test case: when Peter denied Christ, he lived up to his beliefs. And that's our problem. Now, if you have a society that is devoted to desire and the liberation of desire, which is what we have, then—and this can get you into trouble if you say these kinds of things in many settings—but, for example, the church will never deal with the issue of homosexuality until it deals with the issue of sexuality. So now, of course, you have to say something and do something, but you also have to recognize what the issues are in homosexuality and sexuality, how they mix with other desires, disappointments, anger, and so forth. So, the way of the cross says: "You didn't get what you wanted? That's fine. That's okay." Now, are there issues of right and wrong involved here? Well, we have to learn to stand for what is right. But now we've made it a matter of what we want. That's how it's done today. That's why political correctness dominates. There isn't any other kind of correctness left. Political correctness is a matter of desire. So if you don't want certain things that other people do, then they'll attack you, because for them the only problem is a conflict of desire. Churches and ministers should focus on changing people's beliefs rather than focusing on their feelings.

What is giving intellectual assent to the gospel?

We need to break up the social context of the body. And that is why solitude and silence are so important. Because we have to put ourselves in a position where we can come to grips with what we're really doing, what we're acting on. That's what these kinds of contexts can allow us to do. We need to get away from the things that actually control us and govern our lives, and then we can see what really does [control and govern our lives]. One result of this process is that you'll find that you don't really believe a lot of the things you say you believe. And often that is related to the fact that you don't even really understand [the issues involved.] It's just that it's been taught in a social context; you accepted it and learned how to interact linguistically. If we never take time aside like this and discover what we really believe, we continue to go through life experiencing this incongruity between what we say we believe and what we're actually doing. And the only way to get hold of that is to back out of the situation. Often a person just needs rest. But they need enough inner space to begin to track what's going on there, and to be honest with what's really moving them.

What role can the church play?

It's surprising how little talk there is about God that makes sense in our religious circles. What people need to believe above all is that God is the ultimate reality. So talk about it. Explain it. What is God like? How does he relate to people? And now in a scientific age, there is a lot of good work to be done. How does the fact that in Christ all things hold together relate to chemistry? Now, there's a topic that'll hold you for a while. Or to all of the areas of human life? How does Christ relate to business? There really isn't a lot of talk about God. There's a lot of talk about God's word, and about what God says, and all these sorts of things, but what we really need to do is to make sense of God. And in an age in which the predominant theory of knowledge and reality is empiricist, you have to address that issue. Could things be real if they aren't sense-perceptible? That's one of the standing questions of practical religious life. Where is God? So also the problem of evil, for example. This is not just a problem for philosophers, for the real point of the problem is for people who are suffering in this world: and where is God when that happens? What kind of a world is this in which prayer can be answered? What kind of a God would set up a system of prayer? You know, when you think about it, it's kind of strange. So, we need to answer real questions about God and about life and about the Bible. And the real questions are the ones that often people are afraid to ask. So you have to figure out what they are and raise them yourself. Then you have to address them.

CHAPTER 13

What Makes Spirituality Christian?

John Ortberg was a good friend of Dallas's and one of his most public advocates. In this interview, John and Dallas discuss the state of spirituality, the church, and personal faith.

Interview conducted by John Ortberg in 1995
and first published in *Christianity Today*

DALLAS WILLARD LEADS TWO LIVES. IN ACADEMIC CIRCLES HE IS known for teaching philosophy at the University of Southern California, where he has been since the sixties. However, in the evangelical community, he is best known for his work in the area of spirituality. An ordained Southern Baptist minister and an adjunct professor of spirituality at Fuller Theological Seminary, he has been addressing the subject of the spiritual disciplines throughout his adult life. He has also been a mentor to many in this area, including noted author and minister Richard Foster.

Willard's 1988 book *The Spirit of the Disciplines* (HarperSanFrancisco) generated fresh thinking on spirituality among evangelicals and led to the 1993 republication of his earlier work *In Search of Guidance* (HarperSanFrancisco). Here Willard talks about the state of spirituality today and its meaning for the church.

What do you make of the current widespread interest in spirituality?

People hunger to do more than just believe the right things. There is a hunger for some experience of God in their lives. Whether or not this new interest in spirituality leads to much good remains to be seen. There is a danger of spirituality becoming "the new legalism" of our day, so that one of the criteria for advancement in our society will be that you must "be spiritual."

But there are two directions spirituality can take: Christian or general human interest. A great question in our day is whether it will be defined as Christian or non-Christian spirituality.

How are they different?

Much modern thinking views spirituality as simply a kind of "interiority"—the idea that there is an inside to the human being, and that this is the place where contact is made with the transcendental. In this view, spirituality is essentially a human dimension. Christian spirituality is centered in the idea of a transcendent life— "being born from above," as the New Testament puts it. This idea of spiritual life carries with it notions like accountability, judgment, the need for justice, and so on. These concepts are less popular, and they certainly are more difficult, than a conception of spirituality that simply focuses on one's inner life.

Many people have suggested that Evangelicalism lacks a good understanding of spirituality. Do you concur?

That has been largely true in the twentieth century, but it's not true if we go back to earlier periods. Believers in the nineteenth century, for example, were not shallow in this regard. If you look at the practices of the leading figures in that time, you will find that they did not separate their daily life from their faith in the way that has evolved in the twentieth century.

As liberal theology began to degenerate into a mild form of social ethics, the fundamentalist-evangelical movement came to stress the notion that if you believe the right things, it will get you into heaven. So in an effort to preserve the faith, we came to emphasize that what really matters is what you profess. This left believers very little help on how to actually enter into the life that Jesus himself modeled and taught.

Most churches at least offer an occasional class on spirituality.

But it's still in the category of the optional. I believe this reflects a widespread misunderstanding about the true nature of the
gospel. What has come down for us historically is that the center
of the gospel is sin. With the manner in which we treat the gospel,
you'd almost get the idea that if it were not for sin, we'd have no
use for God.

It also reflects a misunderstanding about faith. Faith has been
redefined by social and historical processes so that you can profess
to believe in Christ while being deeply doubtful about the wisdom
of what he says. This is really central to the whole issue of spirituality. If you see faith as merely a mental shift in your mind that
God sees, and thereby determines you will get into heaven, then
spirituality has no place. Once you see that faith is not simply believing certain things about Jesus but also believing that what he
taught about life was right, then you see that faith is much more
than taking advantage of a convenient accounting procedure to get
into heaven.

What is a spiritual discipline?

It is a practice undertaken with the aid of the Spirit to enable us
to do what we cannot do by human effort. And that's the essence
of Jesus's teachings, because if you succeed in obeying Christ, it's a
manifestation of grace. You can never do that on your own.

How does one begin the pursuit of the spiritual disciplines?

First, you must have a clear definition of faith: to trust Christ is
to believe that he was right. This has much deeper implications than
merely believing certain things about Jesus—though, of course, that
is important, too. Second, you must have a working definition of
what makes a disciple: one whose goal is to live the way Jesus would
if he were confronted with your circumstances. Third, you must realize that the Bible simply does not recognize a separate category of
"Christian" over against "disciple."

People sometimes equate deep interest in spirituality with the absence of solid theology. What is the role of theology in spiritual life?

It depends on how you approach theology. Students in my philosophy classes know that their task is to get the right answer. If you were to ask them if they actually believe the things they wrote on the test or if you were to say, "I'm going to give you a C on this test because you didn't believe this," they'd think you had lost your mind. They're not graded for believing, just for getting the right answers.

Likewise, if we're studying theology so that we will know what the right answers are, it is of very little relation to spirituality. If I study a subject like the Virgin Birth so that I'll know the right answer to give on a test, God probably won't be very impressed. But if I'm interested in it because I realize that believing in it totally changes the meaning of human history and life, that's the difference. Being able to give the right answer is not particularly important if, at the level of your "mental map," you don't actually believe it's true.

What about argument that focusing on spirituality leads to a lack of concern about social issues?

There actually is a connection between spirituality and concern for social issues. If you look at the journals of someone like Walter Rauschenbusch—father of "the social gospel"—you will see that he thought of personal spiritual concern and social concern as inseparable. An authentic spiritual life always pushes one back into the world.

How has response to your work on spirituality changed over the years?

In the sixties, evangelicals thought of my work as dangerous: teachings on the spiritual disciplines were thought to be teetering on the edge of Catholicism and salvation by works. Today there is an enormous hunger for this material, and I believe it is evidence of the church's hunger for the reality of God.

CHAPTER 14

Gray Matter and the Soul

———

In this short exchange with David O'Connor, Dallas explains his beliefs on the essence of the soul and the complex interrelations involving the mind, brain, and will with personhood.

Interview conducted by David O'Connor in 2002
and first published in *Christianity Today*

———

It is said that the soul is the seat of emotions, intellect, and will, but the brain is involved in each of these functions. What is the difference or relationship between the brain and the soul?

First it will be helpful to look at where both soul and brain stand in relation to personhood. It is a mistake to confuse the soul and the person; nor is the soul merely that which is "personal" in us. But the soul is such a fundamental dimension of the person that in scripture, poetry, and in common life, *soul* often means the person. *Soul* or *souls* in the Bible sometimes—perhaps most of the time—refers to the whole person, precisely because it represents a deep dimension of the person.

The relation of the brain to personhood, too, is frequently misstated. Because scientists tend to take the brain as central to life, people often construe it as identical with life. This is because the scientific community generally assumes, in practice if not in theory, that only that which is physical is knowable. Scientists often believe they can treat the personal side of life only if it is physical.

Clearly there is in human beings a profoundly important connection between the states and events of the brain and those of personal existence. But the person is not identical with the brain (or the DNA or the body as a whole). Why? Because there are thousands upon thousands of truths about the person that are not truths about the body. And there are many kinds of truths about persons that are not the kinds of truths that apply to the body or any part thereof. Inspect the brain in any way you will, you will not find these truths or even know that they exist from what you do find there. Gottfried Wilhelm Leibniz [1646–1716] pointed this out long ago, and no satisfactory way around it has ever been found.

On the other hand, people's bodies are essential to their identity and life. Through them we have an inner world and become the person we become—forever. The body is not just a container. That is why, in Christian thought, there is to be a resurrection.

While the brain has its role in emotions, intellect, and will, and while people's bodies are essential, we must always remember that the person is the ultimate unit of analysis: you, me. Thought, feeling, action (involving the body, as well as relations to others) are ultimately dimensions of the person. And it is the soul that combines all the dimensions of the person to form one life. It is like a computer system, which runs an entire commercial operation.

When it is broken, you have to attend to it—and in fact, only God can repair it: "He restoreth my soul" [Ps. 23:3]. Law and disciplines can also help heal the soul, but grace—God doing in my life what I cannot do for myself—is the first and last word. And yet law and disciplines are inseparable from grace as they do their part.

So it is the person that ultimately is "the seat of the emotions, the intellect, and the will"—not the brain, as scientists would say, nor the soul, ultimately. The person is the seat of the soul if we mean by "*seat*" that in which the soul is located. The soul is, arguably, the deepest dimension of the person or, as we often say today, of the "self." But it is not the person.

To sum up: The soul is one nonphysical dimension of the person.

A human person is a nonphysical (spiritual) entity that has an essential involvement with a particular physical body. The brain, then—a piece of meat that is of more than usual interest—is one part of the embodied dimension of the human person. It too is integrated by the soul into one life, along with all of the dimensions of the person (at least when all is well).

These matters are especially important as Christians often treat the soul as the recipient of salvation, and the other dimensions of human life are left out—especially the bodily and the social, but also thought and feeling. Redemption in Christ is a retrieving of the entire person from alienation from God and opposition to God.

The soul is not some separable part of us that eventually gets to go to heaven while everything else about it is left out.

CHAPTER 15

Going Deeper

In this interview with *Response* magazine, Dallas discusses the lessons he aims to teach his students, especially in the current intellectual and religious culture. He also offers his opinions about the contemporary church.

Interviewed conducted by Hope McPherson in 2000 and first published in Seattle Pacific University's online magazine, *Response*

ONE OF TODAY'S LEADING CHRISTIAN THINKERS AND WRITERS, Dallas Willard left a Southern Baptist pastorate in the late 1950s because, he says, "I became so convinced of my ignorance about God and the soul that I thought I was a public hazard."

He attended graduate school and, in 1965, joined the faculty at the University of Southern California. Still at USC today, he teaches undergraduates and postgraduates in a secular university that has little regard for Christianity. It's a good place to be, he says. "In a curious way, I'm now the radical," he adds, laughing.

The son of a politician and a schoolteacher, Willard combines his friendly humor with an ardent call to give Christ a new hearing in our increasingly hectic world. That call is receiving great attention. In fact, *Christianity Today* chose his third book, *The Divine Conspiracy,* as its 1998 Book of the Year.

"Dr. Willard is one of the most insightful contemporary commentators on the church in America," says Tim Dearborn, dean of the chapel at SPU. "He combines a deep understanding of the spiritual life, rich insights into scripture, and a grasp of our culture that often leaves me saying, 'That's right, though I've never thought of it that way before.'" Les Steele, professor of Christian formation and chair of the Department of Theology, agrees. "He's tapped into a hunger that's there for deeper, more thoughtful approaches of living out the Christian faith," he says. "I can only hope more people would pay attention to that."

What has been the focus of your life's work?

The strongest impression on my mind has always been the person and teachings of Jesus Christ. That's true from [when I was] a very small child. I can remember clearly how impressed I was in Sunday school. I've never moved away from the basic project of "knowing him and making him known." This is not a particularly religious project; it's a human need. It is out of love of my neighbor, as well as love of God, that I feel the imperative to do this.

And I believe the way to do it is not by being especially religious in the sense that people would normally understand that, but by just being an honest, open, thoughtful human being living among other human beings, depending on the grace of God.

Given that philosophy, do you see the secular university, the University of Southern California, as a good place to be?

Well, I think it is. I'm not here by my good sense because, truthfully, I was pastoring a church and teaching school when I became so convinced of my ignorance about God and the soul that I thought I was a public hazard. That's when I went to graduate school at the University of Wisconsin. I didn't intend to become a philosophy professor or any kind of professor. I thought I would study a few years and then return to the pastorate. But I seemed to be led onward and I did finish the degree. I hadn't even intended to do a degree—just study for my own benefit.

After I finished my Ph.D., they invited me to stay on the following year as a member of the faculty. During that year, the Lord said to me that if I stay in the church, I will be limited to the church and the university would be closed to me. If I went into the university, on the other hand, the churches would be open to me.

Your university, USC, was founded by the Methodist Episcopal Conference in the nineteenth century. But it's a secular university now. Is it a challenge for you as a Christian to teach in that environment?

No, not really. People often say to me, "Oh, isn't it wonderful that you're there as a testimony to the Lord." Now, that's not my first job. My first job is to be a good professor, a good teacher, a good writer. If you do that well, people are open and receptive to you. It is true that there's a significant bias against conservative Christians in the academy. But if you're living it out in person, it's different than if you're looking at it from the outside.

Younger people today who are conservative Christians are apt to have an extremely hard time in some sections of the academy. They can suffer real persecution. But in my case, I'm sort of the old bull moose of the department and the university. I've been the chairman; I've been everything you're supposed to be. A lot of the people in the department were hired while I was there. From my point of view, they're my neighbors. I love them, and a few of them are Christians, others aren't. To make it short, it's not a bad place to be. It's a good place to be. And, after all, I can walk to the center of the campus and point to the top of the building, and there's John Wesley standing with his hand outstretched across the central campus in benediction.

When your students get to know you, are they challenged to think about Christ and Christianity?

They certainly are. Many of them come to me and tell me that their lives have been transformed. But it isn't because I preach in my classes or anything of that sort. I am who I am in my classes. The students do find out [that I'm a Christian] and it's really quite intriguing to them. Some of them can't help coming around saying, "Now, is this really true about you?" It's delightful to see that, and they really do find it refreshing, I think, even if they don't agree with me.

I also represent philosophy positions that are not most common. For example, I wouldn't even be in philosophy (as a writer, especially) except for the issue of realism—realism about the world, about values, about God. Almost no one in philosophy is a realist, so they also find that very intriguing. I think by the grace of God, I am in an ideal place. I can't imagine how I could be in a place that was better.

Seattle Pacific University is serious about pairing rigorous academics with living out our faith in the real world, or "engaging the culture." What advice do you have for Christian faculty members who are serious about doing that?

The most important advice is to put Jesus in the right place. Academics especially have to understand that he, after all, is the smartest man who ever lived on earth. Einstein, or whoever else you want to mention, couldn't hold a light to him. They need to take that very seriously. That means he's the smartest person in their field, no matter what that field is.

They're faced with a situation where knowledge of God—and certainly of Christ—is not thought of as essential for good standing in any profession. That's why we're in the mess we're in today. Nearly everyone—myself included—went for a doctoral degree in an institution that regarded knowledge of God and of Christ as totally irrelevant, or even impossible. So the great challenge in a place like Seattle Pacific is to take that knowledge seriously and find out what it means practically.

What does it mean to be a disciple of Jesus Christ in economics? In mathematics? In business administration? Nursing? Whatever the field is. The task of Christian intellectuals today is to regain the position of Christ in the intellectual and cultural world that is due to him because of who he is. We've got our hands full, haven't we?

What do students need to know when it comes to living out their faith?

Students are trying to find a basis for life in their studies. Hopefully they have already received something good from their family or their church. But this simply cannot be counted on, even if they are professing Christians. Thank God there are exceptions, but by and large, they haven't received it in such a way that it seems to them a solid basis for their life. They've received it as dogma. They've received it as commandments and law and things that they will be punished for if they don't do something about them.

These are the kind of people for whom I've written *The Divine Conspiracy*. It's to say to them: Now take Jesus seriously. Don't just make him an icon of some sort. Take him seriously as a companion in life and become his disciple. Learn from him how to live your life, as he would live your life if he were you.

What you're saying is reminiscent of the book *In His Steps*, in which a town is transformed when people begin asking, "What would Jesus do in this instance?" But some argue that's not a realistic option. What do you say?

My only criticism of *In His Steps* is that it doesn't go far enough. We should grow in our understanding and relationship to Christ to where, in most cases, we wouldn't need to ask what he would do. We would know—and we would be doing it. The problem with the *In His Steps* method is that if you have to stop to ask what he would do, ordinarily you will have already done what he wouldn't do. Life moves very fast, and that's why the point of the book is good but the method is not as good.

We need to go deeper in the method. But if that's the best we can do in a method, that's much better than most of the alternatives. Let's be clear about that. It's much better to do something that sounds a little funny if it will help us, than to not do it. The point is right, [and] I have a little addition to the method. My book *The Spirit of the Disciplines* tries to spell that out.

Have you seen differences between this generation of students and the last in how they respond to Jesus and to issues of faith?

In the last few years there has been emerging in my undergraduate and my graduate students a very different cast of mind, much more serious and thoughtful. I've been teaching since 1960 in the university system, and I came to USC in '65. But for the first time since I entered university teaching, there is a significant body of thoughtful young people, many of whom are professing Christians. But they recognize they have to go much deeper. I think this is an encouraging time in that regard. I'm hopeful that it will be possible for these people to find and appreciate Christ for who he really is.

The media reports spirituality is very "in" today. You seem to have seen it with your students. But is there a danger of it becoming a kind of surface spirituality?

There's a very great danger in it, and it has many aspects. There's the commercialization of it that is just pathetic. Spirituality in itself doesn't mean anything. It depends on which spirit and which spirituality. But, on the other hand, you want to give credit to the fact that there is a sense of need that is driving people to this. That is appropriate and right given human nature, which hungers for a relationship with God.

How would you define a spirituality that's not commercialized?

Definitions are where we want to begin, and most people can't even tell you what "spirit" is. *Spirituality* has come to mean just vague practices, so you have all kinds of spirituality. The spirit is not a *force*. It is a *power* and not a force because it's personal. Being personal, it has demands to make on its own. If you're a Satanist, you know what that means. You know that Satan is a spirit and that he has demands to make on his own.

Christian spirituality is a spirituality that places obedience to Christ at the top of the list. Finding out how to obey Christ is the method of Christian spirituality. Any spirituality that does not place obedience to Christ at the top is not Christian spirituality. Many of our religious groups are misled because they think the aim of spirituality is peace. Christianity is not a peace religion. It has peace as one side effect. But peace is not the aim. Righteousness, meaning the same thing as love, is. But you have to interdefine those so love won't get misconstrued. That's why Jesus says, "Seek first the Kingdom of God and his righteousness." That's the aim. Not peace.

Yet many people in churches hear about peace. They say, "Oh, this is a wonderful thing. Let's have peace. Ah, the Buddhist will show us how to have peace." And they're off running in the wrong direction. It's like Alcoholics Anonymous in a sense. Alcoholics Anonymous is very effective for people who know they're going to die if they don't stop drinking. It's great for that problem. Like it, most of the spiritualities are directed toward some specific problem and not transforming the human soul into righteousness, as defined by Christ.

Will people involved in this kind of surface spirituality eventually run into problems because of it and realize it's not the answer?

They may and they may not. For example, consider a person who has gone through Alcoholics Anonymous and has been sober for ten years. That still won't give meaning to their life or make them a loving person. The issue that may face such a person is precisely, "What are the limits of this spirituality that I have adopted?" We have a lot of illustrations of this in history. For example, a group called the Shakers originated a very powerful spiritual movement that was very Christlike. But now when you think "Shakers," most people think furniture. They make wonderful chairs. Well, that actually is a result of the failure of the spirituality they had to keep its focus on Christ. Every spirituality will have built into it a limit— and the capacity of the human mind to deny and distort and deceive itself is almost unlimited. But the real question that faces us all is, Do I have the goodness of life that I'm intended for, and do I really have knowledge of God?

You spoke to regional pastors while on campus. What do you try to convey to pastors and other men and women in church leadership?

Pastors today have one of the hardest jobs in the world, and most of them are quite discouraged with it. The main thing that I have to say to them is that the resources for doing what they need to do are genuinely available to them in the kingdom of God, which is present with them. They have to hear and accept the gospel of the kingdom of God and minister out of that—not out of their own cleverness and their education and their own strength.

Poll after poll shows that pastors are just being crushed and their families are being broken because of the demands that are placed upon them and because of the low social regard in which they're held. Now is a time when a pastor is not thought of as an important person. Even well into the '60s and '70s, the pastor was often the most important person in town, even in large towns. But that's no longer true.

Is it a problem that a lot of churches feel they need to somehow entertain their congregations?

Yes. Have you ever seen the movie *Sister Act*? *Sister Act* is actually a parable of the churches in our time. A nightclub singer makes the church a success by making it an entertainment center, which then, of course, also reaches out and does good social works in the community.

Today you see people turn to entertainment, especially pastors and church leaders, because they know they must "succeed." When the pastor comes in, he or she is immediately faced with the demand to produce the ABCs of church: Attendance, Buildings, and Cash. If the pastor doesn't produce them, the church will go into default, because it will have already gone into such debt to build the buildings that it can't sustain itself. There's constant anxiety over this.

Instead of living from the kingdom of God in such a way that people are drawn into the ministry of Christ and are converted and grow and become powerful in their communities, people turn to entertainment—which does nothing but to hopefully keep people coming back and putting money in the plate. This is a tragedy of our time. The churches who are turning to this to have success have eliminated their dependence on, and knowledge of, the kingdom of God in the hearts of people.

Does that mean pastors—any Christian, really—should step back and decide to be a servant in order to be a leader?

That's exactly right. But if you don't believe in the kingdom of God being available here and now and under the administration of Jesus Christ, who is the head of the church, you can't step back. If you [do] step back, your people regard you as weak—and you'll be out of a job.

That's the CEO model of the pastor, and it is the one that increasingly has taken over. What we want in our pastor is a person with a Day-Timer and a briefcase—a very, very busy person who succeeds in managing in such a way that we keep our payments up, our building is in good shape, and the people are coming.

It sounds like modern American society has crept into the church.

It has, I think. We are a society that's dominated by models of success and leadership. That's why there's so much talk about leadership as a sort of magic. We look for a leader who's supposed to solve all of our problems. If all our problems are not solved, that means our person isn't leading.

A great turning point in my own life as a young minister was when I saw how the crowds flocked to Jesus and, for that matter, to the apostles. Here I am, trying to get people to come and hear me speak, and Jesus is trying to get away from them. What we need to do is to understand that his method of church growth is far better— even in terms of attendance, buildings, and cash—than the one we're following. You just have to take a different route to get there. It is the route of dependence on the kingdom of God.

Are you planning to follow *The Divine Conspiracy* with another book?

Yes. The title will be *The Disappearance of Moral Knowledge,* which is what has happened now in our culture. I talk a little bit about that right at the opening of *The Divine Conspiracy*. I'm going to tell the story of how that happened.

There seems to be a lot of fodder for, and need for, a book like that in America today.

Desperate need. And many, many people who are trying to do something about it simply haven't gone down far enough to find the foundations of our lack of moral knowledge. I'm thinking of people like [author and previous Secretary of Education] Bill Bennett and others, who are good people. It's just that you can't deal with the problem at that level. You have to go deeper. That's what the book is going to try to make clear. The intent, of course, is so that we can then do something about the problem.

What led you to want to do this as your next book?

A combination of things. One is that I've always taught advanced courses in the history of ethics, and the twentieth century marks the completion of the history of ethics. The other thing is simply the need—on the part of people like legislators, educators, ministers, leaders of all types—to understand what happened to the only possible basis that they can work from, which is moral knowledge. If we don't know what is right and wrong, and what is good and bad, we're nailed as leaders. You cannot lead without it. That's why we're in the condition of drift we're in now. Now, I like to say, leadership is a matter of finding a parade and getting in front of it. That's about all it amounts to.

This sounds like a good book for pastors and people in leadership positions.

I'm hoping it will be. I'm actually thinking that I may have to write two books—one for the academic side and one for people in general, more at the level of *The Divine Conspiracy* where people who are willing to work a little bit can read it. Then on the academic side, the arguments may have to go deeper than I could expect any fair-minded person to follow unless they had an academic interest.

What message do you have for Christians at the beginning of a new century?

I don't think it's possible to sufficiently emphasize the importance of Jesus's message about the kingdom of God and what that means both for time and for eternity. We've come to the end of a so-called millennium and the beginning of another, which I'm sure makes no difference to the cats and the dogs. A lot of people worry about the end of the world. They should know that eternity has hardly begun. It isn't like the universe is going to go out of existence. We have an eternal destiny, and it's in this universe under God. It's very important to understand that at this particular time.

But that's just what the message of the kingdom of God means. After all, it is God who is the king, and he's not going away. As we step into that kingdom, we are a part of something that will last forever. That's why the book of Revelation ends, in the last chapter, the fifth verse, with "And they shall reign forever and ever. Through the ages of the ages."

CHAPTER 16

Spiritual Disciplines in a Postmodern World

Poet and author Luci Shaw has a conversation with Dallas about what concerns them in today's culture. They discuss issues ranging from hedonism to recognizing the signs of the kingdom of God, as well as what gives them hope and inspiration.

Interview conducted by Luci Shaw in 2000
and first published in *Radix* magazine

I understand you're writing a new book.

Yes, I'm working on a book about the disappearance of moral knowledge—that is, about the cultural situation we are in now. I want to explain how that has come about. The book is more theoretical than popular; it deals with where the problem came from.

I want to make very clear what has happened. Of course the point is to be able to go back, or rather go forward, to a situation where we have reliable moral knowledge available in our culture once again. This has been a theme in my teaching for years, and it's time to put it all down in writing.

Are you seeing repercussions from the deconstructionist, postmodern way of thinking and of perceiving reality? Is that a part of the present equation?

Yes, absolutely. That kind of understanding is, however, as much a consequence as a cause of the present condition. The basic idea is that empirical thinking has been elevated, but knowledge of the self is not empirical. It's simply not verifiable by sense perception. Given the triumph of empiricism and the difficulties we have in psychology with making any sense of moral knowledge, the postmodern deconstructionist stuff makes the loss of moral knowledge inevitable. I don't want to try to refute all of those elements, but rather to help people understand how we got here.

What do you see as the cause, the reason for movement in a direction that allows for this loss of moral knowledge?

The deepest cause is the rise of a kind of hedonism, along with an exaggerated individualism. As I put it in more technical, but I hope understandable, terms, the cause of the problem is the triumph of the will. The will is worshiped in our society.

The will, and therefore the self?

Yes, the self. Everyone thinks that we ought to be able to do whatever we want to do.

That's a theme we hear constantly. For instance, on television talk shows, we'll hear a young student proclaim, "I have a dream, and my teachers tell me I can be whatever my dream calls me to be."

Right. We hear that over and over. Even in advertisements for recruitment in the armed services: "You can be whatever you want to be, and we can help!" Given that, we cannot then admit any moral knowledge, because that might get in the way of what we want to do.

Conversely, if someone feels called to a more modest or less prominent role or responsibility, they may be rebuked for selling themselves short, or for lack of ambition.

Imagine a bumper sticker that says: "My child learned humility at school this month," instead of "My child is an honor student at Success Academy." The fact of the matter is this: the essence of morality is to tell you that in some circumstances you must do what you don't want to do. If you have already set it up that you should be able to do whatever you want to do, then good-bye morality. Empiricism will just become an excuse.

This new book of yours will create some controversy, I suspect. Within the academy it should create some waves.

I believe it will. I hope it will. I don't expect it to be read as widely as my earlier works, however.

What are your hopes and prayers for Christians in the new millennium?

This may sound pretty backward looking, but it really is the most forward-looking thing I can imagine. My prayer is that Christians would really come to know what Jesus is up to in this world.

That would reflect the theme of your book *The Divine Conspiracy*, would it not?

Yes, because *The Divine Conspiracy* is about how the kingdom of God is at work, and Christians need to be in on this. Good as they may be in some respects, the ordinary Christian just isn't going to get it.

For those who haven't read this book, what is that "conspiracy" about?

The conspiracy is God's plan in human history to overcome evil with good.

And who are the characters in this conspiracy story? The conspirators? Father, Son, and Holy Spirit?

They are in the original conspiracy, but they now have agents, sometimes working undercover—because the agents are not all Christians; and indeed, not all of them are human.

There are supernatural powers at work?

Indeed. That is what we are told. One reason why angels have become so prominent (and that's not all good by any means) is because of a recognition by people generally that there is much more at work in the course of human events than can be ascribed to human beings.

Do you think that aspects of the "new physics" contribute to this?

Yes, the new physics is moving toward a view of the universe where people can see that it is for the manifestation of the glory of God.

Isn't that amazing? That we can come to that conclusion through human knowledge and experimentation . . .

Although it isn't happening just through human knowledge. One of the fields I worked on in my graduate studies years ago was the history of science. I took a minor in that for my Ph.D. at the University of Wisconsin. The field was just opening up. One of the most interesting things is how much progress is due to what is often termed serendipity, over and over and over. It just bowls you over when you get to know the history of science.

It isn't really just serendipity, is it? Perhaps it was ordained from before the foundations of the world.

Absolutely right. This is God at work in human history. This is a part of the story, and not just in science but in other areas. When you survey the overall scene you realize how little of what we call progress is due to human inventiveness, including the discoveries of Christopher Columbus—who he was and what he thought—and the court around him in Spain. We're being trained to have this vision of how awful he was, subduing native peoples, et cetera, but that is shallow, shallow thinking.

It's accepted because it has become politically correct. That "correctness" is forcing us into false conclusions.

Of course, it wasn't just Columbus. You see the hand of God everywhere, all over. The most powerful force bringing the world together, into a situation where we're going to have to love one another, or die, is business. Business is the primary way that the nations are being drawn together. And then space exploration.

And our ruination of our own planet.

All of those things. I think that's why, in the last church in the book of Revelation, we have that verse about Christ at the door, knocking. We use that image to get people to open the door of their lives to Christ. But it was the door of the church he was knocking at.

Not just the individual heart?

No. Jesus was on the outside. He's always out there, and we're trying to catch up with him, if we're not just sleeping. He comes and knocks on the door of the church and says, "Hey, you in there? If you would open the door, I would come in." But the church gets so ingrown, so self-centered, self-absorbed, it's not listening.

It's so prone to self-analysis, in a pseudopsychological mode.

Yes, and it's a dead end.

In your book In Search of Guidance you talk about the paradox of guidance. What are the elements of that paradox?

Well, the paradox has to do with the fact that on the one hand we talk so much about God's guidance, and we especially want our leaders to be guided by God. Yet, when it comes down to us, we do the humble-mumble and say, "Well, you know, not me. I'm not big enough or important enough for God to bother with."

It's that combination: on the one hand we expect guidance, and we desperately need it, but on the other hand we're not prepared to receive it and we think it wouldn't really be appropriate. You have to be "kicked upstairs" to become a so-called "full-time Christian worker" for it to be appropriate.

Generally, people can't deal with this at all. Christians can't. There's that little joke about: "When we speak to God we call it prayer, and when he speaks to us we call it schizophrenia."[1] It's a curious ambivalence that's driven by our deep need as finite human beings.

It's almost like that story about Joan of Arc. When her accusers said, "Those voices you hear, they're just your imagination," she answered, "Yes. I know. That's how God speaks to me."

That's a very good line. It's by using our natural faculties in a certain way that God speaks to us. In a way, the paradox is the same as in the Incarnation; it's the union of God with human beings in a relationship. The Incarnation's much more than that, but it is that. (By the way, that book on guidance has been renamed. Its title now is *Hearing God*. The third edition has just come out with InterVarsity Press here in the United States and HarperCollins in Britain.)

Is that a title you can live with, or does it short-sell the book?

Well, they did leave me the subtitle, *Developing a Conversational Relationship with God,* and that's what it's about. I don't like the new title as much, because *In Search of Guidance* is indicative of something deep about us. We're looking, longing, for guidance. One of the themes of the book is that we're looking for guidance, but what we really need is something else, which includes guidance: a life lived in a conversational relationship with God.

We really want to hear God.

Yes. So perhaps that title is not so far off the mark. I'm not unhappy with it.

How are the spiritual disciplines to be practiced in community? What are the challenges we face as we attempt to do this?

Well, they are much more effective if they can be practiced in community, and you can't really practice them without community. If you have a community where they are understood as a normal part of our lives, there can be instruction or teaching about them, which brings about a kind of accountability.

In the midst of that, problem solving for individuals is so important. Because while the disciplines are not really complicated, learning them—silence, solitude, fasting, et cetera—is apt to throw you on false courses, and there really needs to be some question-and-answer kind of setup.

As a safeguard?

Yes. We need teaching that will keep people remembering such things as: "I'm not righteous because I do this. I'm not earning points. And when I fail, at whatever—solitude, fasting—I have not sinned." That's one of the most important things of all, because people are so bound by legalism that they think if they fail—suppose they're trying to fast, and the food in the refrigerator gets the best of them, and they break their fast—they feel they've broken a commitment to God.

So, there could be a dark side to the spiritual disciplines. It's possible that they could be applied or enforced in a legalistic, almost abusive way, perhaps in an effort to control or exert power?

Absolutely. It has been done, and that's one reason why in recent years there has been an attempt to recover the disciplines—because, in fact, they were lost, by and large. That is true in places you wouldn't expect it. I have found many Roman Catholics to whom the spiritual disciplines were almost unknown, lost.

There's a wonderful priest in Pittsburgh who has a telephone program. He's called me occasionally when my books have come out, and one time we were on the air discussing *The Spirit of the Disciplines,* when someone called in and asked angrily, "Why don't you people teach these things anymore? When I was young, Sister So-and-So taught us to fast, and taught us to contemplate and be silent, and now it's not taught anymore."

It's true. In many quarters of the Catholic church it isn't taught, or at least not effectively. In Protestant churches, with very little exception, it was totally lost, until back in the '70s, some writings began to appear.

Yes. I'm hearing some grassroots response to this lack in the evangelical community. There are numbers of small movements toward a more contemplative life. I'm part of a California group, Women at the Well, which is an effort to show women in evangelical groups that it's possible to hear God's voice for ourselves—if we know how to listen in silence and solitude. But so many are afraid of silence, and of being alone. They wonder, What if nothing happens? What if God ignores me? Or what if he isn't there? But on a three-day retreat, in gradual steps, and

given some simple tools, people can begin to experience contemplation for themselves, and it's transformative.

Well, that's wonderful. The disciplines are self-validating. Now that I've had a long experience of teaching them and practicing them, I can't remember a case when the disciplines, when seriously practiced, did not validate themselves. That is, I cannot recall a person coming back to me, and saying, "Hey, you know, this doesn't work."

When Saint Paul speaks about a "thorn in the flesh," presumably he had some tenacious weakness or personal defect that he couldn't seem to rid himself of, even with persistent prayer. Is this a sort of caveat to people with a perfectionistic nature? How does this operate with the disciplines that you teach?

Beautifully, really. That passage is about the answer Paul gets from God. Because he does get an answer, not silence. His prayer was answered.

"God's strength is made perfect in human weakness."

That's the key. And the key to the disciplines, because the disciplines are actually learning how to access the strength of God and the power of God.

Paul, in another passage, says, "I glory in my tribulations." How can that be? Well, it was because, in his tribulations, he knew that the life of God was flowing in him. That was the one thing he wanted above all, in Philippians 3: "That I might know him, and the power of his resurrection, and the fellowship of his sufferings."

See, Paul knew this. (I wish I had time to write a book about it.) Paul "got it." Maybe John grew into it later, but Paul understood it, and lived it, and it showed in his behavior. That's why he wouldn't come into town in a limousine, with a large staff and an expense account, enjoying the status of apostle.

He came as a maker of tents. A small businessman.

As we're told in 1 Corinthians 15, he could say, "I was the least of the apostles. But the grace of God worked more effectively in me than in any."

Doesn't this speak to the current ideology of personal empowerment? Think of the "downward mobility" of Jesus in Philippians 2.

That's right, it speaks powerfully to it, because if we want to know what power really is, we have to step into the kingdom of humility. To learn how it works, the disciplines are indispensable.

Solitude is central precisely because it breaks us free of the world in which we're used to exercising power or having power exercised over us. Solitude and silence together, when adequately practiced, form a framework within which we can absolutely and constantly be aware of the movement of God in us, and know it is not us. This is why the disciplines are so essential—because they break away that competing world that we have identified with. We are often just puppets of our own egotism and that of others.

Those disciplines attune us to the wavelength of the word of God and the voice of God, but we have to have our antennae out to receive the messages. Silence and solitude leave us undistracted, so that the messages come through clear and true. But can a Christian believer actually become Christlike? Like Christ? Do you think flawed and finite human beings can really become like the Son of God?

They can become that in such a way that it will be obvious to others that they are followers of Christ. This is the true ecumenism— for people to follow Christ until they become like him. It is not a matter of external behavior. If you try to become Christlike in your external behavior you will simply turn into a devoted legalist, and people will run from you.

But your own self-consciousness about your inadequacies will be exaggerated, because, when you're living to please others by external behavior, everything you do or don't do is magnified in its significance.

That way lies paralysis, futility, and, as Jesus knew, hypocrisy. He warned of the "leaven of the Pharisees," and the reason for that is because when you try to conform at the outward level you fail, but because you're so driven you begin to fake it.

Change of topic: There's the exponentially growing emphasis on spirituality, and on being "spiritual." But the definition of spirituality varies drastically, depending on who promotes it, including those whom we would not acknowledge as Christian. So what are the distinctives of a Christian spirituality?

The distinctive of Christian spirituality is precisely the formation of the inward person, one who becomes like Christ on the inside. The objective is that obedience to Christ would be achieved. But that is not the focus. The focus is on inward transformation into Christlikeness. The old, much-used, but too little applied, statement of Paul in Galatians 4:19 is that "Christ be formed in you."

The short answer is, it's the inner transformation of will, mind, and emotions into likeness to Christ's will, mind, and emotions. We think like Christ, we feel like Christ, we choose Christ's character, and it moves out into our body, our surroundings, and everything we do. But the transformation is essentially inward.

Does that transformation begin to extinguish our human characteristics, or does it make us more fully human?

Well, here I've got to give a more complicated response. If we think, as I do, of the human character, the human being, as creative will (that is, its likeness to God, who is creative will without limit), that means we're designed to create good. Of course, good not just for ourselves but in a more general sense. Now, if we take that to be human nature, our spirituality is the only thing that can make it possible and cause it to flourish.

Currently, to go back to our initial discussion about the loss of moral knowledge, it is a dogma in intellectual and academic circles that there is no such thing as human nature. The practical image of the human being is of a consumer, an individual who does what he or she wants to do, and derives from it a lot of pleasure. . . .

And responds positively to marketing initiatives.

Yes, and that's partly because they're conditioned to think of themselves as consumers. The person disappears, because the true person is not a consumer, but a creative will. We are designed to be creators, initiators, not just receivers. Yet the whole model, the consumerist model of the human being, is to make us passive, and to make us complainers and whiners, because we're not being given what we need. We cook up a "right" to that and then we say we've been deprived of our rights.

We see this in our churches, which pander to consumers. They say, "Come and consume the services we offer, and we guarantee you a wonderful time. You'll go out of the church door feeling good."

Does this have something to say to the so-called seeker-friendly churches?

That language is a manifestation of the tendency to use words to get a leg up on someone else. I can't imagine anyone being more "seeker friendly" than Jesus was, but he didn't pander. He never tried to attract people with a song and dance. You can't imagine him giving away embossed copies of the Sermon on the Mount to his supporters, or to the people who promised to come back to church next Sunday.

What was it about Jesus that people found so magnetizing?

I think it was the authority that people sensed in him: he knew what he was talking about. That was what drew them to him. Then, as they listened to him talking about God, they realized that God was not a condemning God, and that Jesus wasn't about to condemn them. He knew they were already overloaded with condemnation and didn't need him to add to their load. He said, "I didn't come into the world to condemn the world."

So people were encouraged: lepers, and prostitutes, and tax collectors, and Romans, and publicans—those people who were on the fringes. That's really the story of the gospel, how these people were drawn to him.

Dallas, in my own very limited personal contact with you, I've sensed a largeness and a generosity of spirit, which, I suspect, is a reflection of God's largeness and compassion—his grace in your own life. How is God's grace mediated to you in daily living?

Well, this may sound a little irreligious, I'm afraid, but it's primarily through creation. I'm sitting here, enjoying the sight of a lemon tree outside my window. I don't know if it was because I was raised away out in the country where there really wasn't anything other than nature to see, but still, the most vivid images to me are of the abundance of creation. Grace is abundance. It's overflow. It's God giving for the sake of giving.

For the joy of it. Exhilaration.

You know, when I was young and lived away out there, it's the abundant productiveness of nature that sticks with such beauty in my memory. A flock of sheep, and lambs, and cows, and trees, and fruit, and squirrels—I really do draw from that. It's the first thing that strikes me when I get up in the morning. Then mediation comes to me through the word of God in meditation and prayer and the words of others around me.

Those responses to nature are the responses of a poet. That's how poetry comes into being, when there's a sudden excitement and exhilaration of spirit in just observing and being part of that creation, seen in its daily detail and singularity.

And only poetry is adequate to express it. Or perhaps dance.

I think music expresses that same wonder and exuberance. But nonverbally. Or at least with a different kind of language. The genius of poetry is that it verbalizes what many people have felt without quite knowing how to express it.

I know how the experience is mediated to us in English. But even in the Greek, which may very well not have been Jesus's language, it just seems that everything he touches is poetry.

His words sing like nothing else I've ever read. They break through layers and layers of translation and transition from other languages. Perhaps that was what was meant when it was said of him, "This man doesn't teach like the scribes and Pharisees; he teaches with authority."

Another thing—and I believe you might agree with me because you're a poet—I think that if you had to characterize poetry or even art, generally, it has to have that authority. Without that it has nothing.

It has to speak out of the reality of personal experience. That's where its authenticity shows. If you as a reader can feel what the poet is feeling, what the poet is offering to you of an event or insight or emotion, then the transfer is complete. The gap has been bridged.

I love so much a few lines from Robert Frost, a prayer written in his later years: "To prayer I think I go. I think I go to prayer. Along a darkened corridor of woe, and down a stair." You can just feel where he's going, the genuineness of it. I think the lines conclude, "If religion's not to be my fate, I must be spoken to, and told, before too late."

The great thing about poetry is, it doesn't matter what you believe about these issues. When it is poetry, it is on and you get it. Unless you're locked off in some consumerist corner. Regrettably (back to our theme, I guess), even poetry has become a product, and the people who own it treat it as "product." A great painting will make the news only if it's sold for $36 million. It's so distressing.

Everything is quantified, or viewed as quantifiable, in terms of monetary value, which is the lowest common denominator in our culture.

Everything of value culturally, given the loss of moral knowledge, is sucked into this economic vacuum where it's chewed up and spewed out until nothing of value remains. So people wind up eating and drinking and doing all the things human beings do, but in lives stripped of the glory that is a manifestation of grace.

Beauty is, above all, a manifestation of grace, of abundance and generosity. It's the reason why God placed flowers on the earth: to have little voices calling to us constantly about grace. You walk in the field, and here's a flower. Jesus valued the "lilies of the field."

And a flower speaks so . . . radically. (I guess that's appropriate to say in *Radix*. A flower is so literally rooted.) The plant's a parable of transformation, of taking the decay and muck of organic humus and turning it into a thing of color and fragility. Something delicate, and so dramatically different from the soil it came from. That is what grace does.

Getting back to language, I have often felt that it's important for poetry, and for scripture, to be read aloud. Something changes when our voice tones carry those words rather than our eyes reading them in silence, flat on the page. Reading aloud, with expression and understanding, adds a new dimension. It's a resurrection of sorts, a raising of a story, or an image, or an idea, into life. It becomes a living thing.

That happens only when there is a soul capable of reading and hearing. Then the reading takes on awesome power, and the effect is so much greater. You're not dealing just with meanings and abstractions, but with the presence of a living soul adding intonations that can never come from the print on a page. It hooks into a larger reality. Just to hear someone read scripture . . . so much of that is disappearing from our services.

You're right. In many churches the reading of the Bible has either disappeared or been trivialized—it's a formality that has to be endured so we can get to the sermon. But scripture has a power that is beyond the intellectual.

It brings us back not only to beauty, but to the moral insights on which it is based. Such moral insights are integral to Trinitarian reality—the ultimate foundation for morality—the relationships within the Trinity.

Do you see heaven as being radically continuous or discontinuous with our present earthly life?

Continuous. Jesus in John 8:51–53 talks about this: "Those who are involved with my word will never see death."

Will we recognize the kingdom of God when it comes, when it arrives?

I think it will take us some time. I think there will be some great moments of revelation. But if I hesitate in what I say it's because I believe that the kingdom of God is already here, already at work. Jesus told us, "We're not going to say, 'Oh, here it is,' or 'Oh, there it is.' Because it's among you."

I think when we step through death we will be in a different world, and it will suddenly occur to us, "Hey, I'm seeing things I've never seen before." Or, "Oh, here's someone I thought was dead. Aren't they dead?" I think it will come that way. For those who are not companions of Christ I don't think it will be obvious, but that's another story.

But the question is so important. Currently, and for some time now, really, the teaching about heaven and hell has totally lost its impact. That's partly because it hasn't been thought of in any realistic terms. We have thought of it as some sort of celestial fallback, with shelves where the old saints are parked, I suppose, with fabulous images of harps and clouds and so on.

My reading of Jesus is that he understands there to be a radical continuity here. There is almost a casualness, a flippancy, we might say, when he talks about this. Imagine just turning to the thief on the cross and saying, "See you later today, in Paradise."

Almost a throwaway line.

I think it's regarded as not meaning much. But when you go back and read scripture, one of the few things that's recorded in all four Gospels is that at Jesus's baptism "the heavens opened." Of course, in the Old Testament, the heavens opened periodically. I believe that at such moments what had been there all along suddenly became visible.

When it opened for Stephen as he was dying, after being stoned, he simply saw what was there all the time. That clarity never ceased for Jesus. On the Mount of Transfiguration he was just operating in the world that was real for him all the time, and the three witnesses were enabled to get a little glimpse. Of course, Jesus couldn't go around with his face and his clothes shining like that, or the people would have taken him to be some pagan deity.

What about Moses, when his face shone so much as he descended from Sinai that he had to veil himself?

Well, we're supposed to manifest that glory too. I think of the story in Genesis where there's a description of Adam and Eve after their disobedience—they "knew they were naked, and sewed fig leaves together and made coverings for themselves"—I don't think that's about sex, or the human body, but it's about what they were like before that. They were naked, and unashamed; there's no indication that they'd had clothes and lost them; rather, their bodies glowed, as we get a glimpse of in these other incidents.

When you look at a lightbulb, you can't see the lightbulb, but you see the light. When that light's turned out, we're aware of the limitation, the loss.

There seem to be these little hints in the scriptures, these flashes of light. But in a way, heaven is too mysterious, too utterly other, for us to imagine. Words abstract it so, separate it so far from our human lives as we live them, that we honestly don't know how to think about heaven. Or hell, for that matter.

This goes to a very deep issue that we really do need an answer to, or our faith will not make much sense. That is the question, Why isn't God obvious? We would think he could be. (I put on the front page of *The Divine Conspiracy* a quotation from C. S. Lewis that I think helps with the problem. It's actually a remark from Screwtape to Wormwood, and it deals with this issue.)

You see, God doesn't wish to overwhelm us. He's put us in a position where our will can go in either direction. We are responsible for our decision. It's what we choose to see that matters. In order for us to have that choice, God leaves things so that we have to seek them.

Isaiah cries out, "Truly, you are a God who hides yourself." *Deus absconditus.* That's a part of this whole picture. We have to seek, so that the promise of Jeremiah 29 can be fulfilled: "You will find me, when you seek for me with all your heart."

Here's that Screwtape quote: "Our cause is never more in danger than when a human, no longer desiring, but still intending, to do our Enemy's will, looks round upon a universe from which every trace of Him seems to have vanished, and asks why he has been forsaken, and still obeys." That's such a marvelous insight from Lewis.

Isn't that the point? That God puts us here, and in effect says, "What do you want?" If there is a person who says, "I deeply, desperately, want God," then as that soul can stand it, it will find God.

It would almost be like being confronted with a nuclear explosion, wouldn't it? My understanding is that God chooses to reveal himself gradually, in metaphor, in vision, in the imagination, because otherwise we'd be annihilated by his presence.

The standard teaching is "If you've seen God, you're ready to die." Because it will blow you away—kill you. Just the effect on your mind will kill you. People often die of shock, or bad news—they fall dead. Basically the situation is that God mediates himself to us in forms, first of all, that will work, so we can find him that way, but also in ways we can tolerate. This is the background of prophetic writings such as "He is like a refiner's fire, like fuller's soap, and who can stand when he appears?"

But even some of those prophetic visions were enigmatic. Ezekiel particularly. And the revelation of John. There's still a lot of mystery there.

Yes, especially from the ordinary human point of view in a fallen world. Prophetic language is just loaded with imagery that would truly be horrifying if you got near to it. After all, when John saw his old friend on the island of Patmos he dropped down as if he were dead.

And Daniel. Same thing. And that being had to lay a reassuring hand on each of them to allow them to get up and stop being afraid and hear a message from God. It was grace at work again.

That's teaching us that if we're going to deal with God there has to be an infusion of grace that enables us to do what he's telling us to do.

Who takes the initiative here? I know God took the first great initiatives in creation and incarnation. But at what point does the human desire to know God become so compelling that God responds and begins to reveal himself?

I think rather late in the process. We're apt to misread cases like Paul's encounter on the road to Damascus. One of my favorite cases is Isaiah: "In the year that King Uzziah died, I saw also the Lord." King Uzziah was one of the best kings that ever lived in Israel. Isaiah had gained some maturity, and he's realizing now that his eyes hadn't been focused in the right place.

But God had come to him, and even at that point in his life his response is "I am a man of unclean lips and live in the midst of a people of unclean lips, and my eyes have seen the King, the Lord of Hosts." So you see, I think it's pretty late when we begin to have that kind of revelation.

I do believe that God is constantly moving in gentle ways around people (except possibly those who have absolutely hardened themselves in their own self-will to the point where God isn't going to bother them). I think he's constantly eliciting in us the desire for himself.

When it comes to the conscious level (and I certainly have to say this for myself, and in everything I've read from others past and present), the conscious desire for God arrives rather late. Before that, there will be a lot of fumbling, a lot of misfiring, perhaps some very deep and unsatisfied yearnings that are hard to identify or act on.

Hopefully there will be some good input from others—parents, family, and so on—that would stimulate this. But the answers come well down the line.

If you look at George Fox, Martin Luther, or others, it does seem to be that way. The "prevenient grace of God," as the theologians call it, has usually long been at work, and at a certain point it emerges to a conscious desire to know God. A few tender souls may know this much younger, but for others, it will take a while.

C. S. Lewis has a poem that reflects that theme—that we may think we're praying, but really, it's God praying through us, so that he becomes both sides of the conversation.

The thing we have to be careful with is—this doesn't mean we have no part. What it means is that our part is something we cannot imagine separated from God's part. Back to disciplines: if I'm fasting, it's not just me fasting, it's God fasting with me, and through me. In order to do the disciplines in a way that is joyous and strengthening and good, they have to be experienced as an extension of grace to us.

So the "divine conspiracy" is also the divine companionship.

That's where "Lo, I am with you always" comes in. The Roman centurion recognized the divine conspiracy in Jesus when he said, "Lord, just say the word. . . . I know how this thing works!"

Cornelius had intimations of that, too.

You don't get very close to God without picking this up. God will make sure that you are preserved, and you can be preserved only if you don't get into the isolated individualism that many people still regard as true religion.

CHAPTER 17

Getting the Elephant Out of the Sanctuary

In this interview with Gary Moon, Dallas reveals his position on the three theories of atonement: ransom, satisfaction / penal substitution, and moral influence. Dallas also discusses the practical impact these important theological concepts have on the church and personal discipleship to Christ.

Interview conducted by Gary Moon (executive director of the Dallas Willard Center for Christian Spiritual Formation at Westmont College) in 2010 and first published in *Conversations Journal*

Dallas, in *The Divine Conspiracy,* you reference statistics indicating that while most Americans believe in God and claim to have made a commitment to Jesus, Christians seem to differ very little from non-Christians. You say, "Surely something has gone wrong when moral failures are so massive and widespread among us. Perhaps we are not eating what we are selling. More likely, I think, what we are 'selling' is irrelevant to our real existence and without power over daily life."

Let's say that what is being sold is any one of the three primary theories of atonement—ransom, satisfaction / penal substitution, or moral influence. How is your last comment not a cause for being burned at the stake?

Fortunately, being "burned at the stake" is a matter of your social context, and at least here in America we're not quite there yet.

I'm just trying to look out for you.

Now, there is a real problem that you are addressing, and it is deeply rooted in the historical past of the Christian religion. The [thought] is that if you don't get this [your atonement theory] right, you are going to be lost and cause a lot of other people to be lost. And that's why these theories can become such "fighting" issues.

If it's that important, do you think it is odd that after two thousand years we still have at least three (some would say six or more) theories of atonement? Theories, not facts, about what is arguably the most important of all Christian doctrines?

Well, I don't find it strange because there is an objective pull here, and that objective pull is that Christ died for our sins. Now, that is the fact that each of the theories tries to explain, and when you have to deal with a stubborn fact, your theories have a limited range, and I think that is why you have these three basic envelopes. Fundamentally, these are three ways of trying to understand the fact that Christ died for our sins and that somehow we are saved by what he did.

I like it that you say "somehow," but I suspect that might make some nervous. Would you mind commenting on what you believe to be a primary strength and weakness of each of the three most prominent theories / metaphors of atonement—ransom, satisfaction (including the commonly held variation on this theory, penal substitution), and moral influence?

The ransom theory has a great strength to it because it fits a well-known social and even political model of redemption, where someone is captive and an arrangement is made to pay off the one who is holding the captive. Now, there has been a lot of bouncing around as to whether it is Satan or sin or God who has us captive and as to who has to be paid off. But the theme of being a captive and being set free is fundamental to the core of Christian salvation.

Would you agree with Anselm that a major stumbling block might be that if the ransom is paid to Satan, it raises questions as to who is in charge here?

Yes. The ransom theory has been the longest-standing theory overall. But Anselm was concerned with it because he felt there was an issue with reference to God that was left out. The atonement is in the person of Christ, but it has many effects. Deliverance from Satan (even deliverance from sin) is only a part of those effects.

Same question: what do you see as the primary strengths and weaknesses of the satisfaction / penal substitutionary theory?

The strength of this theory is that it solves a problem with reference to God. The great hold of this theory is that it provides a model of something that is present in human experience: the situation where someone has done wrong, and now it needs to be set right. Basically this theory addresses a problem of justice. When wrong is done, things must be made right, and that's the strength of the penal theory.

All of these theories, if they are not taken too narrowly, have an important truth to them. It is true that human beings have sinned, and this sin is ultimately an offense against God. The question is how this can be set right. The penal substitutionary theory—one does need that slash in there, because substitutionary theories need not be penal. And actually, substitution is really present in all of these theories except some very weak forms of moral-influence theories. But, and this is a weakness, once again you see what the human mind does—seizes upon something that it understands and says, "Oh, this is like that." So the theory comes along and says, "Oh, I know what happened. This death on our behalf is like that; that is to say, punishment was necessary as a way of setting right or giving justice to the situation."

And you are saying that when you make the jump to punishment, you are getting into a potential weakness of that theory?

The weakness of the theory is in its understanding of how the death of Jesus did what it did—and we simply don't know that. The weakness is that you can get a mistaken view of the whole thing—as you get further away from the fact, the death of Christ. This is true with the ransom theory too. You can get a mistaken view of the whole thing.

What is the whole thing?

The whole thing is Christ coming into the world in the historical setting he did, and reconciling the difference between God and man by his death and his resurrection. We have to come to that because it is there that people tend to see the death [of Christ] as an isolated aspect of his life. And that is perhaps the weakest part of the penal substitutionary theory.

Please say more.

The weakest part of the penal theory is that it tends to focus on one event in the life and death of Christ and to say that is what did it—that event. And [then it becomes,] unfortunately, a theory that isolates atonement from life.

So, a weakness to the penal substitutionary view—and perhaps all of the three theories we are discussing—is attempting to remove the mystery concerning what the death of Jesus actually accomplished. And particularly with the penal view, I could imagine a parishioner might feel as if he got whiplash by being told that God's wrath is so great, it must be appeased even in this way. But, by the way, God is also the prodigal son's father waiting for you to return home with open arms.

That will really jerk you around. This is one of the problems with [penal substitution]—and I don't mean the actual theory—but how it is popularly taken. It presents God as someone who never [really] forgives.

Right.

If you get off the hook, it's because somebody paid for it.

Yes. "While you—congregant in the pew—must forgive seventy times seven times, I—God—must have my wrath appeased when someone messes up."

That's exactly right. It gives a terrible picture of God, and it isn't reconcilable with scripture or with what Jesus taught about or practiced about God, or what the relationship to God through the ages has meant for those who are alive in Christ. And so, the human mind makes a model and says, "This is like that." And then you are stuck with that if you don't have a larger view and basically one that incorporates all three of the alternatives that you have set out.

Very helpful. What about the moral influence view?

The moral influence view is basically a view that leaves the large cosmic order—whether involving Satan or God—untouched, and it basically says, "Well, Christ came into the world as a moral influence," and that's true. But it depends on how you take it. What people have normally done is make it free of its cosmic setting and make it [as if] Christ is only human and has an influence simply by his excellence as a human being, including giving up his life on the cross. The one-sidedness again is obvious. So, you have a central player in the ransom theory in Satan; you have the central player in the penal theory, of course: God. And the central player in the moral influence theory is man.

What would you say to someone looking at the moral influence theory through a different lens, someone who says that it helps them gain a deeper appreciation of the role of a personal cross?

It's extremely helpful if you take it in that context because actually, Christ's death on the cross is the place where we can join him. Scriptures teach abundantly about how this works, but when most people say "moral influence," they don't include that. Now, that's a terrible mistake. Influence is of little significance in a world that faces the human problem of sin and rebellion, as well as alienation from God and hatred for one another. It's of little significance unless it includes the power of resurrection to life—and this is often left out by those favoring the moral influence theory.

If I had to pick a weakness for all of them, it would be that each stops short of identifying the role of and importance of the Incarnation—both that of Jesus and now, his ability to be incarnate in us. None of them place us beside Mary, outside her little village, praying, "Please be born in me today and live your life through me." That is a strange way to say it, so let me just ask. Do you think each theory deemphasizes the role of incarnation—Christ two thousand years ago and Christ today in us?

Well, you see, a good way of putting this is to say that atonement is basically incarnation. Incarnation is Christ coming into flesh to allow us to identify with him in his life and ministry and on the cross and in life beyond the cross.

Including being able to come into our flesh.

That's absolutely right. Each of these theories has a flaw in that it identifies something and says, "That's the whole thing." That is the underlying mistake when you try to take a fact and force it onto a theory. That's attractive because human beings want to control the fact, and they do that by developing an image or theory that makes sense to them, given the whole background of their ideas and social realities. But that can miss the point. Christ was not just any old person; he was a true prince of the cosmos. His death, then, is not like the death of any ordinary person.

Is there a parallel between these theories or metaphors for atonement and the streams of Renovaré—that is, would we stand to benefit by drinking from the best of each instead of choosing sides?

I think, actually, something could be done with that, but you still have to deal with the "dark side" of each one and its deficiencies, and I think you are always going to be troubled if you stay at the level of theories, even if you have several good ones, because atonement is, in the last analysis, a matter of our fellowship with Christ, the person.

Let's back up a bit. Do you make a distinction between justification, atonement, and salvation?

They are distinct but inseparable. Justification means the restoration of a relationship. And, by the way, I think it's very unfortunate the way we use this word and say, "It's just as if I'd never sinned." It will never be that way. I will always be a redeemed sinner, and that's going to be part of the mental and spiritual furniture that helps me live before God for eternity. It will never be "just as if I had never sinned." Now, there is a resumption of relationship, which you can describe as "peace with God" or "being reconciled to God" or "God being reconciled to man," and that part is justification.

So, if justification is about forgiveness and restoration of relationship, where does atonement come in?

Atonement is God's act that makes this possible, and that act is the giving of his son. The giving of his son is much bigger than his son's death on the cross. When we read John 3:16, [we] have to understand that the whole passage is not about forgiveness. It is about life that comes in our relationship to the son—and that is atonement; that is a gift. It is not separable from our faith in Christ or from justification. This is rather difficult to make clear, but justification is not just a forensic act. It is a declaration before God, but it is not just a credit transfer; it is God's act of entering our life, and that's what John 3:16 is about. It's about life from above, and that is atonement.

This is helpful, but the two still keep running together in my mind—and maybe I should just leave them together and not try to force even a subtle distinction between justification and atonement. But do I hear you placing a little more importance on the Incarnation with atonement?

Yes. You have to see the death of Christ as a necessary part of the giving of his son to humanity. And, as Paul says, there is one God and one mediator between God and man . . . the man, Christ Jesus. So now atonement is the resumption of life.

Do you think Jesus was talking about atonement in all the union passages in John 15 through 17?

Well, that fleshes out the idea of union in one's life.

So please put this in the context of how, as you say, salvation is ultimately our "life with God."

Salvation is, biblically speaking, deliverance. It is a condition of being delivered from sin and, with that, guilt—but primarily the emphasis is on being delivered from sin. How we understand that is what matters. Some people, of course, depending on their theory, understand it as in the penal theory: that now your sins are paid off and you have a kind of contract with God, you will not be punished for your sins. But in the biblical / New Testament picture, I think, what you have presented is salvation as a form of life [with God]. And that, I think, is what John and Paul and the New Testament generally understand it to be . . . that people now have a life from above, and their salvation, their deliverance, is a matter of having that life and living that life with God.

Salvation is participating in a transforming friendship with the Trinity.

That's an excellent way of putting it.

I got that from [twentieth-century British theologian and one of the leaders of the Oxford Group] Leslie Weatherhead.

But as you know, if you aren't careful, you just sort of slip out of the substance of that, and you wind up with a very thin moral influence theory rather than an accompaniment with Jesus throughout your days of life.

You mean if Leslie Weatherhead is not careful . . .

Salvation is the life of the son of God in you. That is where, of course, the "vine and the branches" figure comes in and Paul's constant teachings about our unity with Christ, a kind of dynamic pursuit of Christ, and that involves your whole life. So that is incarnation that has gone through death and resurrection.

Before we leave this, I have a follow-up question. I forget the age of your granddaughter.

She is eleven.

By way of summary, then, if you were sitting down with her and she said, "Grandpa, I'm confused. Can you tell me how justification, atonement, and salvation are different, if they are different?" what would you say so that I—I mean, she—could understand?

I would say that justification is a new beginning for a relationship that has been broken, and it is made right by forgiveness. But that's just the doorway into the resumption of relationship. The relationship [itself] is atonement, and that involves Christ becoming one with us. [Atonement] means that we now [can] walk with him and that he is in us, and we are in him. We have eternal life, and that is what atonement is. The result of atonement is deliverance or salvation. We are not under the power of sin and death anymore. Justification, atonement, and salvation are three aspects of one thing.

And then if she were to say, "Grandpa, what do you mean when you say, 'Salvation is a life'?"

I would talk to her about the life that is in a plant or an animal so that she would understand there is a definite kind of movement in the plant or the animal, and I would talk to her about different kinds of life. Then I would tell her that when we place our confidence in Jesus, he becomes a new kind of life in us, and that means now we think different thoughts; we believe things we didn't believe before, and also we are strengthened and directed by grace, which is now a force in our life that comes from Jesus. And salvation as a life is simply participation in the life that comes from Jesus, who is with us and in us. The basic idea is, there is now a power, a personal power, moving in our lives that comes from God and comes in the form of Jesus.

That was wonderful. In fact, for the rest of our questions, let's just pretend I am your granddaughter asking these. So, with that in mind, if Jesus's death on a cross and resurrection conquered sin, how would you explain the Holocaust to a rabbi? Or more simply, how would you explain the obvious presence of sin in the world after the death and resurrection of Jesus?

Well, the death and resurrection of Jesus do not impose a necessity; they open a possibility. The continued presence of sin in the world, including the horrible dimensions that we have in the many holocausts (Cambodia, Siberia, etc.), means that we're not done with this by any means. The tendency of human beings to kill others en masse is a permanent fixture of a world in which they (human beings) are living on their own in alienation from God.

And that [alienation] is why I like thinking about sin—and I hope this is not heretical—as separation, and salvation as the journey toward union or the experience of union. So Jesus's death on the cross makes it possible for union, the journey of being with him, living your life with him. But even with all that is offered, even if you've gone down front at a Billy Graham crusade, you can still go back to living separate from God?

That is the issue of spiritual growth. So now, let us say you have placed your faith in Christ and he has given you new life—that doesn't mean you are all fixed up. You still have the issue of growth, and it looks like that is an eternal project, and it will go on forever. So, that's where you need the gospel of the kingdom of God and life in the kingdom. And you need to understand all of the aspects of you as a human being (thinking, feeling, choosing, relating, etc.) and how redemption comes into them by your discipleship to Christ and growing in grace and in the knowledge of our Lord and Savior, Jesus Christ. You see, if we have a version of the atonement that is independent of spiritual growth—and frankly, all three theories tend to leave you there—then you are going to sort of say, well, we even have "the finished work of Christ on the cross."

Christ's work on the cross was not the end?
    No.

I knew that, but I'm trying to help you out.
    Christ's work on the cross was not the end. Now, there was something finished. Primarily, it was that, in the biblical sense, the days of his flesh were finished. But to think that redemption was finished or that everything needed for salvation was finished is simply a brutal misunderstanding of the New Testament teaching about the life of Christ.

To follow up on that, in expounding on what you mean by "bar-code faith," you state that "for some Christian groups the 'account' has to be appropriately serviced to keep the debts paid up, because we really are not perfect. For others—some strongly Calvinist groups—every debt past, present, and future is paid for at the initial scan. But the essential thing in either case is forgiveness of sins." "The real question," you continue, is "whether God would establish a bar-code type of arrangement at all and is it we who are in danger; in danger of missing the fullness of life offered to us."[1] Has he? And if not, how would you again describe what he has established?
    Well, let's understand that the "bar-code" picture means it doesn't matter what's in the can. The scanner just reads the bar code, and it doesn't matter if it is dog food in the can or salmon; what appears on the register is whatever the bar code says. My little granddaughter would pick up on that immediately because everyone now knows what bar codes are and they know that it is something on the outside of the can. But what God looks at is what is in the can.
    Again, you know, we have all these wonderful peripheral stories and statements: "Man looks on the outward appearance, God looks

on the heart." Or Jesus's statement in John 4: "God is seeking people who worship Him in spirit and in truth," and so on. God does not make a bar-code arrangement; human beings make those precisely because they can look on the outward appearance. Basically, human beings, in their religion, tend to continue the project of domination and control, and they run on outward appearances that give us all our denominational differences and so forth. God does not look at that. God looks at the heart. What does he look at in the heart? He looks for a person who loves him and trusts him.

And what would you say about the importance of decision in the process—I'm thinking, for example, the classic evangelical altar call?

Well, those are actually two different things—the decision and the classical altar call. For many people, that decision has been made in the form of responding to a call to come forward and confess your faith in Christ—that you have put your trust in him. There is nothing wrong with that unless you identify that [the form] and the decision together, and then you will think that the decision cannot come in any form. But the decision comes in many forms. For some, they more or less wake up and discover that they have decided. And that, too, can be a very real, very good and strong way to do it.

We want to recognize, though, that for most of Christian history the majority of people who have been Christians didn't have an altar-call experience. Altar calls came relatively late; calls to decision did not. Saint Francis of Assisi, a well-known person, really never had an altar-call experience, but he had experiences and he gave his life to Christ, and that was the beginning of a beautiful story.

So, you believe coming to a decision is part of the conversion process, but the context can vary widely. Along those lines, something struck me recently when I read where Jesus asked Peter, "Who do you say that I am?" What hit me was that this was apparently several years into their time together. So, when Peter answers correctly, and Jesus says to him, "Blessed are you

because flesh and blood did not reveal it," well, it would seem that Jesus hadn't taken the disciples through the four spiritual laws on their first night together, if at all. Perhaps it was more important to Jesus that they had entered into an apprenticeship with him than that they immediately knew all the answers to "salvation" questions.

Well, you know, what is not commonly understood is that a rabbi might do that kind of thing and it had a perfectly definite meaning for them. They knew what it meant to follow and be with a rabbi, and there can be very little doubt that these people knew about Jesus before the time he approached them. This is often presented very badly—as if these guys had never seen him before and as if he didn't know who they were. You sometimes are left with the idea that he just said, "Follow me," and they, under inspiration, did it. But the decision to follow a rabbi was about entering a form of life that really, I suspect, in that community was much more commonly understood than today. Now we generally think about this as making a decision for Christ. But they knew what this meant. It meant a decision to leave all, to be with him and to serve him and to learn and to go through a period of spiritual formation, as we would say.

Yes, that is what I was trying to get at. You seem to be putting our journey of salvation back into that context. The disciples made a decision that involved entering into an apprenticeship with Jesus.

Yes, and as I often say, a disciple can be very "green." Being a disciple—or an apprentice—is not an advanced spiritual condition. We tend to think it is today because we have accepted this idea that you can be a Christian (make a decision for Jesus) and not be a disciple of Jesus (enter into an apprenticeship with him).

Thank you. Along those lines, let me run this past you. I was sitting in church this past weekend and observed a very prominent altar. As I studied it I began to think about altars of sacrifice in the Old Testament and the sacrificial death of Christ, but I also

began wondering if it's possible today that we may be placing so much emphasis on the death of Christ—in thinking about salvation—that it may become a way of avoiding focusing on the need for our own death or our own personal cross. What I mean is: Do you think we have underemphasized the importance of our personal cross in the West? And, when I say "personal cross," let me be clearer. I'm not referring to having an unwanted cold sore pop up before an important interview; I mean the pain of desiring to embrace death to any will other than the will of God.

Yes. It is actually the cross of Christ we take [up], and he calls it our cross when he says: "if you take your cross and follow me," and that's the essential part of taking the cross.

So, I wonder sometimes if there can be a tendency to place so much emphasis on the past and the cross of Christ that it may result in an unintended avoidance of living out what it means to daily take up our cross—daily desire to die to any will other than the will of God.

Yes, well, I do think that. When we see the altar in the church, we should think of ourselves upon it. This is our way of identifying with Christ on his cross and, in that way, entering into his life. But I think you are right. Now, when the ordinary person sees an altar in the church they may not have the profound thoughts that were provoked in you, because they think it is simply Christ on that altar. They may never make the connection to themselves. So we really need to emphasize the unity of Christ and the believer in his death. I [too] am dying on the altar. Jesus says, "This is for you, my cross is for you, too."

Okay, now an easy question. Was Abraham saved, and if so, what was the process since it didn't involve the cross?

He was saved.

I was kidding about that being an easy question. Please expound.

He was saved in the sense of being secure in his future with

God—that would include the afterlife. He was saved because he trusted God. Now, the details were that he trusted God to fulfill his covenant to give him a male heir to carry on his line. That is what he trusted God for. When God looked at him and said that he would rather have this than sinless perfection, Abraham believed God and God accounted it to him for righteousness. That is to say, God took that as the basis of his relationship to Abraham.

God would rather have what than sinless perfection—a trusting interactive friendship?

Yes. God was in that world (as he is in this world), and those who trust him and live within an interactive relationship with him are, in fact, a part of what he is doing and therefore, they are a part of his life and his life is an eternal kind of life. Now, we can trust Jesus Christ, in the sense of turning your life over to him for him to do with it what he wants. Then you become a part of him and he becomes a part of you, and that is the basic reality of salvation and of the life that is salvation—that interactive relationship, the intermingling of activities, sharing a life; that's what it's about.

When you go to one of the most important passages [in scripture] and read about atonement (or the "at-one-ment" Christ accomplished—see Romans 5), you realize, Oh, this is about a life. A life that is shared, and as 5:17 says, "Those who receive the abundance of grace and the gift of righteousness will reign in life through the One, Jesus Christ." That's atonement!

So if salvation, theoretically, could have been possible, even prior to the Incarnation or cross, what was the value added by the cross?

The cross is mandated because of sin. Jesus went to the cross for our sakes. That's why the fundamental reality is expressed in terms of "Christ died for our sins." Yes, he did. But, if you want to understand what that was, you have to read the larger context. In Romans 5, for example, you find out that "God commended His love towards us in that while we were yet sinners, Christ died for us." He died for us because of sin, and there was actually no way around that, given the reality of human sin. He accepted the cross in order that he might identify as us, as Philippians 2 explains and also Hebrews 2—"He tastes death for every man"—and without the cross, you cannot imagine what a gospel would look like in a fallen world. So, the cross is necessary.

So what happened at the cross?

Well, I think anyone who thinks they understand that is probably not justified in that belief. One of the things that happened was God was in Christ, reconciling the world unto himself, so one of the things was reconciliation. Obviously, something happened between the Son and the Father also. Now, that's where our problem really arises—with people theorizing about that, and attempting to impose that on the clear statements of the scripture. That's where our theories come in—for better and worse.

So . . .

So, what happened? At a minimum, what happened was something that permitted God, in his wisdom, to act differently toward men than he would have if the death on the cross had not occurred. Now, what was that? I don't think anyone knows what that was.

Thank you for your honesty and for allowing some aspects of theology to remain a mystery.

Yes, to impose more understanding, I believe, is to intrude into the mysteries of the Trinity in ways that I simply think take us "off base" when we try. But I think we should say, it is a fact that there was something that happened between the Son and the Father on the cross that makes possible the plan of salvation. That plan is God's plan; not our plan. That's God's plan, but people often present it as "my plan for how to get saved." The Son poured out his life on the cross. The life is in the blood, so, when we talk about the blood of Jesus, we are talking about his life; or as Isaiah 53 says, "He poured out His soul unto death," and that life is what saves.

And now, mysteriously, he can pour it [his life] into us?

Absolutely; that's exactly right. He poured it out on earth. And the most appropriate symbol for that is his blood, of course, and that ties in with how the gospel is preached through the ages, and to the Eucharist or the Lord's Supper. All of this is deeply important; it's not just symbols. The cross and the blood point to the depth of God's love for the depths of man's sin.

Okay, no more slow pitches. Dallas, what is your concept of hell?

My concept of hell is very simple. It is God's best for some people. It's the best God can do for those who don't like him. The worst would be to make them be with him. Now, what that means is separation from God, because people in hell want to be away from God, and he lets them.

Hell is not something God enjoys. He is not willing that any should perish but that all should come to everlasting life. That is his wish. God is not trying to keep people out of heaven; he is trying to get them in, and I believe that he will admit anyone who, in his judgment, can stand it—and I'm not being funny. That is deadly serious. For God, this isn't playtime. This business of being in heaven is very serious indeed. If you got there and found you didn't like God—well, actually, most people don't like God—that would be a problem. In heaven you're going to be right up against him, constantly, forever. You have to be ready for that. People who don't like God enough to seek him and spend time with him here are very likely to find heaven utterly agonizing.

I've heard you comment on this in a way that reminds me very much of how my Uncle Otis, a faith-healing evangelist, would say it. When he was asked, "Who goes to heaven?" he would answer something like, "Everybody who can stand that much love." And when asked, "Who goes to hell?" he responded, "Only those who will have it no other way."

Yes, that's exactly right.

I knew he got that from you.

You see, the problem is, we have all the imagery that comes to us from an uninspired tradition. A lot of this is pagan, and it's borrowed from pictures of volcanoes and lava flowing, and all that sort of thing—sulfur, and so forth. You don't want to have images of atonement and hell that give us a God who is fundamentally mean.

I used to minister down in Texas with a dear old brother who, when he got to preaching on hell, [made] you [want] to hide under the seats and hope God wouldn't find you. He used to say, "God's gonna skip them sinners across the lake of fire like a boy skips a rock across a pond." He was giving a picture of a God who enjoys the misery of the lost. It was as bad as the picture of a God that has got a big whuppin' in him, and he takes it out on Jesus so we don't have a whuppin' coming.

These are just incredibly terrible images of God, and you end up with people who are thinking the miracle is that God loves me. No, no—the miracle would be if he didn't love you, because he is a God of love, not a God of wrath who occasionally "lets up."

Now, moving to the practical, if you don't mind, what are a few things you do every day in your own apprenticeship program? What is your own way of living out salvation as a life?

Well, the main objective—and I will come back to what I do—is to keep the Lord at my right hand or, to use another biblical image, always before me. So my objective is to go through my day with God.

Now, some of the things that I do [that help with this] are that, routinely, when I wake up in the morning and often before I get up out of bed, I will work through the Lord's Prayer and the twenty-third Psalm a couple of times, and then as I get up, I will make it my practice to be thankful and to ask God to be with me as I go through the day.

Beyond that, it depends on what the day is, but I return to the conscious invocation of God periodically as I go through the day. I

try to keep that alive—and of course, having memorized a great deal
of scripture, being committed to service, to those that I'm with [and
so on], are helpful things to keep that alive.

It sounds like your quiet time gets extended a bit.

My main problem with "quiet time" is that I want my whole day
to be quiet. I don't view quiet time as something that I have and then
depart from into "noisy time." No, my main business is to make the
whole day "quiet time."

So, given the day, I may have an extended time of the study of
scripture or prayer, but that depends upon which day it is, because
some days I simply can't do that. And I don't think there is anything
wrong with that. There would be something wrong if on those days
I took a vacation [from being with God], but I don't do that. Jesus
said he would be with us always, and that's the center of what I try
to do. I try to be with him.

I have other periodic things like fasting. I try to fast some period
of time each week and do longer fasts periodically. Then, of course,
worship and all of the things that we might think about on a periodic basis. But my objective is to have the Lord always with me.

**Dallas, I think I've warned you that I'm a compulsive summa-
rizer. I like to think about salvation and the differences between
justification, atonement, and salvation in terms of verb tenses.
In terms of the past, I see the Incarnation and the cross of Christ
coming into focus. That is where I would place justification and
forgiveness: the Incarnation of Christ, the cross of Christ, makes
possible justification and forgiveness. As you said, "justification
is the front door."**

**In the present, I think more in terms of my own personal
cross. And I'm not talking about "a pebble in my shoe," but
whether or not I am willing to crawl on the altar as a living sacrifice and, in the present, die to the desire for any will apart from
the will of Christ, and the desire for the living Christ—because
of his death and resurrection—to be incarnate in me. I think of**

atonement in terms of accepting my personal cross that my new life can begin with God living his life with and through me, living more and more moments by way of personal incarnation of the power and spirit of Christ in me. I think about the future in the sense that salvation is an ongoing process, but ultimately there is the deliverance—through an ongoing journey with God in which I'm becoming more like him. I love the idea of salvation as a journey toward union with God.

So stop me if I'm wrong, but I've come to view justification a little more in terms of the cross of Christ and forgiveness of sins; atonement is living my life with God in the present, animated by the power, presence, energy, and love of Christ—all looking toward a future where salvation is deliverance and, as John 17:3 states, intimately "knowing" God.

I like that, Gary. It is a manner in thinking about these terms and arranging a number of different things in a coherent relationship. I guess my only worry about doing it this way is if you view justification as only in the past. I believe you must also relate it to ongoing and eventual salvation.

Justification is, then, more than the front door?

Yes, that's why I would [also] consider justification as an effect of regeneration. It has a forensic attitude, but justification is basically the way God treats people to whom he has given life from above. What are you going to do with it? Well, that's where justification comes in. I'm not going to hold their sins against them, because now we have a new principle that is a life, and I think that's how Abraham was justified by faith and so on. So, it depends on how you handle the details of justification, and, of course, there is a lot of room for work on that.

Dallas, thank you for being beyond gracious with your time. Last question: What question do you wish I had asked that I didn't ask?

I honestly can't think of any question that I wish you had asked, but I do think that the main issue with atonement is what it has to do with our daily life, and I think we have gone over that in various ways, but it is essential *not* to equate atonement and justification. You have to fit justification in somehow, but don't do it in a way that leaves it disconnected from the life that includes both sanctification and glorification.

Before we stop, please underline what you mean when you say it is essential not to equate justification and atonement. Is it because if you do that, you might miss the notion of salvation as a life?

You will certainly miss it, and as a result of that, you are going to cut salvation off from life, and I think that, among other things, that is a basic falsification of the message of the New Testament and of the salvation that Jesus himself announced and called people to—of life in the kingdom of God.

That might be the best single answer for why nontransformation is the elephant in the sanctuary, as you put it.

It is now. Theologically, we latched on to the idea that you can accept justification through the death of Christ, and then for the ordinary person there is no connection beyond that to anything else. It doesn't have to be that way, but that's the way it has turned out.

Thank you for being so generous with your time and for offering us both the diagnosis and the treatment for the elephant-in-the-sanctuary problem. If I heard you correctly, the diagnosis is that we can "get saved" without this necessarily meaning that an active agent of change is in our lives—without daily participating in a transforming friendship with the Trinity. We can become "Christians" without becoming disciples/apprentices. The treatment is to approach salvation as a life with God, a life of obedience, incarnate with the presence, power, and love of Jesus. To use your words: "Salvation is the life of the Son of God in you."

CHAPTER 18

The Gospel of the Kingdom
A Conversation with Dallas Willard

In this interview with Keith Giles, Dallas explains how we can better understand spiritual transformation in action and what is needed for a biblical experience of salvation.

Interview conducted by Keith Giles in 2005 and first published online by the interviewer[1]

Dallas, can you explain the difference between the gospel of the kingdom and the more popular gospel of the atonement for us?

The gospel of the kingdom is that you can now live in the kingdom of God, and the gospel of the atonement is that your sins can be forgiven. Those are the respective "Good News"es, I suppose.

So, are you saying there are two gospels? Are my sins not forgiven if I live in the kingdom? Or am I not in the kingdom of God if I accept the gospel of the atonement?

The way it practically works out is this: if you have the gospel of the atonement, and that's all you've heard, the rest of your life you will run on your own and you may or may not think of being a disciple of Jesus or of obeying him or of devoting your life to the kingdom of God. You can still do that, but those things are all optional for you. That is where we really stand in [most of] our Christian culture today. Anything more than forgiveness of sins,

212

and by that I mean "heaven when you die," is optional, and most of our professed believers now do not know that they can live in the kingdom of God now.

By contrast, anyone who is alive in the kingdom of God now knows that their sins are forgiven because they have the life of heaven in them now. So heaven and forgiveness are natural parts of the gospel of the kingdom of God, whereas discipleship and holiness and power and other scriptural evidences are not a natural part of the gospel of the atonement. I want to emphasize that sense of being a natural part.

Here's one of the ways I try to help ministers understand this difference. I ask them, "Does the gospel you preach truly lead to discipleship to Jesus?" and the gospel of the kingdom has that natural connection. It's not trusting the kingdom, it's about trusting Jesus and living in the kingdom with him. So then, for example, the New Birth is the birth from above, and as Jesus was telling Nicodemus, "You must be born again." Now, that's about new life that isn't just atonement. One of the strange things that has happened is that verses like John 3:16 are treated as if it were a forgiveness verse whereas it is really a new life verse. The whole context is about having the life of the kingdom. Nicodemus came saying he could see it, and Jesus said, "No, you can't see it," and helped him to understand why he couldn't.

So, it's the idea of a natural part of the kingdom containing forgiveness, and if you're trusting Jesus, and not just his death on the cross alone, but the person of Jesus, then life in the kingdom comes with that, and as a natural part also comes discipleship, forgiveness, all of the things that any good theology would cover.

So, it seems to me that the reason why the gospel of the atonement is the most readily accepted and understood version of the gospel today, especially in America, is because it's sort of the fruit of the style of evangelism we have employed.

Yes, that's absolutely right. Now, the reason for that, however, is the theology that's in back of it. We do not evangelize for disciples; we evangelize to make Christians and then, maybe, later try to raise the issue of discipleship. Frankly, that's like "bait and switch" in advertising. You'll hear people express that to their pastors and say, "Why are you talking about discipleship? I'm right with God. Why are you talking about obedience?" It's like I talk about in one of the chapters of my book about an upright citizen of the church who came to his pastor and said, "I'm going to divorce my wife because I've fallen in love with someone else," and the pastor, of course, turned purple and said, "You can't do this," and the man said, "Of course I can. You've said that Jesus will forgive my sins if I believe he died on the cross." There's honestly no response to this from the theology of atonement only.

I was teaching on this recently in our home group, and I had a woman, innocently, not trying to be argumentative, but honestly puzzled with me on the subject, who asked me, "What would you say to someone if you wanted to evangelize them? If it's not about going to heaven when you die, then what is it about?" It just seems that once you diffuse the idea of the gospel of the atonement as being an incomplete version of the gospel, it kind of leaves us unequipped now. So, how do we witness if the language of the gospel of the atonement is not part of my script?

That's really an excellent question, and I hope we can get a very clear answer to it because it naturally comes up because of what people have been taught all their lives. The appropriate question then is, "If you don't die tonight, what are you going to do tomorrow?" And the answer should be, "I'm going to trust Jesus with all of my life, with everything," and that will allow you to live in the kingdom of God. Now, if you do die tonight you may go to heaven, but you see, most people are not going to die tonight. They, like the rest of us, have to face life tomorrow and the day after and the day after.

The big question is, Are you going to live life on your own tomorrow and the day after? And if you do, then you're not trusting

Jesus. The evangelistic question needs to be varied a bit, and I use various formulations for it. For example, if it is appropriate I will say to someone, "How are you doing with your kingdom?" and that usually opens up the discussion about how they're handling their lives. I will then let them know that there's a kingdom they can live in that belongs to Jesus and that if they will turn their lives over to him, then they will prosper for time and for eternity, in his kingdom. That's the difference.

It opens up a different landscape on evangelism because it turns out that the people that need to hear the gospel of Jesus the most are the people who are well off and in charge of a lot of things, not just the person living in the box in the alley or the person who is living the life of debauchery. All people desperately need to know about the kingdom of the heavens and their life in it. So, that's how you evangelize: you call people to discipleship by announcing the availability of the kingdom now. That's what Jesus did, and then when people understood him they also understood that he was the king.

The simple gospel is: "Jesus is available to trust, and what you need to do is to trust Jesus." Once you begin to teach this fully, then you begin to realize how great Jesus is and that he is actually running the world and that the cosmos is under his charge. So then, the invitation is to become involved as a disciple.

One way I try to express what salvation is, is to say, "It is participating in the life that Jesus is now living on earth." That is why Paul says, in 1 Corinthians 15, for example: "If Christ is not risen, your faith is in vain and you're still in your sins."

Right, and also that it is not I who lives, but Christ who lives in me.

Exactly. So, it's participating in the life that Jesus is now living. Christ in me, the hope of glory. That was the message to the Gentiles, as reported in Colossians, and that's the message to everyone. The "hope of glory" (Col. 1:27) is the living Christ in you, and that's another way of describing life in the kingdom of God.

I have so many possible questions and directions we could go from here . . . so, I'll just pick one. I'm curious how and when and in what way did this distinction of the gospel of the kingdom become clear to you? Have you just always understood this? Were you raised in a church that taught this? Or did you discover this over time?

Well, I can tell you very easily about that. First of all, anyone who goes through a theological education will be given a version of the gospel, and it will be said that it is different from the gospel that we're supposed to preach. On the Liberal side, the kingdom of God was taken to be a condition of society toward which they were supposed to work. Both the Left and the Right, theologically, share the idea that Jesus was going to bring the kingdom of God, but he didn't. So, the Liberal version [states] that Jesus expected a political order to emerge among the Jewish people and instead they rejected it, and so he was wrong because Jesus thought the kingdom was going to come and it didn't. The Conservative version was the one that was most common among the people in Jesus's own day—namely, that there was going to appear the king, and the kingdom would come, politically, because the king appeared. Well, the king appeared on the cross, and so that's where you get the dispensational teaching. You see it in the old Scofield Bible and elsewhere—the idea that we were then put into this odd thing called the Church Age. So, they believe that the kingdom will come at the end of the Church Age, and that's where you get your *Left Behind* books and so on.[2]

There's no New Testament scholar who would ever tell you that the gospel of Jesus was about anything other than the kingdom of God. What many don't understand is how that connects to the development in the book of Acts, and later in the church, where people come to understand the kingdom through Jesus, and that's where, if you do an inductive study on the kingdom of God in the book of Acts, or of the kingdom, you'll see how that develops. So, for example, in 1 Corinthians 15 where Paul spells out the gospel he preaches, it is presenting the kingdom, in the form of Jesus. That's the way we're supposed to do it. We're not supposed to say, "Won't it be wonderful when the kingdom of God comes?" or whatever.

My theological education took all that in, and I began to serve as a pastor in the Southern Baptist Convention, in the church, as a young man. As I did that I began to see something strange. I spent a lot of time trying to get people to come to church. I looked at Jesus, and I saw that he spent a lot of his time trying to get away from people.

(laughs) Because he had so many people following him around?

Absolutely. When you read the Gospels you see people walking on one another in Luke to just get to hear him and be around him. It wasn't just a signs-and-wonders show; they came because of his teaching. Publicans and sinners thronged around him, flocked to him, to hear him present the kingdom of God because, again, that's all Jesus talked about. But it wasn't a political thing; it was a reality that is here now, and you can, by trusting him, live in that kingdom.

So, all of these zany things he talks about—the birds and the flowers and so forth—that's the presence of the kingdom, and that's what he taught. So, I knew I must find out about this. I knew I must preach what Jesus preached. Although I was far from having his effect. Once I began preaching this way, then this issue of trying to pump people up and come to church and trying to get people to do things—that just disappeared.

I began to say to people, "The real issue is your life when you're not in church, and what are you going to do with that?" Now, then if you want to know how to do that you begin to become a disciple of Jesus. You trust him to the extent that you believe that he knows the best about everything, and you want to learn from him. That means how to run your business, how to run your home, personal relations of all sorts, and so forth come under his control and authority. That's the path of a disciple.

So, to put that long story simply, I just realized that what Jesus was saying in the Gospels is for us now. But to access it we have to trust him with our whole life, and then the whole New Testament lights up and the great passages like Ephesians 3 and 4 and Galatians 5 and Colossians 3—all those, you suddenly realize, "Well, this is talking about life in the kingdom of God." So, it ceases to be laws and becomes an expression of the life you live in Christ.

So, forgive me if this seems like a loaded question, but, is discipleship to Christ necessary for salvation?

If you mean life in the kingdom, it is. If you mean going to heaven when you die, I think a lot of people are going to be in heaven who don't understand this. I think they may have to wear a dunce cap for several million years, but I think people are going to go to heaven in different conditions. I do think that what Paul the apostle says—that "whoever shall call upon the name of the Lord shall be saved"—includes that, and you don't have to understand everything perfectly to be on Jesus's side. See, our situation now is one where we are under a severe misteaching, and I don't think that people under that teaching are going to be automatically condemned for it. God knows their hearts, and I'm sure that many people who wouldn't know how to talk kingdom language if their lives depended on it will be in heaven.

But of course the questions that face us are, "What are we going to do until we go [to heaven]?" and "Is that all just lost?" Many people treat the time before you die as if somehow it had nothing to do with God. God has nothing to do with your life here; we're just hanging on, trying not to sin, and we all fail, and we have a whole teaching that you never make any progress, and that you don't have to make any progress, because you're saved by grace. Grace, to them, relates only to forgiveness; it doesn't relate to life.

This leads right into what I was going to ask you next, which is the whole fascination we seem to have, as a culture, with grace. Although it seems that the version of grace that we're so enamored with isn't the complete, biblical version of grace.

It has almost nothing to do with it. But see, again, that follows this basic line, which I believe is inspired by evil, to keep our lives out of touch with God. If you do an inductive study of grace in the Bible, you would never come to the idea that it has only to do with forgiveness. I have heard nationally known speakers say, and these are the exact words, "Grace is only for guilt." Now, if you take that and, for example, the words of Paul the apostle in Ephesians 3:8—"unto me, who am the least of all saints is this grace given, that I should preach among the Gentiles the unsearchable riches of Christ." Now, just take that context. Does this mean that all that is involved here is forgiveness? Not at all.

What Paul was referring to is that grace was a gift of a ministry of life to the Gentiles. The general idea that fits all the contexts of grace found in both the Old and the New Testaments is that grace is God acting in my life to accomplish what I cannot accomplish on my own. Now then, if you take that idea and you go back to all the passages about grace, you will see that suddenly things begin to light up. Paul in 1 Corinthians 15 is talking about how he was the last one who witnessed the resurrected Jesus. He says he doesn't deserve to be an apostle, even though he was late. He says, "I have labored more abundantly than they all," and he catches himself then and adds, "yet not I but the *grace* of God that is in me."

Now, that wasn't forgiveness. That was God acting in Paul, and then you watch his life and you see what that means. So that when Paul acted, he knew that God was acting with him and through him. Again, grace is God acting in my life to accomplish what I cannot on my own. Of course, it's much bigger than that because it also has, not just an individual, but a social presence in history. Now you come to the very famous passage in 2 Peter 3:18: "Grow in *grace* [and that means to grow in the presence of God in your life, doing what you cannot do on your own], and in the knowledge of our Lord and Savior Jesus Christ." Now, knowledge, biblically, always refers to interactive relationship, and that's grace.

So now I would say that, of all the things for which we have to go back and redo the vocabulary, to get it right, grace is the big thing,

and the next thing is salvation, or, What does it mean to be saved?
Once you get those right, then you see a picture of a life lived in the
kingdom of God, and the kingdom of God is God in action. It's God
reigning. I often say it's where what God wants done is done. Now all
that comes together, and you get a coherent picture of what it means
to trust Jesus, enter the kingdom, be saved, and live by grace.

**Thank you so much for taking the time to go through that de-
scription, that clarification, of grace. I agree with you that we
have grossly misunderstood grace. And then you said that the
second thing we need to understand is salvation. Could you do
the same thing for this concept also?**

Right. What it means to be saved is to be living a life of interaction with Jesus, and that's the only description of eternal life in the
New Testament: John 17:3, where Jesus says, in his prayer, "Now
this is eternal life: that they may know you, the only true God, and
Jesus Christ whom you sent." Now again, *know* does not mean to
know *about* him.

It's not about knowledge.

Biblically, knowledge is interactive relationship. As Mary said
to the angel, "But how can this be since I know not a man?" See,
that word *know* is different than knowledge. What she meant is that
she had not had sexual intercourse with a man; that is called *carnal
knowledge.*

So, it's an intimacy that conceives something, then?

It most certainly does. The intimacy is one of interaction. When
the prophet says, on behalf of Jehovah to Israel, "You only have I
known of all the peoples on the Earth," he's not saying he doesn't
know about the others; he's saying, "You're the only ones that I've
entered into a covenantal relationship with, an interactive relationship." So eternal life, then, is an interactive relationship with God.
That's what salvation is.

Now what about forgiveness? That's a natural part of that interactive relationship: when you trust Jesus, you trust him for everything, including forgiveness. But God's point of view, as Paul says in Romans about Abraham, is "He believed God and it was accounted unto him as righteousness," but if you trust Jesus Christ, God would rather have that than sinlessness. When God saw Abraham's confidence in him, God said, "I like this better," and to be accounted as righteousness means that the proper relationship between a human being and God is now resumed. That is an ongoing relationship in which progress in understanding and practice of holiness and joy and obedience and all these things come together as a part of a life.

So, you don't get a little thing that says you get heaven when you die, and you're left with the option of saying, "Well, shall I obey?" And then of course if you say, "I shall obey," the next step is "I learn to obey," because that isn't done for me—though we do it with God; [obedience] is not something we do on our own. And so that, too, is grace. When the person comes to the place where they can actually love their enemies, that is grace. But it's not passive. That's where we have to learn that true grace is not opposed to effort. It's opposed to earning, but not to effort. Earning is an attitude, but effort is action.

There is a connection, then, as you describe grace as "God helping me to accomplish the things I cannot accomplish on my own . . ."

I would say, "God acting in my life." The wording there is very important.

Okay. So, it seems that this is the necessary fuel for the spiritual formation of a person.

Spiritual formation is a word for the process you go through in a life.

So, spiritual formation should not be optional. It is a natural process that would occur if you were completely trusting Christ.

That's exactly right. It's the process of actually trusting Christ. If you really trust Christ, then he will be your teacher and you will be his student. What will he teach you? About everything that is going on in your life. You will come to the place where, as Colossians 3:17 says, "Whatsoever you do, in word or deed, do all in the name of the Lord Jesus Christ, giving thanks to God the Father."

It seems that, for some people, the spiritual disciplines are too heavy. It's like, "Fasting and solitude are such a drudgery" to most of us.

No, see, that is a person who, whether they know it or not, is still living their life on their own. So, they come to something like these disciplines and they say, "Now, this doesn't fit into my plans, I couldn't do this," or "I don't need to do this," and it's because they are living their life on their own. That, of course, is the basic sin: living your life your way, on your terms.

So, in this case a complete surrender has not taken place?

That's right. Of course, they haven't been taught what that would mean. They haven't been given an opportunity to do that. So, it's almost natural that they would be in that position.

The ordinary preacher, when he goes to his church—what he's actually facing as he looks out at his congregation is a wall of unbelief. Now, of course you might say it's well-intentioned unbelief, and it is. Most of the folks you're dealing with in churches have head knowledge of a lot of stuff. For example, they know there's a Trinity perhaps, but it has no connection with their lives. They never think, "I'm living in a Trinitarian universe," and that's why it does no good for ministers to moan and groan about the lack of involvement or obedience, about how they have to keep entertaining people so they'll come back next week and keep giving and so on. That's the situation these ministers are in. They've now accepted that as normal. Whereas that's not normal.

No. That's not what Jesus works so hard for and died on the cross for and rose again for. Not to create this kind of mediocrity.

Absolutely. We can sing a song about "joy unspeakable and full of glory," but nobody's got it, and the rest of the things that are talked about in scripture are missing. Even the social issues are fundamental to the kingdom—loving our neighbor as our self and so on. But they are not additional things we're trying to tack on; they are more expressions of the kind of life that is moving in us appropriately under our discipleship to Jesus.

I think we touched on this a little bit the last time we spoke, but it seems that the other factor is not just that it's not being preached in our churches, but it's also something that the average Christian could need a role model for, to help them get an idea for how to live this sort of life. I'm not saying it's not happening, but I'm suggesting that the idea of mentoring or discipling one another is a bit of a lost art these days. I guess because it isn't being taught from the pulpit, then it therefore also isn't being practiced.

Well, two things. One is, the kind of so-called fellowship we have in our churches does not allow people to know one another. If it did, they might actually find some people who are remarkably exemplifying life in the kingdom of God. Second thing: we do have cases at a distance—for example, people like Mother Teresa of Calcutta, or Billy Graham, or the late pope, and I'm not talking about perfection here. That's one thing you really have to stay away from in this discussion. We're not talking about perfection; we're talking about doing a lot better.

The fact is, there are many people Christians know at a distance that exemplify life in the kingdom. They recognize this. They know this. They may even have to travel to Calcutta to be with Mother Teresa—and I've met many people who have made that trip—but they're not going to do what she does. They come back and they talk about her, and maybe they are different in some respects, but they don't do what she does. The same way you go to Francis of Assisi and all these people talk about him and what he did, but you don't see anyone doing what Saint Francis did. At a distance we have these exemplars. Jesus himself is the exemplar. We know about Paul and others in the New Testament, and sometimes with their imperfections, because perfection is something you have to put out of your mind. You have to think in terms of learning to do the things that Jesus said to do. The models are there. The problem is, we have this automatic theological adjuster in our minds that says, "That's not for me, that's for special people."

One of the most touching things I observe as I come across people who have read Brother Lawrence's book on practicing the presence of God is that they immediately translate that into feeling at peace and being calm and so on. They don't translate that into obedience. They don't look at the life that Brother Lawrence lived as essentially a servant in the kitchen and apply that to themselves. That's because they have this little theological adjuster; it's like one of these dimmer switches on the wall where it has a knob and you can turn it down. So, they turn it up so they can see Brother Lawrence, but when it comes to themselves they turn it down. And they've accepted that. The main reason why they've accepted that is because they've accepted the idea that salvation is about forgiveness of sins.

Yes, I agree.

Now on the Liberal side, they don't talk about sin or heaven when you die. They don't even talk about that. They talk about getting involved in social issues, and then if you're really serious you'll join [Jim Wallis's] Sojourners and help out in the soup lines and protest the war, and all sorts of things like that. But they're not going to put their lives on the line for that. They have a mild little version of what they would call discipleship, which is about being engaged in, or at least concerned about, social issues.

Both of these, in the whole spectrum, basically leave your life untouched. We need to communicate that what you're doing now is where God wants to be in your life, and you can invite him in and begin to expect him to act, and you will know the kingdom of God, you will know God in action, you will know Christ, and you will be inwardly transformed, progressively, by spiritual formation, as a disciple who is learning to live his life as Jesus would lead his life if Jesus were that disciple.

What I want to ask, now that we've identified this condition, is, What's been going on in American Christian culture? How do we turn this ship around?

By preaching. This is really the heart of the matter, and it's very simple. I say this over and over to people, to pastors: "Just start with Matthew and just preach what Jesus preached." Now, that's going to really jerk you around. You have to avoid things like going to your church and saying, "We're going to keep doing things the same but now we're going to really mean it." That's really what they think, but as long as they do that they're really going to get nowhere. Spiritual formation, as a hope, will flame out within just a few years unless people understand that they really are doing something different than they've done before. So, I say to anyone who asks, "What do we do?"—I just suggest that you just start and teach what Jesus taught and begin to put your own life into it, and progressively you will see people respond. It will take a little while to realize that you really are saying and doing something different. Then when they do that you'll see various reactions, just like the Parable of the Sower: some people will say, "You're not preaching the truth anymore, brother," or maybe that you're teaching salvation by works.

Yeah, that's usually the first comment that rises up.

So, you have to, as a pastor, have the grace of God with you to deal with that. You have to show people that grace doesn't equal passivity; we still do things. My background is Baptist, and I like to rib them a little bit so I'll say, "We'll preach to you for an hour telling you you can't do anything to be saved and then sing to you for an hour trying to get you to do something to be saved." It's really confusing, to tell you the truth.

So the pastor, as he preaches, will begin to react in different ways. In nearly every case, if that pastor does his work from the Bible, the

people will be joyously won over to what he is doing and they will
say, within a short period of time, "Yes, we want to live in the kingdom. We know what trusting Jesus means now. We want to make
disciples. We want to be disciples. We want to teach people how to
do everything he said." But you can't go there and start. You can't go
into the church and say, "Now we're all going to be disciples. If you're
not a disciple you're not one of us," and so forth. That's just terribly
misguided behavior, and it doesn't come from the love of Jesus. So,
you accept the transition and you stay with it, and eventually your
people will come around, but you have to give them time to replace
this whole string of concepts we've talked about like salvation and
grace and so on. The way to go about it is through teaching the Bible.

Here's what I found out years ago, and if I hadn't I would've been
out of the business thirty or forty years ago, and it's this: you don't
have to make it happen. The little parable that Jesus tells in Mark
about the farmer that goes out and sows the seed and then takes a
nap? There's a little phrase there that says, "The farmer knoweth not
how this works." There's a plant coming up out of the dirt, and pretty
soon there's something edible there. But although the farmer doesn't
know how it happens, you can be sure it's going to happen, and that
takes the load off of you. You don't have to make this happen. This
is one of the most important things for pastors to understand. Don't
try to get people to do anything; just speak the word of the gospel,
live as a disciple, lovingly teach, be with people, and it will happen.

**It's funny, last night I was getting ready for bed and I was reading
a chapter from A. W. Tozer's book *The Knowledge of the Holy*.**

Oh, you can't beat that!

**Yeah, it's a wonderful book. There was a paragraph here that
goes along with what you're saying. . . . If you don't mind me
reading this to you, "When viewed from the perspective of
eternity, the most critical need of this hour may well be that
the Church should be brought back from her long Babylonian
captivity, and the name of God be Glorified in her again, as of**

old. Yet we must not think of the Church as an anonymous body, a mystical religious abstraction. We Christians are the Church and whatever we do is what the Church is doing. The matter, therefore, is for each of us, a personal one. Any forward step in the Church must begin with the individual."

That's absolutely correct. The church is a pretty ragged bunch of people, and actually one of the surest signs that the church is on the wrong path is when it tries not to be. I've seen churches die when they try to go around the neighborhood to collect the "right" sorts of people, when the "wrong" sorts of people were right under the shadow of the building but they would not reach out to them and say, "It's okay for you to come. Jesus accepts you and we do too." Of course, Jesus got into more trouble for hanging out with the "wrong" kind of people than almost anything else, but of course those were the ones who were happy to hear. Those were the ones who were breaking down the wall to get in.

That's why Jesus had the response that it's the sick that need a doctor. The point being that all of us are sick and in need of a doctor; it's just that some of us are more aware of our need for the physician than others.

As Jesus said to the Pharisees, it was because they claimed to see that they were guilty of sin. If they had not claimed to see, they would not have been in sin. That's the problem with the leaders of our churches—because they say, "We see," but they are not doing what Jesus says to do. The idea of doing it doesn't even appear on the horizon of most of those who are leading others. They hammer away on righteousness, but often righteousness is defined more in terms of culture (don't smoke or drink, etc.) than in terms of how you live your life as a disciple of Jesus.

Thank you so much, Dallas, for taking the time to sit and talk to me about these very important issues. I'm very grateful to you for this.

We can talk again.

CHAPTER 19

Kingdom Living

In this interview, Dallas reviews several key arguments made in many of his published works. He provides both an overarching summary and important tenets required for abundant living in the kingdom of God.

Interview conducted by Andy Peck in 2002 and first published in *Christianity + Renewal* magazine

Your writings don't make it easy for anyone to pigeonhole you. What do you say when people ask you where you stand?

I try to represent Christ and his teachings and his presence in the contemporary world. I happen to be from an evangelical background, which I am very thankful for, and I happen to be a believer in the use of spiritual gifts in their wider sense. My feeling is that Christ is generally outside the boundaries that we would set for him. In fact, much of what I have to say is an attempt to overcome the boundaries that divide people who have an allegiance to Christ.

If you were to get to the bottom of my theology, you would find me pretty Calvinistic, but my sense of ministry is to judge the lay of the land for your times and shoot where the enemy is. The enemy in our time is not human capacity, or overactivism; rather, the enemy is passivity—the idea that God has done everything and you are essentially left to be a consumer of the grace of God and that the only thing you have to do is find out how to do that and do it regularly. I think this is a terrible mistake and accounts for the withdrawal of active Christians from so many areas of life where they should be present. It also accounts for the lack of spiritual growth, for you can be sure that if you do not act in an advised fashion consistently and resolutely, you will not grow spiritually. We all know that Jesus said (in John 15), "Without me you can do nothing." We need to add, "If you do nothing, it will be most assuredly without him."

Of course we must be concerned about works righteousness. I talk a lot about the value of spiritual disciplines but also the danger of using them as if they help us earn our salvation. But it is crucial to realize that grace is not opposed to effort, but to earning. Earning is an attitude; effort is action. Without effort, we would be nowhere. When you read the New Testament you see how astonishingly energetic it is. Paul says, "Take off the old man, put on the new." There is no suggestion that this will be done for you.

Who has influenced your thinking outside of the Bible?

The people who have influenced me most are long dead: people such as, in the Catholic tradition, Thomas à Kempis, Saint Francis of Assisi, Saint Augustine; in the Protestant tradition, George Fox, John Wesley, Jonathan Edwards, Richard Baxter, Jeremy Taylor.

As far as the content of what I try to present is concerned, it focuses on the gospel of the kingdom of God and becoming a disciple of Jesus in the kingdom of God. So it doesn't merely have an emphasis on the forgiveness of sins and assurance of heaven, as you are apt to find in most evangelical circles. I think that is vital, but it is not the whole story. The issue is whole life; other issues are subordinate to that. After all, Jesus said, "I came that you might have life to the full," which is more than life beyond death.

I have drawn a great deal of encouragement from people like John Owen, especially as my time is spent in scholarly and academic settings. It is important for me to be able to picture Jesus within such settings, and the Puritans like Owen are very good at that. Today evangelicals have a real problem with the intellect. They mistrust the intellect. In the United States, many Christians see the university as an area where human pride and Satan rule supreme and beyond hope. It has been a major part of my own growth and development that this is a terrible mistake. People like Owen and Edwards saw it as a gift of God and an area of redemption.

In your first book, *The Spirit of the Disciplines*, you pose the question, Are we disciples of Jesus or merely Christians by modern standards? Clearly you are concerned about the state of discipleship in the American church. What alarms you most?

That the issue of discipleship is thought of as totally irrelevant to being a Christian, which carries over to obedience to Christ's teaching. The basic question, Will I obey Christ's teaching? is rarely taken as a serious issue. For example, to take one of Jesus's commands that is relevant to contemporary life, I don't know of any church that actually teaches a church how to bless people who curse them, yet this is a clear command. And there is plenty of cursing going on, especially on roads! We must remember that Jesus says, "How can you call me Lord, Lord, but not do the things that I say?"

You say in *The Divine Conspiracy* that there is a lack of teaching in the church on the kingdom.

This is the reason why people, including pastors, don't see the need for discipleship. What you present as the gospel will determine what you present as discipleship. If you present as the gospel what is essentially a theory of the atonement and you say, "If you accept this theory of the atonement, your sins are forgiven and when you die you will be received into heaven," there is no basis for discipleship.

I ask pastors, "Does your gospel have a natural tendency to produce disciples?" By "disciple" I mean someone who is learning from Jesus how to lead their life as he would lead their life if he were in their place. The New Testament defines a disciple as someone who is with Jesus, learning how to be more like him.

But if your gospel focuses on the gospel of the kingdom, that we are invited to live in the kingdom of God, then the basis for discipleship becomes clear. The new birth should be seen as an entrance into the kingdom of God. John chapter 3 is not a "forgiveness of sins" passage but a "new life from above" passage. Forgiveness from sins is essential—but it is not the whole package. One of the main barriers is that people see the teachings of Christ as laws that they have to obey. They are not. They are expressions of the life that comes to you through the new birth and is naturally disposed to develop a new kind of person inside.

So when many look at the teachings of Christ, they are demoralized. They ask, "I have to do these as I now am?" Of course it's impossible, but if you say instead that this is the sort of person I can become, then they open up and appear as things that are good and not an imposition.

This links into what you say in *The Divine Conspiracy* about ways in which Christians, including Bible scholars, have understood the Sermon on the Mount.

I believe that the greatest gift of Jesus, outside the gift of himself and "regeneration," is the Sermon on the Mount. But the way most interpret it actually makes it sound like bad news. This extends, for example, to the Beatitudes. People read "Blessed are the Poor" and say, "Oh, I've got to become poor in order to be blessed." This is a total misunderstanding of his teaching. All of his teaching is about the kingdom of God, entering the kingdom of God through faith in him and the process of being transformed so that the kinds of behavior taught, and indeed the old law, are a natural expression of who we have become.

In the United Kingdom talk of the kingdom was associated with charismatic churches, with supernatural manifestations seen as the sign of the kingdom. This was a theme of Vineyard Church leader John Wimber, for example, when he first visited the United Kingdom in the '80s. Can you explain how you understand the kingdom?

I would not want in any way to cast aspersions on the name of John Wimber, for whom I have enormous respect, but I think that both charismatics and evangelicals have missed the point. The Vineyard had a real problem with obedience, and John knew this very well. "Doing the stuff," as he put it, meant manifestations of the kingdom, but it did not mean obeying Jesus. He personally understood that this was essential, but it did not interfere with going on the street and casting out demons and healing.

As regards the kingdom of God? Theologians such as [George Eldon] Ladd say that the kingdom is both present and absent, but this basically means we focus on the absent! But I didn't come to understand the kingdom through theologians. I came to the understanding when I was a young Baptist minister. I noticed that I spent a lot of my time trying to get people to come and hear me, and other ministers did the same. But when I looked at Jesus, his problem was getting away from people! So I said, "There has to be something different here." So I found what every scholar will tell you—that Jesus's message was the kingdom of God. He proclaimed it, he manifested it, and he taught it. When he sent out his disciples, he didn't send them out to teach (that's the hard part), but to proclaim and manifest (the easy part!). It was very powerful.

When we look at contemporary expressions of this through, for example, the Vineyard movement, we find that the teaching part never came through. The Sermon on the Mount was never taught and is generally as alien to charismatics as it often is to noncharismatics. The proclaiming is also weak, [therefore] the manifestation is thought to be the whole package.

When you look at the Bible you see that the kingdom of God is God acting. It is the range of God's effective will. When I pray "Thy kingdom come, thy will be done," I am praying first that God's will may be done in my own life and then around me. This is the open door for his teachings, for it is his effective will that I bless and don't curse, that I let my *yes* be *yes*, and my *no* be *no*, that I not be motivated by anger and contempt, and so on (as outlined in the Sermon on the Mount). So as someone who is living in the kingdom, I am praying that this may become a true expression of who I am by inner transformation. Discipleship is learning how to do that.

Your teaching on the kingdom highlights some of the differences between the charismatics and evangelicals. Charismatics emphasize manifestation; evangelicals, Bible teaching. Are you saying they are both wrong?

Exactly. If you ask, "How is it wrong?" I would say that neither manifestation nor teaching transforms character. Charismatics flail at the dead horse of experience, evangelicals at teaching, but neither leads to transformation spiritually. The only thing that transforms us spiritually is the action of following Christ. You seek to follow, you fail, and you learn. But in order to engage in following, you have to have a clear understanding of life in the kingdom of God—that you are accepted by the grace of God in Jesus—and that lays the foundation for as much true doctrine as you can manage and as much manifestation of the Spirit as you can stand.

In your book *In Search of Guidance,* you write of the danger of seeing Bible characters as super saints. Some books say that God does not communicate directly to us outside of the Bible and others that he is always speaking to us. You take a different line.

I have read those same books. What we should focus on here is not guidance or hearing from God, but the kind of life within which guidance makes sense. So many people would like to have guidance from God because obviously if you have a word from God, it's the best possible thing. But they don't relate that to life as a whole. Often they want guidance as a way of opting out of the responsibility of making decisions. In the book I point out that one of the main functions of the life in which guidance makes sense is to develop us as people who are capable of making decisions. God may not guide us in an obvious way because he wants us to make decisions based on faith and character. The problem with the What Would Jesus Do (WWJD) movement is that in most cases Jesus would not have to ask the question. He would know. This is what we are expected to grow into.

But having said that, God can and does give clear guidance and clear words. We need this, in part because of the need to evaluate the sort of guidance people may wish to impose on us. It is also invaluable especially when there is a manifestation of kingdom gifts. I think the best single contribution of John Wimber is that we should work with God as we minister, and receive from him words, discernment, in a communicating process. Wimber would pray, interview, listen, and interview again as he helped people. This is incredibly valuable, and I believe it is his greatest legacy.

As a philosopher, what comments would you make on the belief that postmodernism represents a great opportunity for the gospel?

You have to regard postmodernism as a mixed bag. It represents the cultural withering of confidence in what was known as the scientific worldview. It represents an opening that refused to reduce everything to science. The life of the spirit can be known without waving [a dismissive] hand at math and physics. The problem is that when postmodernism is pushed in a certain way it is impossible to have any notion of objective truth. This comes home with reference to scripture, as if God himself can't even break through to your cultural forms. That's pretty tough. This is still a big problem.

Without any access to moral knowledge, you are just left with political correctness. I understand you have institutions here [in the United Kingdom] better able to resist political correctness than in America. But in America political correctness is so big, just because there's no other kind.

PART III

Discipleship

CHAPTER 20

Your Place in This World

Dallas was a frequent commencement and convocation speaker, and he looked forward to these occasions as an opportunity to address graduates—and their families—on the role of higher education in our society. Here, he issues a call to action and an invitation to the kingdom of God to new graduates.

Commencement address given to the graduating class of 2004 at Greenville College in Greenville, IN, and first published in 2005 in *The Graduate's Bible*

NOT SO LONG AGO, YOU PARTICIPATED IN A COMMENCEMENT SERVICE. I don't altogether like the word *commencement* because the word suggests a "beginning." It doesn't do justice to what you have already done. Nevertheless, there is a certain point to the word. You're going through a change, and in that way you are commencing. I think perhaps the words that best capture the nature of this change are found in words like *responsibility, effectiveness,* and *opportunity.* You're going out into the world and finding your own path in a way you haven't before. That is what you were created to do. Consider the wonderful words in Ephesians 2:10:

> For we are His creation—created in Christ Jesus for good works, which God prepared ahead of time so that we should walk in them.

That should be a tremendous encouragement and a great aid in helping you understand who you are. Not that you should go off and become an isolated individual, indifferent to others, like one of the Three Little Pigs, going out into the world to seek your fortune. Rather, you are called to take your place alongside others in a community under God and devote your life to the causes of God among all of humanity and within your specific generation. That is your special work and what we celebrate today as you commence on your path now, carrying a distinctly different quality of wisdom and judgment.

Jesus, you may recall, gave a commencement address to his students as well. He spoke to them just as they were entering a new phase of responsibility, effectiveness, and opportunity. His commencement address is found in the Gospel of John, chapters 13 through 17. It ends with a lengthy prayer that makes up most of chapter 17. Here are some of the words that we have already heard read:

> I am not praying that You take them out of the world, but that You protect them from the evil one. They are not of the world, just as I am not of the world.

He goes on to say:

> Sanctify them by the truth; Your word is truth. Just as You sent Me into the world, I also have sent them into the world.

Notice Jesus's use of the concepts *in* and *of*. Being in the world for Christ today. *In* but not *of*. This is an interesting distinction. Keep it before your mind for a few minutes. How are we to think of *in* but not *of*? Think of a desert landscape. Dust and dryness as far as you can see. But right in the middle of it a spring of water bubbles up, forming a pool of life and refreshment for all who come by. Do you have that picture?

Now, the spring and the pool are *in* the desert but they are not *of* it. They do not partake of the nature of the desert but of rain and snow and limpid streams on faraway mountains that feed the springs through hidden passageways in the earth. We know how that works. Think of this applying to you. Indeed, it applies to everyone who makes contact with Jesus Christ and draws life from him.

This is what Jesus was talking about with Nicodemus (John 3). Jesus was trying to convey to Nicodemus how God's Spirit works—how the Spirit comes and moves in the life of an individual. People see the results, but they can't see what causes the results. This is abundant life in its fullest sense: life lived from hidden sources that come into the soul from God and his kingdom. Such abundant life is possible no matter where you are or what you happen to be doing.

Being in the world is not a bad thing; it's a good thing. The world is—in the end—God's creation. The world is the place where God has appointed you to live. Your birth and life to this point haven't taken God by surprise. God has prepared this time and this place for you. We find this place prepared through our family, through our country, and through our education. You have been prepared to rule for good. That's the purpose for which God made you.

> Let Us make man in Our image, according to Our likeness.
> They will rule the fish of the sea, the birds of the sky, the animals,
> all the earth, and the creatures that crawl on the earth. (Gen. 1:26)

God made you similar to him and made you to rule over all the earth. This is a command that extends throughout scripture, beginning in Genesis and continuing into eternity. This is the place you have in God's order—to be the person he intended you to be—forever.

You aren't alone in the place God prepared for you. God placed you with other people, beginning with your family. God's intention is that your family bless and serve you, giving you a solid foundation for blessing and serving them. Blessing and service don't stop with one's family but become a settled way of life with all of those whose lives we touch. Our character is formed for that purpose.

Sometimes we don't receive the blessing God intends from our family or the community in which we grow up. Sometimes much healing is needed, and, thank God, healing is available. If healing remains to be done in your life, know that it is available.

Whether you feel weak or strong, whether you have been well prepared or poorly prepared for taking your next step in life, Jesus's invitation is for you: "Repent, because the kingdom of heaven has come near!"

Jesus invites you to live in his kingdom.

Repent means to change the way you've been thinking and acting. Notice how you've been thinking, and then add to those thoughts the fact that it is now possible for you to begin living in God's kingdom right now, right where you are in this time of change and transition.

In the world but not *of* the world.

As you take your next steps and find your place in this world, you will find yourself in the middle of much that isn't good or right. Still, you can know the action of God in your place. You can live the presence of God in the midst of a spiritual wasteland. Your soul can be both a conduit and a receptacle of those refreshing streams that come from the mountain heights and course through the earth's hidden passageways. Repent. Change your thinking. Seek God's kingdom first. Seek his righteousness. He promises that everything else will be added when you put first things first. This is what he promises in Psalm 23: "The LORD is my shepherd. There is nothing I lack." That's the provision of God for those who seek his kingdom. To seek his kingdom simply means to find out what he is doing and join him in it.

How do I know what God is doing? The source of this knowledge is God's written word, the Bible: "The Bible is the unique written Word of God. It is inerrant in its original form and infallible in all of its forms for the purpose of guiding you into a life-saving relationship with God in His kingdom" [*Hearing God*, p. 141]. The Bible contains a body of knowledge without which human beings cannot survive: "It reliably fixes the boundaries of everything God will ever say to humankind" [*Hearing God,* p. 142].

Knowledge is fundamental to life in God's kingdom. Knowledge is the capacity to represent things as they are—the basis for thought and experience. You will find more than ever in the days to come that the real battle in our world today is over knowledge. Who knows? Who has knowledge? Underlying most of the conflicts in public life is what counts as knowledge. Christians have sometimes made the mistake of allowing the secular world to define what counts as knowledge. Christian knowledge is often marginalized when people say, "It's only tradition. It doesn't count as knowledge." This is one of the challenges you will face as you take your next step in the place God has prepared for you.

The organ of spiritual knowledge is obedience. Just as you open your eyes to see colors, you know the presence of the kingdom of God by obeying. You act on the knowledge you have. And in acting you encounter the reality of the kingdom. This is not some esoteric knowledge but claims that can be tested publicly. These knowledge claims are verifiable. As you obey, you yourself will be tested—at times severely. In those times, hold fast to the idea that you do have knowledge. As you do, you will come to know the goodness and rightness of the teachings of the Christian faith.

Simply obeying Jesus will bring into your life the reality of the Trinitarian presence and action. As Jesus said in his commencement address:

> If you love Me, you will keep My commandments. And I
> will ask the Father, and He will give you another Counselor to
> be with you. . . . The one who has My commands and keeps
> them is the one who loves Me. And the one who loves Me will be
> loved by My Father. I also will love him and will reveal Myself
> to him. (John 14:15–16, 21)

In obedience we come to know. You have received knowledge

from generations of faithful, obedient believers. Now, this knowledge must be renewed and made actual in your time by your own obedience. This knowledge will shape every dimension of your life: intellectual, emotional, social, and professional. It's your turn to take the baton.

Neil Anderson, a well-known author, says the greatest problem in Christian education in our day is the fact that doctrine rather than character transformation has become an end in itself. Character transformation requires right belief and right doctrine, but we don't stop with right doctrine. Right belief and doctrine must be expressed in thought, decision, and action. In action we meet the kingdom of God. Love and adoration of Jesus and confidence in him assumes right doctrine. But there is much more. And it's this that leads us beyond mere consumer Christianity, where we see ourselves as merely consuming the merits of Christ and the services of the church. What Christ has done for us calls forth something from us—daily and hourly discipleship.

Isaac Watts gets it. Contemplating Jesus's death on our behalf, he cried out:

> Love so amazing, so divine
> Demands my soul, my life, my all.

His work for us, then, becomes his work in us. The goal is that we will be just like him. As his disciple, Jesus teaches you to live your life as he would live your life. That leads to inner transformation, the transformation of character resulting in godly service in the kingdom of God. Transformation moves from the inside out. You take on his thoughts, his beliefs, and his judgments. They become yours. You feel as he did. Your body acts as he did. Your social relationships bear the imprint of his character, and the depths of your soul are renewed in a likeness to his.

This transformation into his likeness is a lifelong process. Here are four things to remember as you make this journey.

1. Remember who you are. That's not as easy as it sounds. Remember who you are before God. You are an unceasing spiritual being with an eternal destiny in God's great universe. Say it: "I am an unceasing spiritual being with an eternal destiny in God's great universe." Memorize it. Say it to your friends. Tell it to people you meet. Strong currents in our society will attempt to keep you from realizing who you are before God.

Some months ago someone did a study of a certain type of chimpanzee. They discovered that this chimpanzee possessed 99.4 percent of human DNA. What's the conclusion you are supposed to draw? You know what it is. It's certainly not that you are an unceasing spiritual being with an eternal destiny in God's great universe. The conclusion you're supposed to draw is that you're very much like a chimp.

I've talked to some of my colleagues and suggested that we try giving a chimp a Ph.D. Certainly if chimps have 99.4 percent of human DNA and DNA is what we are, then some chimps should do better on tests than humans! But no one who thought about it would suggest that 99.4 percent of human DNA translates into 99.4 percent of human experience. What conclusion should we draw? We humans are a great deal more than DNA. You are a spiritual being. I emphasize that and encourage you to stay connected to this truth, because you will be continually challenged on this. Remember to say it to yourself, to your friends. Get them to say it to you. You may even want to write it on your bathroom mirror.

2. Remember to keep God before your mind.

> You will keep in perfect peace the mind that is dependent on You, for it is trusting You. (Isa. 26:3)

David says:

> I keep the LORD in mind always. Because He is at my right hand, I will not be shaken. (Ps. 16:8)

Set the Lord before you. Keep him in your mind. You can learn to do this. You can bring God before your mind constantly and train yourself to have him there always. One simple approach is to train yourself to go through the morning repeating to yourself, every minute or so, "Hallowed be your name" or some other phrase that's meaningful to you.

3. Remember to live sacrificially. On January 20, 1961, John F. Kennedy was inaugurated as the thirty-fifth president of the United States. During his inaugural address, this, the youngest man ever elected president, said that "the torch has been passed to a new generation of Americans." In this context, President Kennedy issued the following challenge: "Ask not what your country can do for you, ask what you can do for your country."

This simple statement, delivered with great fervor, drew forth an amazing current of sacrificial giving from people. This is built into our hearts. We know it's right. And as Christians we're the ones who really know what it means and how it can be done.

Don't strive to advance yourself. Let God advance you. This is a deep psychological and sociological truth as well as a profound theological teaching. If you try to save your life, you'll lose it. Give it away. God will give it back to you. Don't make it your aim to get what you want. Serve others. Remember, God gives grace to the humble. He calls us to submit ourselves to the mighty hand of God so that, when the time is right, he will lift us up.

I need to add that it's not safe to be a servant unless you know who you are and unless you stand before God. On the night of his betrayal, just before he shared the Passover with his disciples,

> Jesus knew that the Father had given everything into His hands, that He had come from God, and that He was going back to God. So He got up from supper, laid aside His robe, took a towel, and tied it around Himself. Next, He poured water into a basin and began to wash His disciples' feet and to dry them with the towel tied around Him. (John 13:3–5)

Because Jesus knew who he was, because he was secure in his relationship with his Father, he was able to do the work of the most menial slave.

Remember who you are. Keep God before you. Then serve sacrificially. When you serve others, you're really serving God. Because you are serving God, you give the best of service to other human beings.

4. Remember you need a plan of discipline. Living the Christ life requires it. What's normally thought of as church activities is not enough, even if you're one of the leaders. Put together and follow a plan of solitude and silence, scripture memorization, fasting, prayer, and worship.

If you regularly do these things, Christ will grow in you and his character will become your character. Then you will routinely and easily do the things he did and said to do out of love, joy, peace, and power.

The people who are in the world but not of the world are people who simply do the right thing routinely, easily, with peace and joy. Their picture is drawn repeatedly in the scriptures (Eph. 4, Col. 3, Phil. 2). What you see in these passages is true. It works. It's accessible to everyone. And there's nothing in this world that compares with it. People like this are the answer to Jesus's prayer at the end of his commencement address.

> I have given them the glory You have given Me.
> May they be one as We are one.
> I am in them and You are in Me.
> May they be made completely one,
> So the world may know You have sent Me
> and have loved them as You have loved Me.

This is what the world is waiting for. Paul says that all creation is groaning, waiting for the sons and daughters of God.

Now take your God-given place in this world. Be Christ to those around you.

CHAPTER 21

The Evolution of Discipleship

This article provides an in-depth history of one of the central tenets of Dallas's corpus: discipleship. Here he examines some key evolutionary moves within Evangelicalism during the twentieth century in America and the biblical background that shaped his own definition of discipleship.

First published in 2010 in *The Oxford Handbook of Evangelical Theology* as "Discipleship"

How one thinks of discipleship within Evangelicalism depends upon how one draws the line around that movement. If one draws the line, as is now common, to include only the "Evangelicalism" that emerged from the conservative-to-fundamentalist churches of North America after World War II, then there is very little to say about discipleship there except what is anecdotal—and there is not a lot of that. There has simply been no consistent general teaching or practice under the heading of discipleship among evangelicals of this period: none that would be recognizable as discipleship in terms of biblical teaching or of the Christian past.

In the post-WWII period the strongest association of Evangelicalism was with evangelism, and for many citizens of North America the only thing they knew of evangelicals was that they are evangelistic. And indeed they were. They were intent upon proclaiming a gospel of "salvation" and upon winning converts to Christ. The most visible evangelical of the period was the world-renowned evangelist Billy Graham. And the subgroup of evangelicals most associated with programs of discipleship, the Navigators, was focused upon winning converts—converts who were explicitly recognized by them as not being disciples until an optional further stage in commitment. Being a disciple was, for them, to be in training to become a soul winner, and discipleship was the process of training you underwent (under the direction of "workers," people of a third stage of commitment and development) to enable you to win converts.[1] The slogan of the Navigators was "To know Christ and to make Him known." Their aim, as they said, was "to produce reproducers."

This vision was firmly tied to the version of the gospel and of salvation that dominated Evangelicalism during the period. It was strictly a gospel of forgiveness of sins and assurance of heaven after death upon profession of faith in Jesus Christ—or, minimally, profession of faith in his having suffered the penalty for our sins upon the cross. If you believed in his death as your substitute, you were a Christian, even though you never became a disciple. Many of the Navigators were certainly among the finest followers of Christ from any period of Christian history. Their founder, Dawson Trotman, was an ardent disciple of Jesus by any sane standard and one of the greatest of twentieth-century Christ followers.[2] But as disciples, Navigators were far better than their theology and their program. They have blessed and continue to bless the earth with their lives and testimonies. Nevertheless, in them the essential disconnection between post-WWII Evangelicalism and discipleship prevailed and still prevails today.

RELYING ON CORRECT BELIEFS ALONE

During the mid- to late twentieth century, Evangelicalism came to define itself in terms of the profession of correct belief alone. Holding correct doctrine was standardly presented as the condition of forgiveness of sins. Obsessed with threats from modernism and liberal theology on the one hand, and from the looming presence of an allegedly "scientific" worldview on the other, Evangelicalism undertook to "contend earnestly for the faith which was once for all delivered to the saints" (Jude v. 3). This meant to defend the truth of doctrines taken to be essential to a "saving" faith in Christ. Ironically, this phase of Evangelicalism developed—as a social form—into a particular version of "nominal Christianity." It had traditionally defined itself in opposition to nominal Christianity, emphasizing as it did an individualized "birth from above" and an ongoing personal experience of God. But its actual "nominal" status is the reality back of the statistics, often quoted at the beginning of the twenty-first century, that show little or no behavioral difference between the lives of contemporary evangelicals on the whole and the lives of those outside its circles. Being a Christian in evangelical terms came to be a matter of professing belief in time-honored tenets of traditional Christianity, with a few additional points about the nature and authority of the Bible and about eschatology.[3]

CALLED TO A CLOSER WALK

But that left a deficiency that came to be deeply felt—especially among evangelicals most seriously devoted to Christ. This felt need for experience of God, for a life in God, expressed itself in various ways—ways always in some tension with the prevailing theology and with the most prominent evangelical leaders and teachers of the time. This tension has been an enduring problem within modern Evangelicalism. It has expressed itself in various ways: for example, through interest in what was viewed as "higher life" or "deeper life" teachings. The Keswick Movement (associated with the Keswick Convention, running from 1875 to the present)[4] was centered on these teachings, and interest in them was cultivated by such authors as Andrew Murray (1828–1917) and F. B. Meyer (1847–1929). A slightly older work by Hannah Whitall Smith, *The Christian's Secret of a Happy Life* (1875),[5] was very influential in this vein, along with numerous similar writings, and more contemporary works such as Rosalind Rinker's book *Prayer: Conversing with God* (1959),[6] which presented prayer as a lively conversation with God. These and similar works revitalized the "devotional life" of many evangelicals, often taken by them to be "discipleship" itself. Still older Catholic writers such as Thomas à Kempis (*The Imitation of Christ*) and Brother Lawrence (*The Practice of the Presence of God*) stoked the hidden fires of evangelical devotion—simultaneously confirming the grim suspicions of many leaders and teachers that the "deeper life" seekers and teachers were not properly evangelical.[7] They were not satisfied with just believing the essentials or with "the pure milk of the word."

The Charismatic Movement—breaking out in the early twentieth century in its "Holiness" form, and reviving in the post-WWII period without the emphasis on holiness—was yet another challenge to the adequacy of this most recent "official" form of evangelical Christianity. Many evangelical leaders simply rejected the charismatic experience, and taught (some still teach) that charismatics are misled and dangerous to the faith. This was largely for fear that their "experiences" were not biblical and would undermine the authority of the Bible. But the hunger for and reality of an interactive life with God (the Holy Spirit) was not to be denied to people generally, and today the most effectual carriers of "evangelical truths" to the world are in fact charismatics. However, the focus upon spiritual gifts that characterizes the charismatic groups and teachers still does not include a realistic and theologically coherent teaching and practice of discipleship. It is still true of them that to be a Christian—even a "Spirit-filled" Christian—does not require that you be a disciple of Jesus Christ, or that you, through the course of discipleship, take on the character of Jesus Christ in your life as a whole.

The widely felt inadequacy of the official twentieth-century evangelical teachings to life (however effectual for death and judgment) also expressed itself by the emergence of "Christian Psychology" among evangelicals in the 1960s. This movement was a tacit acknowledgment that teaching the truth, and eliciting profession of the central doctrines, did not solve the problems of Christian living. As a result, it was strongly resisted across a broad range of evangelical life. By the twenty-first century, however, it had burgeoned into a vast profession, with extensive training and higher academic degrees available from the most prominent of evangelical educational institutions. It clearly intersects in aims and in some of its methods with what would have counted as discipleship or training in following Christ at other times and places. Many of the larger evangelical churches and groups now provide psychological counseling as a major part of their ministry.

Currently, Christian psychology is interacting with yet another significant tendency in evangelical life. The emergence of "spiritual formation" among evangelicals toward the end of the twentieth century was also a response to the felt need of many for a spiritual life, in addition to correct beliefs and outward practices. This need was associated with the increasing failure of "denominational distinctives" to constitute a spiritual existence or a life for the individual. It is rare to find evangelicals within these churches who could make a life of being a Presbyterian, Baptist, Catholic, Lutheran, Pentecostal, and so forth. By contrast, "spiritual formation," like discipleship itself during some periods of the past, was associated with learning to live a remarkably different kind of life: one of pervading spiritual reality and transformed character. In its quest, spiritual formation among evangelicals reached out to learn from the church and from Christians across the ages on the one hand, and it also turned the individual's focus toward redemption of their life as a whole.[8] "Spiritual formation" edged—however obscurely or unintentionally—toward thinking of salvation, the essence of Christian deliverance, in more comprehensive terms than the afterlife alone. Once again, prominent evangelical spokespersons were uneasy. But how one understands salvation turns out to be the key to what one makes of discipleship, as well as to any possible renewal of Evangelicalism as a redemptive force for the future. Post-WWII Evangelicalism simply had no essential place for discipleship in its view of salvation.

EVANGELICALISM FROM WESLEY TO FINNEY

We must draw the line around Evangelicalism beyond post-WWII America if we are to see any close connection between its vital core and discipleship to Jesus Christ. It is sometimes said that evangelical Christianity began in the eighteenth century, with people who were willing to preach out of doors at a time when that was a very radical step. The reference to "preaching out of doors" picks out the ministries of George Whitefield (1714–70) and John Wesley (1703–91), but also of many preachers who followed after them in the settlements and frontiers of America. Jonathan Edwards (1703–58), though he did not regularly "preach out of doors," is often regarded as historic Evangelicalism's most competent theologian. (We must not forget his overlap with Puritanism.) Some have even thought of evangelicals as an American brand of Protestant Christianity. This unfortunately results in seeing contemporary Evangelicalism as having a greater continuity with the evangelical past than it actually has. The "revivalism" of George Whitefield, John Wesley, Jonathan Edwards, and even up to Charles Finney (in the first half of the nineteenth century) was a very different kind of thing from the "revivals" of the twentieth century, which were almost entirely focused upon converting the lost. The revivals of the 1800s gradually transmuted into evangelistic campaigns or "outreach." The earlier evangelical "revivalists," by contrast, focused upon "stirring up" Christians or church members, and urging them on to overall holiness of life and devotion to God.[9] That is why the word *revival* was used by them. What they did naturally led into a process of learning and growing in holiness and power, as the New Testament clearly presupposes. Evangelizing was a natural side effect of the revival of slumbering Christians, and the evangelizing of this earlier period easily saw discipleship to Jesus as a natural development from conversion and confidence in Jesus Christ as Lord, and therefore master and teacher.

New Testament language fits well with this earlier phase of Evangelicalism, as compared to today's: "Work out your salvation with fear and trembling; for it is God who is at work in you, both to will and to work for His good pleasure. Do all things without grumbling or disputing; that you may turn out to be blameless and innocent, children of God above reproach in the midst of a crooked and perverse generation, among whom you appear as lights in the world" (Phil. 2:12–15). This calling and reality was not thought by earlier evangelicals to be for a special group of Christians—perhaps "full-time Christian workers"—but as the opportunity and obligation of everyone who placed their hope in Christ. It was a shift away from this viewpoint that opened the way for twentieth-century Evangelicalism, dominated by a particular version of "Calvinist" theology and its peculiar soteriology. Eighteenth- and nineteenth-century Evangelicalism made an essential place for holiness and wholeness, for transformation of character, and for ordinary occupations as divine calling. An excellent place to see this at its best is in the sermons and writings of Phillips Brooks (1835–93). It was entirely natural to the underlying theology of the earlier period that Wesley and Finney, both "revivalists" in the earlier sense, developed and applied elaborate, scripturally based accounts of Christian perfection as something continuous in its nature with Christian salvation. Their theology was essentially Arminian, and thus their understanding of grace and salvation was quite different from that of their twentieth-century counterparts. While discipleship could be seen as a natural part of salvation as they understood it, the later evangelicals have been more careful to avoid "perfectionism" than to avoid sin. They favor bumper stickers that say, "Christians are not perfect, just forgiven." *Just* forgiven? There lies the problem for contemporary Evangelicalism with respect to discipleship. What does discipleship have to do with forgiveness? With saving faith?

THE SOURCES OF EVANGELICALISM IN LUTHER

To respond to these questions adequately we must push the time line further back, to the point in Western history where the terminology *evangelical* enters the stream of Christianity. The language originates in sixteenth-century Germany, amid the turmoil and violence of the Protestant Reformation. People became known as "evangelicals" because of their appeal to the Gospels—the "Evangels"—of the New Testament, against the authority and power of traditional institutions and sources. It was at Martin Luther's (1483–1546) suggestion that the new churches emerging out of the turmoil called themselves "evangelical" (*evangelische*). Philip Melanchthon (1497–1560) drew up a standard form of "evangelical" worship service, with Luther's approval; and Luther himself wrote out his "Shorter Catechism" in 1529. Preaching became the centerpiece of the public meeting, and church architecture changed to accommodate that and make it easier for the attendees to hear the sermon. Congregational singing was introduced, and Luther became a writer of great hymns. For many people throughout Europe still today, *evangelical* simply means "Protestant."

What lay at the heart of evangelical religion at its origin? Two things: (1) devotion to the Bible as the ultimate source of authority and divine life, and (2) personal experience of conversion to God and of practical communion with God. These, with the fundamental tensions built into them and with all of the blessings and problems they present, are the bedrock of evangelical religion, today as in the past. They in fact are what have sustained and driven evangelical religion, for individuals and for groups, up to Evangelicalism's latest surges of charismata and "spiritual formation." The followers of Luther soon drifted from these two basic elements in various ways, into splintering "orthodoxies," institutional deadness, and social conformity. The landscape of history is littered with the skeletons of these "orthodoxies," and even with the skeletons of further movements that arose to revive those skeletons. Pietism (seventeenth century) soon arose, to counteract or revive the Lutheran orthodoxy that settled over much of Europe within a century or so after Luther. Then there is a current of continuity running from the radical faith of Luther himself, through the great Pietist teachers Philipp Spener (1635–1705) and

August Hermann Francke (1663–1727), to the Moravians, on to Wesley, and to the holiness, "Deeper Life," and charismatic streams running through or alongside the later evangelical churches, right up to the "spiritual formation" impulses of the present times. Basic Evangelicalism is a *theologia cordi*, "a religion of the heart," joined in an unstable relationship to the exclusive authority of scripture. The influence of this basic Evangelicalism on other social formations and denominations of the Christian church remains constant and irrepressible. Its ever-present insistence that being a Christian is a matter of a life one lives founded in biblical teachings and consisting in personal interaction with God and the various facets of his kingdom connects with deep hungers of the human soul. The effort to force the basic genius of Evangelicalism into the armor of a more particular orthodoxy—a recurring tendency running rampant on the heels of Luther and painfully oppressive at later times, including post-WWII America—is perpetually resisted by the stream of spiritual life flowing from scripture and from the intermingling of human life with the Trinitarian presence.

THE NEW TESTAMENT PICTURE OF DISCIPLESHIP

Evangelicalism always looks to the Bible as the point of reference from which concepts are defined, practices legitimated, and principles adopted. So we must ask what can be made of discipleship and of the disciple of Jesus as seen in the life of the New Testament. Indeed, as it turns out, the New Testament "disciple" is by no means a peculiarly "Christian" innovation.[10] The disciple is one aspect of the progressive and massive decentralization of Judaism that began with the destruction of the first Temple (588 BC) and the Babylonian exile, and proceeds through the dispersal of the Jewish people among the nations that followed the destruction of Jerusalem in AD 70. During this period the synagogue emerges as the center of the local

Jewish communities, devotion to the Torah becomes the focus of the synagogue, and the rabbi or "great one" stood forth in the role of interpreter of Torah: "By degrees, attachment to the law sank deeper and deeper into the national character. . . . Hence the law became a deep and intricate study. Certain men rose to acknowledged eminence for their ingenuity in explaining, their readiness in applying, their facility in quoting, and their clearness in offering solutions of, the difficult passages of the written statutes."[11] The rabbi with his coterie of special students was a familiar feature of Jewish religious practice by the time of Jesus.

There was no one way in which to become a rabbi in the Jewish society of Jesus's day. It is true that most of those who became rabbis did so by studying under a rabbi, and having a "formal" training had some obvious advantages. But there was no "licensing" process, and an element of the Old Testament prophet carried over to the role of rabbi. A rabbi could, like the prophet, be "from nowhere." His was a performance-based status, and public recognition as a rabbi was a response to the power of the individual's words and deeds, not to their "credentials." The usual path of advancement seems to have been through the schools for young people around the synagogue. Some students did very well, memorizing huge portions of scripture and listening to interpretations by teachers. Then, if they wished, they might approach a rabbi, requesting him to take them as their disciple. If accepted, there would follow a lengthy period of close association with their rabbi—hearing, observing, and imitating. They were simply with their rabbi, serving him and becoming like him in thought, character, and abilities. Jesus's observation that "a disciple does not rise above his teacher; but everyone after he has been fully trained will reach his teacher's level" (Luke 6:40) was both a commonplace observation about the nature of the rabbi/disciple relation and—as the context makes clear—a warning about the limitations and dangers of that arrangement. ("Can a blind person guide a blind person? Will not both fall into a pit?" [Luke 6:39].)

JESUS AND HIS DISCIPLES

However, Jesus did not simply fit himself into the more or less standard model of the rabbi. He had no "formal" education beyond the synagogue schools and did not become a disciple of a rabbi. He did receive a (very unorthodox) stamp of approval from John the Baptizer, but not as his disciple. He was known to the people around him as uneducated. Amazed at the depth and power of his words, they exclaimed: "How does this man have such learning, when he has never been taught?" (John 7:15). Also, Jesus did not accept disciples upon application, testing them to see if they were "worthy." He personally selected—though not from "the best and the brightest" in his community—those he would especially train. There was a larger outer circle of people who seem to have just showed up in his presence and received training of various degrees (the "other seventy" of Luke 10:1, for example, and the group in the "upper room" of Acts 1:13). Often would-be disciples were subjected to severe discouragement by him (Matt. 8:18–22; Luke 9:57–62; 14:26–33). He also leveled scalding criticisms at the proud practitioners of the law in his day (Matt. 23:13–33; Luke 11:39–52) and prohibited his followers from being called "rabbi" and using other "respectful greetings" exchanged among those who took themselves to be highly qualified as teachers (Matt. 23:1–12). He was not "one of the boys," nor were his disciples to be.

Nevertheless, the basic nature of the rabbi/disciple relationship of his day was retained by Jesus and his disciples and, arguably, remains normative to this day. That relationship is very simple in description. His disciples were with him, learning to be like him. "With him" meant in that day that they were literally where he was and were progressively engaged in doing what he was doing. Jesus moved about the Jewish villages and towns, primarily around the Sea of Galilee, with occasional forays beyond that and especially to Jerusalem. His main disciples ("apostles") were with him in all of this, and no doubt at considerable hardship to themselves and their families. Peter on one occasion plaintively remarks: "We have left everything to follow you" (Matt. 19:27). It was no doubt a thought that often occurred to his disciples.

As they traveled about he did three things in the synagogues, homes, and public areas: he announced the availability of life in the kingdom of God, he taught about how things were done in the kingdom of God, and he manifested the present power of the kingdom by amazing deeds (Matt. 4:23; 9:35; Luke 4:18–44). Then, after a period of training, he set his disciples to doing the things they had heard and seen in him—continuing all the while to evaluate their work and to teach them as they progressed. This continued through his trial and death, and during his post-resurrection presence with them when he trained them in how he would be with them after his ascension, without visible presence. His instruction as he left was for his disciples to make disciples of all "nations"—of all types of people—and his promise was that he would be with them always until the end of the age (Matt. 28:19–20).

THE METHOD OF "BEING WITH" PASSED ON THROUGH DISCIPLES

While the charge was to make disciples of Jesus and not of the disciples, the basic method—teaching, example, and imitation—remained the same as his immediate followers proceeded to do what he had told them to do. The method was to gather a group of people by telling the story of Jesus, featuring his resurrection and pending return; to show by example what it meant to live with him now, already beyond death; and to lead others into such a life of being "with Jesus, learning to be like him." No New Testament text better fills out what this life of learning was than Colossians 3:1–17.

The role of example and imitation in the learning community of disciples is often stressed in the New Testament. Numerous statements from the apostle Paul concisely state the strategy of being and making disciples. In one of his earliest letters to groups of disciples he reminds the readers of how "our gospel [proclamation] did not come to you in word only, but also in power and in the Holy Spirit and with full conviction; just as you know what kind of men we proved to be among you for your sake. You also became imitators of us and of the Lord, having received the word in much tribulation with the joy of the Holy Spirit, so that you became an example to all believers in Macedonia and in Achaia" (1 Thess. 1:5–7, NASB).

Paul proceeds in this letter to spell out how he and his fellow workers lived "pure, upright, and blameless" in their conduct toward the believers, and to encourage them to "lead a life worthy of God, who calls you into his own kingdom and glory" (2:10–12). In 1 Corinthians he exhorts the believers to imitate him, to be "reminded of my ways which are in Christ" (4:16–17), and to "be imitators of me, just as I also am of Christ" (11:1). In 2 Thessalonians he indicates that the readers "know how you ought to imitate us." He reminds them of how he led a disciplined life and worked hard to support himself, "not because we do not have that right [to support from them], but in order to offer ourselves as a model for you that you might imitate us" (3:7–9). To the Philippians he said: "Keep on doing the things you have learned and received and heard and seen in me, and the God of peace will be with you" (4:9). He elsewhere reminds Timothy that he had "observed my teaching, my conduct, my aim in life, my faith, my patience, my love, my steadfastness, my persecutions and suffering the things that happened to me in Antioch, Iconium, and Lystra" (2 Tim. 3:10–11). And in an earlier letter he directed him to "show himself an example to those who believe" (1 Tim. 4:12). The writer of the letter to the Hebrews counsels his readers not to be sluggish, "but imitators of those who through faith and patience inherit the promises" (6:12). They should "remember your leaders, those who spoke the word of God to you; consider the outcome of their way of life, and imitate their faith" (13:7). As it was for "your leaders," the writer assures them, it will also be for you, and that is because "Jesus Christ is the same, yesterday and today and forever" (vv. 8–9). The point of this much misapplied verse is, as the context makes clear, that the nature of discipleship to Jesus and its outcomes does not change.

TRANSFORMATION THROUGH
THIS KIND OF DISCIPLESHIP

Now, this practice of discipleship in the communities of Christ followers—being with Christ, learning to be like him, in part by being with those who are further along on that same path—is what lends realism and hope to the glowing pictures of his people that stand out from the pages of the New Testament. Such passages as Matthew 5–7, John 14–17, Romans 12, 1 Corinthians 13, Ephesians 4–5, and Colossians 3 readily come to mind. These are not just passages stating required behaviors, as laws might do—"Turn the other cheek" and so forth—not a new and sterner legalism. Rather, as expressing what lies "beyond the righteousness of the scribes and Pharisees" (Matt. 5:20), they are indications of what life becomes for those who are devoted disciples of Jesus Christ within the fellowship of disciples and under the administration of the word and of the Holy Spirit. A life of this quality is the "output" of disciples of Jesus who make disciples wherever they go, gather them in Trinitarian reality, and teach them in such a way that they come to do all that Jesus told us to do out of transformed personalities. What is now generally regarded as "normal Christianity" drops away with the "cleaning of the inside of the cup" (Matt. 23:25–26). Discipleship is the status or position within which spiritual (trans)formation occurs.

As we have noted, post-WWII Evangelicalism does not naturally conduct its converts and adherents into a life of discipleship, nor into pervasive Christlikeness of character—with the routine, easy obedience that it entails. What this most recent version of Evangelicalism lacks is a theology of discipleship. Specifically, it lacks a clear teaching on how what happens at conversion continues on without break into an ever fuller life in the kingdom of God. How, to cite Paul's language, does "the grace of God that brings salvation" discipline us, train us, in such a way that we turn from "ungodliness and worldly lust" to live lives that are "sensible, righteous, and godly in the present world" (Titus 2:11–14; cf. Phil. 2:12–15)? How is it, exactly, that he who gave himself for us also "redeems us from all iniquity and purifies for himself a people of his own who are zealous for good deeds" (v. 14; cf. Eph. 2:10)? To such questions contemporary Evangelicalism has no answer. Its doctrine of grace and salvation prevents it from developing an understanding of discipleship that makes discipleship ("being with Jesus, learning to be like him") a natural part of salvation. The basic genius of Evangelicalism as such, however, is never content to leave the matter there.

For Further Reading:

Dietrich Bonhoeffer, *The Cost of Discipleship* (New York: Macmillan, 1966).

Michael D. Henderson, *A Model for Making Disciples: John Wesley's Class Meeting* (Nappanee, IN: Francis Asbury Press, 1997).

Wes Howard-Brook and Sharon H. Ringe, eds., *The New Testament: Introducing the Way of Discipleship* (Maryknoll, NY: Orbis Books, 2002).

Bill Hull, *Choose the Life: Exploring a Faith That Embraces Discipleship* (Grand Rapids, MI: Baker Book House, 2004).

———, *The Disciple-Making Church* (Grand Rapids, MI: Baker Book House, 1998).

William Law, *A Serious Call to a Devout and Holy Life: Adapted to the State and Condition of All Orders of Christians* (London: Griffith Farran & Co., n.d. Many editions).

Richard N. Longenecker, ed., *Patterns of Discipleship in the New Testament* (Grand Rapids, MI: Eerdmans, 1996).

Michael U. Wilkins, *The Concept of Disciple in Matthew's Gospel* (Leiden: E. J. Brill, 1988).

———. *Following the Master: Discipleship in the Steps of Jesus* (Grand Rapids, MI: Zondervan, 1992).

Dallas Willard, *The Great Omission* (San Francisco: HarperSanFrancisco, 2006).

———, *The Spirit of the Disciplines* (San Francisco: Harper & Row, 1988).

CHAPTER 22

Discipleship How-To

The following piece identifies what Dallas believed were the essential qualities of a disciple of Jesus. He argues that intentional discipleship is a necessary predicate to living a Christlike life in our workplace, and here he uses the New Testament Gospels as a foundation for learning this practice.

Adapted excerpt first published in 1998 as "How to Be a Disciple" in *The Christian Century* from chapter eight of *The Divine Conspiracy*

BEING A DISCIPLE OR APPRENTICE OF JESUS IS A DEFINITE AND OBvious kind of thing. To make a mystery of it is to misunderstand it. There is no good reason why people should ever be in doubt as to whether they themselves are his students or not. And the evidence will always be quite clear as to whether any other individual is his student, though we may be in no position to collect that evidence and rarely would have any legitimate occasion to gather or use it.

Now, this may seem very startling, even shocking, to many in our religious culture, where there is a long tradition of doubting, or possibly even of being unable to tell, whether or not one is a Christian. The underlying issue in some traditions has been whether or not one was going to "make the final cut." And that has, in turn, often been thought a matter of whether God has "chosen you" and you are therefore "among the elect." Or else it is a matter of whether or not you have sinned too much, or are good enough. Needless to say,

those would be difficult questions to answer with much assurance—
perhaps impossible to answer at all, because we are in no position to
inspect the accounting books of heaven.

It would take us far out of our path to enter into those hoary controversies. But fortunately there is no need. It is almost universally
conceded today that you can be a Christian without being a disciple.
Further, we can be assured that anyone who actually is an apprentice
and co-laborer with Jesus in his or her daily existence is sure to be a
"Christian" in every sense of the word that matters. The very term
Christian was explicitly introduced in the New Testament—where,
by the way, it is used only three times—to apply to disciples when
they could no longer be called Jews, because many kinds of Gentiles
were now part of them.

Now, people who are asked whether they are apprentices of a
leading politician, musician, lawyer, or screenwriter would not need
to think a second to respond, as would also be the case for those
who are studying Spanish or a trade such as bricklaying. Formal ap-
prenticeships are hardly something that would escape attention. The
same is all the more true if asked about discipleship to Jesus.

But if we were to inquire as to whether one is a *good* apprentice of
whatever person or line of work is concerned, they very well might
hesitate. They also might say no. Or, yes with the qualification that
they could be a better student. And all of this falls squarely within
the category of being a disciple or apprentice. For to be a disciple in
any area or relationship is not at all insinuating that one is perfect.
One can be a very raw and incompetent beginner and still be a disciple or apprentice.

It is a part of the refreshing realism of the Gospels that we often
find Jesus doing nothing less than sternly correcting his disciples.
That, however, is very far from rejecting them. It is, in fact, a way of
being faithful to them, just as chastisement is God's way of showing
that someone is his child (Heb. 12:7–10). A good "master" takes his
apprentices seriously and therefore takes them to task as needed.
Therefore, a good working definition of a disciple or apprentice is

simply someone who has decided to be with another person, under appropriate conditions, in order to become capable of doing what that person does or to become what that person is.

How does this apply to discipleship to Jesus? What is it, exactly, that he, the incarnate Lord, does? What, if you wish, is he "good at"? The answer is found in the Gospels: he lives in the kingdom of God, and he applies that kingdom for the good of others and even makes it possible for them to enter it themselves. The deeper theological truths about his person and his work do not detract from this simple point. Discipleship is what he calls us into by saying, "Follow me."

The description Peter gives in the first "official" presentation of the gospel to the Gentiles provides a sharp picture of the master under whom we serve as apprentices. "You know," he says to Cornelius, "of Jesus, the one from Nazareth. And you know how God anointed him with the Holy Spirit and power. He went about doing good and curing all those under oppression by the devil, because God was with him" (Acts 10:38).

Likewise, as a disciple of Jesus I am with him, by choice and by grace, learning from him how to live in the kingdom of God. This is the crucial idea. That means I am learning how to live within the range of God's effective will, with his life flowing through mine. Another important way of putting this is to say that I am learning from Jesus to live my life as he would live my life if he were I. I am not necessarily learning to do everything he did, but I am learning how to do everything I do in like manner to that in which he did all that he did.

My main role in life, for example, is that of a professor in what is called a "research" university. As Jesus's apprentice, then, I constantly have before me the question of how he would deal with students and colleagues in the specific connections involved in such a role. How would he design a course, and why? How would he compose a test, administer it, and grade it? What would his research projects be, and why? How would he teach this course or that? That my actual life is the focus of my apprenticeship to Jesus is crucial. Knowing this can help deliver us from the genuine craziness that the current distinction between "full-time Christian service" and "part-time Christian service" imposes on us. For a disciple of Jesus is not necessarily one devoted to doing specifically religious things as that is usually understood.

To repeat, I am learning from Jesus how to lead my life, my whole life, my real life. Please note, I am not learning from him how to lead *his* life. His life on earth was a transcendently wonderful one. But it has now been led. Neither I nor anyone else, even himself, will ever lead it in that particular manner again. And he is, in any case, interested in my life, that very existence that is me. There lies my need. I need to be able to lead my life as he would lead it if he were I.

So as his disciple I am not necessarily learning how to do special religious things, either as a part of "full-time service" or as a part of "part-time service." My discipleship to Jesus is, within clearly definable limits, not only a matter of what I do, but of how, why, and from what resources I do it. And this necessarily would cover everything, "religious" or not.

Brother Lawrence, who was a kitchen worker and cook, remarks,

> Our sanctification does not depend upon changing our works, but in doing that for God's sake which we commonly do for our own. . . . It is a great delusion to think that the times of prayer ought to differ from other times. We are as strictly obliged to adhere to God by action in the time of action as by prayer in the season of prayer.[1]

It is crucial for our walk in the kingdom to understand that the teachings of Jesus do not by themselves make a life. They were never intended to. Rather, they presuppose a life. But that causes no problem, for of course each one of us is provided a life automatically. We know that our life consists exactly of who we are and what we do. It is precisely this life that God wants us to give to him. We must only be careful to understand its true dignity. To every person we can say with confidence, "You, in the midst of your actual life right here and now, are exactly the person God wanted."

The teachings of Jesus in the Gospels show us how to live the life we have been given through the time, place, family, neighbors, talents, and opportunities that are ours. His words left to us in the scripture provide all we need in the way of general teachings about how to conduct our particular affairs. If we only put them into practice, along the lines previously discussed, most of the problems that trouble human life would be eliminated. That is why Jesus directs his teaching in Matthew 5–7 toward things like murder and anger, contempt and lusting, family rejection, verbal bullying. This is real life. Though his teachings do not make a life, they intersect at every point with every life.

So, life in the kingdom of God is not just a matter of not doing what is wrong. The apprentices of Jesus are primarily occupied with the positive good that can be done during their days "under the sun" and the positive strengths and virtues that they develop in themselves as they grow toward "the kingdom prepared for them from the foundations of the world" (Matt. 25:34). What they, and God, get out of their lifetime is chiefly the person they become. And that is why their real life is so important.

The cultivation of oneself, one's family, one's workplace and community—especially the community of believers—thus becomes the center of focus for the apprentice's joint life with his or her teacher. It is with this entire context in view that we most richly and accurately speak of "learning from him how to lead my life as he would lead my life if he were I."

Let us become as specific as possible. Consider just your job, the work you do to make a living. This is one of the clearest ways possible of focusing upon apprenticeship to Jesus. To be a disciple of Jesus is, crucially, to be learning from Jesus how to do your job as Jesus himself would do it. New Testament language for this is to do it "in the name of Jesus." Once we stop to think about it, we can easily see that not to find our job to be a primary place of discipleship is to automatically exclude a major part, if not most, of our waking hours from life with him. It is to assume to run one of the largest areas of our interest and concern on our own or under the direction and instruction of people other than Jesus. But this is right where most professing Christians are left today: with the prevailing view that discipleship is a special calling having to do chiefly with religious activities and "full-time Christian service."

Therefore, we must pursue how, exactly, one is to make one's job a primary place of apprenticeship to Jesus. This is not accomplished by becoming the Christian "nag-in-residence," or the rigorous upholder of all propriety, and the deadeye critic of everyone else's behavior. This is abundantly clear from a study of Jesus and of his teachings in the Sermon on the Mount and elsewhere.

A gentle but firm noncooperation with things that everyone knows to be wrong, together with a sensitive, nonofficious, nonintrusive, nonobsequious service to others, should be our usual overt manner. This should be combined with inward attitudes of constant prayer for whatever kind of activity our workplace requires and genuine love for everyone involved. As circumstances call for them, special points in Jesus's teachings and example, such as nonretaliation, refusal to press for financial advantage, consciousness of and appropriate assistance to those under special hindrances or struggles, and so on would come into play. And we should be watchful and prepared to meet any obvious spiritual need or interest in understanding Jesus with words that are truly loving, thoughtful, and helpful.

I do not believe it is true that we fulfill our obligations to those around us by only living the gospel. There are many ways of speaking inappropriately, of course even harmfully—but it is always true that words fitly spoken are things of beauty and power that bring life and joy. And you cannot assume that people understand what is going on when you only live in their midst as Jesus's person. They may just regard you as one more version of human oddity.

I once knew of a case in an academic setting where during the lunch hour a professor very visibly took his Bible and lunch to a nearby chapel to study, pray, and be alone. Whereas another professor would call his assistant into his office, where they would have sex. No one in that environment thought either activity to be anything worth inquiring about. After all, people do all sorts of things. We are used to that. In some situations it is only words that can help clarify our understanding.

But, once again, the specific work to be done—whether it is making ax handles or tacos, selling automobiles or teaching kindergarten, engaging in investment banking or holding political office, evangelizing or running a Christian education program, performing in the arts or teaching English as a second language—is of central interest to God. He wants it well done. Assuming, of course, that the job is one that serves good human purposes, it then becomes work that should be done, and it should be done as Jesus himself would do it. Nothing can substitute for that. In my opinion, at least, as long as one is on the job, all peculiarly religious activities should take second place to doing "the job" in sweat, intelligence, and the power of God. That is our devotion to God.

Our intention with our job should be the highest possible good in its every aspect, and we should pursue that with conscious expectation of a constant energizing and direction from God. Although we must never allow our job to become our life, we should, within reasonable limits, routinely sacrifice our comfort and pleasure for the quality of our work, whether it be ax handles, tacos, or the proficiency of a student we are teaching.

And yes, this results in great benefit for those who utilize our services. But our mind is not obsessed with these benefits or perks alone, and certainly not with gaining appreciation from them. We do the job well because that is what Jesus would like, and we admire and love him. It is what he would do. We "do our work with soul [*ex psyche*], to the Lord, not to men" (Col. 3:23). "It is the Lord Christ you serve" (v. 24). As his apprentices, we are personally interacting with him as we do our job, and he is with us, as he promised, to teach us how to do it best.

If one does not know this way of "job discipleship" by experience, he or she cannot begin to imagine what release and help and joy there is in it. To repeat the crucial point: if we restrict our discipleship to special religious times, the majority of our waking hours will be isolated from the manifest presence of the kingdom in our lives. Those waking hours will be times when we are on our own on our job. Our time at work—even religious work—will turn out to be a "holiday from God." On the other hand, if we dislike or even hate our job, a condition epidemic in our culture, the quickest way out of that job, or to joy in it, is to do it as Jesus would. This is the very heart of discipleship, and we cannot effectively be an apprentice of Jesus without integrating our job into the kingdom among us.

If, as we have seen, a disciple of Jesus is one who is with Jesus, learning to be like him, what is the condition of soul that would bring us to choose that condition? What would be the thinking— the convictions about reality—that would lead someone to choose discipleship to him?

Obviously we could start with a disciple having great admiration and love for Jesus—in fact, so much so that it would be appropriate to believe that Jesus is the most magnificent person who has ever lived. This would lead to becoming quite sure that to belong to him, to be taken into what he is doing throughout this world so that it becomes your life, is the greatest opportunity one will ever have.

Jesus gave us two parables to illustrate the condition of soul that leads to becoming a disciple. Actually it turns out to be a condition that we all very well understand from our own experiences. The parables also illustrate what he meant by saying that the "scribe" of the kingdom teaches from the ordinary things of life, "things both old and new."

In the first parable, Jesus states, "The kingdom of the heavens is like where something of extreme value is concealed in a field. Someone discovers it, and quickly covers it up again. Overflowing with joyous excitement he pulls together everything he has, sells it all and buys the field" (Matt. 13:44, PAR). The second parable is similar: "What the kingdom of the heavens is like is illustrated by a businessman who is on the lookout for beautiful pearls. He finds an incredible value in one pearl. So he sells everything else he owns and buys it (Matt. 13:45–46, PAR).

These little stories perfectly express the condition of the soul in one who chooses life in the kingdom with Jesus. The sense of the goodness to be achieved by that choice, of the opportunity that may be missed if not chosen, the love for the value discovered, and the excitement and joy over it all is exactly the same as it was for those who were drawn to Jesus in those long-ago days when he first walked among us. It is also the condition of the soul from which discipleship can be effectively chosen today.

Only with such images before us can we correctly assess Dietrich Bonhoeffer's famous phrase "cost of discipleship" of which so much is made today. Do you think the businessman who found the pearl was sweating over its cost? An obviously ridiculous question. What about the one who found the treasure in the field—perhaps crude oil or gold? Of course not. The only thing these people were sweating about was whether they would be included in such a "great deal." That is the appropriate condition of the soul in a disciple of Jesus. No one enters reluctantly or sadly into a discipleship relationship with Jesus. As he said, "No one who looks back after putting his hand to the plough is suited to the kingdom of God" (Luke 9:62). No one goes in bemoaning the cost. They understand the immensity of the opportunity. And one of the things that has most obstructed the path of discipleship in our Christian culture today is this idea that it will be a terribly difficult thing that will certainly ruin your life. A typical and often-told story in Christian circles is of those who have refused to surrender their lives to God for fear he would "send them to Africa as missionaries."

Here is the whole point of the much-misunderstood teachings of Luke 14. There Jesus famously says one must "hate" all one's family members and one's own life also, must take one's cross, and must forsake all one owns or one "cannot be my disciple." The entire point of this passage is that as long as one thinks anything may really be more valuable, and therefore misses a full appreciation of what fellowship with Jesus in his kingdom provides, one cannot learn from him. People who have not gotten the basic facts about their life straight will not do the things that make learning from Jesus possible and will never be able to understand the basic points in the lessons to be learned.

This is similar to a mathematics teacher in high school who might say to a student, "Verily, verily I say unto thee, except thou canst do decimals and fractions, thou canst in no wise do algebra." It is not that the teacher will not allow a student to do algebra because the student is a bad person. Rather, the student just won't be able to do basic algebra if they are not in command of decimals and fractions. Therefore, counting of the cost is not a moaning and groaning session that sounds something like, "Oh how terrible it is that I have to value all of my 'wonderful' things (which are probably making life miserable and hopeless anyway) less than I do living in the kingdom! How terrible that I must be prepared actually to surrender them should that be called for!" Instead, the counting of the cost is to bring us to the point of clarity and decisiveness. It is to help us to see.

Counting the cost is precisely what the persons with the pearl and the hidden treasure did. Out of it came their decisiveness and joy. It is decisiveness and joy that are the outcomes of the counting. This passage is about clarity, not misery or some incredibly dreadful price that one must pay to be Jesus's apprentice. There is no such thing as a dreadful price for the "pearl" in question. Suffering for him is actually something we rejoice to be counted worthy of (Acts 5:41; Phil. 1:29). The point is simply that unless we clearly see the superiority of what we receive as Jesus's students over every other thing that might be valued, we cannot succeed in our discipleship to him. We will not be able to do the things required to learn his lessons and move ever deeper into a life that is his kingdom.

Given clarity about the condition of soul that leads to choosing discipleship, what are practical steps we can take to bring strongly before us the joyous vision of the kingdom? It is true that that vision can come to us at God's initiative, through experiences that may be given to us. In fact, God's initiative will always be involved, for to see Jesus in his beauty and goodness is always a gift of grace. And then, of course, there may also be a role that other people play. But these are factors over which we have no direct control. What we want to know is what I can do if I have come to suspect it would be best for me to apprentice myself to Jesus. How can we come to admire Jesus sufficiently to "sell everything we have and buy the pearl of great value" with joy and excitement?

The first thing we should do is emphatically and repeatedly express to Jesus our desire to see him more fully as he really is. Remember, a primary rule of the kingdom is asking. We ask to see him, not just as he is represented in the Gospels, but also as he has lived and lives, through history and now, in his reality as the one who literally holds the universe in existence. He will certainly be aware of our request, just as you would be aware of anyone expressing his or her desires to come and dwell in your house. We should make our expression of desire a solemn occasion, giving at least a number of quiet hours or a day to it. It will also be good to write down our prayer for his help in seeing him. We should do this privately, of course, but then we should share what we have done with a knowledgeable minister or friend who could pray with us and talk with us about what we are doing.

Second, we should use every means at our disposal to come to see him more fully. Several things might be mentioned here, but there are two in particular, and they are keyed to one of the most well-known statements Jesus ever made. In John 8 he says to those around him, "If you dwell in my word, you really are my apprentices. And you will know the truth, and the truth will liberate you." As the context makes clear, he is saying that we will be liberated from all of the bondage that is in human life through sin, and especially from that of self-righteous religion. Positively, we will be liberated into life in the kingdom of God.

It is then important to understand that "dwelling" or "continuing" in his word is to center our lives upon (a) his good news about the kingdom among us, (b) his wisdom regarding who is really well off and who is not, and (c) true goodness of heart and how it expresses itself in action. To dwell on these realities, we would need to fill our minds and souls with the written Gospels, devoting our attention to these teachings, in private study and inquiry as well as public instruction. On the negative side, we will refuse to devote our mental space and energy to the fruitless, even stupefying and degrading mess that constantly clamors for our attention. We will attend to it only enough to avoid it.

However, dwelling in his word is not just intensive and continuous study of the Gospels, though it is that. It is also putting them into practice. To dwell in his word, we must know it, know what it is, and what it means. Ultimately, we actually dwell in the teachings of Jesus by putting them into practice. Of course, we shall do so very imperfectly at first. At that point we have perhaps not yet come to be a committed disciple and are still at the level of only thinking about how to become one. Nevertheless, we can count on Jesus to meet us in our admittedly imperfect efforts to put his words into practice. Where his word is, there he is. He does not leave his word to stand alone in the world, for his loveliness and strength will certainly be personally revealed to those who will simply make the effort to do what his words indicate.

In these efforts to see Jesus more clearly we should not dabble but be thoughtfully serious and intentional. We should find a reliable and readable version of the four Gospels. If we can plan a week in a comfortable retreat, or at least several days, then we can read through the four Gospels repeatedly, jotting down notes and thoughts on a pad as we go. If over a period of several days or weeks we were to read the Gospels through as many times as we could, consistent with sensible rest and relaxation, that alone would greatly assist us to see Jesus with clarity and start the full transition into beginning discipleship. We can count on him to meet us in that transition and not leave us to struggle with it on our own, for he is far more interested in it than we can ever be. He always sees clearly what is at issue. We rarely do.

There are also a few other things we can do that will help us toward discipleship to Jesus—not the least of which is seriously looking at the lives of others who truly have apprenticed themselves to him. Often Jesus's radiance in such people gives us very bright and strong impressions of his own greatness. To look closely at Saint Francis, John Wesley, David Brainerd, Albert Schweitzer, or one of the many well-known Teresas, for example, is to see something that elevates our vision and our hope toward Jesus himself. We should, however, make sure to soak our souls in the Gospels before turning to lives of his other followers.

Perhaps the most overlooked yet crucial step in becoming a disciple is the act of decision. We become a life student of Jesus by deciding to. When we have achieved clarity on "the costs"—on what is gained and what is lost by becoming or failing to become his apprentice—an effective decision is then possible. But still it must be made. It will not "just" happen. We do not drift into discipleship.

This may seem a simple point, but today it is commonly ignored or disregarded, even by those who think of themselves as having a serious interest in Jesus and his kingdom. I rarely find any individual who has actually made a decision to live as a student of Jesus in the manner I've discussed. For most professing Christians, that is simply not something that has presented itself clearly to their minds. Current confusions about what it means, and the failure of leaders and teachers to provide instruction on it and to stress the issue of discipleship, make that almost inevitable. But in the last analysis we fail to be disciples only because we do not decide to be. We do not intend to be disciples. It is the power of the decision and the intention over our life that is missing. We should apprentice ourselves to Jesus in a solemn moment, and we should let those around us know that we have done so.

In William Law's book *A Serious Call to a Devout and Holy Life*, the author asks "why the generality of Christians fall so far short of the holiness and devotion of Christianity."[2] To set the scene for his answer to this question, he raises a parallel question. Vulgarity and swearing were then an especially prominent feature of male behavior, even among professing Christians. So he asks, "How comes it that two in three men are guilty of so gross and profane a sin as this is?"[3] It is not that they do not know it is wrong, he points out, nor is it that they are helpless to avoid it. The answer is that they do not intend to please God in this matter:

> For let a man but have so much piety as to intend to please God in all the actions of his life as the happiest and best thing in the world, and then he will never swear more. It will be as impossible for him to swear whilst he feels this intention within himself as it is impossible for a man that intends to please his prince to go up and abuse him to his face.[4]

And it is the simple want of that intention to please God, Law points out, that explains why "you see such a mixture of sin and folly in the lives even of the better sort of people."[5]

It was this general intention that made the primitive Christians such eminent instances of piety, that made the goodly fellowship of the saints and all the glorious army of martyrs and confessors. And if we would stop here and ask ourselves why we today are not as pious as the primitive Christians were, our own hearts would likely tell us that it is neither through ignorance nor inability, but purely because such a life was never thoroughly intended.

Now, perhaps we are not used to being spoken to so frankly, and it might be easy to take offense. But on the other hand, it could well prove to be a major turning point in our life if we would, with Law's help, ask ourselves if we really do intend to be life students of Jesus. Do we really intend to do and be all of the high things we profess to believe in? Have we decided to do them? When did we decide it? And how do we intend to implement that decision?

CHAPTER 23

How to Live One Day with Jesus

In this presentation, intended for a conference on spiritual renewal, Dallas provides a practical guide for daily exercises and goals for living as a disciple of Jesus. It is unique in that it is anchored in personal experience and practice and is intended to be a helpful guide for beginners and those interested in renewing their faith.

Presented at the 1991 Renovaré National Conference on Personal Spiritual Renewal (previously unpublished)

THE SECRET OF THE BLESSED LIFE IS: GOD WITH US. WHEN GOD is with us we live and experience a life without lack. This is just as Psalm 23 describes: "I shall not want." What an interesting possibility! There are other great passages that describe God "with us" such as Genesis 5:22; 21:14–22; 28:11–21; 39:3, 21–23; Exodus 4:1–15; 1 Samuel 18:12–16; 2 Chronicles 15:2, 15; Ezra 8:22, 31; Psalms 37 and 121; Matthew 28:20; John 14:16–17; and Hebrews 13:5–6. But of course, if God is really going to be with us, we should expect that our lives will be extremely different from ordinary human life. To which we should ask ourselves the question, Do we want this? Most of religion is organized around keeping God at a distance, allowing us to "go see him" when we want. We say things such as, "Lord, this morning we come into thy presence," to which God might be saying, "Really? Where have you been?" For God has always been present. Our answer might be, "Well, taking care of things. Naturally." God really being with us works like the manna worked for the Israelites in the desert: one day at a time. We have enough until the next day. If we can live one day with Jesus, we can lead every day with him, each one as it comes.

PRELIMINARIES (YOU'LL NEED THESE THINGS FIRST)

Placing our faith in Jesus's gospel means we are placing our confidence in the availability of heaven's rule now. This begins with our honest desire. We must not attempt to fake it. God knows whether we really want and deeply desire Jesus to be with us or not. Many regard Jesus as necessary, but not desirable. We should ask ourselves, "Am I really 'nuts' about Jesus or only prepared to put up with him in some degree, even though I don't really like him very much?"

The second item we must engage is our willful decisions. We must make the decision to have Jesus with us, to be with him. We cannot drift into a life of constant companionship with Jesus. A decision is an inward resolve that we will do whatever is necessary to bring something to pass. If we have made the decision to invite Jesus to be with us always and to do all that is necessary to make that happen, we may feel a little claustrophobic. Or we may want a little more room to "be ourselves" and to live on our own. Some may want to reserve a few little "vacations" from God so they can do a few things that might be embarrassing if Jesus sat beside them. That's understandable. He understands. The question is whether or not we are willing to work this out. If we are, then we make arrangements. Arrangements or plans come from a decision to implement steps toward a specific goal.

SOME STEPS TO TAKE AT THE START OF THE DAY

Here are a few ideas about how to intentionally devote an entire day to the presence of Jesus. The biblical day, God's day, begins at sundown—the early evening, we might call it. God appoints an end to man's labors with darkness. Mr. Edison's invention of the lightbulb has not put asunder what God joined together (Ps. 104:19–24). Therefore, in darkness, at the end of our day, we gather, we recollect, we praise, we dream, in the security God has given to us. Above all, we rest. Rest is an act of faith, especially today. Few people today get the rest God has appointed for their natures. We need to both get our rest and arrange for proper rest. Second, we might resolve to lay to rest any and all household conflicts as appropriate. Leaving nothing of ill will between you and another. We don't let the sun go down on any lingering anger. Last, as we retire we commit to meet with God first thing when we awake, and go over in our mind how that will be. This is a wonderful way to fall asleep in prayer. We can very effectively use the simple prayers of childhood or the Lord's Prayer or the twenty-third Psalm to lead us into restful sleep.

WAKING IN THE MORNING

We arise to meet the new day with praise to God. This will be natural (supernatural) if we decided to retire in faith and prayer. As soon as possible we might seek seclusion to kneel for five or ten minutes and welcome the presence of Jesus, renewing our invitation to him to be with us each moment. Ask him to remove all evil and fill you with his love for your life and all that enters it. Specific concerns for the day should be called out and submitted. Finally, we can declare our dependence upon him to realize his presence with us all day long.

VIEW LIFE FROM GOD'S POINT OF VIEW

During the day we can continually settle our minds into the "God's-eye view" of our world and what is transpiring around us (Ps. 33:13–22). By constantly renewed effort, we choose to "retain God in your knowledge" (Rom. 1:28) and "set your affections on things above, not on things on the earth" (Col. 3:2). This is a habit we can develop and is something Frank Laubach testified to and experienced. As things arise during the day, invite Jesus into each new situation or relationship. Expect him to accomplish the goods of God's love in these occasions. Watch for them and give thanks. As we engage with others we can *will* or desire the peace and joy that we are experiencing to pass from us like living waters to those we are engaged with. Such peace and joy is in us, in our bodies. We can will it to enter others and watch it happen. Sometimes it occurs by benediction or "good speaking," sometimes in complete silence.

Then every two or three hours during the day take ten minutes to lift a fully concentrated heart and mind to God in thanksgiving and petition, alone if possible. Sometimes you may do this by looking at the beauty of a flower or the sky or listening to beautiful music. At the end of the day take fifteen minutes to review or examine the day. Give thanks for the successes, and try to understand why any failures took place. Ask Jesus for guidance in continuing the project. Don't make this a part of your evening exercises, for they are a part of the practices of the new day.

KEEP IN MIND

If lapses from these practices occur, do not berate yourself. Just thank Jesus for being a good friend and resume your course. Don't fuss over your failures. He doesn't. You have better things to do. It is okay to succeed with your project of walking through the day with Jesus. God isn't used just to dealing with our sin. He would have a place in our life even if we had never sinned. Life isn't about sin. The kingdom of God is righteousness, and peace, and joy in the Holy Spirit (Rom. 14:17).

The above arrangements are designed to be used in our ordinary workdays. Days of special devotion to God for special purposes of discipline and/or service will have a different nature and organization. Such days are a vital requirement of our walk with Jesus. Add what you think has been omitted here from a proper set of "arrangements" for one day with Jesus. You may wish to compare the above with Jeremy Taylor's instructions on how to "Practice the Presence of God," in chapter 1, section 3, of his book *The Rule and Exercises of Holy Living.*[1] Be experimental and inquiring as you learn how to walk constantly with Jesus. He will have some things for you alone.

CHAPTER 24

Discipleship as Apprenticeship

This piece follows the stages of growth for living as a disciple of Jesus. Dallas identifies three specific dimensions of learning to live a Christlike life and encourages the reader to "grow in grace."

First published in 2009 in *Radix* magazine as "How Does a Disciple Live?"

HOW THE DISCIPLE LIVES NATURALLY COMES OUT OF WHO THE disciple is. As Jesus's disciple, I am his apprentice in kingdom living. I am learning from him how to lead my life in the kingdom of the heavens as he would lead my life if he were I. It is my faith in him that led me to become his disciple. My confidence in him simply means that I believe that he is right about everything: that all that he is and says shows what life is at its best, what it was intended by God to be: "In him was life and the life was the light of men" (John 1:4, NASB).

Being his apprentice is, therefore, not a matter of special "religious" activities, but an orientation and quality of my entire existence. This is what is meant by Jesus when he says that those who do not forsake all cannot be his disciple (Luke 14:26, 33). The emphasis is upon the *all*. There must be nothing held of greater value than Jesus and his kingdom. He must be clearly seen as the most important thing in human life, and being his apprentice as the greatest opportunity any human being ever has.

When this orientation of the whole life has come upon us and been accepted, then the grace that brought it can begin to move throughout every aspect of what we are and do. Grace is God acting in our lives to bring about what we do not deserve and cannot accomplish on our own. But we are not passive in this process. We are commanded to put off the old person and put on the new (Col. 3:9–10; Eph. 4:22–24). We are told to "grow in the grace and knowledge of our Lord and Savior Jesus Christ" (2 Pet. 3:18). This is something for us to do, and, although we cannot do it on our own, it will not be done for us. Being alive in Christ means that we can do whatever it is we need to do to increasingly take on his character and live in his power.

The ultimate outcome of this process is expressed by Paul the apostle: "Whatever you do in word or deed, do all in the name of the Lord Jesus, giving thanks through Him to God the Father" (Col. 3:17). And again: "Whether, then, you eat or drink or whatever you do, do all to the glory of God" (1 Cor. 10:31). My entire life is to be caught up in the life that Jesus Christ himself is now living on earth and will continue throughout eternity. And that is why being his apprentice is the greatest opportunity any human being ever has. That is how grace possesses our whole life. That is how those "saved by grace through faith . . . are His workmanship, created in Christ Jesus for good works, which God prepared beforehand, that we should walk in them" (Eph. 2:10).

Living as Jesus's disciple, I am learning from him how to lead my life in the kingdom of the heavens everywhere I am, in every activity I engage in. There are three dimensions of this learning.

First, I am learning to do the things that Jesus explicitly said to do. It is quite literally nonsense to call Jesus "Lord" and not do what he said. "Lord" means nothing in such a case (Luke 6:46–49). But because I do accept him as Lord, his instructions on behavior are my treasures for living life. Of course I cannot do what he said by just trying. I must train! I must, through appropriate courses of action, become inwardly transformed by grace to become the kind of person—in my inmost thoughts, feelings, attitudes, and directions of will—who will routinely do the kinds of things he said to do. I will then not be governed by anger, contempt, or lust. And I will be able to bless those who curse me, love my enemies, and so forth, because I am one in whom the character and power of Christ have come to dwell through the processes of discipleship to Christ.

Second, I am learning to conduct the usual activities of life—in home, school, community, business, and government—in the character and power of Christ. Jesus himself, of course, spent most of his life on earth as an "independent contractor" or businessman. Jesus could have led the ordinary life of the ordinary citizen in all of its legitimate respects. He can show us how to live now, as a mother or father, banker or computer programmer, teacher or artist, in the kingdom of the heavens. His character and power and personal guidance will lead us into life as it should be in all of these areas of human existence.

Third, I am learning to exercise the power of the kingdom—of Christ in his word and spirit—to minister good and defeat evil in all of the connections of earthly existence: "God anointed Jesus of Nazareth with the Holy Spirit and with power, and He went about doing good, and healing all who were oppressed by the devil; for God was with Him" (Acts 10:38). Apprenticeship to Jesus means that, in tiny steps, we learn to exercise this power seen in Jesus. Growth in character is primary, for power requires substance of character if it is to be used for Christ's purposes. Christ had no character problems, but we do. Prayer, in its aspect of training for kingdom life, is primarily a matter of learning to exercise power in a way that is both profitable and safe. Through it, in the usual case, we take our first steps in "receiving abundance of grace" and "reigning in life by One, Jesus Christ" (Rom. 5:17). So character is more important than power for us, but it does not replace power. The fruit of the spirit (thoroughly Christlike character) flourishes only in a context of regular communal manifestation of the gifts of the spirit. And this manifest power of the spirit in life is not something restricted to "church services."

In this matter also, Jesus is our example and our teacher. He acted with the kingdom wherever he was. The "rivers of living water" that, as he said, "shall flow from the center of the believer's life" (from his "belly," John 7:38) will continually flow from us, as they did from him, wherever we may be.

Now, growth in grace—in God acting in our life—is something we must plan for by regular engagement in activities that enable us to receive God's grace in all areas of our spirit (will), thoughts, feelings, body, social relations, and the deepest depths of our soul. We have been thoroughly "occupied" by sin—which is mainly just exaltation of "me," and the consequences thereof. Our intention as apprentices of Jesus is to become the kind of person who lives in the character and power of Christ. We must, then, do those things that will enable us to become that kind of person, from the inside out—through appropriate actions and practices.

Such actions and practices are "disciplines for the spiritual life." They are well known from observing Christ and his people. They include such practices as solitude, silence, fasting, study, worship, fellowship, prayer, and so forth. There is no complete list of such practices, though some are better known and widely practiced than others, because they are more central to breaking the power of indwelling sin and increasingly filling our life with grace. Disciplines are, in essence, activities in our power that enable us, by grace, to do what we cannot do by direct effort—by "just trying." We cannot, by just trying, succeed in loving our enemies and heartily blessing those who curse us. But by a wise practice of disciplines in the presence of Christ, we can become people who will routinely and easily do so.

In practicing disciplines we need to be informed and experimental. They are not righteousness, but wisdom. We must be practical with them, and not picky. We must not be "heroic" or think we are earning anything from God. Disciplines for the spiritual life are places in which we meet with Jesus to be taught by him, and he is our guide into how they are best practiced. We should not be overly concerned about how others do them. In a very short time Jesus will lead us into the practice of them that is best for us.

The crucial thing is that, as disciples, we have a plan for carrying out the decision we have made to devote ourselves to becoming like our master and lord—to increasingly live in the character and power of Christ. Disciples are those who, seriously intending to become like Jesus from the inside out, systematically and progressively rearrange their affairs to that end, under the guidance of the word and the spirit. That is how the disciple lives.

CHAPTER 25

The Disciple's Solidarity with the Poor

The topic of wealth and poverty is essential to the larger subject of discipleship and the Christlike character. In this piece, Dallas dissects some of the more difficult ideas within traditional evangelical theology regarding the nature of wealth and poverty in relationship to the ethos of the kingdom of God.

Written in early 1981 (previously unpublished)

Blessed are you who are poor, for yours is the kingdom of God. (Luke 6:20)

The brother in humble circumstances ought to take pride in his higher position. But the one who is rich should take pride in his low position, because he will pass away like a wild flower. For the sun rises with scorching heat and withers the plant; its blossom falls and its beauty is destroyed. In the same way, the rich man will fade away even while he goes about his business. (James 1:9–11)

AMONG SERIOUS CHRISTIANS OF "COMFORTABLE CIRCUMSTANCES" there is today widespread uneasiness concerning their responsibilities to the poor and the needy. Commonly the uneasiness focuses— when it focuses at all—upon the mere fact that they do enjoy a relatively high degree of affluence, while many others on the earth starve or live and die homeless in the streets of Calcutta, New York, Cairo, and Los Angeles. The channels available to them do not seem to permit them to express that concern and solidarity with the poor that was so clearly seen in the life of Jesus and is so repeatedly commanded throughout the scriptures.

In part this difficulty is caused by vast social changes that have altered communal relations and shattered our traditional images of poverty and of assistance to persons in need. Except for a few isolated areas, the very meaning of *poverty* and *need* is no longer so obvious as it was when the world was a simpler place. Moreover, the pervasive anonymity that blankets our human contacts makes meaningful interaction with the poor very difficult, though modern communication media also make it impossible for us to put them out of our minds.

THE KINGDOM VIEW OF WELL-BEING

But the deeper root of current uneasiness among well-provided Christians lies in a failure to understand and accept the evangelic order of life in God's kingdom, together with the radical character of the gospel of Jesus Christ. We have not heartily entered into the vision of human well-being presented throughout the scriptures, with its implications for the relative life status of the poor and the rich.

The essential point can be put in one shocking statement: under the rule of God, the rich have no special advantage over the poor with regard to well-being, in this life or the next. The financially poor, addressed in the "beatitudes" of Luke 6, as well as those poverty-stricken in things spiritual, addressed in Matthew 5, have available to them now and forever all of the resources of God's reign. No matter what kind or what depths of poverty may possess them, as they make it their highest goal to live under God's rule and to have the kind of righteousness or goodness that he has, all that they need is provided, in life or in death (Matt. 6:33).

Of course the rich, too, can be blessed. But if they are, their blessedness will not consist in their possessions, any more than that of the poor consists in their lack of possessions. Blessedness is in either case entirely a matter of provision enjoyed at the ever-present hand of God.

The beatitudes are not a list that one must be on in order to be blessed, nor is the blessing they announce caused by the condition of those said to be blessed. Poverty, for example, is not the cause or reason for blessedness. Only entry into the kingdom of God provides such blessing. Instead, in the beatitudes we have a list of those commonly regarded among humanity as being unblessable, just as in the "woefuls" of Luke 6:24–26 we have a list of those usually thought blessed beyond all doubt. In these teachings Jesus lays his ax to the root of the merely human value system and proclaims irrelevant those factors that humanity invokes in deciding who is and who is not well off.

SUGGESTION OF REVOLUTION?

Because he set aside the human reference points of evaluation and decision, his words were perceived as revolutionary. Social and political order in the present world is based totally upon false assumptions about who is better off than others. Simply to tear aside those assumptions would throw life into chaos. The common people to whom Jesus spoke saw their religion as certifying all the worldly assumptions about well-being. Thus he knew that those who heard his beatitudes would think that he had come to set aside the law and the prophets. The beatitudes clearly imply that common and undistinguished people from the cursed rabble that "knows not the Law" (John 7:49) could also serve as the light of the world and the salt of the earth. Therefore, Jesus quickly adds: "Do not think that I have come to abolish the law or the Prophets; I have not come to abolish them but to fulfill them" (Matt. 5:17).

THE DEEPER RIGHTEOUSNESS

At this point in the Sermon on the Mount our Lord does something that has the most profound of bearings upon his followers' relationship to the poor. He moves from his explanation of blessedness to the more fundamental issue of righteousness. True blessedness is of course founded upon true righteousness. The poor and others can possess the kingdom that is their blessedness only by contacting it at the level of the heart or innermost personality. But in his fallen condition man identifies being right and good with the externals of behavior rather than with the aims and attitudes of his heart, the source of his life and personality. This is similar to the way in which being well off is usually identified with possessions, power, good times, and good feelings. Externalization of blessedness and righteousness leaves them subject to manipulation, so that humanity can maintain the illusion of control over them.

But Jesus pointed out that entry into the rule of heaven, the experiential reign of God over our existence, comes to us only when we seek our righteousness beyond the field of specific action, where the scribe and the Pharisee play, at the level of fundamental aims and attitudes (Matt. 5:20). It is at this point that the law and prophets see their intent realized. Here they can be fulfilled, and not abolished. Attitudes of heart inspired by faith's vision of good in God's living rule over us, a vision brought to stunning focus in the death and resurrection of his son on our behalf, reshape all of human relationships.

It is this vision of human relations under the loving rule of God that is the only possible foundation for a life of faithful service to our neighbors, including those who are poor. No amount of charitable action—even the surrender of all our possessions, or consuming devotion to the formation and application of charitable laws or institutions—can serve in place of a heart completely immersed in that vision. Such actions without the vision will only prove to be more of the righteousness of the scribes and Pharisees. They will not yield solidarity with the poor, which can be achieved only through life in the kingdom of God. Paul gave complete expression to the mind of his master and said the final word on this subject: "If I give all I possess to the poor and surrender my body to the flames, but have not love, I gain nothing" (1 Cor. 13:3).

RESPECT AND HONOR TO THE POOR

So the indispensable first step in right love and care for the poor and needy is to be conscious of them, to see them as God's creatures of equal significance with anyone else in the divine purpose: "The rich and poor have this in common: The Lord is the Maker of them all" (Prov. 22:2). As we are to honor all human beings (1 Pet. 2:17), so we are to honor the poor. We are to respect them and show them our respect. The distinction between rich and poor is permanently affixed to human life. It is the natural and inevitable consequence of differentiation within peoples' histories and family contexts, as well as of differences in genetic endowment that are an arrangement instituted by God, which explains why scripture never suggests that poverty is to be abolished. On the other hand, it always insists that the needy are to be cared for, that the poor are not to be taken advantage of but defended, and that they are to be taken into consideration in all aspects of life. Pure and undefiled religion essentially involves that we "look after orphans and widows in their distress" (James 1:27), they being the poorest of the poor under usual circumstances.

The overarching command is to love, and the first act of love is always attention. Therefore, the poor are not to be avoided and forgotten. The apostle Paul tells us: "Do not be proud, but be willing to associate with people of low position. Do not be conceited" (Rom. 12:16). Jesus Christ "did not consider equality with God something to cling to, but made himself nothing, taking the very nature of a servant" (Phil. 2:6–7). The vision of kingdom blessedness and righteousness both directs and enables the disciple to extend the incarnational model into all phases of his or her life. In this way they let his mind be in them through their association with people of all conditions.

When we are well formed by the gospel and by the pattern of our Lord, any advantages we may have within the world's set of evaluations do not mislead us or affect the quality of our human associations. Because of our vision of faith, we are comfortable with the poor and the other "unblessables" and are able to be with them in a spirit and manner that does not set them off from us. We share the human condition gladly and without affectation, as did our savior, whose spirit has pervaded us.

By contrast, those without the mind of Christ make distinctions between people that the mature disciple would never make. They cannot respect the poor within their value system. Even their special efforts, no matter how "charitable," break or emphasize their lack of solidarity with the poor. They are, of course, trying to "be big about it." But the disciple, whose very life is a gift of incarnation, really sees nothing special in his actions toward the unblessables. He is not "being big about it" because he truly sees nothing to be big about in the situation. That is why his left hand is unconscious about what his right hand is doing (Matt. 6:3).

THE CENTRALITY OF THE CROSS

So our problem is not primarily with how we see the poor, but is mainly with how we see ourselves. If we still think, or convey in the immediate responses of our mind and body, that in some way we are different as persons from the man sleeping in the discarded boxes in the alley, we have not been brought with clear eyes to the foot of the cross and seen our own neediness in the light of it. We have not learned to live always and thankfully in the cross's shadow. From that vantage point alone is solidarity with the poor to be realized.

Does it take great and awkward effort even to acknowledge the presence of the needy person, to speak to her (if some purpose is served), or to take her hand or help her with managing her few possessions? Are we frightened of the homeless though the circumstances in which we encounter them are perfectly safe? Do we shrink from being seen near them or dealing with them? Is his smell and dirtiness alone enough to repel us? Or, if he is not in this extreme condition, does the fact that he is without work or an apartment or an automobile make us treat him as if he were "different" or wholly other? Then we have not truly beheld our own lost and ruined condition, and because of this we cannot heartily love our brother and sister.

RICH OVER POOR IN THE CHURCH

James addresses a case all too familiar to us today: "A man comes into your meeting wearing a gold ring and fine clothes, and a poor man in shabby clothes also comes in" (2:2). The rich man receives much attention and is given a good seat, while the poor man is hustled off to stand in a corner or to sit on the floor. In such cases, James says, we insult the poor, whom God has chosen to be rich in faith (v. 5), and fail to care for our neighbor as we would be cared for. We fail to keep the "royal law" of neighbor love, and therefore are lawbreakers on a level with the murderer or adulterer (vv. 8–11).

What an indictment! And yet one hardly ever finds a church or a Christian free from knee-jerk favoritism toward those who are impressive in the world's scale of values. It is heartbreaking to behold. Our most biblical of churches are permeated with favoritism toward the rich and comfortable, the beautiful and famous—or, at least, toward "our kind of people." Yet many will insist that this is necessary for the advancement of the cause of Christ. We cannot sustain our programs, we are told, unless we can attract and hold the right kinds of people. It seems forgotten that the church's business is to make the right kind of people out of the wrong kind—who more often than not are precisely the "right" kind by the world's standards.

ASSOCIATE WITH THE POOR AND NEEDY

Thus, the main cause of uneasiness in the hearts of many well-provided Christians today is the inadequate vision of well-being in the kingdom of God that prevails in Christian circles and produces an anemic faith. But once solidarity with the poor is vividly realized in the Christian's faith, through adequate preaching and teaching of the gospel, there is much to be done. Opportunities to serve people of impoverished and weakened condition will come to us every day. The cup of cold water must be kept ever ready, for our vision of kingdom realities will make us much more sensitive to occasions to help and to give. It may also lead us to make a point of discovering need, rather than always waiting for it to be thrust upon us.

Remembering that we are, overall, as needy as those we serve, and that to receive is not as blessed as to give, our deeds of giving, though frequent, will naturally be low-key and unassuming. Perhaps we will easily find ways in which the need may be known and met without anyone knowing the source, "so that our giving may be in secret" (Matt. 6:4).

But it will also prove very useful for us to experience the life of the poor in some further measure. No adequate elaboration of practical strategies can be undertaken here. But, depending upon our family and other circumstances, we might do some of our ordinary business in the poorer districts of our community. It may even be as simple as getting out of our cars and onto the public transportation system. One of the great social and economic divisions in many parts of the world is between those who must ride public transportation and those who can transport themselves. We must take care not to force such things upon our dependents, but shopping, banking, even living in the poorer districts of our area will do much to lend substance to our grasp of how the economically deprived experience their world—and ours. This will add a great substance to one's understanding, prayers, and caring that can never be gained by an occasional "charity run" or by sending money to organizations that work with the poor.

Remember, Jesus did not send help. He came among us. He was victorious under our conditions of existence (Rom. 8:3). That makes all the difference. We continue on the incarnational model when we follow the apostle's command to "associate with people of low position" by in some measure walking with them in the path of their daily affairs, not just on special occasions created because of their need.

THE TEMPTATION TO ASSUME POVERTY

However, there are dangers of which we should be aware. In their zeal for the poor and needy, many experience the temptation to act— to dress or speak, for example—as if they too were poor, or even to undertake poverty. But to follow such a course will rarely if ever increase our unity with or service to the poor, or to God. That temptation falsely presupposes that it is necessarily better to be poor than to be rich, when in fact, as we have seen, neither is in itself better than the other to the clear eye of faith. It also may come from a false guilt over material possessions as such, as if the mere possession of ample goods were wrong. It is not.

There is no special virtue (or vice) merely in being poor, as there is no special vice (or virtue) merely in being comfortably well off or rich. Each is an estate ordained by God through the larger order of things, at least for the present condition of humanity. Each has its special advantages and disadvantages.

Surrender to temptations to act or become poor also involves much deception, even self-deception. Obviously we should never pretend to be other than we are. If we are well off in material terms, or even rich, we have no less reason to trust God than do those who are poor (1 Tim. 6:17). Perhaps we have even more reason, since we have vastly greater responsibilities. We are to accept all that is placed at our disposal and carefully use it in a life of love to God and to the neighbors he has given us.

POVERTY "VOWED" AND
POVERTY ROMANTICIZED

We should note that there is a great deal of playing at poverty to be found in the history of the church. "Poverty" voluntarily assumed is never the same thing as the inescapable and involuntary want from which most people in our world suffer. "Religious poverty" never amounts to the crushing, squalid deprivation and helplessness that grip the truly needy. Vows of poverty usually allow one to continue to enjoy the security, provision, and care of the religious community. Moreover, they assign one a special status in the eyes of the surrounding world, with corresponding encouragement and assistance. None of this is available to the poor of the earth. Poverty as it is "vowed" only amounts to forgoing formal ownership of things, not access to the use of them—which, in fact, the vow usually guarantees.

Poverty has been romanticized by both the Catholic and Protestant alike. In his journal for September 6, 1750, John Wesley notes a published account of the passing of "one of our preachers." The deceased had hardly enough possessions to pay for his funeral, and Wesley observes with gratification: "Enough for any unmarried preacher of the Gospel to leave to his executors!"[1] Clearly he thought it good that the man have so little at his death. But would it not have been equally well, even better, had the man been found to have great possessions carefully managed for the good of man and the glory of God? Surely it would have. While certain individuals may have a specific call to poverty because of a specific type of ministry, we may say in general that being poor is one of the poorest of ways to help the poor.

WESLEY'S LAMENT OVER
PROSPEROUS CHRISTIANS

Wesley, like many today, was deeply troubled about the relation of riches to Christianity. He saw that the form of life that resulted from his preaching made his converts prosperous, which then resulted in their becoming selfish, indulgent, and lacking in self-denial. In his touching sermon titled "The Inefficacy of Christianity" he cries out, "I am distressed! I know not what to do!" He even suggests that "true, scriptural Christianity has a tendency, in process of time, to undermine and destroy itself."[2] It begets diligence and frugality, which make one rich. Riches, in turn, "naturally beget pride, love of the world, and every temper that is destructive of Christianity."[3]

THE FLAWED SOLUTION

For all of his insight, he could not understand the possibility of a Christian teaching and discipline that would produce people capable of holding possessions and power without corruption (1 Tim. 6:17–19). People who have money need not love it and so have in them the root of all evil (1 Tim. 6:9–10). And, in fact, few love it so much as those who do not have it. But Wesley somehow failed to see this, and had recourse to a deeply flawed solution:

> I can see only one possible way: find out another who can. Do you gain all you can, and save all you can? Then you must in the nature of things grow rich. Then if you have any desire to escape the damnation of hell, give all you can; otherwise I can have no more hope of your salvation, than that of Judas Iscariot.[4]

Of course giving must have a great place in the life of the disciple on any account. But giving cannot replace keeping, using, and controlling as responsible stewards of God's creation for our individual time in his world. Here Wesley, with many others, went sadly wrong. His formula must be supplemented to read: Get all you can; save all you can; use all you can within the confines set by a properly disciplined spiritual life; control all you can for the good of humanity and the glory of God; and then give all you can.

SERVING IS MUCH MORE THAN GIVING

Serving is only a part, and by no means the largest part, of stewardship before our Lord. The poor are much more to be benefited by the godly controlling the goods of this world than by a pious hand washing that abandons those goods to the servants of Mammon. It is as great and difficult a spiritual calling to run the factories and the mines, the banks and the department stores, the schools and government agencies for the kingdom of God as it is to pastor a church or serve as evangelist. The division of vocations into sacred and secular does incalculable damage to our individual lives and to the cause of Christ.

The Christian must be taught how to own without treasuring (Matt. 6:21); how to possess without, like the "rich young ruler" (Mark 10:22), being possessed; how to live simply, even frugally, though controlling great wealth and power. But because we continue to be misled by the world's view of well-being, which holds riches to be well-being, we react by thinking of possessions as inherently and essentially evil. Thus we fail to develop adequate teaching and example for those who prosper. We can only suggest that maybe they ought not to prosper.

GRACE FOR ABUNDANCE

The apostle Paul certainly knew better. The usual Christian quotes his words "I can do everything through him who gives me strength" (Phil. 4:13) only when facing hard times. But that is not Paul's meaning. In the previous verses he said, "I have learned to be content whatever the circumstances. I know what it is to be in need, and I know what it is to have plenty. I have learned the secret of being content in any and every situation." Thus, when he adds that Christ gives him strength for everything, he is saying also that Christ enables him to abound, be full, and prosper.

He succeeded in abundance because of his relation to Christ just as much as he succeeded by grace in his times of need. Few people understand that they need help to abound. Once again, our pastoral ministry is tragically defective at this point. I have never heard anyone exclaim, upon coming into great wealth, "I can do all things through Christ who strengtheneth me!" But this is one of the most serious errors that can be made in the spiritual life—against which only an unprejudiced, full, and constant presentation of the gospel and a full use of the disciplines for the spiritual life can protect us. The gospel is for the up-and-in as well as the down-and-out, equally so, and equally needed, from God's point of view. The church's solidarity with the poor cannot be realized until spirituality has a place in the boardrooms and factories, the universities and government offices, equal to what it has in the church house, the religious retreat, or the rescue mission.

It has never been said better than by William Law, in the opening words of his *Serious Call to a Devout and Holy Life.*

> Devotion is neither private nor public prayer; but prayers, whether private or public, are particular parts or instances of devotion. Devotion signifies a life given, or devoted, to God.[5]

And,

> He, therefore, is the devout man, who lives no longer to his own will, or the way and spirit of the world, but to the sole will of God; who considers God in everything, who serves God in everything, who makes all the parts of his common life parts of piety, by doing everything in the Name of God, and under such rules as are conformable to His glory.[6]

VISION, WALK, AND WORK

The disciple's solidarity with the poor has, then, three major dimensions:

Vision: a clear and well-worked-out vision of the kingdom of God
and its meaning for human well-being.

Walk: an awareness and association with people from all conditions of life, made deep and natural by the kingdom view of
well-being and well-doing.

Work: a control of "the Mammon of unrighteousness," or worldly
wealth (Luke 16:9), so far as it in any way lies under our direct
or indirect influence, to ensure that the needy are protected
and cared for and that the economic order serves godly ends so
far as is in our power.

To the individual Christian uneasy in prosperity, no neat formula
will be given. By study, prayer, fellowship, and experience, however,
we can find confidence and peace in our individualized place where
we are to stand as light and salt. The church can help us to achieve
full-fledged solidarity with the poor and needy if her ministers will
constantly preach and teach the gospel that Jesus himself preached,
and do so in the manner in which he preached it. From him and his
truth we shall draw the knowledge and strength to be humble and
trusting, safe and effective in the midst of poverty and in the midst
of wealth alike.

PART IV

Theology

Spiritual Formation as a Natural Part of Salvation

This essay, which was originally a lecture delivered at Wheaton College, may well be the single best representation of Dallas's thought on the objective of the Christian faith. He once said to me, "As leaders of the church we need to understand that we are in the salvation business. The whole of the gospel is intent on deliverance. Our opportunity, and our problem, is making sure we understand exactly what salvation means. All of it." This work clarifies many of the key details about the existential reality of eternal life that Jesus manifested and that the writers of scripture illustrate.

Presented at the 2009 Wheaton College Theology Conference and first published in *Life in the Spirit: Spiritual Formation in Theological Perspective*

Test yourselves to see if you are in the faith; examine yourselves! Or do you not recognize this about yourselves, that Jesus Christ is in you—unless indeed you fail the test. (2 Cor. 13:5, NASB)

THE ANNOUNCED THEME OF THIS CONFERENCE IS "LIFE IN THE Spirit: Spiritual Formation in Theological Perspective." Earlier indications from some of the organizers of the conference said that we would be concerned with "the deeply spiritual and practical aspects of following Jesus." I would like to use my time to address a central issue in theology (specifically, soteriology—the understanding of salvation) that, given prevailing understandings, poses almost insurmountable barriers to (trans)formation of professing Christians into Christlikeness, which is the meaning of spiritual formation in Christ.

Simply put, as now generally understood, being "saved"—and hence being a Christian—has no conceptual or practical connection with such a transformation. There is plenty of talk about transformation in the New Testament (2 Cor. 3:18; Rom. 5:1–5; 12:2; Eph. 4:14–16; Col. 3:4–17; 2 Pet. 1:2–11; 3:18; etc.) that is presupposed in its massive descriptions of normative behavior. It also shines in the lives of acknowledged "great ones" in the way of Christ and in the literature spun off by the church through the ages. But all of this appears to the ordinary Christian today like near or distant galaxies in the night sky: visible, somehow, but inaccessible in the conditions of life as we know them. Hence, you will rarely meet an individual Christian who is seriously engaged in the transformation (spiritual formation) depicted in the Bible and in church history, or who even has a hope for anything like it this side of heaven. And while you might think that Christian organizations would have such transformation as their central focus, that simply turns out not to be true. They are doing something else.

So let us start out with some clarification of "spiritual formation." As I have explained in various writings, spiritual formation in Christ as portrayed in the Bible and the "great ones" is not primarily behavior modification, though modification of behavior certainly is an outcome of it. Especially, it is not being trained into one or another outward cultural form of the Christian religion: Lutheran, Benedictine, Quaker, and so forth. That is how it has often been approached, but to suppose that it is identical with such training will only result in another form of "the righteousness of the scribes and Pharisees" (Matt. 5:20), which leaves untouched the inward character of the person, the "heart," the source of action and outward bearing (Mark 7:21–23). It is not entirely misleading to regard this inner dimension of the self as the "spiritual" side of the human being, and then to think of "spiritual formation" as the process of reshaping or redeveloping it until it has, to a substantial degree, the character of the inner dimension of Jesus himself. Of course this is a process to which the agency of the Holy Spirit is indispensable, along with other instrumentalities of God and his kingdom. One can think of the process as formation of the human spirit as well as formation by the divine Spirit, for it indeed is both.

What this looks like is indicated in various ways in the teachings of Jesus and his early followers. When asked by a scribe to state the most foundational commandment of all, Jesus replied in terms of recognition of Jehovah as the one God, and of our loving him "with all your heart, and with all your soul, and with all your mind, and with all your strength, and loving your neighbor as yourself" (Mark 12:29–31). This would be the outcome or "product" of the process of spiritual formation in Christ. In various wordings, that is the uniform testimony of the New Testament. High points are, of course, 1 Corinthians 13 and 16:22; Romans 5:5; Colossians 3:14; and 2 Peter 1:7.

The behavioral outcome of such a spiritual formation is assured: "He who has My commandments and keeps them, he it is who loves Me. . . . He who does not love me does not keep my words" (John 14:21–24). Paul remarks that "love does no wrong to a neighbor; love therefore is the fulfillment of the law" (Rom. 13:10). John says bluntly: "The one who says, 'I have come to know Him,' and does not keep His commandments, is a liar, and the truth is not in him" (1 John 2:4). But one must understand that the sequence is important in these sayings, or otherwise they will throw us into a legalistic frenzy—as has happened over and over in the history of Christ's people. Accordingly, the practical aim of the one who takes obedience seriously is not to obey, but to become the kind of person who easily and routinely does obey as a result of devotion to Jesus and consequently of taking him as Lord, teacher, and friend. The practical aim is to know him, to be devoted to him, in this inclusive manner.

What, then, does "being saved" have to do with such a transformation? We should perhaps start with recognition that, for almost everyone today in Western Christendom, being saved has nothing essentially to do with transformation. We might find "being saved" and such transformation conjoined in an individual here or there, and that might be regarded as admirable; but it is not normative for being a Christian, and when it does happen it has to be accounted for in terms other than the basic nature of the salvation presumed. All notable theological and ecclesiastical positions with which I am familiar in the contemporary world hold that you can be right with God in ways that do not require transformation and in ways that do not routinely support and advance transformation. These ways may involve (1) the professing of right doctrine, (2) a specified formal association with a denomination or group, or, on the more liberal side, (3) a kind of vague—or even intense—sympathy with what one takes Jesus to stand for. There are, of course, many ways in which this can be spelled out, which I have tried to deal with in more detail elsewhere.[1] But together these three "paths"—frequently overlapping—pretty much take in the ways in which North Americans at least, along with many Europeans, think of themselves as "Christian." This seems to me to be a merely descriptive point or matter of fact, which would be borne out by statistics.

Now, within this broad range of Christians, a narrower group—many Roman Catholics, Orthodox, and evangelicals—think of "salvation" or "being saved" as strictly a matter of having one's sins forgiven and of having heaven "nailed down" as a result. In what follows I am going to speak mainly to this group. The problem we are addressing then arises from a soteriology that equates being saved with having your sins forgiven. And our question then comes down to how having your sins forgiven relates to spiritual formation as process and as outcome. The background assumption is that justification is the entirety of salvation. If you are justified—your sins forgiven—then you are saved and you will be "okay" after your death. I submit to you that this is what is offered, in still more specific forms, by current efforts ("evangelism") to convert people to Christianity, and it is what people generally understand to be essential to the transaction. It is how many people "come into the church." Other words may be used—such as "giving your heart to Jesus," or "taking him into your heart," or even "accepting Jesus as lord of your life"—but what is essential, no matter the words, is receiving forgiveness by counting on the merits of Christ to cover your sin-debts.

To get the complete picture you have to explain how grace is understood in this context. Salvation is by grace through faith. That is a foundational truth. But it is usually understood to mean that nothing you do contributes to salvation. With this, a pervasive passivity enters the scene. You will even be told by some that your very faith in Christ as the sacrifice for your sins is not something you do, but something God just produces in you (or not). It is not just that grace is "unmerited favor," but that it is something exterior to you— an event involving God in heaven, a transfer of merit from Christ to your "account." When that is done, it is done. Salvation is complete.

Some soteriologies require you to service the account in various ways if you are going to make it in—faithfulness to the sacraments, for example, or periodic repentance and efforts to do better, perhaps, or even rebaptism—but in only a very few cases is there an insistence that you have to be significantly transformed into Christlikeness to "get in." In one tradition it is said that gratitude for forgiveness will in fact make you adhere to Christ in such a way that transformation and obedience will follow. That has happened, and perhaps still happens in some instances. But if you simply observe the groups that propose this, you will see, I think, that the rate of radical transformation in them is quite low, and usually no higher than in groups that do not hold their view.

The conclusion I draw from all of this is that a view that takes salvation to be the same thing as justification—forgiveness of sins, and assurance of heaven based upon it—cannot come to see spiritual formation as a natural part of salvation. The result of that will be the routine omission of spiritual formation unto Christlikeness as a serious objective of individuals and groups who hold a mere "justification" view of salvation. Further, it seems to me, adherence to this view of salvation is what accounts for the transformation of evangelical Christianity into a version of nominal Christianity over the course of the twentieth century, even though, historically, Evangelicalism has strongly opposed nominal Christianity.

But is there a recognizably Christian view of salvation—one prominent in scripture and history—that does have spiritual formation as a natural part or outgrowth of "salvation," understood to be an identifiable status (sometimes, at least, associated with a specific event)? You will perhaps not be surprised to hear me say that there is such a view, and that it comes in the form of the theological concept of regeneration.[2] This is the event of a new type of life entering into the individual human being. The kind of life that the human being has on its own—its "natural" life, so to speak—is a kind of "death" compared with the type of life that begins to move in us at "regeneration." Once this is mentioned, I believe the person familiar with the New Testament writings will recognize the passage from "death" to "life" as a constant biblical theme, where "life" is a real and powerful presence in the regenerate individual (Eph. 3:20; 2 Tim. 2:1).

John the apostle states, as a sure indication, that we have "passed out of death into life, we love the brethren. He who does not love abides in death" (1 John 3:14). And also: "He who has the Son has life" (1 John 5:11–12). *Life* is perhaps John's favorite term for what happens when one comes to Christ. It is the entire point of "the birth from above" as discussed in John 3—a passage that is desecrated by the usual reading of it as focused upon forgiveness of sins. There the "life" is associated with seeing and entering the kingdom of God. "Birth" and "life," of course, go together. Paul describes the action of God in saving us: "For He delivered us from the domain of darkness, and transferred us to the kingdom of His beloved Son" (Col. 1:13). To enter the kingdom is to have the life "from above." That life is the principle of kingdom inclusion. It is otherwise described by Paul as sharing in the resurrection life of Jesus himself: "You have died and your life is hidden with Christ in God" (Col. 3:3). Again: "You were dead in your trespasses and sins. . . . But God . . . , even when we were dead in our transgressions, made us alive together with Christ [by grace you have been saved], and raised us up with Him, and positioned us with Him in the heavenlies in Christ Jesus" (Eph. 2:1–6). That is what the birth "from above" does.

Simple inductive study of the New Testament will, I believe, convince anyone that the primary way of understanding salvation according to the scripture is in terms of a divine life that enters the human being as a gift of God. There is then a new psychological reality that is God acting in us and with us. Eternal life is said by Jesus to be knowledge. Knowledge in biblical language is an interactive relationship, and in this case with "Thee, the only true God, and Jesus Christ whom Thou hast sent" (John 17:3). Eternal life in the individual does not begin after death, but at the point where God touches the individual with redeeming grace and draws them into a life interactive with himself and his kingdom. A new, nonhuman activity becomes a part of our life. Our life is now interwoven with his and his (amazing grace indeed!) with ours. Speaking thus we must make it clear that we are not just "talking something up," but referring to the concrete reality of regenerate existence.

What is life? What is a new life? Not to attempt here a definition of life, but observation will show that life is a self-initiating, self-directing, self-sustaining activity of some kind and to some degree. That is what distinguishes living things from nonliving things, and things that are still alive from things that have died. An important part of the activity that is life consists of the living thing's interaction with its environment, and, indeed, the kind of life that is in a thing determines what counts as its environment. The life that is in a plant makes soil, water, and sunlight the major factors of its environment, and when it dies it ceases to interact with those factors by appropriate activity. A kitten has a different kind of life in it and interacts with different types of things in different ways: small rubber balls, mice, and other kittens, for exam-

ple. A dead kitten is totally indifferent to those things, as the plant
is indifferent to them while it is alive. And so on through the scale
of living things. A human being, in comparison to other living
things, has a real or possible environment of fantastic proportions
not yet revealed (Isa. 64:4; 1 John 3:2).

The human being is by nature meant to function on the basis of
interaction between itself and God at the very center of its life. The
sufficiency of God to the human being (Rom. 8:31–39) is adequate
to the "fantastic proportions" of human abilities and aspirations. To
lose that central reality is what it means to be "dead in trespasses
and sins." Life activity of a sort continues on in the human being for
a while, but defined in terms of the reverse trinity of the world, the
flesh, and the devil (Eph. 2:2–3). But that activity draws from limited, chaotic, and self-destructive resources. Its condition of spiritual
death ends in total death (Rom. 8:5–6).

God alone has life in himself (John 5:26), and it is he who gives
life to all things (1 Tim. 6:13). He alone can say, "I am that I am"
(Exod. 3:14). (Not, please, "I am *who* I am"! Such a statement makes
no distinction at all.) The presence of life in anything, other than
the life of God, is always limited and dependent on other things—
ultimately upon God. In regeneration God, utilizing various instrumentalities, imparts his own life to the fallen life of the human being
apart from God. The self-initiating, self-directing, self-sustaining
activity of God now penetrates the darkened world of the human
soul and begins to act in it and around it. It has rarely if ever been
better said than this:

> Long my imprisoned spirit lay
> Fast bound in sin and nature's night;
> Thine eye diffused a quick'ning ray,
> I woke, the dungeon flamed with light;
> My chains fell off, my heart was free;
> I rose, went forth, and followed Thee.
> Hymn, "And Can It Be That I Should Gain?"—Charles Wesley, 1738

Salvation, being saved, is then not a meager, merely human existence here, but one with a heavenly account flush in the transferred
merits of Christ. It is a human existence, to be sure—meager as it
may be—but one in which the currents of divine life have at least
begun to pulsate. It is: "Christ in you, the hope of glory" (Col. 1:27).
It is: "He who began a good work in you will perfect it" (Phil. 1:6).
It is: "God, who is at work in you both to will and to work for His
good pleasure" (Phil. 2:13). It is: becoming "partakers of divine
nature, having escaped the corruption that is in the world by lust"
(2 Pet. 1:4). It is: "Your life is hidden with Christ in God" (Col. 3:3).

Now, life of whatever kind has a natural development. This is the
absolutely crucial point for our discussion here. The "activity" that is
life is poised for a specific order of development. It can be deflected
or stunted, but its natural course is set by the kind of life it is. The
same is true with the new life "from above" that enters the human
being, however degraded, upon regeneration.

The first clear manifestation of heavenly life in the individual is
recognition, hearty confidence, that Jesus really is the anointed one,
Christ, Lord. This is not primarily a profession. It is a gripping realization of what is the case. It is not possible for the unaided human
being to arrive at such a condition. When it gripped Peter, the Lord
told him that only divine assistance could have brought it to him.
Not "flesh and blood" (Matt. 16:16–17). That was not a point upon
which error could be tolerated. Jesus went on to say that the rock of
this realization would be the foundation upon which his triumphant
εκκλησίαν would prevail and stand, with access ("keys") to the resources of the kingdom of the heavens. Paul, in helping the Corinthians come to an understanding of where God was really present,
pointed out that "no one can say, 'Jesus is Lord,' except by assistance
from the Holy Spirit" (1 Cor. 12:3).

When one understands the realities involved here it will be clear
why: "If you confess with your mouth Jesus as Lord, and believe
in your heart that God raised Him from the dead, you shall be

saved" (Rom. 10:9). (To "confess" is to own up to a condition of your soul; to profess is to put forth an understanding of something.) Confidence in Jesus as absolute maestro of the universe is the first indication of regeneration. It is this, not a mere credit transfer, that constitutes a "personal relationship with Jesus."

The natural consequence of this confidence is apprenticeship to Jesus in kingdom living. We will not say that failure to become the apprentice or disciple of Jesus is a metaphysical impossibility for one who has confidence that he is lord of the universe. A certain degree of understanding of "what comes next" is presupposed, and in the midst of confused teaching and example, things might not proceed as they naturally would. Life in all its forms permits distortion within limits, of not becoming what it was meant to be. But in the nature of the case, one who really understands who Jesus is sees their own situation in a realistic light and wants to take measures to remedy their condition by staying as close to Jesus as possible. Discipleship is a natural part of confidence in Jesus as he really is.

What exactly is a "faith" that does not naturally express itself in discipleship to Jesus? It would be that of a person who simply would use something Jesus did, but "has no use" for him. This is the person I have outrageously called the "vampire Christian." "I'll take a bit of your blood, Jesus—enough to cover my debts—but I'll not be staying close to you until I have to." Wouldn't heaven be hell for a person stuck forever with the company of someone (the magnificent Jesus and the Trinity) that they did not admire or even like enough to stay as close to them as possible? There is no way you can say that such a person has faith or confidence in Jesus Christ. This is not "the faith which works by love" (Gal. 5:6), or the faith through which Christ dwells in the heart (Eph. 3:17). It is not the faith that is a natural part of regeneration as life from above.

Discipleship may be loosely described as staying as close to Jesus Christ as possible. It is life with him, which from the reverse side is his life with us. As his disciples we are learning from Jesus how to live our life here and now in the kingdom of the heavens as he would live our life if he were we. Now, the locus of our life with him as disciples is precisely obedience where we are. Our "obedience" to start with will be ragged, messy, and inadequate. But we are not trying to be "righteous" anyway. All hope in that direction has been abandoned, and we do not deal with ourselves or with others on the basis of "righteousness."

Our faith in Christ, now that we understand what it is, is the basis upon which our interactive relationship with God in Christ is based: "Abraham believed God and it was reckoned to him as righteousness" (Rom. 4:3). That is to say, God based his relationship to Abraham upon Abraham's confidence in God, not on Abraham having always done or continuing to do "the right thing." So with us. Obedience to Jesus Christ is not how we earn anything; it is simply the place where the kingdom of God is in relation to us. It is where we know it and where we know him. Merit is not the issue. Life is the issue: life beyond merit.

That enables us to get grace right. Grace is God acting in our life to bring about, and to enable us to do, what we cannot do on our own (2 Tim. 2:1). Inductive study of scripture, once again, will make this unmistakably clear. Grace is inextricably bound up with discipline in the life of the disciple or apprentice of Jesus. Discipline in the spiritual life is doing something in our power that enables us to do what we cannot do by direct effort—because in this way we meet the action of God (grace) with us, and the outcome is humanly inexplicable. This is what it means to speak of discipline as "a means to grace." Thus Jesus tells his puzzled and frightened friends that if they love him they will keep his commandments, and God will give them "another Helper" that will always be with them (John 14:15–16). Loving him, keeping his commandments, and Trinitarian cohabitation are inseparable parts of the life into which regeneration "naturally" develops (14:9–28).

Thus the famous statement of Jesus about truly being his disciples: "If you abide in my word, then you are truly disciples of mine, and you shall know the truth, and the truth shall make you free"

(John 8:31–32). The "abiding" here is "dwelling in" or living in. The word is μείνητε. It is the same basic term used in the great teaching of John 15:1–7: abide in me, as the branch dwells in the vine. But what does it mean to "abide in his word"? It means to put his words into action, to act according to them. When we do that we "inhale" the reality of the kingdom. That is what it means to be his "disciples indeed." And one who does this will come to know the truth, the reality, of the kingdom and of God's action with them, and that in turn will enable them to live free from the bondage of sin. This is exactly the situation that Paul is spelling out in Romans 6: "For sin shall not be master over you, for you are not under law, but under grace" (v. 14; "grace," of course, as an active agency in the psychological and biological reality of the disciple).

So we think like this: being a disciple (apprentice, student) of Jesus is the status into which regeneration naturally brings us, just because of the nature of the belief in Christ through which regeneration expresses itself. Discipleship to Jesus has as its natural outcome transformation of character—the hidden realities of heart, mind, soul, body, and social atmosphere—in such a way that conformity to his commands becomes the easy, routine, standard way the well-developed disciple comports himself or herself. (We of course are not talking about legalistic perfection, or perfection in the way it has been taken in most of the battles over that subject. And, of course, when we say "natural" here, we mean it in such a way that it does not exclude, but actually requires, the supernatural—as should be clear from what we have already said.)

It should be clear that we, with all our faults and failures, have an indispensable role in both discipleship and spiritual formation: "Be on the alert, stand firm in the faith, . . . be strong" (1 Cor. 16:13). Once we are clear that the issue is no longer merit, but life—that grace is not opposed to effort but to earning—this responsibility should cause no problem. We are quite prepared to hear the ceaseless admonitions to action set down in scripture, to welcome them, and to undertake the corresponding actions—as best we can, learning as we go. Paul's admonitions to "put off the old person and put on the new" now present themselves as something we are to do! James's directive to "prove yourselves doers of the word, and not merely hearers who delude themselves" (1:22) is completely appropriate. Jesus's own picture of the foolishness of those who hear him but do not do what he says (Luke 6:49) makes utter sense: "The grace of God which brings salvation" does not offer us a cushion, but "instructs us to deny ungodliness and worldly desires and to live sensibly, righteously and godly in the present age . . . zealous for good works" (Titus 2:11–14). That looks like the only way for a believer in Jesus to go anyway.

The key to it all, from the point of view of action, is indirection. We want to obey Jesus, and we know that we cannot do this just by trying to do what he said. We understand that we are broken—not only wrong but wrung, twisted, with parts that do not connect up right. We realize that our feelings, embedded in our body and its social context, are running and ruining our life, and producing godless and destructive actions under the direction of false ideas and images and messed-up patterns of thinking. We know that we must, instead of just trying to obey, find a way to become the kind of person who does, easily and routinely, what Jesus said—does it without having to think much about it, if at all, in the ordinary case.

It is here that disciplines come to our rescue, always encompassed by grace. In engaging disciplines, we go to the root of the tree of our life, the sources of behavior. We do the things that will transform our minds, our feelings, our will, our embodied and social existence, even the depths of our soul, to "make the tree good, and its fruit good" (Matt. 12:33). We cultivate and fertilize the tree (Luke 13:8). We don't try to squeeze fruit out of the ends of its branches. In doing this we use tried and true methods of Christ's people, as well as any sensible means at our disposal, including "professional help." And in this way we become, by divine grace, the kind of person who does the things Jesus said to do and avoids what he said not to do. From the point of view of our assemblies of disciples, we "teach disciples to do everything Jesus commanded" (Matt. 28:20).

So all of this—if we "get it"—can give us a practical hope when we look at remarkable New Testament passages such as 2 Peter 1:1–11, Colossians 3, and 1 Corinthians 13, or at the landmark literature of discipleship and spiritual formation generated by the lives of disciples throughout the Christian ages (Francis of Assisi, Hudson Taylor, Amy Carmichael, etc.).

In 2 Peter 1 the writer addresses "those who have received a faith of the same kind as ours by the righteousness of our God and Savior, Jesus Christ." He then prays that "Grace and peace be multiplied to you in the knowledge of [or "interactive relationship with"] God and of Jesus our Lord." He cites the fact that "through genuine knowledge of Him who called us to Him by His own glory and virtue . . . divine power has granted to us everything pertaining to life and godliness" (v. 3). All of this means that "He has given to us His precious and magnificent promises, in order that by them you might become partakers of divine nature, having escaped the corruption that is in the world by desire." (*Desire* is also translated as "lust"/επιθυμία.) This brings fully before us the picture of salvation as leading a life that is caught up in the kingdom of the heavens, or in what God is doing in human history. It is a life in which "God works all things together for good to those who love him and are absorbed into his purposes" (Rom. 8:28, PAR). It is a "resurrection life": a life already beyond death (John 8:51–52; 11:25–26; Col. 3:1–4).

And then there comes as a "natural part" of such life the active response of discipleship and spiritual (trans)formation. "Now for this very reason," the writer continues—or, "Because all of this is so"— "also, applying all diligence, in your faith achieve moral excellence ["virtue"/αρετήν], and in your moral excellence achieve knowledge, in your knowledge achieve self-control, in your self-control achieve endurance, in your endurance achieve constant adoration [ευσέβειαν], in your adoration achieve kindness to others [brotherly love], and in your kindness to others achieve divine love [αγάπην]" (2 Pet. 1:5–7).

We do not have time and space here to discuss each of these in turn, but an adequate course in discipleship and spiritual formation would go into each of these "additions" and explore how each lays a foundation for the later ones, and how each of the later ones enriches and strengthens the earlier ones. Also, such a course (should it not be the standard curriculum of our local assemblies and denominations?) would go into detail as to how, starting from faith, one achieves virtue, from virtue one achieves knowledge, and so forth, always presupposing divine assistance, grace, in the human progression. This would be done in a way that includes practical directions, training sessions, and disciplines, not just "information"—though the relevant information is crucial and currently is sorely lacking. Such details were not laid out in the New Testament because they were conveyed by the examples and practices of the communities arising out of the original fellowship of Jesus and his apostles.

The writer of 2 Peter, in any case, clearly assumes that "these qualities are yours and increasing," and that "they render you neither useless nor unfruitful in the genuine knowledge of our Lord Jesus Christ" (v. 8). That would be the natural progression and outcome of spiritual formation in the disciple. Diligence in this direction makes one sure of his "calling and election," "because as long as you practice these things, you will never stumble, and because in this way the entrance into the eternal kingdom of our Lord and Savior Jesus Christ will be abundantly supplied to you" (vv. 10–11). We should not assume that this latter "entrance" refers primarily to the famous "gates of splendor"—though that entrance is certainly grand and important, and is also included in the package. It, too, is a "natural part" of the life in question. Rather, the eternal kingdom mentioned, as the context should make clear, is the one Jesus announced as already "at hand," from which the regenerate person is drawing "the life that is life indeed" (1 Tim. 6:19).

Now, with all of this before us we can perhaps make good practical sense of the parting admonition of 2 Peter: "Grow in the grace and knowledge of our Lord and Savior Jesus Christ" (3:18). Grace, we have said, is God acting in our life to bring about results beyond human ability, and knowledge, biblically, is interactive relationship with what is known. They are two aspects of one reality in the concrete existence of the disciple of Jesus living out the process of spiritual formation. But for our purposes here it is vital to understand that we can, by our attitudes and actions, actually increase the amount of grace and knowledge of Christ that is in our lives. "Be strong in the grace that is in Christ Jesus," Paul instructs Timothy (2 Tim. 2:1). To increase in grace and knowledge is to open our life ever more fully to the presence/action of God with us in all we are and do. This is something we intentionally undertake and learn to do as we go. In Old Testament language it is to "acknowledge him in all our ways" (Prov. 3:5–7). It is increasingly to "humble ourselves under the mighty hand of God." On prevailing understandings of grace and salvation, however, 2 Peter 3:18 seems to remain in the category of pretty words without practical implications. "Christian education" now has the mandate to change that.

So, just to review and reemphasize: Regeneration, entry of God's nature and life into our real existence and identity, has, as a natural progression or part, entry into the status of discipleship to Jesus Christ in the power of the new life. Living in the status of disciple has, as a natural part and progression, spiritual formation in Christlikeness. Progression in spiritual formation in Christlikeness leads to easy, routine obedience to the commandments Christ brought to us, and to living the public life—from the inside out—that any sincere and thoughtful person would expect from the biblical record and the track record of the "great ones" in Christian history. In practice all of this is, no doubt, more ragged and messy than I have, for the sake of simplicity, made it look here, but the basic structure is clear and holds up in the demands of actual human existence.

But this leaves us with difficult practical problems facing the project of spiritual formation in Christlikeness in our local assemblies and in the larger units of Christian organization—even, indeed, in the "Christian" atmosphere of thought still pervading the Western world. We have to deal with a massive population of churched and unchurched people who think of "being saved" or "being right with God" merely in terms of some picture of justification, not regeneration. Being "born again" is usually understood now not in terms of being animated by a "life from above," but in terms of a profession of faith—often a profession of faith in the death of Christ as bearing the punishment for sin that otherwise would fall on us. This understanding usually prevails in ways that do not involve—may not even make mention of—participation in divine life. (And, of course, one can mention it without engaging it.) Then, of course, the otherwise natural progression into discipleship and its spiritual (trans)formation does not occur, and the churches and surrounding society are flooded with discipleshipless Christians whose lives seem not to differ profoundly, if at all, from those of non-Christians.

Because of human hunger for something deeper than a strictly physical existence, we then see multitudes who say that they are not religious (not "churched," they usually mean) but nonetheless are "very spiritual." Most often these are people who think they have seen, and seen through, the authentic Christian way. (Ironically, the "spirituality" they practice commonly has little or no bearing on their character, for they despise "morality" almost as much as they do "religion," and morality now is often lumped together or confused with religion: treated as "the same thing.")

For evangelical Christians, turning around the ship of their social reality, and restoring the understanding of salvation that characterized Evangelicalism from its beginnings in Luther, and periodically after him, will be very difficult if not impossible. It would primarily be a work of scriptural interpretation and theological reformulation, but modification of time-hardened practices will also be required. Radical changes in what we do in the way of "church" will have to be made.[3] This in turn will demand the utmost in loving character, humility of mind, and dependence upon the hand of God in a "with God" life.[4] But that is the way it is supposed to be anyway, is it not? It can be done and has been done, providing some of the most brilliant periods in the history of Christ's people.

I will suggest two steps on the way forward. One is that responsible leaders at all levels of Christian activity begin to exemplify and teach, in their official activities, spiritual formation in Christlikeness as something essential to the condition of "being saved"—not as a precondition but as a natural development. How that is to be worked out, avoiding "works righteousness" and legalism, is something that must be carefully elaborated in scriptural, theological, ecclesiastical, and psychological terms. The other is that efforts in evangelism and toward increasing "church membership" be very purposively reoriented toward bringing people to the point of regeneration and discipleship. The work of turning people to Christ is not done until that point. If we continue to make "converts" or "Christians," instead of disciples animated with the life from above that comes at "new" birth, spiritual formation and obedience to Christ (doing "all that he commanded") have little prospect other than that of a passing fad, which will certainly disappoint or will fade into diverse legalisms and vacuous "spiritualities"—things that fall entirely within human abilities, otherwise known as "the flesh."

The future of vital Christian life lies in the hands of the pastors and others who teach for Christ—especially including those who teach pastors. What will they do? The greatest field open for discipleship evangelism today is the North American and European churches and seminaries ("divinity" schools). They are full of people hungering for the real life that, surely we all know, is offered in companionship with Christ in his kingdom.

For Further Reading:

Richard J. Foster, *Life with God* (San Francisco: HarperOne, 2008).

Bernard Koerselman, *What the Bible Says About a Saving Faith* (Newton, KS: Berean Publishers, 1992).

Martin Luther, *Preface to St. Paul's Epistle to the Romans,* trans.
Charles E. Hay (Philadelphia: Lutheran Publication Society,
1903), especially the sections on what faith is.

Henry Scougal, "The Life of God in the Soul of Man," in *The Works
of the Rev. H. Scougal* (Boston: Crocker & Brewster, 1833).
First published in 1677. Reprint, Kessinger Publishing, ISBN
0548154732.

Dallas Willard, *Renovation of the Heart* (Colorado Springs, CO:
NavPress, 2002).

CHAPTER 27

The Faith of Unbelief

One of the main themes in Dallas's writing and ministry was the importance of language. He believed that the definition and use of words mattered deeply since words can either clarify or confuse crucial aspects of Christian life and thought. Here Dallas attempts to define *faith* and *unbelief* and examines the consequences when these crucial Christian concepts are not properly understood.

(Previously unpublished)

FIRST OF ALL, DISCUSSING THE ISSUE OF UNBELIEF NEED NOT BE A *tu quoque* session. That is, it isn't necessary to reproach the unbeliever for not having faith as a way of trying to justify religious belief. Faith here is understood not as a profession of something you do not believe, but as belief, trust, and reliance upon something. You believe in A, or that P, if and to the degree that you are ready to act with reliance upon A or as if P were the case. Thus we can state that we always "live up to" (or "down to," but really . . . right at) the level of our true beliefs. We can also state that unbelief, in the context of the present discussion, is not simply a lack of belief, in the sense that I now have no beliefs at all about most individual things that exist. Rather, *unbelief* here will refer to what is more properly called disbelief: a readiness to act as if certain things were not so. Thus unbelief is a species of belief involving negation.

More precisely still, by unbelief in the present context we are referring to belief that a certain set of claims made by traditional Christianity—roughly, what C. S. Lewis referred to as "Mere Christianity"—are false. We are thinking of the person who is set to act as if they were false, and this personality set is what we mean here as speaking of the faith of unbelief.

The idea that there is an ethics of belief and unbelief is founded on the subassumptions that:

1. We ought to do what is beneficial for human life.
2. Our beliefs can cause great good or harm, especially with regard to their truth or falsity, and truth may be regarded as good in itself, regardless of consequences.
3. We have, indirectly, some degree of control over the beliefs that we have, and hence some responsibility to see to it that they are true or at least rational.

In his essay "The Ethics of Belief," W. K. Clifford claimed that it is always wrong to believe anything on insufficient evidence.[1] To which William James effectively replied (in his "The Will to Believe") that such a claim is too stringent. There are many issues that cannot be decided on the basis of "sufficient" evidence, where much of value is at stake, where we must decide (to take the plane or not, for example, or to believe in God or not) and we have a preference. Here James says,

> Our passional nature not only lawfully may, but must, decide, . . . for to say, under such circumstances, "do not decide, but leave the question open," is itself a passional decision—just like deciding yes or no—and is attended with the same risks of losing truth.[2]

James saw that you could "lose the truth" by not believing as well as by believing, and that it is irrational to think it is better not to believe than to believe, given only that you lack sufficient evidence on the positive side. Clifford actually expresses the contemporary prejudice that the one who doubts is automatically smarter. James saw that one has to earn the right to disbelieve as much as the right to believe. Basically: disbelief is a form of belief. Pascal made essentially the same point much earlier with his famous "Wager."[3]

Let us give this much to Clifford: that we should make a sincere effort to ensure that our beliefs are true, that we are morally obliged to do so, and that to do anything less, to be careless about the truth of significant beliefs, is to be legitimately subject to moral censure. The believer or disbeliever who is careless about truth and evidence is less than they should be, for they are careless of human good.

Since truth is not always manifestly attainable, we do not have an obligation to have true beliefs. *But we always have a moral obligation to do what is possible to ensure that our beliefs are true.* That is, to be irrational is to be morally irresponsible, and to be morally admirable we must be rational because of the fundamental importance of true beliefs to human welfare.

But who is the rational person? Persons are reasonable in the degree to which they conform their thinking, talk, and action to the order of truth and understanding or are effectively committed to doing that so far as is possible. They will characteristically endeavor to reason soundly (validly, from true premises), and be open-minded and inquiring about the issues that require a response from them. They will seek the best concepts, classifications, and theories, testing those concepts, classifications, and theories by relating them to each other and to the world given by their experience and the experience of others. They will respect facts more than theories, and take pains to determine the facts relevant to their beliefs. (This is only an attempt to characterize the rational person, not to give necessary and sufficient conditions of being a rational person.)

By contrast, the unreasonable person characteristically: does not thoroughly inquire into the basis for his beliefs, contradicts himself, rejects known means to his chosen goals or ends, demands the impossible, refuses to test or consider criticisms of his beliefs, and fails to seek better means of ascertaining the truth.

Turning back to the "faith" of "unbelief" explained above, we currently experience that "unbelief" rarely holds itself responsible to be rational as we have described it about the following issues:

1. About the nature of ultimate reality or about which reality is ultimate—specifically, the Christian view that reality is ultimately personal and subject to personal will that is intelligent and loving. By contrast, a rather typical statement: "Christianity lost its credibility by and large in the course of the eighteenth century. . . . Such Christianity as did survive was no longer secure even within the Christian churches. . . . The leading thinkers and artists of Christendom were virtually all de-Christianized even before Darwin in 1859 provided a credible alternative to Creation."[4] Darwin provided what?

2. About the historical claims of the "biblical" tradition. For example, that there was a person whom we call Jesus Christ. That he was human and more. That he was killed and continued to exist, resuming personal contacts—though admittedly of a rather unusual character—with those who knew him before his death.

3. About the current experience of human beings in the life of belief. For example, "miracles" of various kinds, as acts of God in response to prayer or action. You rarely ever find anyone who rejects such "miracles" who has made a point of examining a single one that thoughtful Christian reflection has marked as such. As the bishop said to Galileo, "I don't need to look. I already know."

4. About the ethical superiority of Christ's teachings and of life conforming thereto. Generally speaking, it is assumed that you can safely omit serious thought about this matter and stick to John Stuart Mill or John Rawls. Jesus is at best an irrelevant idealist; at worst the sponsor of the ethical disaster that is Western Civilization.

There really is no reason in the general nature of reality why "Mere Christianity" or any other view should or should not be true.

This constitutes what older thinkers used to refer to as the "antecedent credibility" of Christianity (or other views).

This leads to the suggestion of a thesis regarding the nature of the faith required of unbelief: most of "the faith of unbelief" that exists today in the concrete form of individual personalities is morally irresponsible—because not rationally sustained—and would be recognized as the superstition it most often is, but for the fact that it is vaguely endorsed by the socially prevailing intellectual system. One might be rational, as above defined, and not believe, in my opinion. But I think this is highly unlikely, and am sure it rarely ever actually occurs. (This opens up another set of issues about belief in relation to evidence.)

If, now, one says that current belief is just as morally irresponsible as current unbelief, or even more so, we can only ask: "And how does that help?" Do we not, whoever we are, owe it to ourselves and those around us to be serious about questions of major importance to human well-being?

CHAPTER 28

Lessons from the Life of Jesus

In concert with his investigations of soteriology, the study of salvation, Dallas's theological reflections tended to focus most deeply on the subject of Christology. The following essay focuses on the means by which Jesus revealed life "from above" within his specific cultural contexts, and the unequaled ethical framework his life and teachings provide for all humanity to follow.

First published in 2011 as "Jesus," chapter six
of the *Dictionary of Christian Spirituality*

CHRISTIAN SPIRITUALITY HAS AT ITS CENTER JESUS OF NAZARETH, acknowledged by believers to be both savior and Lord. To be a Christian, then, is to follow this Jesus. To appreciate what this has involved, and must continue to involve, it may be helpful to consider very briefly the dynamics that explain and shape all human spiritualties. For spirituality, viewed broadly, is indeed a universal dimension of human life. It arises out of the human quest for a place, an identity, and powers that are more than the "mere facts" of human existence. It seeks to make meaningful contact with, and draw substance from, that "more," that "higher power." Such a quest is the source of religions as we find them in our world, but it is not limited to religion. It constantly overflows and renews religion—very often by opposing what religion has become.

325

In their origin and development religions are profoundly shaped by the spiritual journeys of individuals. In the case of Christianity, this has been supremely the life story of Jesus. In turn each religion, as a concrete social reality, makes a distinct spirituality available to those in significant contact with it, and that spirituality always has two main dimensions. These two dimensions are dependent upon and simultaneously in tension with each other. They are, first, the human forms, outwardly recognizable patterns of behavior, events, and equipage that yield the many different "spiritualities" familiar to us; and second, the transcendental interconnection that lies outside of and within human forms and institutions, inhabiting them but always challenging, correcting, and modifying them.

Through the centuries distinctively Christian spirituality has involved the endeavor to conform individual and social life to what Jesus did and said—more deeply still, to who he was and is. He lived out in his own person a spirituality that had both a human and a transcendental dimension. His followers through the ages, in adoration of him, have sought to penetrate to the core of his spirituality and to make it their own. Sometimes this has been a very explicit quest, as in the famous work of Thomas à Kempis, *The Imitation of Christ* (1471), and in the *Imitatio Christi* tradition generally, but it has always been an implicit reality of the Christian life.

In its outward dimension (i.e., in the part necessarily expressed in human society and culture), the spirituality of Jesus was that of a serious Jewish young man—eventually a rabbi—living in the period of mature, post-exilic Judaism. He was brought up and lived for the most part in outlying areas of the Jewish homeland under Roman occupation; but he was thoroughly immersed from his youth in the teachings, traditions, and official practices of the Jewish religion of his day. He lived and died within the outward forms of that religion, even while, as a true son of Israel, he drew from "the law and the prophets" a vision of the whole world under God's rule (Isa. 49:6; Ps. 46:10).

Freeing human life from the tyranny of certain specific cultural—especially religious—forms was one of the main thrusts of his life and ministry, and a major part of the task his followers inherited from him. Staying within the Jewish forms of his day, at many points he challenged those forms as practiced around him, but always from within the resources of the law and the prophets. He constantly contrasted the heart of the law, or God's intent with his laws, to the distortions and misapplications those laws had undergone at the hands of the "power people" or authorities of his day—"the scribes and the Pharisees." They used and abused "the law" to shut people away from God and to impose, for their own advantage, impossible burdens upon the masses of simple people they were supposed to serve. By critiquing them, Jesus continued the ancient prophetic tradition of Israel: that of the insider who is also an outsider, standing among people in the presence and power of God.

The spirituality of Jesus Christ was in that precise sense incarnational. To use that word, however, is not to refer only to the metaphysical nature of Christ, as is usually done. Rather, it is an indication of two different realms coming together to form a unique kind of life, in which human life in the world is an expression of divine life surpassing the world. The fullest expression of this "incarnation" is perhaps given in Jesus's prayer of John 17: "I have given them your word, and the world has hated them because they do not belong to the world, just as I do not belong to the world. . . . As you, Father, are in me and I am in you, may they also be in us, so that the world may believe that you have sent me" (vv. 14, 21, NRSV). Christ followers are, it is often said, "in the world but not of it." In the words of the apostle Paul, "Our citizenship is in heaven" (Phil. 3:20).

The spirituality of Jesus Christ and of his followers is therefore a twofold life. It is, on the one hand, an ordinary human existence of birth, family and social context, work, and death, shared by all human beings, including Jesus himself. That is what it means to be "in the world." The spirituality of Jesus is not flight from the world.

But it is also a life of knowing God by interactive relationship with him as we live in the world. It is eternal living (*aionios zoe;* John 17:3) here and now. It expresses itself within ordinary human life through understandings, events, and characteristics that cannot be explained by the natural capacities of human beings or the natural course of events in "the world." It is accordingly "of the spirit and not of the flesh." This distinction, along with the warfare of spirit and flesh, is a focal point of the spirituality of Christ and the Christ follower, and a direct consequence of its incarnational nature.

The language Jesus used to express the spiritual side of the two-fold life was the language of "the kingdom of the heavens" or "the kingdom of God." The kingdom of God, which is exercised from "the heavens" around us, is the domain of God's action: it is where what he wants done is actually done. Jesus worked and spoke in terms of the kingdom of God. He proclaimed or "preached" the direct accessibility to all of life in this "kingdom of heaven" (Matt. 4:17; Mark 1:15), he manifested the presence of God's action with him through deeds of power, and he taught about how things were done, what life would be like, for those living under the rule of God. (On this threefold ministry of proclaiming, manifesting, and teaching, see Matt. 4:23, 9:35.) Thus one of his most oft repeated phrases is: "The kingdom of the heavens is like . . ." After his resurrection he was in and out among his friends "during forty days and spoke about the kingdom of God" (Acts 1:3). The message of the kingdom's presence and availability through faith in Christ was committed to the disciples and carries on through the book of Acts (28:23, 31) and beyond.

So the spirituality of Jesus was a twofold life: Jewish in outward form, but drawn, on the divine side, from the kingdom of the heavens, as a domain of reality in which one lives now. In the life of Jesus as presented in the Gospels, his spirituality was characterized by a number of traits that have also been prominent in the lives of his followers.

INDEPENDENCE FROM HUMAN AUTHORITY

That he had authority—that is, the power, and not just the right, to direct thought, action, and events around him—was never in doubt. The effects of his power were obvious, and that is repeatedly brought out in the Gospels. That it did not derive from human sources was also obvious, for human authority was mainly set against him, and eventually caused his death. He was questioned concerning the source of his authority (Luke 20:2), but no one doubted he had authority. His implicit reply to the question was that his authority came from heaven. John the Baptizer had authority from heaven, and his "endorsement" of Jesus put the stamp of "heaven" on Jesus.

Jesus was, however, not the disciple of John, or of any other prophet or rabbi. Jesus's effects in speaking and acting manifestly originated from the God who was "with him" (Acts 10:38). That was an essential part of his spirituality. He endowed his followers with that same authority (Luke 9:1–2; Acts 1:7–8). Independence from human authority—so often exercised, unfortunately, in the name of God, yet in a manner contrary to his character and purposes—is nonetheless a constant factor in Christian spirituality, from Jesus and his first followers up to the present day. Its watchword in this respect is always, "We must obey God rather than any human authority" (Acts 5:29, NRSV; cf. 4:20).

THE GREAT INVERSION

"What is prized by human beings is an abomination in the sight of God" (Luke 16:15, NRSV). And, it was also clear to Jesus that what is prized by God is often an abomination in the sight of men. The two sides of the twofold life offer very different vantage points on what is good and what is important—on what "success" in life really amounts to. This was a note often struck in the Old Testament, but Jesus relentlessly drives it home in every aspect of his life and teaching. He repeatedly emphasizes that "many who are first will be last, and the last will be first" (Matt. 19:30, NRSV). His most remarkable statements on this point—and perhaps the most misunderstood— are the "beatitudes" of Matthew 5 and Luke 6. He himself was among the humanly "unblessables" in his birth, life, and death—as the great "kenosis" passage of Philippians 2:7–8 so clearly spells out. But he was blessed before God nonetheless. Down in the human order (poor, mournful, etc.) may well be up (among the blessed) in the divine order. Up in the human order (rich, popular) may well be down ("Woe to . . .") in God's order. Well-being is not at all what humans routinely take it to be. But anyone alive in the kingdom of God, no matter what their circumstances may be, is blessed, well off. The servant is regarded by human beings as among the lowest of the low. But in the spirituality of Jesus, "the greatest among you must become like the youngest, and the leader like one who serves. For who is greater, the one who is at the table or the one who serves? Is it not the one at the table? But I am among you as one who serves" (Luke 22:26–27, NRSV).

THE PRACTICE OF THE PRESENCE OF GOD

The spirituality of Jesus is unthinkable apart from the presence of God with him. In the times when he was alone from the human point of view, God was with him (John 8:16, 29; 16:32). On the cross, apparently, he was allowed to experience being forsaken by God, as he "taste[d] death for everyone" (Heb. 2:9). But his oneness with the Father was unbroken. The covenant people from Abraham onward had lived interactively with the God who was with them. That accounted for the manifold types of extrahuman effects and accomplishments that characterized individuals as well as the people of Israel together. The tabernacle in the wilderness was an arrangement made in order for God to dwell among the children of Israel and be their God: "And they shall know that I am the Lord their God, who brought them out of the land of Egypt, that I might dwell among them; I am the Lord their God" (Exod. 29:46, NRSV). God was so manifestly with Isaac, for example, that his powerful neighbors asked him to move away—and then came to ask him to move back, because "we see plainly that the Lord has been with you" (Gen. 26:16, 28, NRSV). Looking back upon the career of Jesus the apostle, Peter explains "how God anointed Jesus of Nazareth with the Holy Spirit and with power; how he went about doing good and healing all who were oppressed by the devil, for God was with him" (Acts 10:38, NRSV). The "practice of the presence" is today one of the strongest themes in Christian spirituality.

COMPLETE SECURITY AND A WORRY-FREE EXISTENCE

Jesus taught and practiced a life of peace and joy in the knowledge of God's complete nearness and care, and he offered that life to his disciples as well. Such life lay at the very heart of his own spirituality. His mastery over events and people through faith in God, and the presence of God with him, never left him at a loss, no matter the situation. Though sometimes saddened to tears, or exasperated by the ineptitude of his students, only in the supernatural struggle with evil in Gethsemane, on the way to the cross, and then upon the cross, do we witness his vulnerability—his "passion" (John 12:27). No doubt it was from him that Paul learned how to be "afflicted in every way, but not crushed; perplexed, but not driven to despair" (2 Cor. 4:8, NRSV).

He could enjoy the company of "publicans and sinners." He could continue his nap in the storm, though the boat was filling with water and his disciples were scared out of their wits. After calming the storm he asked them: "Why are you afraid? Have you still no faith?" (Mark 4:40, NRSV). Surely his friends must have wondered at these questions. They simply did not yet see what he saw.

He knew that there was no reason to be afraid of those who can kill the body but after that have no more that they can do

(Luke 12:4). "Whoever keeps my word," he said, "shall never see death" (John 8:51, NRSV). "Keepers of his word" will have already passed from death to life. There also is no need for them to worry about food or clothing or the material provisions for life (Luke 12:22–31). One has only to devote oneself to living in the kingdom, and every provision will be made—though perhaps not to the world's taste. Provisions for this life and beyond are made by the Father, who watches over everything and is always with us. Joy, the pervasive sense of well-being, is the condition in which we live the kingdom life.

The early believers knew the secret: "Keep your lives free from the love of money, and be content with what you have; for he has said, 'I will never leave you or forsake you.' So we can say with confidence, 'The Lord is my helper; I will not be afraid. What can anyone do to me?'" (Heb. 13:5–6, NRSV). Writing to the Philippians from his prison cell, citing the fact that "the Lord is near," Paul echoes the instruction of Jesus (Matt. 6:25–34) not to worry about anything. Rather, "in everything by prayer and supplication with thanksgiving let your requests be made known to God. And the peace of God, which surpasses all understanding, will guard your hearts and minds in Christ Jesus" (Phil. 4:4–7, NRSV).

SUBVERSIVE OF "THE WORLD"

The picture of Jesus's spirituality that emerges from the above points naturally leads to appropriate subversion of merely human arrangements, which are largely based on fear. Subversion was the charge that led to the death of those early Christians who would not worship Caesar, and it is the charge that has been repeated through the ages, up to today in many parts of the world. The charge upon which Jesus was crucified was, essentially, that of subversion of the religious and political orders. In his encounter with Pilate, Pilate said to Jesus: "Do you not know that I have power to release you, and power to crucify you?" Jesus answered him: "You would have no power over me unless it had been given you from above" (John 19:10–11, NRSV). The source of governmental power is the same as the source of the "new birth" (it is *anōthen* [Greek, "from above"]).

Then Jesus proceeded through death to destroy the one who has the power of death, and thus to set "free those who all their lives were held in slavery by the fear of death" (Heb. 2:15, NRSV). The primary human instrument of repression and control—the fear of death—is set aside by Jesus and his good news about eternal living now in the kingdom of God. He "abolished death and brought life and immortality to light through the gospel" (2 Tim. 1:10, NRSV). The Christ follower honors those to whom honor is due, but always "under God." It is because they stand under eternal authority and power that they more than any others stand for what is good, whether with or against those who have responsibility in human affairs. This, too, is the spirituality of Jesus Christ, and it is radically subversive. The ultimate "subversion" would of course be at the coming of "the day of the Lord," when the "kingdoms" of this world would have become the kingdom of our God and of his Christ.

DEATH TO SELF

Unlimited abandonment to God is essential to the spirituality Jesus lived and taught. He did not have to go to the cross. No one made him. It was his choice when there were other paths he could have taken. Choice is sacred to God, but what is best to choose? Faced with options, he saw that "unless a grain of wheat falls into the earth and dies, it remains just a single grain; but if it dies, it bears much fruit. Those who love their life lose it, and those who hate their life in this world will keep it for eternal life. Whoever serves me must follow me" (John 12:24–26, NRSV). Abandonment to God is the fruitful way to experience good under God. It means relinquishing "our way." It means not being angry or resentful when things do not go our way. It means that in God's hands we are content for him to take charge of outcomes. And in that posture we make way for him to occupy our lives with us, and achieve what is best for us and for others far beyond anything we can even imagine. "I am crucified with Christ." His abandonment becomes our abandonment. "Nevertheless, I live" (Gal. 2:19–20). His resurrection becomes our resurrection—even before our "physical" death (Col. 3:1–4). Death to self is not ultimately a negation, but a rising up into the very life of God (2 Pet. 1:4). Thus our life is saved by his life (Rom. 5:10).

The positive aspect of the "if it dies" is "bears much fruit." The death he chose was for the sins of the world. It was not just to lose life, but also to give life. This is what prevents his death, and Christian "death to self," from being morbid. It was for the "joy that was set before him" that he "endured the cross, despising the shame" (Heb. 12:2, NRSV). According to the ancient prophecy, he "saw the work accomplished by his suffering and was satisfied" (Isa. 53:11). "He died for all, so that those who live might live no longer for themselves, but for him who died and was raised for them" (2 Cor. 5:15, NRSV). The mark of his disciples, accordingly—that they "love one another just as he loved them" (John 13:34)—is simply the outflow of transcendent life that comes through self-giving death.

These are a few outstanding points in the incarnational spirituality of Jesus Christ, which he shares with us today. Many people will find them surprising, because they have come to think of him and his spirituality, roughly speaking, in "monastic" terms. This widely shared vision of him sees him as withdrawing from the world and from "natural" human existence in order to be "spiritual." But for all of the virtues that may be found in monasticism, Jesus and his students were not monastics. Theirs was a spirituality of engagement with the world—a spirituality of stewardship, which hears the words "Do business with these until I come back" (Luke 19:13, NRSV) and rises up, in the face of all opposition, to conduct normal human affairs in the power of God.

To succeed with this indeed requires a life disciplined under grace. We learn to follow Jesus by entering into the activities he practiced. Effectual spirituality in the manner of Jesus demands wise, nonlegalistic spiritual disciplines that nurture spiritual formation in Christ. But practicing spiritual disciplines is not itself spirituality. Spirituality is the life from God flowing through our life, which spiritual disciplines, rightly used, can help to facilitate. Indeed, the kingdom walk with Christ is no life as usual among human beings, but an intelligent and spiritually informed course of regular activity that maximizes interactive relationship with the Trinity in the two-fold life.

For Further Reading:

William Barclay, *Jesus as They Saw Him: New Testament Interpretations of Jesus* (Grand Rapids, MI: Eerdmans, 1978).

Alfred Edersheim, *The Life and Times of Jesus the Messiah* (New York: Longmans, Green, 1904).

Otto Karrer and Nora Wydenbruck, *St. Francis of Assisi: The Legends and Lauds* (New York: Sheed & Ward, 1948).

Malcolm Muggeridge, *Jesus, the Man Who Lives* (New York: Harper & Row, 1975).

Jaroslav Pelikan, *Jesus Through the Centuries: His Place in the History of Culture* (New Haven, CT: Yale Univ. Press, 1985).

Joseph Ratzinger, *Jesus of Nazareth* (New York: Doubleday, 2007).

Dallas Willard, *The Spirit of the Disciplines: Understanding How God Changes Lives* (San Francisco: HarperSanFrancisco, 1991).

N. T. Wright, *Jesus and the Victory of God: Christian Origins and the Question of God* (Minneapolis: Fortress Press, 1992).

CHAPTER 29

The Foundations of Moral Realization

As a philosophy professor, Dallas came from an intellectual background that was concerned with ethics and truth. His religious writings reflected this interest in morality. Here, Dallas defines the essential Christian virtues as they stand on their own and as they compare to the virtues of other world religions.

Written as "Faith, Hope and Love as Indispensable Foundations of Moral Realization" (previously unpublished)

Inclining apparently to avoid moral trespassing and seeking above all to be scholarly, not admonitory and didactic, the ethicists, philosophical and religious, have left out what is crucial—the primary ethical stuff. For the depiction and pursuit of actual virtues, the terribly homely business of learning how to be polite in difficult circumstances; always prompt; courageous when threatened: temperate when zig-zagging looks right; "just" when advantages lie in injustices: these and more are the achievements, the habitual achievements, that make up the virtues. Without these, there simply is no primitive working content for the moral life. Surely there is, then, no clarity about moral concepts either.

—Paul Holmer[1]

THIS ESSAY WILL ENDEAVOR TO UNDERSCORE THE UNIQUENESS OF Christian ethics. Yet I presume that the issue before us is not merely the uniqueness found in a Christian form of ethics—which, after all, might consist in some relatively trivial point of behavior, even one marking the way of Christ as ethically inferior to other moral traditions or outlooks. Rather, it seems to me that what is of primary importance here is whether the moral system (including a properly ethical or theoretical component) of the way of Christ is significantly superior to systems associated with various other religious and secular traditions. If so, then a Christlike perspective on ethics will most certainly be unique.

Perhaps it is not proper to say it in today's social and intellectual atmosphere, but I confess at the outset my belief that from the traditionally accepted teachings of Christ (including his example) there can be drawn a morality and an ethical theory that are significantly superior to the other systems that have been concretized in the history of the earth. In what follows I shall try to explain why I stand by this. I will also confess that I have been socially conditioned to believe in the significant superiority of the ethics of Christ. But it does not follow that there are no good reasons to sustain that belief. We are socially conditioned to accept many beliefs that are also rationally supportable, as well as many that are not.

Finally, I confess that it would be very surprising if the disciples of Jesus did not agree with me. Perhaps I shall be surprised. But I find it difficult to imagine this particular subclass of the population concurring with some such comment as the following:

"Well, it is true that one is no better off morally for being a Christian. The relation (whatever it may be) of God to our lives as disciples of Jesus in the kingdom of God has no general tendency whatsoever to help us understand moral reality better or to realize that reality more fully in our individual lives. The degree of understanding and realization of moral ideals has no regular connection with being a Christian or not. Nevertheless, I choose to continue my life as a practicing Christian and to recommend such a life for adoption by others."

Not that the moral advantage (if there is such) is the only thing

that matters about Christian faith and life. Prudential, social, aes-
thetical, and possibly other considerations, such as historical truth
or pure cosmological theory or ontology, well might be cited in
an overall comparison of the Christian way with others. Nor do I
suggest that Christians base their relationships to God or to other
personal beings upon moral superiority. Precisely not, according to
the view of Christ and his friends! But on the other hand it is not
clear to me what it would mean to be a follower of Christ and yet to
allow that the possibilities of moral understanding and life are equal
to or better than, say, a Buddhist or Mohammedan, or as a strictly
secular Marxist or hedonistic utilitarian, or as an existentialist of
the Sartrean variety. In any case, it would certainly make news if
Christians were to decide that there is no moral advantage associated
with the Christian religion. (Less worthy of note would be a decision
that we cannot know the way of Christ to be ethically superior, or
that there is no objective scale of comparison against which such
judgments could be made.)

If there is a moral advantage to being (in some sense) a Christian, what is it? Clarifications are required before we can respond to
this question. First of all, we are not speaking of an advantage that
automatically accrues to all who sincerely apply to themselves the
term *Christian*. We do not suggest that every person who identifies
with Christianity is in a better moral position than anyone who does
not. A recent poll reports that four out of five people in the United
States now identify themselves as Christian. This could easily throw
one into despair. Kierkegaard's poignant question presents itself: "If
we are Christians—What then is God?"[2] So, in short, I do not here
wish to make any claims about the moral superiority of Christianity
as a cultural identification—though the moral significance of that
identification as contrasted with others might also prove interesting
to explore.

But if our question is not about the moral advantage of Christianity as a general cultural form, what is it about? It is, I suggest, best
understood by reference to a certain picture of the good person and

of praiseworthy action that is derivable from "the definitive Christian moral teachings." Without belaboring the point in the manner it deserves, I will take this vague but necessary phrase to refer primarily to the central New Testament texts that deal with what we ought to be and do. These include Matthew 5–7 and 18; Mark 8:34–38 and 12:28–34; Luke 14 and 15; John 13–17; Romans 8 and 12–14; 1 Corinthians 13; Galatians 5 and 6; Philippians 3 and 4; Colossians 3 and 4; and 1 John. But I also mean to include among the definitive Christian moral teachings the time-tested interpretations and expressions of these and similar passages from the Bible as a whole that have developed during the history of the church and that have found a broad constituency among those who thoughtfully and deliberately accept, as the overriding imperative of their lives, to be like Christ. From these writings and traditions there emerges, it seems to me, a moral ideal for personality that is superior to comparable ideals from other traditions. What does this mean?

William Frankena and of course many others regard morality as (whatever else) "an instrument of society as a whole for the guidance of individuals and smaller groups."[3] In my view, however, the moral guidance offered by society always has to do primarily with what sorts of persons we must be in order to be good persons. Our actions certainly are important and are morally significant in numerous ways, but our character is of much greater importance morally than are our actions, to others as well as to ourselves. The moral quality of my actions as my actions, and not merely as an instance of some general type of action, is dependent upon my character: the pervasive and long-range governing tendencies of feeling, thought, and will that I have acquired through the experiences and choices that determine my life as a whole and of which my actions are only a very partial expression.

Now, Aristotle, as is well known, pointed out that "actions . . . are called just and temperate when they are such as the just or temperate man would do; but it is not the man who does these that is just and temperate, but the man who also does them as just and temperate men do them."[4] Kant emphasized the distinction between acts that are right (those with universalizable maxims) and those that are praiseworthy (those where the respect for law present within them is the determining ground of the actions).[5] But increasingly in the modern period we have come to emphasize the (presumed) moral worth of the right action as an abstract type, treating actions as having a moral quality separable from the moral praiseworthiness that involves the action's ground in the life of the agent. (The excessive emphasis on rights that, it seems to me, is so characteristic of contemporary moral thought is at least highly consistent with this drive toward moral externalism.)

No doubt some good purposes are served for moral theory by singling out and specifying the general types of actions that are characteristically done by the good person. This may be especially attractive in an age that places as little stock on inward states as ours does, and finds it almost impossible to comprehend the idea of an ineluctably hidden or implicit self or soul as a significant factor in human life and morality. But I am inclined to think that the mere action correctly identified as the just, temperate, and so forth act, or the "right" act generally, has no moral worth at all as distinctive from a certain prudential and social value. ("Honesty is the best policy.") Whatever is left over to count as "rightness" once the moral substance of the agent is extracted from the action should perhaps not be treated as a moral value.

All moral considerations aside, of course, my neighbor will prefer that I not lie to him, steal his auto, or molest his children. It certainly is also in my interest not to do these things. To be able to single out the abstract type of act and understand its significance for society is obviously important for human life. But I am unwilling to agree that that importance is a moral one, or that morality is seen at work in the guidance that society gives merely to secure acts of the abstract types characteristic of the good person. I would like to reserve moral significance for what essentially contributes to or constitutes a part of the moral worth of persons, what makes them good as persons; and the mere (even frequent, even exceptionless) commission of acts that are the same in abstract type as those characteristically performed by the good person does not do so.

The morally good person will usually be, I would argue, "useful" to himself or herself, and to society, as are no others. One recalls Aristotle's observation that the virtues are chosen "for themselves (for if nothing resulted from them we should still choose each of them), but we choose them also for the sake of happiness, judging that by means of them we shall be happy."[6] Nicolai Hartmann insightfully comments on how good persons are also goods:

> Persons are goods for one another and just because of their moral quality; to his fellow-citizens the just man is a good of a higher order, likewise the friend to his friend. But to be a good in this way presupposes the morality of the person. It cannot therefore constitute it. The goods-value depends upon the moral value. For the person has the moral value in himself, in his purely inward, secret disposition, independently of whether he becomes a good to anybody.[7]

The morally good person is, I suggest, to be thought of as one who is admired and imitated just for what he or she is, and without any essential reference to specific relationships, talents, skills, or useful traits they may have. Kant spoke of the moral character that he called "good will," and contrasted it with natural qualities of mind or temperament and gifts of fortune. He noted that talents and gifts of fortune "can never give pleasure to an impartial, rational spectator" if they are unaccompanied by goodwill.[8] The pleasure here in question is not just any pleasure, but the special one associated with the attitude of admiration. (We greatly envy the person who is fortunate or talented without admiring them, and those we admire may have or exemplify nothing that we would envy—that is, that we would like to have while remaining otherwise just the same sorts of persons we are.) And Kant's "spectator" should, of course, not only be impartial, but also sensitive, intelligent, and well informed about the possibilities of human personality. But, with these additions, I think it correct that there is a widespread and penetrating insight into human goodness (not rightness of action), quite accessible to ordinary persons of good sense. My claim is that, to the type of common moral insight that Kant had in mind, operating under ideal conditions, the Christian model of the good person will commend itself both as unique and as better on the scale of human goodness than the historically developed alternatives.

Henry Sidgwick's general concept of good as the desirable may also prove useful here:

> Meaning by "desirable" not necessarily "what ought to be desired" but what would be desired, with strength proportioned to the degree of desirability, if it were judged attainable by voluntary action, supposing the desirer to possess a perfect forecast, emotional as well as intellectual, of the state of attainment or fruition.[9]

The good person might then be thought of as the desirable one, in the sense of the one we would desire to be "if it were judged attainable by voluntary action, supposing the desirer to possess a perfect forecast, emotional as well as intellectual, of the state of attainment or fruition."

But is it possible to say anything more about the good person than that he or she is the type of person one would desire to be, given certain ideal conditions? I think that it is, and that much more has been said, by teachers of religion and outstanding literary figures, as well as by the great moral philosophers. The discussions of human virtue by Aristotle, Hume, and, in our century, Nicolai Hartmann are representative of the philosophers. What does not seem to me to be possible is to find an illuminating general formula that comprehends all of human moral excellence or, as Hume puts it, "personal." Aristotle's attempt to find such a formula in the doctrine of the mean, if that is what he is doing there, does not, finally, serve that purpose well. It is drawn from considerations of how one trains for excellence in any art,[10] and no doubt also expresses some significant truth about how those acknowledged to be masters of "the art of life" calibrate feeling and action to avoid excess and defect in the given situation. But I do not see how we can eliminate "intellectual" virtue either from Aristotle's account of human virtue or from any adequate account, and the mean is of no use in explicating it.

Hume also is troubled by a dichotomy within virtue. He "defines virtue to be whatever mental action or quality gives to a spectator the pleasing sentiment of approbation; and vice the contrary."[11]Among these pleasing mental features he distinguishes those that are useful and those that are agreeable, either to himself or to others.[12] But it seems possible that some mental traits that please might well have nothing to do with moral worth: cleverness, for example, or intellectual creativity (genius). Indeed, Hume includes just such traits in his lists of moral qualities. Also, the relation of usefulness to moral worth or value is and has been one of the main problems for moral theory, and much the same could be said for agreeableness or pleasantness. Moreover, the relation between the useful and the agreeable is unclear, and there is no reason given to suppose that the disjunction "agreeable/useful" is complete. (From Cudworth on, the moral "intuitionists" have thought not.) One suspects that instead of a definition or formula of essence for personal merit, one is being offered only a two-membered list.

Possibly an open-ended list of virtues is as close as we can come to a statement of what the good person is like. That seems to me to be precisely the case. Aristotle in one place lists as "the forms of virtue, . . . justice, courage, temperance, magnificence, magnanimity, liberality, gentleness, prudence, wisdom."[13] So far as I can tell he never commits himself to having a complete list of the virtues, and other virtues than the above are mentioned in various passages. Hume's list is much longer, including under the useful such traits as justice, fidelity, honor, veracity, allegiance, chastity, humanity, benevolence, lenity, generosity, gratitude, moderation, tenderness, friendship, industry, discretion, frugality, secrecy, order, perseverance, forethought, judgment; and under the agreeable such traits as serenity, cheerfulness, noble dignity, undaunted spirit, "facetious wit or flowing affability," and "a delicate modesty or decent genteelness of address and manner."[14] He also makes no pretense at a complete list. Hartmann discusses such virtues as justice, wisdom, courage, self-control (the "Platonic" virtues, he calls them), along with others from Aristotle's list. To these he adds brotherly love, truthfulness and uprightness, trustworthiness and fidelity, trust and faith, modesty, humility, aloofness, sociability; and, as a third group of moral values, love of the remote, radiant virtue, personality, and personal love. But he explicitly indicates that one cannot exhaustively list all that falls into the realm of moral values.[15]

Let us suppose, then, that when we speak of the moral uniqueness and superiority of Christian ethics we are primarily referring to alternative models of the good person. We are saying that among these models one can be identified as the Christ model. If that model is one that contains certain character traits or virtues not found in the others, then it will be in that respect unique. And if it is one that as a whole would be chosen over the others by persons in conditions ideal for the making of the choice, then it is morally superior to the others. Corresponding to the unique character traits in the Christ model will of course be certain duties or moral obligations. Actions that offend against those obligations will be wrong, and all others will be innocent or right. The virtues and duties peculiar to the Christ model of goodness will of course be reflected in patterns of practical reasoning peculiar to the Christian.

But what are the peculiarly Christian virtues, the character traits that constitute the good person on the Christian model? Certainly it is easy enough to mention in this connection the three so-called theological virtues of faith, hope, and charity, made much of in the moral philosophies of Augustine, Aquinas, and other Christian philosophers.[16] However, it seems to me that if we are to find anything distinctively Christian about faith, hope, and love—and what religious tradition could possibly just omit them, especially at this point in history—we must view them in specific concretizations, in peculiar ways of having faith, hope, and love (or ways of them having us). In any case, I suspect that they are better understood as attitudes, not character traits at all; for I doubt that they are characterizable as behavioral dispositions, as is the case with, say, honesty and courage. The New Testament depiction of love as the fulfilling of the law seems to preclude it from being one character trait among others and to place it in the position of an overall quality of life within which the various character traits that are virtues, along with their corresponding actions, are sustainable and even "natural." Likewise, for faith and hope. We shall return to this again later.

To locate the specifically Christian virtues, we must look at the paradigmatic situations in the Gospels where Jesus is teaching people how to live. There is none more crucial for this purpose than the one recorded in the Sermon on the Mount, of Matthew 5–7, or in its companion sermon on the plain, of Luke 6, verses 17 and following. The overall tendency of these discourses is to upset the notions of well-being ("blessedness") and of righteousness that dominate under the rule of earth (of man) and to substitute for them notions that apply when people turn in to the rule of heaven (the "kingdom" of God). The theme of the first (in man's way) being last (in God's) and the last (in man's way) being first (in God's) is the focus of much of what Jesus taught and did. It has to be kept constantly in mind as his words are read. Thus the "blesseds" of Matthew 5 and Luke 6 are taken from among those usually regarded as the cursed, and the "woefuls" of Luke 6 from among those usually regarded as blessed.

Following the "blesseds" of Matthew 5 we have the declaration that common people, not just the great and the glittering, can be the salt of the earth and the light of the world. Jesus then immediately has to forestall the idea that he came to destroy the law and the prophets (5:17), which his hearers understood as in effect sanctioning the human kingdom's view of who is blessed and who is woeful.

Jesus's way of preventing harmful misreading of his intent with his gospel of God's rule over human life is to say that to enter that rule one does not set aside or destroy "the righteousness of the scribes and the Pharisees," but one goes through and beyond it (vv. 17–20). Then come his great illustrations of what this "going beyond" means.

These illustrations fall into five major areas of life, and are designed to make clear, without systematic exposition, what the "righteousness beyond" is like. First are illustrations from situations where the aggressiveness of the male human being is displayed: toward other men (5:21–26), toward women (vv. 27–32), and toward God (vv. 33–37). Second are illustrations that deal with situations of harm (vv. 38–42) and threat (vv. 43–48). Third are illustrations bearing upon religious practices: alms deeds (6:1–4), prayer (vv. 5–15), and fasting (vv. 16–18). Fourth are illustrations of how we are to relate to material goods and provisions (6:19–34). And fifth are illustrations of how we are to "manage" other people: not by condemnation (7:1–5), not by forcing good things upon them (v. 6), but through God (vv. 7–12).

It is in these and similar passages, if anywhere, that we will find the distinctively Christian virtues. Of course we must remember that illustrations are not laws, and that the letter kills. The approach of Christian ethics is entirely to the inward personality. It does not say, for example, "Sure, I'll turn the other cheek, and then I'll knock your head off. I've done what Jesus commanded." It doesn't insist on going the second mile for someone who does not need it, "because Jesus said to." But it seeks to foster the kind of persons for whom such behavior will be reasonable and even agreeable in appropriate circumstances—for whom it would then seem quite "natural," quite "in character," as it was for Jesus himself.

With reference to these central teachings of Jesus, I shall comment now on what I take to be two uniquely Christian virtues: One unique trait of good persons on the Christian model is their active generosity toward those who harm them or are hostile to them. By this is not intended a mere nonretaliation, nor an abstract benevolence toward all persons, including, incidentally, those who harm and threaten us. The concreteness of the situations used by Jesus to convey his teaching on this point must be felt or vividly imagined by extrapolation from our own experiences—the stinging pain combined with unalloyed good-seeking for the one inflicting it—in order to understand the uniqueness of this virtue:

> Love your enemies, do good to them which hate you, bless them that curse you and pray for them which despitefully use you. And unto him that smiteth thee on the one cheek offer also the other; and him that taketh away thy cloke forbid not to take thy coat also. Give to every man that asketh of thee; and of him that taketh away thy goods ask them not again. (Luke 6:27–31, KJV)

There is here a progression from love, to doing good, to going beyond ourselves (in blessing and prayer) for the benefit of those harming us, to giving over and above what is taken. It seems likely that there is also a progression on the other side: one of evil—from being hostile toward us (an enemy), to hating, to cursing (verbal abuse), to mistreating through physical abuse and the taking of our possessions. The generosity commended and commanded is further characterized by how it responds to those who only ask for our goods, and how it does not later seek the return of goods taken from us.

It is necessary to reemphasize that these words of Jesus are not laws, but are illustrations. One who can think of morality and moral goodness only in terms of laws will find the teachings of Jesus simply outrageous or impossible. As I see it, these teachings are indications of what children of the kingdom will be constrained to do, and be able to do, in many circumstances, perhaps most, because of the faith, hope, and love—not precluding understanding—present in them. We are not here dealing with behaviors of weak and wimpy, depressed and gloomy people. (No blessings through grinding or gritted teeth, if you please! And how dreadful to be "loved" by people who are not loving. "Love bombing" is a technique now used by certain cults to brainwash inductees.) The call is for and to people who know God well and live well and who act in truth, with a cheerful confidence and strength that would impress Nietzsche. As Robert Adams comments in his valuable corrective to Susan Wolf's disastrously flawed analysis of "moral saints":

> The substance of sainthood is not sheer will power striving like Sisyphus (or like Wolf's Rational Saint) to accomplish a boundless task, but goodness overflowing from a boundless source. Or so, at least, the saints perceive it.[17]

A second unique trait in the peculiarly Christian configuration of virtue is certainly presupposed in the active generosity toward enemies and others just sketched. That trait is forgiveness, which more than anything else characterizes the moral character of the Christian. I am not, of course, referring to God's forgiveness of us, with its well-understood priority in Christian teachings, but to forgiveness as a human disposition and activity. The emphasis of Jesus upon forgiveness between human beings is quite reasonable, in view of the fact that without forgiveness merely decent human relations become for the most part impossible between persons close together in the events of life. The lack of a constant flow of forgiveness goes far to explain why family and other contexts so frequently prove to be disaster areas. Jesus seems actually to have even made God's forgiveness of us contingent upon our forgiving one another (Matt. 6:12; 14–15). I suspect that this is because forgiveness is not a unilateral action, not an imposition of one person upon another, and can be received from God only by one who lives in a pervasive orientation of forgiveness.

His drumbeat emphasis on forgiveness (always involving straightforward dealing with the offending person and the community, it seems) finally evoked from his disciples the (typically legalistic and therefore totally wrongheaded) question: "How often shall my brother sin against me and I forgive him? Till seven times?" No, came the reply, "until seventy times seven" (Matt. 18:21–22). Of course the legalist will conclude that on the 491st time we are free to not forgive. That isn't the point, however. The point is that we are to be constantly disposed to forgive, to not base our future relation to others on grievance over past injuries. It is this disposition that stands out as a unique trait in the overall pattern of Christian virtues, and is to constantly display itself in the day-to-day activities of the Christian.

Now, I certainly do not hold that only in Christianity do we hear of generosity toward enemies or of forgiveness. No one who has read the Bhagavad Gita (Hindu) or the Dhammapada (Buddhist) and the sermons of Gautama could possibly think that. Nevertheless, it seems to me that such generosity and forgiveness as is exhibited and taught by Jesus is qualitatively very different from that in Hinduism and Buddhism. It is affirming and optimistic in a way impossible to outlooks that are world- and life-negating, to use Schweitzer's terminology.[18] Divestment of passion,[19] extinction of desire,[20] and extinction of the sense of individuality, if not individuality itself,[21] simply do not yield a generosity or a forgiveness that equates to what is sponsored in the person and teachings of Christ. But these two (of course closely related) traditions come as close to Christ's teachings about generosity to enemies and forgiveness as any, to my knowledge.

Various Stoic authors of antiquity also emphasized generosity and forgiveness, but, it seems, mainly as a counsel of prudence— the smartest way to "get through it." Though I do not put it forth as a proven fact, it seems to me that we have here two significant respects in which the Christian ethic is unique. I would, even more diffidently, suggest that they also constitute a distinct superiority for the Christian ethic, in the sense explained above.

Perhaps the strongest objection to what I have thus far said will be that generosity to enemies and forgiveness of the sort advocated by Jesus Christ is just not possible: that the Sidgwickian condition on the good—that it be "attainable by voluntary action"—obviously fails for the two traits in question vis-à-vis real human existence. "To err is human, to forgive is divine," don't you know, and ergo not human. But "attainable by voluntary action" does not mean attainable by totally unaided voluntary action. When told that they must forgive a brother seven times in a day the apostles cried out: "Lord, increase our faith!" (Luke 17:5). They were exactly right in doing so. Faith, love, and hope must be given. That, by the way, is why they are, fundamentally, not virtues, which are, as Aristotle correctly saw, acquisitions or attainments. I do not suggest that faith, hope, and love enter those who do nothing to receive them. The merest gift must, after all, be accepted, received, in some way. But the New Testament teaching clearly places them all much more on the side of gifts or graces than on the side of attainments, even attainments divinely assisted. Thus, faith is created in our hearts, we are told, as we listen to the word of God in the gospel of the kingdom (Rom. 10:8–17; cf. 1:16–17). Hope, the joyous expectation of those good events that our confidence in God's rule causes us to anticipate, rises as experience of trials certifies our faith (Rom. 5:3). We are saved by hope (Rom. 8:24). And this hope does not let us down or "make us ashamed," for as we live in it "the love of God is shed abroad in our hearts by the Holy Ghost which is given unto us" (Rom. 5:5).

Love as a presence in us thus presupposes, includes, faith and hope, as is clear from Saint Paul's language when he invites us to consider what love (agape) does:

> Love is patient; love is kind and envies no one. Love is never boastful, nor conceited, nor rude; never selfish, not quick to take offence. Love keeps no score of wrongs; does not gloat over other men's sins, but delights in the truth. There is nothing love cannot face; there is no limit to its faith, its hope, and its endurance. Love will never come to an end. (1 Cor. 13:4–8, NEB)

It is to be noted that this does not say we do, or are to do, these things. (A well-meaning minister once suggested that I should put my name in the place of the word *love* and then read these verses. It took weeks for me to emerge from the cloud that came over me.) Another New Testament writer tells us that God is love. No doubt he is capable of the things Paul here attributes to love.

In any case, love (inclusive of faith and hope) now reenters the moral arena as the "condition of the possibility of" the realization of the specifically Christian pattern of virtue, including of course active generosity to enemies and forgiveness. It is a "presence" (the ontology of all this is not clear) that is communicated to us through a course of experience that we have a part in but cannot reduce to a formula. It is a power in its own right, in us but not "of" us, with which we can more or less willingly and intelligently cooperate as we "work out our own salvation with fear and trembling," sensing that "it is God which worketh in us both to will and to do his good pleasure" (Phil. 2:12–13). Christ is "in" us and, being divine, communicates to us, in a good Athanasian manner, the divine nature, making "attainable by voluntary action" what would otherwise be out of the question for us. God's "can" now implies our "ought." Faith, hope, and love are, in this way, the foundation of the highest moral realization.

There is surely required some comment on where this leaves the non-Christian. Without the "can" they obviously do not have the "ought." They might seem to be absolved of responsibility for the Christian virtues (though I would prefer to say they are deprived of the opportunity). But we should perhaps say instead that, while they do not have the "can" of the indwelling divine love, they nevertheless can obtain it. They have, in Aristotle's language, the potentiality for receiving divine love. Somewhat as a child who cannot do numbers can learn to do them, or the person who cannot drive safely while drunk can (at least in some cases) avoid drinking, and thus drive safely.

If it is true that the superior pattern of moral goodness includes virtues supportable only by indwelling faith, hope, and love from Christ, does not that obligate every person to obtain that indwelling if at all possible? In simple language, is there a moral obligation on every informed person to follow Christ? To defend an affirmative answer to this question would at least require a demonstration that one's moral pattern is the superior one for all human beings, and I certainly have not done that here. But I will suggest that any ethical system should be considered inherently hypocritical—perhaps not in intent, but in effect—if it does not impose the duty of adopting appropriate and necessary means for getting into position to do what it holds one is morally obliged to do. One has not only the duty to be truthful, but also the duty to do what lies in one's power to become (able to be) truthful. And if only eating beans (*pace* Pythagoras) made one able to be truthful, then one ought, one has a duty, to eat beans—at least so long as they are available.

It is not my intention to be inflammatory. Moral superiority or even uniqueness can be a most infuriating topic for many, especially when associated with religion. But it is at least an interesting question of fact whether Christian faith, hope, and love are indispensable for realization of the specifically Christian virtues (if there are any), or are indispensable, even, for the realization of "secular" virtues, such as honesty, justice, and benevolence, to the degree demanded by secular morality itself.

I conclude with an observation about "saints." There is something oddly wrong, unfocussed, about the picture of the saint as occupying the strenuous upper reaches of moral attainment, and the resultant association of *saint* with *hero*. I believe this to be because what most characterizes the saint—pervasive faith, hope, and love—are really conditions of significant moral attainment, which are even found in the raw but earnest beginner—one who has not yet the settled dispositions of, say, guilelessness or courage, much less those of generosity toward enemies and forgiveness. Indeed, who ever attains these virtues as fully as they desire and as they ought? Thus the saint more comfortably fits in the category of the child than in that of the hero, though there remains something heroic about the saint only because what is in them lifts them above the course of "ordinary" human behavior.

CHAPTER 30

The Problem of Evil

When Dallas wrote this previously unpublished article, he intentionally omitted the word *theodicy* because he believed it was often misused and misunderstood. The danger he perceived was the growing assumption that human beings have a legitimate claim or right to judge God, thus holding God to account for his actions. In spite of his concerns, Dallas found that the questions raised by theodicy help open discussions about God's character, action, and nonaction as good, loving, and just. Thus, while avoiding the term *theodicy,* this piece addresses the ultimate questions of moral evil in the world and how human beings can better understand and experience God's loving character despite suffering and difficulty.

Written as "God and the Problem of Evil" (previously unpublished)[1]

THERE ARE VERY FEW PEOPLE WHO DO NOT ASK "WHY?" WHEN confronted with the terrible things that have happened in history and continue to happen day by day. This is because we nearly all believe, to some degree, that there really is a God who is conscious of human beings, who is good, and who has sufficient power to prevent bad things from happening. Unless there is such a God, there is no "problem of evil" as usually understood. If there is no God, the only answer to the question "Why are children starving in Somalia?" is

"Why not?" We would have no reason to think that they shouldn't be starving. The occurrence of evil would no longer be strange, and might even seem quite natural—though we would still have the "other" problem of evil, the problem of how to get rid of it.

Certainly the Christian faith is committed to a picture of God and the world that makes every event ultimately redeemable, and therefore permissible, by a personal God who is both willing and able to nurture into being a creation that cannot be improved on. It does not hold that every event is good in itself. Bad things, even horrendous moral evils, do come to pass. But in the vision of Jesus Christ, communicated to his people, all human beings—and yes, even the sparrows and the lilies—are effectively cared for. Every person is invited to say in faith and obedience, "The Lord is my shepherd, I shall not want."

But how can we resolve the classical thorn in the side of such faith, which insists that if God were both all-good and all-powerful, he would not permit the evil things that do happen to occur at all? Therefore, we shall concentrate here on the evils that human beings do or cause, the moral evils. They pose the most serious problem. And we shall ask why God permits human beings to do evil, for it would seem that God cannot be both all-good and all-powerful, if moral evil exists, and that we are forced to let one (omnipotence) or the other (omnibenevolence) go.

In resolving this dilemma, the first step is to affirm that a universe that permits the development of moral character—one that makes it possible for persons to become the immeasurably precious and even glorious beings that they sometimes demonstrate—is of greater value than any world that does not allow for such potential. A world containing only minerals, or minerals and plants, for example, would be of much less worth or intrinsic value than one that also contained human beings as we know them. If personality is not to be regarded as having a very great value, it would clearly be wrong of God to permit the actual suffering and wrongdoing that occur in order to procure human existence.

But the moral development of personality is possible only in a world of genuine freedom. To nurture moral perfection, horrendous moral crimes must be permitted by God—though he himself never approves of them, actualizes them, or requires them. Nurturing moral perfection (within a suitable world) and not allowing wrong-doing is impossible. If a child is never permitted to do wrong, it will never become capable of developing a nature or character that resolutely chooses the good. Good persons must live in a world where doing evil is a genuine choice for them.

But does this not mean that God is limited in power, that there is something he cannot do? Not at all, *for the impossible is not something that could be either done or left undone.* If the janitor does not sweep the room after a lecture, his supervisor can rightly point that out to him, and require that he do it. But the supervisor cannot require that he both sweep the room and not sweep the room. Sweeping the room and not sweeping the room is not something that can be done or left undone. It is nothing at all. The fact that the janitor "cannot do it" does not mean that the janitor is limited in some way, as he would be if he had no arms and could not hold the vacuum or broom.

To hold God to be limited because he does not nurture moral character while simultaneously preventing choice is like regarding the janitor as limited because he does not both sweep and not sweep the room. Producing people with character without giving them choice is impossible because the capacity to choose is a part of character. So it is not something God "left undone," for it is not anything at all. It is not something he cannot do, because it is not "something." Period. God remains of unlimited power. He can do anything that might either be done or left undone.

Hence the presence of moral evil in the world does not mean that God is lacking in goodness or in power. The classical dilemma is dissolved by setting existing evil in the context of the good that God achieves in permitting (but not producing) moral evil.

While this may seem like a "merely logical maneuver," it in fact yields the conclusion that permits us to see the suffering of individuals, ourselves or others, in the larger world of a great and good God, who has all eternity, and resources beyond our wildest imagination, to ensure that the life of every individual who suffers, in whatever way, is ultimately one that even that individual will receive with boundless gratitude.

If all the individual has is "this" life, then clearly evil, pain, and frustration are not redeemed. But seen in the context of God's world as a whole, seen as but a part of a life that never ends and endlessly becomes more and more glorious, there is no evil that individuals may suffer that can prevent them from finding life to be good, and God to be good. Theirs is the perspective of Saint Paul, who speaks of great suffering as "our light affliction, which is but for a moment and which produces for us a weight of glory far greater than it" (2 Cor. 4:17).

The child dying in famine is ushered immediately into the full world of God, in which the child finds its existence good and its prospects incomprehensibly grand. There God is seen, as he now surely is not seen, to be good and great without limit, and every individual received into his presence enjoys the everlasting sufficiency of his goodness and greatness. There is no tragedy for those who rely on this God.

It is the hearty assurance of this for the individual—which we here do not attempt to prove, but only to show that it is not automatically ruled out by the presence of evil in our world—that empowers the individual to deal with the "other" problem of evil: namely, how to get rid of it. If I am truly concerned about moral evil in the world, I should at least worry as much about my responsibility for it as about God's. By ceasing to do evil I can make a significant impact on the moral evil that is in my world. By trusting the goodness and greatness of God, I can turn loose of the chain that drags me into moral evil, along with the chain of self-deification, which puts me in the position of the one I trust to take care of myself. Nearly all evildoing is done under the guise of "necessity": "I wouldn't lie, cheat, steal, hurt others but for the fact that it is necessary to secure my aims—which of course I must bring about."

By contrast, if I rely upon God, I can relinquish the realization of my aims to him. I can stop doing what I, and everyone else, knows to be wrong, and I can calmly cease cooperation with immoral behavior occurring around me. I also can stand against the evils in my world, unconcerned about what is going to happen to me if I do. We need not try to be perfect. We can concentrate on just doing a lot better. That is the surest way of vastly improving the world we live in.

By far the best way of taking this stand is by simply relying on Jesus Christ to guide and help us. The life that is in him is the best life that has ever been given to human beings. The surest sign that God is who we hope he is, is the presence of Jesus Christ in human history. By trusting him the best we know how, we will begin to share in the eternal kind of life that belongs to God. We will begin to live in the world of the twenty-third Psalm, where we "fear no evil," where "goodness and mercy shall follow me all of the days of my life, and I shall dwell in the house of the Lord forever." That will be given to us in response to our trust. Experience will confirm it to us.

Because I make my living as a university professor and philosopher, I am frequently asked, in so many words, "Why do you follow Jesus Christ?" My answer is always the same: "Who else did you have in mind?" I am open, I am willing, and I continue seeking to know more. But so far I have found no one who remotely compares with Jesus Christ as a practical guide to how things are and should be in human life. He proves to be one who is in touch with reality in depth and who guides me evermore into a life that comes to terms with evil in all of its dimensions. He brings us into the path leading to an experiential solution for the problems of evil.

CHAPTER 31

Christian Thought for the Everyday Practitioner

> Throughout his career, Dallas sought to answer important questions from laypeople in his local congregations and in his classrooms. His theological quest was to always be relevant to everyday life. This short essay on Christology and the deity of Jesus is intended for such an audience.
>
> First published in 1998 in the *Student,* a publication of the Southern Baptist Convention, as "How Can Jesus Be the Son of God?"

MANY YEARS AGO, ANOTHER GRADUATE STUDENT AND I WERE waiting for our university library to open one Sunday afternoon. We fell into a discussion of religion. He commented that he could accept most of what Christianity taught, but not that Jesus was divine. That, he said, was something he just could not understand. Perhaps he expected me to present him with an explanation or an argument. Instead, I simply asked him how much time he had spent trying to understand it. Laughingly he replied: "About ten minutes."

His was an honest response. Rejection of Jesus's divinity is seldom based upon deep and sustained thought about the matter. Unfortunately, the same is true for acceptance of it. It is rare to find a believer who has any view at all concerning how Jesus, the incarnated Christ, could be the Son of God and therefore be divine.

In order to understand Jesus's divinity, we must keep clearly before us what human fatherhood and sonship involves. Fatherhood has three dimensions: the father originates (inseminates) the physical organism in the womb of the mother, conveys his personal character to the child ("Like father, like son," we say), and gives the child entry into the life that he has established in the world—usually by helping the child step into the many legal, social, and/or professional relations where the father stands. These three acts or processes, roughly or incompletely, illustrate the concept of fatherhood.

Likewise, to be the Son of God, then, Jesus must meet three conditions. First, God must have been the cause of Jesus's origination as a physical organism in the physical world. Second, Jesus must have the character of God, the "family resemblance." Third, he must have at his disposal the resources of God as he enters into the work of God. That is how Jesus can be the Son of God.

When we look at the New Testament documents and the tradition of church teaching, we see that Jesus is presented precisely as meeting each of these conditions. Mary was with child of the Holy Spirit (Matt. 1:18, 20). The angel indicated that there would be a specific moment when "the Holy Spirit will come upon you, and the power of the Most High will overshadow you" (Luke 1:35, NASB). In that moment the spiritual agency that created all things acted to supply the biological materials that would, in Mary's womb, become the physical body of Jesus. Thus Jesus is God's only *begotten* son. If God is able to intervene in the course of physical nature as he wills, there is nothing incomprehensible about the physical birth of Jesus by God's act.

But then Jesus also manifested the character of God. When he said, "He who has seen me has seen the Father" (John 14:9, NASB), he made reference to a view of God's nature, which clearly emerges from the Old Testament writings, a view of supremely loving personal rightness and goodness, with no lack of power to accomplish its goals. The followers of Jesus found this to be his character also.

Finally, Jesus was "at home" in the work of God the Father. He said: "My Father is working until now, and I myself am working"

(John 5:17, NASB). The authorities of his day recognized this to be a claim of equality with God and tried to kill him. But he simply insisted that his action was God's action as he worked in his father's "business" (v. 19). Moses, by contrast, was merely a faithful servant in the "household," the business establishment, of God. But Christ was faithful over God's household as a son of the family (Heb. 3:5–6).

There is, then, little real mystery about how Jesus could be the Son of God. His sonship is a question of fact, which each person must settle by considering Jesus himself—his life, his teaching, his effect. Abstract thinking about the nature of God, the nature of man, and about what obstacles there might possibly be to their coming together in one person are of little use. In its place we must ask, "What more could reasonably be demanded of someone, in order that they should be the Son of God, than what is found in Jesus?" The real question was asked by Pilate, "What shall I do with Him?" (Mark 15:12, NASB). Everyone must answer that question.

For Further Reading

Elton Trueblood, *A Place to Stand* (New York: Harper & Row, 1968). Chapter 2, "The Center of Certitude," gives an excellent statement of major points on the divinity of Jesus as stated by modern apologists such as C. S. Lewis.

William Temple, "The Divinity of Christ," in *Foundations: A Statement of Christian Beliefs in Terms of Modern Thought* (London: Macmillan and Co., 1913), chap. 5. Temple carefully explores the major issues. Philosophically sophisticated.

Malcolm Muggeridge, *Jesus, the Man Who Lives* (New York: Harper & Row, 1975). Incisive critique of humanistic views of Jesus and of life, by one who has seen through them.

CHAPTER 32

Truth in the Fire
C. S. Lewis and the Pursuit
of Truth Today

Dallas was supremely dedicated to the concept and pursuit of truth. As postmodern thought and constructivism entered academic and religious discourse, he believed that the concept of Christian truth needed to be defended. He called constructivism a "Midas touch" epistemology because for him, the idea that we create the objects of our perception conflicted with Christian thought. In these prepared remarks, Dallas draws from C. S. Lewis to describe how the nature of truth is critical to engaging the reality of our lives and, by implication, the nature of the gospel itself.

Remarks initially prepared for the 1998 C. S. Lewis Centennial Celebration in Oxford, England, and first published in 2005 as "C. S. Lewis and the Pursuit of Truth Today," in *Sacred History* magazine

---

C. S. LEWIS WAS DEVOTED TO THE PURSUIT OF TRUTH, AND WAS sure he had captured or been given a great deal of it. His confidence in this respect did not make him arrogant and closed-minded but was, to the contrary, the foundation of his remarkable humility and openness. In his third BBC lecture, under the heading, "The Case for Christianity," later published in *Mere Christianity*, he responds to those who might think he had been too hard on human beings in his previous lecture. There he had pointed out that human beings constantly fail to behave as they expect others to behave. He says to the potential objector: "I am not concerned at present with blame; I am trying to find out the truth. And from that point of view the very idea of something being imperfect, of its not being what it ought to be, has certain consequences."[1]

This is a very characteristic statement for Lewis. He understood the pursuit of truth to require devotion to logic as well, and hence to the following out of the consequences of truths discovered. Lewis took logic very seriously as a primary means of securing truth and avoiding falsehood. In the third BBC course of lectures, titled "Christian Behavior," he comments that "we are now getting to the point at which different beliefs about the universe lead to different behavior." "Religion," he continues, "involves a series of statements about facts, which must be either true or false. If they are true, one set of conclusions will follow about the right sailing of the human fleet: if they are false, quite a different set."[2]

The Christian tradition, as well as its alternatives, must—in his view—essentially contain claims about reality, which are either true or false. The fundamental task we face is to determine which claims are true and what logically follows from them. Only so can we come to terms with reality and successfully direct our lives into harmonious relationships with it.

In response to anticipated complaints about the difficulty of basic Christian doctrine, he remarks further in his BBC lectures: "Christianity claims to be telling us about another world, about something behind the world we can touch and hear and see. You may think the claim is false; but if it were true, what it tells us would be bound to be difficult—at least as difficult as modern physics, and for the same reason."[3]

Now, Lewis held what has traditionally been called the "correspondence theory of truth." This could properly be called the classical theory of truth, because it was broadly held with little exception up to the nineteenth century. In other words, Lewis contended that truth is a matter of a belief or idea (representation, statement) corresponding to reality. In the course of rejecting the view that moral laws are mere social conventions he insists that they are, to the contrary, "Real truths." "If your moral ideas can be truer, and those of the Nazi less true," he says to his reader, "there must be something—some Real morality—for them to be true about. The reason why your idea of New York can be truer or less true than mine is that New York is a real place, existing quite apart from what either of us thinks. If, when each of us said, 'New York,' each meant merely 'the town I am imagining in my own head,' how could one of us have truer ideas than the other? There would be no question of truth or falsehood at all."[4]

THE CONTEMPORARY DISDAIN OF TRUTH: "POSTMODERNISM"

The case for "Real truth" is, unfortunately, much more complicated and harder to make stand up (or even get a hearing) now than it was when Lewis wrote these words in the early 1940s. Not intrinsically or in itself, of course; for that does not change. But in terms of numerous popular presumptions that have arisen, mistakenly, against "Real truth." Nowadays truth itself, in the sense in which Lewis and most of his contemporaries still thought it to be of central human importance, is in the fire.

To be sure, this is not exactly a new thing. David Hume long ago (mid-eighteenth century) consigned truth to the flames in the famous passage at the end of his *Enquiry Concerning Human Understanding*. There he advised us to look through our libraries and ask of each book whether it deals with matters mathematical or sense-perceptible (feel-able). If it does not, he said, we should "commit it then to the flames: for it can contain nothing but sophistry and illusion."[5]

Truth, of course, is not a matter of quantity, not mathematically describable; and it also is not sense-perceptible or "feel-able." Truth is not something physical or "naturalistic," as we would now say. And our general intellectual, artistic, and academic culture has by this time caught up with Hume in rejecting "Real truth." Two centuries of cultural development were needed for that. Truth, along with goodness and beauty (both of which David Hume manipulated into something "feel-able" or sentimental), are no longer generally thought of as realities independent of human attitudes. And that, of course, is simply what it means to say they are not "objective." Lewis believed they were objective, and spent much of his time explaining and defending their objectivity.

In the face of present attitudes, however, even earnestness about truth—also about goodness and beauty—is definitely uncool. It might be tolerated in a university freshman. But he or she would be expected to wise up quickly, and might pay a stiff price for not doing so. The idea of devoting one's life to truth, goodness, or beauty is now quaint if not ridiculous, on the campus as in the corporation. They are not considered to be objective realities against which human life is or can be measured.

That is certainly the message that comes to us from the polymorphous clouds of postmodernism(s) that hang over all our intellectual, artistic, and cultural life now. Christopher Norris, one of the very best writers on these subjects, points out that in postmodernism's most emphatic representatives, such as Jean Baudrillard and Richard Rorty, "the ideas of truth, validity or right reason simply drop out of the picture."[6] There is for them no possibility of achieving "an accurate match between real-world objects or states of affairs and concepts of pure understanding."[7] "The idea that one can criticize existing beliefs from some superior vantage-point of truth, reason or scientific method," Norris continues, is considered a self-delusion deriving from the Enlightenment period of Western thought—by now supposedly shown by history to be a delusion.[8]

Of course Baudrillard and Rorty still believe that their own views of truth, validity, and reason are true, valid, and reasonable. They believe that their own views of how language and thought relate to reality present us with how things really are. (Let them simply state the contrary if they do not.) And I have noticed that the most emphatic of postmodernists turn coldly modern when discussing their fringe benefits or other matters that make a great difference to their practical life. They also—on many occasions during each day—discover that some of their ideas, beliefs, and statements about very ordinary matters do (or do not) match up to the actual condition of what those beliefs and statements are about. They share this with every competent human being. (They thought their keys were on the table, for example, but found that they were wrong.) But a powerful thrust of the zeitgeist such as postmodernism is not to be impeded by little details such as these.

A DEVIL'S ADVICE

Lewis clearly saw the early stages of the present situation, though I doubt he could have begun to imagine the attitude toward "Real truth" maintained now by its contemporary "cultured despisers." In the fabulous Screwtape's first letter we find him advising his nephew devil, Wormwood, that argument is not the way to keep his (Wormwood's) "patient" from the Enemy's (God's) clutches. "That might have been so if he had lived a few centuries earlier," he says. "At that time," Screwtape continues, "humans still knew pretty well when a thing was proved and when it was not; and if it was proved they really believed it. They still connected thinking with doing and were prepared to alter their way of life as the result of a chain of reasoning. But what with the weekly press and other such weapons, we have largely altered that," Screwtape points out. "Your man has been accustomed, ever since he was a boy, to having a dozen incompatible philosophies dancing about together inside his head. He doesn't think of doctrines as primarily 'true' or 'false,' but as 'academic' or 'practical,' 'outworn' or 'contemporary,' 'conventional' or 'ruthless.' Jargon, not argument, is your best ally in keeping him from the Church. Don't waste time trying to make him think that materialism is true! Make him think it is strong or stark or courageous—that it is the philosophy of the future. That's the sort of thing he cares about."[9]

Instead of argument, which, Screwtape says, "moves the whole struggle onto the Enemy's own ground," Wormwood is advised to hold his patient's attention—just as David Hume would have it—to the "stream of immediate sense experiences," and to "teach him to call it 'real life' and don't let him ask what he means by 'real.'"[10] In that stream of sensations, of course, neither truth nor logic is to be found.

ON FACTS AND REALITY

One gathers from all this, I think, a clear and accurate impression of Lewis's outlook on truth and its vital importance for human existence. Now we turn to some reflections—in the spirit, if not with the power, of this friend of truth—on the contemporary situation of "Real truth," as it stands in the flames of current disdain and ridicule. We begin with some clarification of what a fact is, what it is to be real, and then what a truth is.

We all have, as a part of the equipment necessary to enable us to navigate the course of our existence, the ability to discern properties things have and relations things stand in. A child quickly learns to distinguish milk from Coca-Cola, and to tell which bag of candy or scoop of ice cream is larger. As time goes on children learn to articulate what goes into such differences, and to distinguish not just milk from Coca-Cola, but the different properties—flavor, color, and so on—that enter into such differences as that between milk and Coca-Cola, or a dog and a cat.

Our education as human beings largely consists in becoming able to identify and interrelate the very large number of properties and relations that are distributed over the various types of entities that make up our self and our world. Such ability is essential to human competence. One could hardly cross the street, much less hold a job of the simplest sort, without it. Here we must hold on to these ideas of properties and relations as we continue.

If an entity, regardless of type, has a particular property or relation, it's having that property or relation make up what we here call a "fact." This is an extremely common notion, and one that has received much attention from philosophers.[11] It is, for example, a fact that I am standing before you now or that you are reading this paragraph. Reality, then, taken as a whole, is the sum total of facts. And to be real, to exist, is to be a constituent in a fact. Please bear with me a moment longer on these painfully abstract, but crucial, points.

Any object of thought or discourse that actually has properties or relations exists or is real; and, conversely, any object that exists has some properties and relations. To illustrate, an object—for example, Pegasus, the winged horse of mythology—does not exist, is not real. That means that the relevant properties we associate with Pegasus (horse-ness, wing-ness, etc.) do not belong to anything in unison. If they did, that thing would be Pegasus, and Pegasus would exist.

But please notice: being a fact has nothing to do, in general, with being "thought" of, or being "mentioned" or being "described" or, as the philosopher W. V. Quine would say, "being in the range of a bound variable."[12] Currently this is widely denied. Many people now take facts and their constituents to be created by consciousness (individual or collective) or by language or culture. Wondrously creative powers are attributed to human thought.

But upon careful reflection it is surely clear that a universe just like ours except devoid of conscious beings and their languages would still be a universe of facts and existents—facts such as the relative sizes and positions of the planets in our solar system, or the structure and habits of gastropods, or the inner structure of carbon atoms. Thought and language, being what they are, have no ability to produce or to restructure the objects that they are about: that is, to "construct" them. Of course thought and language (culture) are themselves facts or realities, and as such they have real consequences in the real world. But that is a very different matter from constructing objects by merely thinking or speaking of them.

There is, I know, a long and influential constructionist story running from Descartes to Nietzsche and the logical positivists. Modern philosophy is burdened with fundamental errors about the connection between the mind and its world of objects. We cannot detail them here. But it is one of the ironies of contemporary thought that the very thinkers who have the strongest appreciation of the follies of so-called representationalism in modern philosophy nonetheless remain constructionist in their own outlook.

In summary, then: facts are a matter of properties actually belonging to certain things, and facts are not produced by our mere thoughts or judgments of them.

THE INTRANSIGENCE OF FACT AND TRUTH

Now let us consider the relationship of facts (and truth) to action. With respect to human action, facts are totally unforgiving. One might in a preliminary way define reality (or fact) as what you run into when you are wrong. The collision is usually painful. When you assume or believe your car to be well supplied with gasoline when it is not, you may find yourself in great danger or discomfort. This is true even in the real lives of postmodernists such as Baudrillard and Rorty.

When you believe in or trust a crooked or incompetent financial advisor to be honest and capable, you may wind up depending upon your relatives or the state and have to kiss your golden years goodbye. Reality, facts, or how things actually are, do not say: "Oh, well, since you believed there was gas in the tank or that the advice was sound, it shall just be so." All roads do not lead to Rome or anywhere else. Beliefs must come to terms with facts, not facts with beliefs.

A *New Yorker* cartoon recently showed a man in a business suit being turned away by Saint Peter at the gates of heaven. He was saying to Saint Peter: "Don't you realize you are criminalizing a policy difference?" But facts make even less allowance for what you believed than God or Saint Peter. There is no such thing as a fact that accommodates itself to what is merely believed about it or to how it is thought of. Some facts can be changed, no doubt, but never by belief alone, nor—we should add—by wish or desire alone. Some facts can be changed or abolished by will and action, but in many instances even these cannot be changed.

Now, among the facts and the things that are or exist, there are, precisely, beliefs and statements themselves, with their properties of truth or falsity and their logical relations. Beliefs are states or acts of persons, and statements are linguistic correlates of such states and acts. They are very real and very important. Our lives for the most part run on the rails of our beliefs, going where—and only where—our beliefs go. This is something that C. S. Lewis often emphasized.

Beliefs are, or at least involve, dispositions or a readiness to act as if something were the case or were a fact. For example, the readiness to act as if there were gas in your tank or as if your financial advisor were reliable, or as if the person sitting next to you were an unceasing spiritual being with a glorious destiny in God's great universe.

But, as we have already noted, it is a part of the precarious human condition that acting or being ready to act as if something were so does not guarantee that it is so. We can act as if something were so-and-so when it is not, and when we do we have a more or less unpleasant collision with reality. An entire society, culture, or historical epoch can do this and has done so. We can get smashed by the car running the stoplight, or acquire AIDS from a supposedly faithful lover. Reality makes no allowance for our beliefs, desires, or good intentions. It just says: "Here is how things are. Now you have that to deal with."

We all discover this at an early age, and with it we discover truth and falseness. Our thoughts, beliefs, hopes, and expectations, as well as what we and others say, often do (or do not) match up with what those thoughts, beliefs, and so forth are about. This fact, this "matching up," is truth. It is something quite independent of all theories. No matter what your theories are, you will experience it and identify it as such. This is how we learn to speak of truth, learn the "language game" of truth.

Of course this "matchup" is not a mathematically quantifiable fact, nor is it sense-perceptible, or "feel-able," in any sense other than that we are often conscious of it. It is not an "empirical" reality. Thus, as Lewis well knew and emphasized, it does not suit the prejudices of our naturalistic age about what facts must be.[13]

But then those empiricist/naturalistic prejudices about what kinds of facts and realities there can be are not themselves mathematical or empirical—not verifiable by mathematical calculation or sense perception—and so are self-condemned at best. They do not meet their own requirement of intellectual respectability. They have only current fashions on their side. In addition, they are refuted by abundant countercases: by the reality of various familiar facts that are neither mathematical nor empirical—such as, precisely, the truth or reasonableness of a given idea or belief.

Naturalism, as Lewis repeatedly argued, cannot be a rationally defensible position precisely because it rules out "Real truth," and reason based thereon. He agrees with much of the postmodern critique of modernity. I doubt he ever read a line of Heidegger, but he had no need to. He understood on his own grounds—the study of human thought and imagination—the ravages of atomism, scientism, technology, and the modern loss of rootedness in the "Tao" of absolute value. But he realized, as many of our contemporaries do not, that it was no solution to the disasters of modernity simply to drop absolute truth, reality, and values.

Besides, one cannot actually just drop them. Their presence remains in the thought and life of all who try, such as Nietzsche and Derrida. It is one of the characteristics of most late-nineteenth-century and twentieth-century philosophy that it denies the very conditions that alone make philosophy possible. But then it assumes those very conditions in that it rejects them precisely on the basis of philosophical arguments. Essences and their accompanying claims about what must be the case are inevitable, and the writings of Nietzsche, Derrida, Richard Rorty, and others are full of them. The result is either the surrender of philosophy as a cognitive enterprise;

the surrender of "Real truth" claims about language, consciousness, and the world; or the continuation of such claims in bad faith. The latter is the course usually chosen—for example, by Wittgenstein, Quine, and Derrida.

All this puts us in position to see that, while belief is relative—a fact or statement is believed only if someone believes it—truth is not relative. One believes something, one does not truth it or fact it. Again, we can and should experiment with this. Try getting your car to run by believing gas is in your tank, or by also enlisting others to believe it, or by generating a social movement in favor of it. One million Frenchmen (or Americans, etc.) can be wrong, and adding a million or two more will make no difference—although they may be helpful in getting the government to pay for the consequences of being wrong.

All of this Lewis understood very well. On several occasions his writings turn to stating and defending at length antiempiricist (antinaturalist) views of truth and reason. His view was that meaning, from which truth and reason derive, "is a relation of a wholly new kind, as remote, as mysterious, as opaque to empirical study, as soul itself."[14] The relations of meaning, truth, and reason he knew to be totally indifferent to what anyone may think or feel about them. They are objective in the strongest of senses. That just means they cannot vary with what we think or feel about them. And yet, like the Tao itself, they are in general quite comprehensible even though nonempirical. They—relations of meaning, truth, and reason—are realities, facts, in the sense we have explained.

At this point a general comment about empiricism is needed. Empiricism (now usually called "naturalism") is, roughly stated, the view that reality (facts) and knowledge are limited to the sense-perceptible and what can be logically derived from or, more loosely, based upon the sense-perceptible—for example, subparticle physics. Empiricism was perhaps historically inevitable. But it has, in many ways, certainly been an unfortunate episode in the career of Western thought, and now lies like a blight upon world culture. It is self-refuting, as already noted, in that it is a claim that cannot be verified empirically. Empiricism is simply a stipulation, not a discovery, of what is to be counted as real and knowable; and from the very beginning, in Hobbes and then in John Locke's *Essay Concerning Human Understanding,* it was ideologically driven—driven by certain social needs as understood by its advocates.

All of this remains true of the later formulations of empiricism, such as classical positivism (Comte, Mach—really, Nietzsche), logical positivism, and linguistic analysis. They are all movements of a distinctly missionary and salvationist tone, and are exercises in ideological imperialism. Of course any comprehensive outlook, including "mere Christianity," runs the risk of becoming merely ideological in the hands of its advocates. But, be that as it may, it remains a stubborn fact that much of significant human interest—including, most importantly, human knowledge (including science and truth) itself—cannot be accounted for in empiricist/positivist terms or in terms of the "Natural" world.[15] One might be excused for thinking that the course of human thought has now made this clear, but there remain many well-known thinkers who still hope that "science," interpreted naturalistically, will eventually answer all questions that can be answered. Perhaps one can only wonder at the strength of their faith.

WHAT TRUTH IS

And now let us go back over some of the ground we have just covered to make explicit the nature of truth. When the object of our belief or statement is as we believe or state it to be, when it "matches up" to that object in the familiar way already indicated by cases, our belief or statement is true. Truth is just this characteristic of "matching up." Otherwise our belief or statement is false. Truth and falsity are, then, objective properties of beliefs and statements—more precisely, of representations and propositions—but this is technical language, which we cannot trouble to introduce here. They are objective ways in which beliefs and statements differ and show resemblance among themselves, just as colors (red, yellow, green) and sizes are objective ways in which apples and other things differ and show resemblance among themselves.

There are here three major points we must attend to:

(1) In many cases the truth-property (or the falsity) of a belief or statement can be directly confirmed by examining what the belief (or statement) is about and comparing it with the belief. These cases are the ones where, as children, we all learn what truth is.

Once while in a meeting of the Faculty Senate at the USC/LA County hospital, my automobile was stolen. I still believed that it was where I parked it and acted accordingly. When, upon leaving the meeting, I came to the place where I had parked it by the curb, I experienced the shocking incongruity of my belief (that the car was there) with the facts. I believed my car was there, but now saw it was not as I believed. I lived through the incongruity of belief with fact and was strongly conscious of that incongruity. I directly knew, was aware of, that incongruity, which is falseness, just as in other cases I have known the congruity ("correspondence") that is truth.

We characteristically say, "I don't believe it!" in such cases, because we don't believe it—that is, we don't believe the fact that presents itself to us in place of the idea that we are in the course of acting upon. It takes a while for our beliefs to adjust to reality. Then we do "believe it," and trudge our way to the police station and report how things are.

A child becomes competent very early at directly determining the truth and falsity of beliefs and statements, just as it does with multitudes of other qualities and relations. It frequently knows that what you believe or tell it is true or false, as the case may be, by direct comparison of your beliefs and statements with what they are about—so long, of course, as the subject matter is indeed open to examination and comparison with the beliefs and statements in question.

The child very soon learns what it is to lie, and learns to detect lies by examining the subject matter in comparison with statements made to it. A dignitary such as Pontius Pilate or a university professor can well say, rhetorically, "What is truth?" But that is never accepted as a response from a child being interrogated about vanished cookies, nor will a child accept it as an explanation of a broken promise. They know what truth is very well, even though, as they also know, it is not easy to determine in some cases. Is it true there is a Santa Claus, for example, or a tooth fairy?

(2) Now, what we find truth (or falsity) to be in the cases where we can compare beliefs or statements to what they are about is exactly what truth is in the cases where we do not or cannot directly compare belief or thought with its object. For example, whether a certain candidate won an election, or whether Milton in *Paradise Lost* really intended to glorify rebellion. That, in a given case, we cannot confirm truth by direct comparison, or that we cannot confirm it at all—for there very well may be beliefs or statements that are true (or false) but (for whatever reason) can never be confirmed by human minds to be such—does not change the nature of truth itself for such cases. The truth of a belief or statement is not created by verification, but discovered by it. Otherwise we could prevent a belief from being true by refusing to verify it. In the cases most difficult to verify, truth remains "correspondence" of the general type we came to know in the verified cases.

For a belief, thought, or statement to be true is simply for its subject matter to be as it is represented, or as it is held to be, in that belief, thought, or statement. When we confirm that a hitherto unconfirmed belief or statement is true, we do not create the relation (correspondence) it actually has to what it is about, any more than we create the fit of a wrench to a bolt head by placing the wrench on the bolt head, or the fit of a door to a frame by putting the door in the frame. The wrench fits the bolt head (or does not) even if it is never placed upon the bolt head, and the door fits the frame (or does not) even if it is never placed within it. And, similarly, a representation that is true is true even if it is never verified—by direct comparison with its object or otherwise. Truth is not the same thing as verification, nor dependent upon verification, any more than the fit or "correspondence" of the wrench to the bolt head is dependent upon the juxtaposition of the wrench upon the bolt head.

(3) Moreover, truth, as we have seen in the case of fact and reality, is totally unyielding in the face of belief, desire, tradition, and will. There is no such thing as a belief or statement whose quality of truth or falsity is modified by mere belief or disbelief, desire or aversion, habit or tradition or social practice or professional opinion, or will and intent. We state it once again: belief is relative, as are our perceptions, but truth is not. Truth is a relation, a "correspondence," but not one that depends upon belief or attitude. It is a relation, but it is not "relative." It pertains to the mind in a certain sense—as a property of beliefs and statements—but it is not "subjective" in the sense that it varies with our attitudes about it or would not exist unless those attitudes did.

A book was recently published under the title *Truth Is Stranger Than It Used to Be.*[16] But now we can see, I hope, that truth is exactly what it used to be, and will always be so. It is a certain property or relation-like structure, and as such it is not the kind of thing that can change, any more than gray and yellow or sister or brother can—which is a totally different matter than how we choose to use the words *gray, yellow, sister,* and *brother.* When philosophers of the last two centuries have suggested that truth—this relation-like structure of correspondence that we all become acquainted with in our early years—is "really" the logical coherence or practical utility of beliefs or statements, their suggestion is no more worthy of serious consideration than would be a suggestion that yellow is really an odor or that being a sister is the same thing as being a seamstress. Their suggestion was in fact based on the assumption that we cannot compare beliefs and statements with what they are about—an assumption that is refuted by the fact that everyone constantly does it.

Now, my hope is that these points will reassure each of us concerning our own individual knowledge of what truth is in its very nature, and permit us not to be deflected from appreciation of its real-life seriousness by the confusions of its current cultured despisers.

LIFE DEPENDS ON TRUE BELIEF

But why is truth of such fundamental importance for life? Why is it so important as to warrant the high regard traditionally given to truth? The importance of truth as a property of belief—and, by extension, the importance of knowledge of such truth—for human well-being lies chiefly in the role of belief and representation in our actions. Lewis and many others have suggested that truth is of intrinsic—possibly aesthetic—value.[17] And there is, I think, a certain beauty and inherent desirability to truth. Most people do in fact strongly prefer to grasp things as they are without reference to whether or not it is useful to do so. But however that is, our representations and beliefs also are the indispensable means by which we "aim" our actions toward future states of our existence, individual and collective. If they are true, then—given no external intrusions—we "hit" the situation intended. For example, if our beliefs about what materials and structures in buildings will preserve the buildings in a 7.2 earthquake are true, then, by following them out in action, when such an earthquake strikes, the buildings we build remain standing. The survival of the buildings in the earthquake is literally due to the truth of the beliefs we relied on in constructing them. If those beliefs had been false, things would have turned out otherwise than they did.

Our representations and beliefs are, in relation to our actions and expectations, comparable to the sighting mechanism on a rifle or artillery piece. The sight, when appropriately set, indicates where the bullet or projectile will strike. Our belief is, similarly, supposed to indicate where action will strike, and, if true, it does so. If false it doesn't. In many ordinary cases, as we have seen, it is possible to determine if our beliefs are true by comparing them to what they are about, or by careful inference, or even by acting on them, just as we can check in various ways whether the sighting mechanism on a rifle is "true"—possibly by firing it and comparing the result with the setting of the sighting mechanism.

On the other hand, many beliefs—and, indeed, many of those most important to human life—cannot be in any direct and immediate way "compared" to what they are about, and sometimes in no way at all. This is certainly true in the political sphere. Is it, for example, true that the passage of a certain law will lead to the consequences that its advocates claim? Are their statements about the proposed law true? Time will, perhaps, tell—though even it may not. It has recently been said that "the overwhelming sense among people in power in Russia today is that the revolution which established the Soviet republic was a conspiratorial *coup d'etat* that shunted the country off the track of democracy, onto a tragic trajectory which took 74 years to reverse."[18] Alas for the human blood that must be spilled to find out if grand social theories are true or false!

But as we have said, "Real truth" retains its basic nature as correspondence to the respective reality, outlined above, even in the case of ideas and statements that cannot be directly verified, or possibly cannot be verified at all. Tests applied to determine truth where "direct comparison" is ruled out—tests such as "coherence" or "workability" or "scientific acceptability"—do not, when correctly used, introduce different notions of truth. Rather, they introduce different ways of identifying the presence of truth, precisely in the sense of correspondence or "Real truth." It can only confuse matters to try to equate coherence, usefulness, and so on with truth. They obviously are not the same thing as truth. Similarly, for equating "true" with "true for me." "True for me" just means I believe it. But as we have already seen, what is "true" for me is often false, does not "fit."

There is, then, nothing inherently enigmatic about truth itself. It is only enigmatic for those who have previously adopted a philosophy of mind, language, and reality that makes it impossible or inaccessible. And the overwhelmingly common direct experience of "matching up," as described above, explains why the understanding of truth as a kind of correlation or harmony—"correspondence"—between a thought and its object dominated human thought for so long. Plato's *Theaetetus* and Aristotle's *Categories* both advance what is clearly a "correspondence" account of truth. Aquinas uses the Latin formula "*Veritas est adaequatio intellectus et rei,*" which remained familiar and widely accepted into the present century.[19] For Kant, "truth consists in the agreement of knowledge with its object" or "the conformity of our concepts with the object."[20]

Hegel and other post-Kantian figures begin to speak of truth in ways that certainly involve more than correspondence, or even rule it out entirely. However, yet more recent thinkers such as G. E. Moore and Bertrand Russell, or Edmund Husserl and Alfred Tarski, provide strong representation for the correspondence account of truth in the twentieth century. Even Martin Heidegger adopted a fairly straightforward correspondence account of the truth of assertions. And in the latest discussions of truth in analytic philosophy, correspondence at least shows up as one of the most serious alternatives in analyzing it. We have already identified Lewis's view of truth as a correspondence view.[21]

TWO OF THE MAIN ARGUMENTS AGAINST "REAL TRUTH"

But if all of this is so, what is it that, today, has turned the worlds of thought and culture so strongly against "Real truth" in the sense of correspondence with reality? There are various political ideas that resist "Real truth." In some quarters it is actually believed that democracy depends upon the relativity of truth to belief and upon no one being in possession of "Real truth." But I shall not consider the political issues and shall mention here only the two main lines of argument that must be successfully dealt with if "Real truth" is to resume its rightful place at the center of human life and thought. I must beg forgiveness for here stating in very simple terms matters of profound complexity and difficulty.

(A) First, there is the widespread conviction now that human consciousness (representation, thought) simply must be interpreted in naturalistic terms. This conviction has only increased in strength since Lewis's day. But of course he was fully informed and especially concerned about it, and we know his attitude toward it. Practically speaking, naturalism means that consciousness must be understood as a feature either of the brain or of language as a social practice. What drives this view, I think, is the still deeper level conviction that knowledge must be unified into one whole, and that it all somehow derives from physics: the mathematical analysis of the sense-perceptible world.[22] One of the significant contributions of postmodernism is its rejection of the hegemony of physics, but then postmodernism also has the strong tendency to treat consciousness as linguistic, and hence as cultural and social.

The difficulty with this naturalistic view is that brains, as well as units of language, simply do not have the "semantic" properties that consciousness manifestly has: most importantly, meaning (intentionality), truth or falsity, and logical relations. This is not an unknown fact. Thinkers such as Richard Taylor and John Searle make much of it, and rightly so.[23] But then, driven by their own naturalistic faith, which remains intact, they are forced to assign the properties of consciousness to the brain or body anyway—with no intelligible account of how this could be. They only say, in effect, "Why not?" Why not allow that the human body (or brain) just is the kind of physical object that has these properties? This, I think, is not a very successful account of the mind, and to continue to call it "naturalistic" is a mere tour de force at best.

As for language, it too does not exhibit the basic properties of human consciousness when analyzed from a strictly naturalistic point of view. Utterances, linguistic acts, and sentences give no indication, considered in themselves—have a close look at them—that they mean or are about anything, or that they are true or false, or reasonable or unreasonable. That is why one cannot learn a language, or discover linguistic meanings, just by hearing or looking at the units of language.

Quite generally, it is only if we already know what consciousness is on other grounds—mainly from our own self-awareness—that we can begin to think of brains and language in connection with consciousness at all. This is the great Cartesian fact that no one can, finally, avoid.

Matters I am only briefly mentioning here are part of long and difficult discussions, of course. But it is clear that at no known level of naturalistic analysis does a brain state or event reveal that it is or has consciousness. And, on the other hand, if consciousness were truly linguistic, how odd that more than two millennia of thinking, by some pretty intelligent people, yielded no inkling of it. It is an interesting exercise to try to pinpoint the exact place in our recent history where the linguistic nature of consciousness was discovered, and how, precisely, it was discovered. Because, in fact, it was not discovered!

What one finds in that effort is that the linguistic interpretation of the human mind arose as an unproven presupposition in order to accommodate the demands of the naturalistic—presumably "scientific"—worldview.[24] And we could all agree that if naturalism is true, then it would be reasonable to think that consciousness must be either physiological/chemical or social/linguistic. But that is no good reason to think that naturalism is true, in spite of its over-whelming popularity in academic circles today.

(B) The second main argument against "Real truth" rests upon the widespread assumption that consciousness (language, history, culture) transforms its objects in "touching" them, so that they are never "in themselves" what we take them to be in becoming aware of them or knowing them or introducing them into language. It is useful to call this the "Midas touch" epistemology, because of the similarity, in this account, of consciousness/language to the mytho-logical King Midas, who turned everything he touched to gold.

Jean-Paul Sartre called this same epistemology a "digestive phi-losophy," according to which, the spidery mind trapped things in its web, covered them with white spit and slowly swallowed them, reducing them to its own substance. What is a table, a rock, a house? A certain assemblage of "contents of consciousness," a class of such contents. O digestive philosophy! . . . The corpulent skeletons of the world were picked clean by these diligent diastases: assimilation, unification, identification. The simplest and plainest among us vainly looked for something solid, something not just mental, but would encounter everywhere only a soft and very genteel mist: themselves.[25]

Because of this widespread assumption of transformation by the mind or language, statements such as the following by John Hick are very common today: "The world is indeed there, and is as it is; but we do not have access to it as it is in itself, unperceived by us. We are aware of it only as it impinges upon us and is perceived and inhabited by us in terms of many kinds and levels of disposition meaning."[26]

In one version or another this view is defended by such philosophers as Carl Hempel, Brand Blanshard, Donald Davidson, W. V. O. Quine, Michael Williams, Ludwig Wittgenstein, Hilary Putnam, and of course the numerous postmodernist writers. Hick's position is actually close to Kant, who also admits a "thing in itself" beyond our cognitive grasp. But many (e.g., Nietzsche, Ernst Mach, and the logical positivists) have seen no point in retaining such a useless addendum and have maintained that there is only the world we construct by our interpretations.

This has now become such a point of "common sense" that you may be amazed that anyone could question it. But the air of commonsense reasonableness disappears once you probe into exactly how language (or the mind) does to its objects what it is alleged that it does.

In any case, the "Midas touch" view of the mind (language, culture) makes access to "Real truth" impossible—and for the more radical thinkers makes "Real truth" itself impossible, if not ridiculous. And it is this second main line of argument from the transforming power of mind and language—sometimes combined with the first—that leads the charge against "Real truth" as correspondence with a "real world" in which we have to find our way and become the kind of person we are going to be.

A BRIEF CRITIQUE OF THE "MIDAS TOUCH" VIEW

This transformational or "constructionist" view, however, is called into serious question by two points:

First, it actually presents itself as a bit of "Real truth": as the "Real truth" about the mind in relation to its world. It does not say: "As I or we think of or experience the world, the world is a construct of the mind, but it might not be that way at all." It says simply, "The world is a construct of the mind," and even "The mind constructs the world—including the mind." And it means it. It intends to give us the very essence of the world/mind relationship as it is independently of how anyone may or may not think of it. But of course this cannot be done if the constructionist's own theory is correct. For in thinking about that relationship one modifies it, one "constructs" it.

And second—as was pointed out in our discussion of facts—it has never been explained how, precisely, the mind (language, culture), being what it is, could actually make or construct a world of things such as solar systems and blades of grass, being what they are. From the beginning of the effort centuries ago, we have many, many explanations of how and why we think of or perceive things in the world as we do. But that is, simply, quite another topic. Certainly our "thinkings" and "perceivings" themselves are, in a sense, made by us; but that is not so of what our "thinkings" and "perceivings" are about or of—our objects, our subjects.

This critical point is as true of objects such as historical events, literature, and moral values—the "fuzzy stuff" of life—as it is of the "hard" objects such as bricks and planets. The elements of the political, the moral, and the artistic certainly are different in nature from the physical world, and they pose problems for knowledge that are peculiar to them. But how they—as distinct from our inquiries and thought and discourse about them—could be created or formed by mind or language has never yet been explained, and no explanation seems forthcoming.

Candidly examined, the mind or culture of the human being simply has no hermetically sealed "inside," such as the advocates of the Midas touch epistemology would have us accept. We are in a world other than ourselves, and we are equipped to deal with it as it is, correcting our mistakes and misperceptions as we go. But here, as with the first main line of argument—"naturalism"—that comes against "Real truth," there is much work for us to do if we are to sustain the methods and objectives of C. S. Lewis.

THE UNFINISHED TASK

Of course, Lewis cannot be expected to give us responses to the challenges of our own day. Each generation must fight its own battles, though it must learn much from the past. Today the main task before us is nothing less than the redemption of reason, of the intellect itself—within the academy, and then across the broad range of human life. It is reason itself, not just truth, that is now fighting for its life. And it, like truth, is lost as a resource of human existence unless it can be identified and used independently of the adoption or rejection of political and cultural outlooks deemed proper or improper.

Although it is not a theme for this talk to develop, the loss of competent reason in our culture manifests itself mainly in the fields of law and education. These two fundamental areas have collapsed, or are collapsing, under the impact of desire and will unchecked by reason. That is but a natural outcome of the disappearance of "Real truth," for without it reason has nothing to serve but the ends of desire and whatever power it can bring to bear to realize them.[27]

Human desire is of course not bad in itself. It is good. But unchecked by reason and reality, it always opposes truth as "Real truth" that puts us in touch with reality; for desire unchecked always demands more than reality can give. Therefore, there is a deep human drive toward setting truth aside, and what better way to do this than by just denying its reality altogether—or at least its accessibility. Naturalism, as Lewis saw so well in *Abolition of Man* and so forth, is in the end the slave of desire, which, if allowed to rule unchecked, will destroy humanity. For desire to have its way through the instrumentality of naturalism, truth must go, precisely, into the fire.

What we must be sure of now, and must act upon, is that only through the rescue of truth—"Real truth" as correspondence with fact—can reason itself be salvaged, and thereby human life sustained in the power and dignity it cries out for by its nature and divine appointment. The excesses and mistakes of modernity should not be allowed to obscure this fundamental point. None, I believe, would be more emphatic about it than C. S. Lewis himself.

CHAPTER 33

Postmodernism and the Christian Faith

Dallas's career was centered during the rise of postmodernism and modern constructionism. As a realist, he believed that constructionism was problematic because it maintains that all things, including truth, are social and mental constructs. This essay is a response to the modern/postmodern epistemological duel and provides an evaluation and comparison of both while also describing the potential effects both have on contemporary evangelical theology.

Written as "What Significance Has 'Postmodernism' for Christian Faith?" (previously unpublished)

WHAT MAKES POSTMODERNISM SO INTERESTING TODAY IS THAT IT lets us get on with business that we firmly believe we ought to be getting on with: careful discussion of those things that matter most in life. It arose not in response to modernism generally, or to that of a Descartes, Locke, or Kant, but in response to the culturally paralyzing empiricist variant on modernism that defines itself through David Hume, John Stuart Mill, and the so-called "logical" positivism of the mid-twentieth century. With this variant there came the view of knowledge as restricted to "science" and "scientific theory," always interpreted with a bias toward the sense-perceptible world. Modernism preached, "There is one reality, the natural world, and physics is its prophet."

Postmodernism takes the scientistic bull by the horns and says: "Theorizing in science is just another one of the social practices that you find going on in our world. There are other practices such as literary criticism, politics, biblical theology, handicapping horses at Hollywood Park. . . . They all have their own internal standards of meaning and correctness. And physics with all its techniques of discovery has no more hegemony over them than they have over it." The postmodern response to empirico-positivist modernism is essentially a "you too" response. All social practices persist as the continuation of a more or less stable set of interconnected activities. To the "scientific" critique that says to systematic theology or political science, for example, that it does not meet criteria that would stamp it as a respectable intellectual enterprise, the postmodern response is that systematic theology and so forth has its own language, traditions, texts, problems, and methods.

Further, postmodernism argues that, while physics or formal logic of course has all these conditions as well, it has nothing more. Physics cannot, in particular, lay claim to be the form that its own knowledge must take—to possess the essence of knowledge—and it cannot claim to have an exclusive window on reality, one allowing it to report that "the other guys" aren't dealing with anything that is real.

Why can it not? It is at this point that we come to the intellectual substance of the postmodernist position. This actually consists in nothing less than an account of what the conscious life consists of. As much as postmodernists like to insist that theirs is not just another philosophy, they cannot avoid the reality that they are engaged in exactly the same task as all of the clear cases of modern philosophy—that of analyzing the nature of human consciousness. They have three main points:

1. Consciousness is a linguistic activity.
2. Language functions by its internal dynamics alone. What governs the "cognitive" and other moves in the cultural process,

marking them as successful or not, are interrelations within the process itself, and these alone.

3.   Language is a social life. With my language, I and others share a world we are already involved in—through "rules"—in whatever consciousness I may have. The first two points stand in radical disagreement with the great "moderns," while the third would have seemed to them a simple irrelevance.

There are three corresponding negations to the postmodern positions stated above:

1.   Consciousness is not a purely inner or spiritual or mental life, such as the "Platonic" or "Cartesian" self was supposed to enjoy. It is important to secure this, for if nonlinguistic consciousness were allowed, the next thing might be that it would claim direct access to how things really are, undistorted by the communal linguistic filters: a distinctively "modern" idea. Postmodern philosophers do not tend to be greatly worried about where this leaves God's consciousness.

2.   Language is not tied to a reality lying "outside" it, to which it must conform and which it "mirrors" when correct. If this is not granted there is always the possibility of a perspective outside the "language game" criticizing the moves made within the game in terms of their lack of adequacy to how things "really" are.

3.   There is no "private" language. If this is not granted, then I might very well have knowledge that is totally removed from rational appraisal by others, and, conversely, I am threatened with skepticism, since my consciousness might then have no essential connection with anything beyond my self.

Given all of this, one can very well say, "On with the show!"— whatever the show may be. If it is physics or literary criticism, evangelizing urban pagans or Muslims in the Philippines, or discussing postmodernism, the moves in the game are guided by and subject to criticism, but only by reference to standards that are themselves part of the cultural activity in question. This, I think, is the primary significance of postmodernism for the Christian gospel, and for the many subpractices and disciplines that fall under its unifying thrust in world history.

Some questions will arise. Doesn't this mean that the secular humanist, the Buddhist—or for that matter a woman sacrificing chickens to her god in Los Angeles or New York City—has just as good a game as an evangelical minister trained in the best evangelical seminaries? Their game can, according to postmodernism, be judged as deficient only by rules internal to the life game they are playing. The non-_____ (whoever) is in no position either to know or to show that they are wrong about God or reality. The Christian who would be postmodernist surely has the task of explaining the Great Commission of Matthew 28 in postmodernist terms: "The heathen in his blindness bows down to wood and stone."[1]

And what about revelation in the postmodernist view? Did the patriarchs and so forth just start one cultural tradition among others, or did they, within some limits, find God as he really is apart from all languages and pass the objective truth on through the centuries to us. In John 14, Jesus explained to his little graduating class that the "world" cannot receive the spirit of truth because "it neither sees nor knows Him." "But," he continued, "you know him for he resides with you and shall be in you." He talks as if the "world" were blinded to a reality that is there all the same, their empirical language game notwithstanding. Is Christian revelation, and Christian experience today, access to a reality by which the adherents of all language games are to be judged, or not? Acts 17:30–31 suggests it is.

And then how can the postmodernist reconcile his interpretation of knowledge with itself? Indeed, it is clear that he (Rorty, Toulman, MacIntyre, Lyotard) intends to lay clear before us the absolute nature of knowledge (language, consciousness). Yet in the nature of his case his interpretation of knowledge (his knowledge of knowledge) can only be more talk about the talk in which knowledge consists, whether it be biblical theology talk, physics talk, or whatever. So why should a modernist accept the language of the postmodernist about knowledge? The postmodernist cannot consistently say: "Because that's how knowledge is!" He cannot, even though he clearly intends just that. He cannot officially deal with objective essences. The modernist can at least consistently affirm that he is stating what knowledge really is, even if he turns out to be wrong. The postmodernist can only say: "We find it works best for us to talk about knowledge in our way."

Finally, postmodernism is actually a return to the authority of social practice as the basis for all critique, which means that social practice in general cannot be subject to critique. This is abundantly clear from, for example, Rorty's *Philosophy and the Mirror of Nature*[2] as well as Lyotard's *The Postmodern Condition*.[3] Such ancient precepts as "Thou shalt not follow a multitude to do evil" (Exod. 23:2) can be applied in specific cases, but postmodernism hardly leaves you a logical leg to stand on to oppose such a "professional practice," much less the spirit of the age.

CHAPTER 34

The Failure of Evangelical Politics

In this essay, Dallas outlines the history of American Evangelicalism and its shortcomings in the areas of moral knowledge, ethics, and integrity in public life. He cautions readers about the consequences of a disciple-less church and the impact of Christian leaders who have missed or ignored the larger vision of God's "Divine Conspiracy" in our world.

First published in 2009 as "The Failure of Evangelical Political Involvement in the Area of Moral Transformation" in *God and Governing: Reflections on Ethics, Virtue, and Statesmanship*

THE HEART OF THE QUESTION BEFORE US IS QUITE SIMPLE: WHY after twenty-five to thirty years of evangelical political involvement, at a high level of visibility and influence, is there little or no improvement in the ethical quality of American political discourse and practice? I'm not going to question the assumption of the question—namely, that there hasn't been any improvement. It seems to me that this is obvious. The words *integrity* and *maturity* were used in my assignment, and those are good words, but they don't cut very deeply today without some explanation. Integrity becomes an issue in public life, of course, as does maturity; but you need to spell out what they mean. And in this context maturity means you have grown up ethically. It means the ideals that are honored in discourse about the ethical or the moral life have increasingly come into possession of you. Integrity would mean, among other things, that you don't have to run different processes in your life—that you're transparent and all parts of who you are hang together, are consistent, so you don't have to keep parts of yourself hidden. You don't live in the dark. But when you speak about growing up morally, you are also actually talking about the ability to lead on important matters of life.

For example, I so appreciated David Wells's discussion of debt.[1] Debt is a primary problem for life, as is repeatedly emphasized in all "Wisdom literature." "The borrower becomes the lender's slave" (Prov. 22:7). Debt, if not handled with the utmost caution, undercuts the ability to live and to lead. It becomes a great destructive force. The greatest threat to the indispensable virtue of prudence in America is the credit card and "easy" credit: the ability to gain possession of things without paying for them. It is equally harmful at the level of government. John Maynard Keynes is mainly the one who brought deficit financing into "respectable" governmental practice. Some used to object to him that sooner or later you'd have to pay the debt; and his brilliant reply was, "Sooner or later we'll all be dead." Of course, after that you don't have to pay your debts; someone else does. Debt is a relentless burden, rarely well handled, though those who sell it present it as a wonderful opportunity. It is a constant threat to well-being and character, to maturity and integrity.

I want to address the question of the recent failure of evangelical involvement in politics as directly as I can, by way of three related factors:

First I will discuss the lack of connection between the evangelical "gospel" now and character development. The fundamental message that is heard now from evangelicals is not what we have always heard from evangelicals and other Christians. Evangelical Christians have a long history, and pre–World War II Evangelicalism, especially in the eighteenth and the early nineteenth centuries, was, quite simply, a different kind of religion—with very different practices and theological assumptions.

Second, I will describe the disappearance of moral knowledge from the "institutions of knowledge" in our society. The institutions of knowledge are primarily the universities, including higher education generally, and the church. You may find it strange to hear the church listed as an institution of knowledge, but if you do, that is precisely a part of our problem, and we have to deal with it.

Finally, we will conclude with the general withering of professional ethos: following upon the previous points, the professional's life is no longer tied to an exalted vision of dignity and public good.

THE EVANGELICAL "GOSPEL" AND THE LACK OF CHARACTER DEVELOPMENT

The current evangelical understanding of salvation has no essential connection with a life morally transformed beyond the "ordinary." Evangelicals are good at what they call "conversion." They're not good at what comes later, because what is preached by them as the gospel has no necessary connection to character transformation. Post–World War II Evangelicalism is, basically, fundamentalism in doctrine minus the pugnacious attitude. Unfortunately, fundamentalism defined itself in terms of correct belief, but not in terms of practice. Correct beliefs were a big and important issue and still are. I don't question that. But now we must understand that we've developed a doctrine and an understanding of belief that does not entail action. It's psychologically false, and biblically false in terms of the language there used, but that's just the way Evangelicalism has developed. "Saving faith" has no necessary implication for becoming Christlike. The idea of Jesus as "Teacher," as "Master," and so on, became code language among liberals in the pre–World War II era for "merely human." So if you talked about Jesus as a teacher, that meant you were dismissing him as divine Lord, and "teacher" disappeared from the fundamentalist (and then the evangelical) vernacular. And, of course, where you don't have teachers you can't have students. So discipleship gradually disappeared during the twentieth century. Discipleship has historically been the process of association with Jesus and his people in which you become like him. That disappeared from evangelical practice.

Now, there are tons and tons of problems with this. This view is founded on a whole hermeneutic that set aside the Gospels and said that our gospel for today is Paul's gospel, which was different from what Jesus preached. The upshot is that now we have this lovely little bumper sticker: "Christians aren't perfect, just forgiven." The former is fine; the latter is not. Christians aren't perfect. The focus on perfection distracts from the real issue—character transformation and obedience; and we've avoided obedience long enough to no longer know how to obey. We have adopted this position under a misreading of the gospel among evangelicals, which says, "Just forgiven." That's it.

How do we grow in Christlikeness? What does it look like? I will give you a couple of verses here just as illustrations of where such growth comes out. "Do nothing from rivalry or conceit, but in humility count others more significant than yourselves" (Phil. 2:3). Now, just think of the effects of that, and of what it would be like to learn it to the point where doing it is easy—where it was not a strain but was an expression of who you really are—to habitually see others as better than yourself. Further on in that same chapter: "Do all things without grumbling or disputing, that you may be blameless and innocent, children of God without blemish, in the midst of a crooked and perverse generation, among whom you shine as lights in the world" (Phil. 2:14, 15). That's basic Christian life from Paul's point of view. That's a life that wins the world and provides a model of life under God. That's a life that has to explain its source to an inquiring public, because it stands out and is so different. That's the New Testament vision. We're talking about taking 1 Corinthians 13 and saying, "Yes, that's for me. I will do that. I will let love dwell in me to the extent that, because love dwells in me, I suffer long and am kind. Love also does not envy, does not puff itself up, does not exalt itself, and so on. That will become my natural character." But in the evangelical gospel preached today there is no natural connection between what is preached as the gospel among evangelicals and the Christlikeness described in these verses.

There are three "gospels" heard today. The first is that believing Jesus suffered for your sins brings forgiveness and heaven. That's the standard version of the gospel among evangelicals. Is it true? Yes, it's true, but that's not the gospel. It's actually one theory of the atonement, and it does not make up the whole of the gospel. Did Jesus die for our sins? Yes, he certainly did.

The second gospel is that Jesus was in favor of liberation and deliverance from oppression, and you can stand with him in that. This is roughly the gospel of the theological left, and it pretty much turns out to be what the political left also thinks. Is that true? Yes, that's true. A well-known preacher of other days, Vance Havner, used to say that Jesus was not crucified for saying, "Behold the lilies; for they toil not, neither do they spin," but for saying, "Behold the Pharisees, how they steal."[2] And from a human point of view, that's what happened. He got under the skin of the oppressors. He was in favor of liberation.

I call the third gospel preached today "churchmanship." Basically, you take care of your church and your church will take care of you. Today that's widely practiced in Christianity—much more widely than people think, and, unfortunately, that "gospel" isn't even true. Now, "churchmanship" is important, and that's why my wife and I continue to be deeply involved in our local congregation. A lot of people get disillusioned with the church and they don't know quite what to make of it. People sometimes ask me why, since I'm such a "profound thinker," I'm still involved in church. I sometimes reply, "Well, the Bible says you're supposed to love your enemies, and you'll find a few there." I mean to be humorous, of course, but I usually sense some recognition when I say that. Actually, however, that's what the church is. It's a place where you can get really mad at people and not run off and leave them. It's a place where anger and contempt can be unlearned. It's a place to learn the deep things of a fellowship in Christ that lovingly endures disagreement, anger, and injury. "Churchmanship" in that sense is important. It's vital. It's in God's plan, and nothing is going to take the place of it. The church is intended to be a school of love.

But what we've arrived at in North America is wall-to-wall nondiscipleship Christianity. The three gospels that I've mentioned do not produce disciples who naturally move into progressive character transformation. They don't do that, and we all can know that through observation. The three gospels define discipleship in different ways—if they deal with it at all—but always in a way that will not include character transformation and routine obedience. These gospels produce only consumers of religious goods and services, not apprentices to Jesus in kingdom living.

We need to ask, If the gospels preached today were the ones originally preached, would there be such a thing as Christianity now? I don't think so. It is now accepted that you can be a Christian forever and not become a disciple. A disciple is someone who is with Jesus learning to be like him. That's a disciple. Actually, that's a disciple in any area. A child in third grade learning long division is a disciple of their teacher. They're with them learning to be like them with respect to a certain discipline. That's what discipleship is. If I'm a disciple of Jesus, I'm learning from him how to lead my life in the kingdom of God as he would lead my life in the kingdom of God if he were I. How would he do that? I'm learning from him. I'm not learning to lead his life. He did very well with that, and that's done and over with and we don't need to do that again. What is at issue now is my life. How am I going to lead my life?

This brings us back to the issue of the evangelicals in political life. If you're involved in politics, how do you do what you do there: as a judge, a state representative, or chairman of a committee in a political campaign? How would Jesus do that? You must exalt him in your mind to the point where you believe he would actually know how to do the job and do it well. So, in so many ways the great old text "What think ye of Christ?" is always the question before us, and if you think of him rightly you will naturally (supernaturally) become his student. You'll become his apprentice, and you'll believe that he's the best man in your field, whatever your field is. So this takes him out of the category of merely a sacrificial lamb and puts him in the category of master of the universe. People who are running for the presidency are trying to get a job from Jesus. Did you know that? Jesus is actually now the king of the kings of the earth (Rev. 1:5). He's not waiting for the millennium, though that will change the scene radically. But this is now, and how would you be president of the United States and do it as Jesus would do it under present conditions?

We have managed, curiously enough, for evangelicals to become "nominal" Christians. This is a real historical curiosity, because one of the things that have been distinctive of the evangelicals through the ages—from Luther on—is their resistance to nominal Christianity. But now it is possible for evangelical Christians to differ from non-Christians only, or very largely, in terms of what they're called. So, when we ask that question we started with—"Why after twenty-five to thirty years of evangelical _____ . . ."—we have this nominal Christianity as our answer. The lack of a noteworthy difference in the moral character of public and political life is to be expected from the very nature of contemporary Evangelicalism.

An outstanding church recently discovered that involvement in church activities is no measure of spiritual growth! I love these people dearly; they're wonderful followers of Christ. But my heart bleeds for them and for us, and I wonder how they could have missed this for so long. Thank God they knew something was not working right and they went out of their way to make a very elaborate study. But it is the gospel that is preached that establishes the background for evangelical practice, and you cannot "plow around it." You simply can't. That language comes out of frontier days when you deadened trees to plant crops and just "plowed around them" until they fell over. But you can't plow around the central message we are preaching. It determines the result we get. We have to come to grips with that. What are we preaching? What is the message?

The result we get is the natural outcome of the basic message we are preaching, and that outcome is shocking to some people. What is the alternative? Well, we can try preaching the gospel Jesus preached in the way he preached it. We could try that. In my own life as a young, very green Southern Baptist pastor, it came as a shock to me when I realized that Jesus was not preaching what I was preaching, and then I realized that I had been taught that I was not supposed to preach what he was preaching. In fact, in one way or another, that teaching has become standard. We today do not know how to preach what he preached. The idea grows up that Paul had one gospel and Jesus had another, which is patently false once you look at the texts. You'd never get that idea from the New Testament unless you were told it must be there.

THE DISAPPEARANCE OF
MORAL KNOWLEDGE

Around the middle of the last century (after World War II), knowledge of good and evil, right and wrong, virtue and vice, ceased to be available from our schools (especially higher education), and then from our churches. We often get the order of events wrong when we start to talk about what has happened in education with the elimination of Bible reading and prayer from public schools. That elimination comes a long way down the line. It only happened because of what had happened in higher education decades before. After the Second World War, the change in climate of thought began to hit street level and the court system. But the real issue here was the disappearance of the knowledge of good and evil, right and wrong, from society. And I emphasize "knowledge" because we're talking about moral knowledge: about knowing what is good, what is right, what is wrong, and so on. This knowledge ceased to be available as knowledge from our schools, but it had much earlier already dropped out of the position of knowledge in elite intellectual circles and in higher education.

Toward the end of the 1800s the university system began to distance itself from the church, as is well known; and one essential way it had of doing that was to interpret theology and morality in such a way that they were no longer to count as knowledge. This process started with some "theology" and with other "ecclesiastical" matters that were taught at the various colleges but were, in fact, just traditions. Usually the particular schools or universities had some denominational identification, and they were each trying to teach their "faith and practice" as a whole as if it all amounted to knowledge—though it was largely just tradition. When the emphasis on research came along in higher education, the traditional material often did not stand up to critical examination, and so, rather than sorting it out progressively, to distinguish the sound from the unsound, there simply arose a redefinition of what knowledge was. Institutions of "knowledge" ceased to make the traditional moral knowledge—of what kind of persons we ought to be and of what we ought to do—available.[3] The universities no longer explicitly undertook to teach people how to live. (They certainly continued to do so implicitly.) Gradually there disappeared any responsibility on the part of universities to teach what is right, wrong, good, evil, and so on. The background assumption or excuse was that there is no knowledge of such things, so "Why not?"

Some may wonder, for example, how we've arrived at the point of teaching "tantric sex" on a certain campus, when something like that couldn't have happened before. Some may think, "Well, it's just because we used to be governed by prejudice and now we're open-minded." But the things that occur on campus now actually come into a vacuum left by the disappearance of moral knowledge. We have moved from the age of "Why?"—seeking a good reason for what we do—to the age of "Why not?" No one in an official position is prepared to go to the people who are doing morally questionable things and even ask, "Why?" I won't begin to tell you stories about what happens in the classroom itself, because in the classroom it's perfectly all right to be radical and to relentlessly teach a "radical" morality or religion. You can't be traditional, but you can be radical—that is even a "plus" to most minds—and then in a pinch you can pass that off as political, not as moral. The political, as we know, does not require knowledge. It only requires advocacy, and that opens the door for things like tantric sex and almost anything else.

So, in fact, higher education and the elite professional groups continue to pressure and teach on moral matters—good, bad, right, wrong—and if you don't believe it, just get crossways of what is advocated as morality by them and you will be subjected to full-blown moral opprobrium. That's because in fact no one can separate life from morality. Moral sentiment and moral opinions are always in full force, and perhaps more so now than ever, because they are not subject to rational criticism in open discussion. One of the things that used to happen in higher education and elite circles, though certainly not in a perfect way, was that moral teachings were surfaced, talked about, and subjected to rational criticism. Now they're not. What is taught is taught by example, tone of voice, selection of subject matters, and so on—often by unguarded explicit statements—but there's no rational criticism directed at them because it's not taken to be an area of rationality or knowledge. Pressure, however, abounds.

Why does it matter whether or not there is moral knowledge? This is really the heart of the matter: Knowledge alone confers the right and responsibility to act, to direct action, to set policy, to supervise policy, and to teach. Sentiment does not do that. Opinion does not do that. Tradition does not do that. Power does not do that. You expect people who act to know what they are doing, don't you? You probably would not take your car to a shop with a sign in front of it that reads "We are lucky at making repairs," or "We're inspired," or "We feel real good about it." This is not a matter of convention. It is how knowledge actually works in human life, and it's very important to understand that. Without moral knowledge there is no moral authority. Hence there is only "political correctness," even though it looks and feels every bit like morality and often assumes a distinctively moral tone and force.

The upshot is that we fall into calling evil good and good evil. One way of doing that is to say it's all the same—as "diversity" has a way of dictating. In the absence of public knowledge of good and evil, right and wrong, and virtue and vice, human leaders have no moral basis upon which to lead in terms of what is good, and so any attempt at leadership in the political, legislative, or other realm immediately becomes a matter of a political or legal contest. There's no acknowledged basis, no public knowledge, of right and wrong, good and evil, in terms of which leadership could be exercised. There's no basis upon which to guide the leader's personal life and public choices, and as a result leaders tend to abdicate to public or internal pressures, with no basis to support them in goodness. Desire, pleasure, and success guide them. Personal integrity rarely survives; still less does effectiveness in leading for what is good and right.

Today, equality is not actually regarded as a matter of human dignity and value. That is very hard to defend. Rather, it is regarded as a doorway to freedom. Freedom itself is not regarded in terms of the inherent dignity and value of human beings, but rather as opportunity. Opportunity is not regarded as opportunity to do what is good and right, but to get what you want. We talk a lot about them, but the basic values in our society are not equality and freedom—they are pleasure and "happiness." And these are interpreted in sensualistic terms. Our society is a society of feeling. That is why debt conquers common sense. Feeling is our master. That's why we have so many issues about abuse of one kind or another: abuse comes out of frustration over feeling. That is why we are such an addictive society. Also, watch your commercials for automobiles and so forth, and see how much of it is predicated upon feeling. Feeling runs our society. It also runs our massively failing educational system. It is the only acknowledged ultimate value. That explains why we do so badly in areas of learning that require sustained discipline—which doesn't "feel good."

Our society basically has two values, which come together. One is doing what you want to do—mistaken for freedom—and the other is pleasure. Sometimes people say happiness is one of our values, but happiness now means nothing that would have been recognized as such by the great thinkers from Aristotle to John Locke, for it translates into pleasure—having a good time. That is what Bill Clinton learned about sex—what is and is not "sex with that woman"—which he learned as part of a legalistic religion. The disappearance of knowledge of moral values leaves us open to all sorts of delusions. On freedom, I want to recommend a writing by a man named Thomas Hill Green, called *Lectures on the Principles of Political Obligation.*[4] What you find in Green are the efforts of a man who was raised an evangelical and grew more liberal as he went on in his life, but he retained a sense of what freedom should mean: Freedom is not just freedom from. Freedom is the "exercise of abilities to attain the good in community."[5] If you want to see real freedom made visible, watch Pavarotti in performance. That's freedom. Watch a highly disciplined athlete, sans drugs. You'll see freedom. "Freedom is the exercise of abilities to attain the good in community." If you follow the idea of freedom that is in Green's writings, you will understand that this connection between freedom and good is an area of knowledge. We must learn to represent it as such.

PROFESSIONAL CALLING FAILS

In the past, human beings had access to the support of a religious outlook like the one that characterized classical Evangelicalism, in people like Richard Baxter and John Wesley or William Wilberforce. When we think of Wilberforce, it's important to remember that there were two objectives on his part. One was the abolition of the slave trade. For this he is admired today. But there was also the "reformation of manners," as he called it. It is important to look at his book that was written to address the issue of "manners" and ask yourself how many evangelicals of today would be comfortable with what it says.[6] It's written out of a specific theological context. John Wesley and John Newton shared and promoted its outlook, and it presents a very different perspective on "real Christianity" from anything we would recognize as "evangelical" today—no matter how heartily we sing "Amazing Grace."

With the absence of publicly available knowledge of the good and the right, and of any essential relationship with the Christian gospel, the traditional understanding of professional devotion to the good one's profession serves is lost. When knowledge of good and devotion to God cease to be the governing principles of professional life, then professional integrity collapses or shrinks down to mere technical competence. Now, in the theory of the professions as it's being done today, you see the gradual but inevitable disappearance of any idea of devotion to the public good. It's very interesting to see how "market theory" enters the picture. The only obligation of the professional, it is increasingly said, is technical expertise, and in the context in which individuals use and exercise that expertise—we vainly imagine—the market will sort out who's good and who's bad, and competition will make things all work for the best for the public. Yes, and about then another cow flew by.

The Rotary Club's slogan, by contrast, is "Service Above Self"— still displayed at their meetings. You don't have to wonder where that came from, right? That's Jesus, and people knew that and honored that when they started the Rotary Club, and thus they had a moral vision of professional life, which remained very strong in this country up until quite recently—again, finally caving in to the influence of the academy. But what could the slogan mean today? With the demise of Christian moral understanding as a bulwark of public life, it certainly means nothing with power to oblige. Really, it means hardly anything at all. Still, "service above self" is the idea back of traditional professionalism, and if you have a Christian vision of life in the kingdom of God as a disciple of Jesus—and on the basis of that you have moral knowledge and a corresponding moral life— then you're prepared to become a very different kind of person in public service. You won't live for your self-advancement above all, but to advance the causes of what is good and right in your special field of activity—the political above all.

IS THERE A WAY BACK?

You will not be surprised to hear me say that there is. There is a way back, but it is the way of Jesus Christ understood now in the generous but rigorous way in which it has been understood for much of the past in this country, and in other countries in other parts of the world. There is a way back, but evangelical leaders (pastors, teachers, writers) must lead. They are the ones who have to lead the way back. They will find many others to join them if they will but lead. One of the things that will happen for those who follow Christ fully and grow in their relationship to him is that they will stand out in such a way that people will look to them for leadership. There's a very interesting example in the history of the Huguenots. For many centuries there's been an ongoing battle between Islam and the rest of the world. It is not a new thing. There was a period in which those under Islam ran sea galleys around the Mediterranean—ships run by oars, and those oars pulled by slaves. It's interesting that on those galleys the Huguenots were the ones that everyone trusted. If they had anything of value to be kept, they put it in the care of the Huguenots. If there was any issue of truth or righteousness, the Huguenots on board were the ones who were looked to for right judgment. That is an example of what we were looking at in Philippians 2 above, of shining out as lights in a darkened world.

Our point of attack and of service today must be the presentation of the basic biblical truths as knowledge of reality. What the world has done is to negotiate the church into a position of saying that it does not have knowledge. Christians just have faith, and faith is an irrational leap. The world assumes Archie Bunker's definition of faith: "It's what you wouldn't believe for your life if it wasn't in the Bible." This is a total misunderstanding of faith. Although faith often goes beyond knowledge, it never works—on the biblical model—outside of a context of knowledge. Many of the things we as Christians have faith in are things we actually also know—or can know. That will seem almost cognitively incoherent for most people today, because they've had it ground into them that when it comes to faith, knowledge is simply ruled out. That's why it is hard to make any sense of "separation of church and state" as it is discussed today, in comparison to how it was understood in the writing of the Constitution, which makes perfect sense. People today think of something other than knowledge when you say "church." If the church brought vital knowledge to human existence, there would be no more talk of separation of church and state, in its current meaning, than there would be separation of chemistry and state. In the past it was assumed that the church did bring vital knowledge to human existence.

It was basically the decision of the church itself to let knowledge go, in the 1800s and 1900s, and to undertake to present something other than vital knowledge. That decision set the scene for where we stand now. I'm talking about knowledge as you require it in your dentist, your auto mechanic, your brain surgeon, your politician (I hope), and so on. You have knowledge of a subject matter when you are representing it (speaking of it, treating it) as it is, on an appropriate basis of thought and experience—including a proper use of "authority." Most of the things we know, scientific or otherwise, we know on the basis of authority. Somebody told us. Nothing wrong with that. What is presented in the Bible on fair interpretation, and verifiable in life, is knowledge of reality: especially of the spiritual and moral life in Christ. So if you're going to turn things back to genuine character transformation, you have to resist the temptation to shy away from presenting the basic things—let's call it "Mere Christianity," it's a good phrase—as knowledge. You have to shy away from treating these things as something else, such as feelings, opinions, traditions, and power plays. You have to know and accept and present Mere Christianity as a body of knowledge.

What do I mean? To repeat: you have knowledge of a subject matter where you are representing it as it is, on an appropriate basis of thought and experience. So, let's try the Apostles' Creed: "I believe in God the Father almighty, Maker of heaven and earth, and in Jesus Christ, His only Son," and so forth. Is that knowledge? What do you say? The challenge is to stand up for Christian knowledge. Not with dogmatism or close-mindedness, but with all humility of mind, with all openness, ready to hear anything from anyone; but you must represent it as knowledge if you are going to find the way back to an Evangelicalism that is routinely transformational. The disastrous mistake was that the church backed away from knowledge in the last two centuries, and piously proclaimed "faith" as something superior to and indifferent to knowledge. But the Bible is all about knowledge. Just read the texts with that in mind. Do an inductive Bible study on "knowledge." Even eternal life is knowledge, as Jesus said (John 17:3), and as we see in 2 Peter 1:2–5, where we are told that we've been provided with "everything that pertains to life and godliness through the true knowledge of Jesus Christ." It's all founded upon knowledge, though there is more to discipleship to Christ than just knowledge.

Vital knowledge is, of course, never what we now call "head knowledge," and that's the way the Bible treats it. It is interactive relationship. When Jesus says, "This is eternal life that they would know you, the only true God, and Jesus Christ, whom you have sent," he's talking about interactive relationship. That's knowledge, biblical knowledge. Now, of course, "head knowledge" can come out of that, but life knowledge is always interactive relationship.

There is also the idea of "secular knowledge" that must be confronted. Allowing the secular world to define knowledge meant there would be no knowledge of God, and the Christian would be left with mere scraps of "tradition" and "diversity." But what business does a university have being secular? Think about it a moment: secular university? Is reality secular? George Bernard Shaw used to say that "Catholic University" is an oxymoron. What he had in mind, that clever but shallow man, was that if you were Catholic, you had to be close-minded. Well, maybe he needed to broaden his acquaintance with Catholics. There certainly are close-minded ones, as with people of every group including the secular. But if "Catholic University" is an oxymoron, then why isn't "secular university"? I submit to you that it is just that, and if you ever want to see close-mindedness and thoughtlessness, step into the atmosphere of a secular university. Is reality secular? Has someone shown that it's secular? No. There isn't even a division of the university that's called "The Reality Department." They don't even have one. It's a little presumptuous for a university to pronounce itself "secular," isn't it?

Having lost knowledge, then, people today are no longer in a position to deal seriously with moral issues. The basic content of moral knowledge is actually love. Love is so central that you cannot ignore it, and everyone knows that it is somehow the mark of a good person. We want to be tough intellectually, so we don't want to use that word very much in "serious" academic contexts. Thus, twentieth-century ethical theory can be accurately characterized as an effort to have morality without a heart. We've surely seen how that "works." Remember the saying by John Dewey: "We want to be good, but not 'goody.'" Everyone's busy not being "goody," and good disappears as a factor governing rational life.

The good person is one permeated with agape love. Right action is the act of love. To love is to be devoted to the good of what is loved. I love those around me as I am working for their good, and of course mine, too, under God; and Jesus and his followers deal with the details of this at great lengths. No one has ever come close to spelling out what love means as he did. We have a terrible time understanding love because we confuse it with desire. We say things like "I love chocolate cake." Now, for sure you do not love chocolate cake. You want to eat it. That's different. I suppose you could imagine someone who actually loved chocolate cake. They'd just go around taking care of chocolate cakes, watching out for their interests. We have an awfully hard time today making sense of love because we're so confused on these matters. But once we pay attention, we realize that desire is not love, and often is opposed to love. In this country every fifteen seconds, I think it is, some woman is badly beaten—maybe killed—by someone, usually one who says he "loves" her.

The path to moral goodness comes through Jesus Christ. The path toward becoming a thoroughly good person, dominated by love, is apprenticeship to Jesus Christ in the kingdom of God. A disciple of Jesus is one learning from him to live their life as Jesus would lead their life if he were they. And now we're back to the issue of who has the responsibility for bringing this out, and it is the pastors and the teachers—primarily of the evangelical Christian churches. Unfortunately, many other Christian groups have fallen completely under the sway of the university system with its moral blindness. The good news in the gospel of the New Testament is that we can now enter the rule and reign of God by relying upon Jesus for everything. We do that by becoming like little children, as Jesus said, by going "beyond the righteousness of the scribes and Pharisees" (beyond "performance" into the depths of the heart), and by being born "from above." Those are words chosen from Jesus's teachings about entering the kingdom of the heavens or the kingdom of God.

Salvation then becomes not something about the afterlife, but about the life that comes into us now—enters us by the spirit of God from above. "Above" is right here. It is resurrection life. That is salvation. Paul says in 1 Corinthians 15:17, "If Christ has not been raised, your faith is futile and you are still in your sins." Redemption does not stop at the cross; it moves on from there. In 2 Corinthians 5:14–15 we read, "One has died for all, therefore all have died, and He died for all that they who live should no longer live for themselves, but for Him who died and rose again on their behalf." A good evangelical is supposed to say, "so that people can be forgiven and go to heaven." Do you see the difference? If you have a theory of the atonement that does not take into account our life now, then you don't have right what Christ provides in the atonement. Moral maturity and integrity come through growth in the grace and knowledge of our Lord and Savior Jesus Christ (2 Pet. 3:18).

Grace itself is God interacting in our lives. It's interactive relationship, the very place of knowledge of God. You grow in the grace and the knowledge of our Lord Jesus Christ as your life is increasingly dominated by interactive relationship to Christ in everything. That's what it means to grow in spiritual and moral maturity. The things that Jesus teaches in the Sermon on the Mount simply illustrate the life of the person living and growing in the kingdom of God. They show that where that life comes out as we study under him is routine, easy obedience. We shift out of where people are now, standing in ordinary "fallen" relationships, where they might, for example, wonder why you would want to tell the truth if it might cost you something. Instead you honestly come to think and say, "Why would I want to tell a lie? Why? Why would I want to mislead someone since I'm standing in the kingdom of God?" Since God is with me and I'm growing in his kind of life, "Lie not one to another seeing you have put off the old man with his deeds" (Col. 3:9).

Spiritual disciplines—necessary components of life with Christ—are simply activities that we undertake, activities in our power. They are something we do that enables us to disrupt evil habits and patterns in our lives and receive grace to enable us to grow increasingly toward easy, routine obedience to Christ. They are not laws. They are not righteousness. They are simply wisdom. They are age-old and life tested, and we need to use them in our relationship with Christ. The grace of God will then flow more richly into our lives. Solitude, silence, fasting, worship, fellowship—all those are disciplines that help us receive more of divine life in our human circumstances.

Now, my final hammer blow here is that evangelical pastors and teachers are in a position to bring to their people and to the public a knowledge that will guide life into the goodness and blessedness of the kingdom of the heavens. That was Christ's intention in giving us his "Great Commission." He said in the Kingdom Proclamation: "I have been given say over all things in heaven and earth. As you go make disciples, surround them in Trinitarian reality" (Matt. 28:18–19, PAR). That's what you do with disciples. You don't just get them wet while you say, "In the name of the Father, Son, and Holy Spirit" over them. Jesus said, "Where two or three have gathered together in my name, there I am in their midst" (Matt. 18:20). We use that passage when only two or three show up. But actually it's true in the case where two or three thousand are gathered in his name—if they truly gather in his name and he's the one running the show.

They're then in a position to teach disciples to do everything that Jesus said. That's the natural progression. Then—as in past times—you will see emerging a people stunningly different from those who are children of darkness and who walk in the kingdom of darkness. The pastors are to be the teachers of the nations. The Christian writers and teachers are to teach the nations. That's their call. They teach the nations their knowledge—their knowledge of God, their knowledge of the human soul. They have to stand in the dignity of that calling and insist upon it, not out of arrogance but out of humility, and out of the firm realization that they must bring to human beings something that is both absolutely essential and something that no one else can bring.

The Christian schools (Christian "higher education") have to stand with the pastors in that posture. Perhaps the greatest issue facing the church today is whether or not the Christian schools will say loudly and clearly that they have essential knowledge that non-Christian schools do not have. There is a great resistance to this among Christian educators. The old-line, sometimes called mainline, churches were betrayed by their schools. A great issue facing us today is whether or not the evangelical church will be betrayed by its schools. The great issue is whether or not the evangelical schools will say, "We have knowledge. Knowledge that the world and the so-called secular universities do not have. We have knowledge. We're not just 'nicer,' and rather odd."

The ancient writers such as Plato and Aristotle believed that the administration of law and political life was the highest of merely human callings. The highest, because in it the greatest good (and evil!) was at issue. But we should know now that it is a calling that can only be carried out in a wisdom and power that is beyond the human. The evangelical message and life in its classical forms—not post–WWII—show how that can be done. There is no real alternative in human existence. It isn't because evangelicals are superior in any other respect. And it isn't that people we call "evangelicals" are the only brand of Christians who must and can do this. Os Guinness has expressed all of this so well in a paper, "An Evangelical Manifesto," that he and others published in 2009: "This is the call of Christ," he says. "It isn't the call of the evangelicals, and the words in response have to be the ones of those long ago, 'To whom shall we go? Thou hast the words of eternal life'" (John 6:68).[7]

CHAPTER 35

Hermeneutical Occasionalism

Dallas's concern with the study of hermeneutics fell directly in line with his investigations of epistemology and the postmodern assumptions regarding language. Here he responds to one of the premier academic theologians and hermeneutists, Kevin Vanhoozer. This also represents what many scholars have suggested was in short supply—namely, Dallas's engagement with academic theologians.

First published in 1997 in *Disciplining Hermeneutics: Interpretation in Christian Perspective*

IN HIS INTRIGUING PAPER TITLED "THE SPIRIT OF UNDERSTANDing: Special Revelation and General Hermeneutics,"[1] Kevin Vanhoozer takes the position that general hermeneutics, or the principles that govern the study of literary meaning as such, are not sufficient as a basis for the understanding of the biblical texts. Rather, a special kind of guidance, generally accessible to individuals within the faithful community, is required. This is the guidance of the triune God through the offices of the Holy Spirit. Guidance from the believing community is, for him, valid only insofar as it is an expression of the action of the Spirit: "There is a danger in tying the fate of the literal sense too closely to community consensus" (p. 149). And: "I see no reason why cognitive malfunction could not be corporate as well as individual" (p. 150). And: "The Bible will only be heard as God's

411

Word . . . if we are enabled to hear it as such by the Holy Spirit" (p. 155). Further, the understanding of the word is not something separable from the application of it in action. Application completes understanding. "The Christian understanding . . . is one that follows the Word. . . . Understanding is our ability to follow the Word. . . . The role of the Spirit is to enable us to take the biblical texts in the sense that they were intended, and to apply or follow that sense in the way we live" (p. 157).

I am largely, if not completely, in agreement (or at least in close sympathy) with the position that emerges from Vanhoozer's discussion. I hope that this will be kept in mind in what follows, for my intent is to raise some of the most difficult issues his type of position faces. To sharpen these issues quickly I shall use the phrase *hermeneutical occasionalism* as suggestive of both the content and difficulties of the position.

Occasionalism, we recall, was a post-Cartesian interpretation of mind/body interaction, most strongly associated with the name of Nicolas Malebranche (1638–1715). Under Descartes's descriptions of the mind or soul and the body, they were of distinct and separable essences. But being of such radically different kinds, how could they possibly interact? Of numerous positions that developed in response to this question, some held that they did not interact but only ran parallel, while Malebranche and some others thought that they did interact, but only indirectly. Without divine assistance they could not influence one another, but God could interact with each side in turn and thereby allow what happens in one realm to determine what happened in the other. For example, when the flesh in your foot is separated by a tack you step on, God takes note and produces a pain and other relevant phenomena in your mind. Or when you resolve to lift your arm, God notes this mental event and (through whatever mechanism) brings it about that your arm rises.

My hope is that the application to the hermeneutical situation will be immediately and intuitively clear. The problem is to get the (or a) right interpretation or understanding of the "text"—here, for simplicity sake, a biblical text. Vanhoozer seems to make authorial intent or use authoritative: "The witness of the Spirit is connected with the effectual use of the Scripture. But—whose use? Not the community of readers, but the author's. The Creed says, after all, that it was God the Father who spoke by the prophets" (p. 156). So getting the right interpretation or understanding of the text will be a matter of capturing for ourselves God's thought in expressing himself through the text in question. (Here many hairs need to be split, but I hope not for present purposes.)

Now, is it possible for us to achieve this if we are limited to the resources (1) of unbelievers operating from within the relevant social/historical contexts, or even (2) of all that plus the Christian community within which we live, however that is to be spelled out? I believe that Vanhoozer holds this to be impossible. Of course we must live in (1) and may also live in (2). But that will not be enough to allow us to achieve a right understanding of God's thought in expressing himself through a given biblical text, any more than, under the Occasionalist view, the intent to raise my arm is enough to make it go up.

I suspect that in adopting this position Vanhoozer is accepting the view—fundamental to the entire discussion and far beyond—that the "cultural context" (most importantly the language, rituals, and cosmic assumptions of the respective group or groups) makes it impossible to determine "how things are in themselves." True, he states, and I applaud it, "Language does not bar us from reality." But he adds as a part of the same sentence, ". . . though reality comes mediated by language" (p. 158).

The problem is: How to spell out this latter clause in such a way that the former can be true. How to have mediation without modification. If in his clauses we replace the word *language* with the word *experience* or *consciousness* or even *thought,* we find our location in the problematic arena of modern thought, persisting ever since Descartes "discovered" consciousness. Once you "discover" it you get out only by a miracle. (Descartes of course "got out" by discovering within his own consciousness an idea, that of a perfect being, of such grandeur that only its object [God] could have caused it. But only his rationalism allowed him to escape the toils of representationalism—a way out no longer available to us, I dare say.)

Quite true to the Occasionalist pattern, now, we find him saying that "the Spirit does not alter biblical meaning." Just as God's mind can move my arm though my mind can't, so his Spirit can bring the true meaning of the text to my mind though my (embodied, culture-bound) mind and body can't. He is able, as it were, to bypass the serpentine routings that my mind on its own must take and that, apparently, do invariably alter the biblical meaning if left to themselves.

In language that I like very much Vanhoozer states:

> The Spirit progressively disabuses us of those ideological or idolatrous prejudices that prevent us from receiving the message. (Again, this aspect of the Spirit's work too aids understanding in general.) In so doing, the Spirit renders the Word *effective*. To read in the Spirit does not mean to import some new sense to the text, but rather to let the letter be, or better, to apply the letter rightly to one's life. The Spirit of understanding is the efficacy of the Word, its perlocutionary power. According to John Owen, the Spirit is "the primary efficient cause" of our understanding of Scripture. Yet the Spirit's illumining work is not independent of our own efforts to understand. (I must *try* to raise my arm or it won't go up!) "It is the Spirit's activity, effected through our own labor in exegesis, analysis, and application, of showing us what the text means for us." (pp. 162–63)

Difficulties for Occasionalism begin to emerge when we ask the question, Why is it that God's mind can make my arm go up but my mind can't, since they are both minds? The answer seems at bottom to be nothing other than that God can do anything, and hence he can make my arm go up. Cannot he who spoke worlds (including my arm) into existence make my arm go up? And cannot this same one cause me to get the right interpretation of a text that he has produced? On pain of blasphemy we can only say, "Yes, surely he can!"

But then we must acknowledge that from the fact that he *can* do it, even though it does not follow that he *does* do it. And we also must wonder, occasionally, what exactly it is that he does in overriding our culture-bound condition to get the message to us. Or: How does he do it? And, finally, the frightening question: How do we know when (or that) he is doing it?

If we say in answer to this last question—with Vanhoozer in his section titled "Unsolved Questions"—that we recognize the presence of the Spirit in people by their confession that Jesus has come in the flesh, is that not circular, in that it is a criterion derived from the New Testament text itself, which we—it is said—can get right only by the aid of the spirit? Or if we say (as he continues on p. 29) that the mark of the Spirit in people is their obedience to the commands, promises, warnings, and narratives in the text, is that not also circular, in that it presupposes that we have got the right understanding of the commands, promises, and so forth?

The basic idea seems right, and it is not a wholly new one. In his *De Magistro* Saint Augustine argued that the understanding of words required the presence of the inward teacher, Christ the Logos, to lead us along; for words as sounds and marks are inherently dumb things at best.[2] But saying exactly how it works, and how we know when it is working, is a daunting task.

One might say, utilizing the language of John Owen quoted above, that God just causes us to have the right understanding of the text. No doubt he could do this. But if that is all there is to it, we still might not know we had the right understanding, for we might not know whether in a given case he is causing the interpretation that we have. Also, that would simply dispense with hermeneutical activity as a human undertaking. We are reminded here of preachers who say (usually shout): "I'm not telling you what I think! I'm telling you what God says!" The operant idea here is that of altogether circumventing human consciousness with its deadly contaminations. But then of course we lose the personal nature of God's relationship to us. We are simply—at least in the moment of inspiration—a keyboard on which God plays, without even our knowledge that it is he that is doing the playing. We could only guess.

The only alternative to this model of manipulation from behind the scenes is one where the Spirit "guides" us into the right interpretation through what he places before our minds, whether it be burning bushes, angels, audible words, inner images, feelings, or thoughts, or the nonphysical "presence" of pure spirits. But of course this means that we will have to be capable of and responsible for the interpretation of what is thus placed before us, and we are back in the fire. Either we can get this right on our own or we can't. If we can't, the Spirit must help us. But then . . .

A way out might be along the following lines: We could abandon representationalism as a general theory of human consciousness, and defend a realism in the light of which it does not follow from the fact that I am conscious of something that it appears to me to be what it is not in itself. Does Vanhoozer have something like this in mind with his "realism principle"? This is, of course, basic philosophical work, and the conclusion is contrary to nearly every prominent writer in the philosophy of mind and language, as well as in epistemology, today.

Then we might do painstaking phenomenological work on putative experiences of the divine word and presence, moving toward a systematic description and analysis of the various kinds of experiences involved and of how the cases of the actual presence of God to us and with us are to be distinguished from cases of absence as well as cases of false presence and false absence. An astonishing amount of this type of work has already been done in the spiritual literature that has been produced by the church through the ages.[3] We need not achieve infallibility on whether or not the Spirit is moving with a particular interpretation or event or tendency, but only sound judgment, practiced in historical/community contexts. Note that the phenomenology of the Spirit's presence would have to be done in such a way that it did not presuppose we have got the right interpretation of texts. Some would say this will be impossible, but we should be willing to see whether or not it is so in fact. And I want heartily to second Vanhoozer's stress on practice. The presence of the Spirit will, I think, mainly be known as we act on the biblical texts, especially those assigned to Jesus himself. It is by action that we enter the reality of the world that the Bible is about. It is residing in Jesus's word that permits us to enter the reality of God's rule and become free from domination by other realities (John 8:31–32; cf. 14:15–16). Just as by acting on knowledge of electricity we become agents in a world where it has play.

Armed with this knowledge of the experience of God, it may be that we can find a way around the impasse that gives rise to hermeneutical occasionalism. Perhaps we can learn the presence of God in such a way that what he places before our minds, in certain cases, as well as the construal given it, can be known to be from him. Stephen Stell's idea, which Vanhoozer seems to adopt, "that the present reality of Jesus Christ is defined not only by the narrative framework 'but also by particular experiences in our current existence,'" might be given a workable form. But there will always be a battle over such possibilities so long as intellectual culture is dominated by the view of consciousness (language) as necessarily distortive of what comes before it as an object.

Professor Vanhoozer makes many excellent points, which I must leave untouched. His thesis of the primacy of the theological for all understanding is, I think, precisely right, and is of tremendous importance not only in the academic/scholarly context, but in today's political, social, and personal contexts as well. It is a major part of the redemptive message, which the people of Jesus must bring to the current world. But I must leave off with that.

One of the background problems that make the philosophical elucidation of interpretation so difficult is that there is no agreed-upon picture of what constitutes understanding of a text or action. I am going to proceed from the assumption that understanding involves the attainment of a certain commonality between the "author" of a certain "text"—where *text* is taken in a broad sense, but paradigmatically includes written language such as we find in the Bible—and the "reader." Certainly the commonality in question cannot be sameness of experience. This is not required even of two "readers" who correctly understand the same "text." Their experiences may differ strongly, and may again differ strongly, and in characteristic ways, from that of the author, while the understanding of the relevant text is accurate and complete. Or so I shall say, and say because it seems to me all of this actually does happen, and happens as a rule in human affairs. Misunderstandings do occur, in various dimensions and degrees. But, everything considered, they are by far the exceptions, which we often seem to forget when we engage in professional discussions of "hermeneutics."

At least a core part of the commonality can be specified in the familiar Fregian terms of sense and reference, or Mill's concepts of denotation (extension) and connotation (intension). Looser ordinary language might speak of what was mentioned and what was said about it. Someone who, in general, is unable to tell what is being mentioned or what is being said about it in a given context either does not know the language, is lacking in relevant experience or information, or worse. But given relevant qualifications, one is able in general to share with the author and other readers what is being referred to and what is being said about it. Within that framework there always arise special cases where the two dimensions of this core part of understanding have to be worked out. This is the work of inquiry, inference, and recourse to relevant principles, which is not a component of the usual situation where understanding occurs. If my wife had to have recourse to inquiry, inference, and special principles of interpretation to understand me when I say, "I'll be home for dinner tonight," something would certainly be amiss.

I would like to speak of the core part of the understanding that makes up the commonality to be achieved in communication as a unit of information. I agree that information is not everything, but it is something, and something very important—something without which, it seems to me, nothing in the way of communication can occur.

PART V

Leadership

CHAPTER 36

The Roles of Women in Ministry Leadership

Dallas was often reticent to publically engage in doctrinal or denominational controversies. However, there were some issues wherein he held deep convictions and felt compelled to engage. One such issue was the role of women in ministry, and he strongly believed that women should hold leadership positions in the church. This essay addresses that debate and the ways in which misinterpretation of scripture influenced the exclusion of women in church leadership.

First published in 2010 as the foreword to *How I Changed My Mind About Women in Leadership*

WHEN ALAN JOHNSON KINDLY ASKED ME TO CONTRIBUTE A CHAPTER to *How I Changed My Mind About Women in Leadership,* I had to tell him that I had not changed my mind on this point, and thus could not contribute. All through my young life—from Mrs. Roy Rowan, at the First Baptist Church in Buffalo, Missouri, to Mrs. Flood and others at Shiloh Baptist Church in Rover, Missouri—those who had taught me most "at church" were women. Actually, I knew that, in many cases, there would have been no church at all if it hadn't been for women; and, beyond church, life in my environment was mainly anchored in strong and intelligent women who—often with little or nothing in the way of "credentials"—simply stood for what was good and right and directed others in the way of Christ.

Of course I knew that in my church the "official" pastors were men, but the issue of women teaching men and "preaching" had not hardened in that time and place, and, if need required—as was frequently the case—certain women could do very well at "bringing a message." Also, I was fortunate to be in significant contact with Wesleyan and Holiness tendencies where women were in leadership roles—quite "officially." As I grew older, and began seriously to study the Bible and the way of Christ, I of course became aware of the gender issues and of the biblical passages that, in the minds of some, occasion difficulties concerning "women preachers." But it seemed clear to me that those passages were not principles themselves, but were expressions of the principle that Christ-followers should be "all things to all men," in Paul's language. They were no more part of the righteousness and power of Christ than not eating blood or being saved by bearing children.

The contributors to this volume have, taken together, covered every point of theology, biblical interpretation, and spiritual life that is of substantial relevance to the issue of women in Christian leadership. They have done it with the best of scholarship, intelligence, sensitivity, pathos, and humor. If you have decided to work the matter through, you cannot find a better place to begin than by reading this book. It will bring light to your mind and joy to your heart—though at some points you will be saddened at how much hurt and harm can be imposed through warping the gospel and its ministry into cultural legalism in the name of God. At the risk of overdoing what has already been done, I would like to emphasize three points.

First, those gifted by God for any ministry should serve in the capacities enabled by their gift, and human arrangements should facilitate their service and provide them the opportunities to serve. There is no suggestion whatsoever in scripture or the history of Christ's people that the gifts of the Spirit are distributed along gender lines. It is clearly something that does not even appear on the mental horizon of the inspired writers. And, if it had done so, can one even imagine that they would have failed to state it clearly? Especially if it is as important as those who oppose female leadership make it out to be. You have to put the fact that, in discussing the distribution and ministry of gifts by the Spirit, nothing is said about gender down alongside the fact that many men are allowed to serve in official roles who manifestly are not supernaturally gifted. Then you realize that official leadership roles, as widely understood now, are as much human artifacts as they are a divine arrangement.

Second, it is misguided and unhelpful to try to deal with the issue of women in leadership in terms of rights and equality alone. Rights and equality are not the main considerations involved, and we will make little progress in understanding or practice so long as they are allowed to define the terms of the discussion. Equality is an extremely crude instrument to apply to human relations, even in a secular context, and much more so in the context of spiritual life and ministry for Christ. People simply are not equal when it comes to their talents, to their ministerial gifts, or to their experiences with God. To try to work out arrangements in those terms is to accept a secular model as the basis of a divine order, and to reduce leadership in the body of Christ to a level that omits the power of God.

It is not the rights of women to occupy "official" ministerial roles, nor their equality to men in those roles, that sets the terms of their service to God and their neighbors. It is their obligations that do so: obligations that derive from their human abilities empowered by divine gifting. It is the good they can do, and the duty to serve that follows, that impels them to serve in all ways possible. Women and men are indeed very different, and those differences are essential to how God empowers each to induce the kingdom of God into their specific life setting and ministry. What we lose by excluding the distinctively feminine from "official" ministries of teaching and preaching is of incalculable value. That loss is one of a few fundamental factors that account for the astonishing weakness of "the church" in the contemporary context.

Third, the exclusion of women from "official" ministry positions leaves women generally with the impression that there is something wrong with them. Perhaps that is a mistaken inference on their part, and some may manage to work around it without being deeply affected. But if God indeed excludes women from leadership of the church, there must be some reason why he does. What could it be? And if leadership, speaking, and so on is good work, and work manifestly in need of good workers, what, exactly, is it about a woman that God sees and says: "That won't do." Or did he just flip a coin and men won? This line of questioning of course affects all women, and not just those with aspirations to official ministry positions. It is noteworthy what a hard time those who oppose leadership by women have in saying exactly what it is about women that excludes them from such positions, and how that puts an unbearable weight upon what was already a very weak hermeneutic.

So the issue of women in leadership is not a minor or marginal one. It profoundly affects the sense of identity and worth on both sides of the gender line; and, if wrongly grasped, it restricts the resources for blessing, through the church, upon an appallingly needy world. The contributors to this volume have served well in allowing us to see the paths of study and experience through which their minds were changed, and may the change abound.

CHAPTER 37

A Cup Running Over

One of Dallas's most evident and enduring passions was ministering to pastors. He never tired of giving all he could to build up ministers through equipping, teaching, and encouraging spiritual leaders, teachers, and spokespersons. From his own days as a struggling pastor, he knew how difficult and even desperate ministry life can become for pastors in their valiant attempts at living and leading others into life "from above." These next three pieces present his very practical advice regarding the care of one's own soul and the nature of pastoral leadership, both of which he knew all too well were essential but often neglected requirements of the ministerial profession.

First published in 2005 as "A Cup Running Over: Why Ministers Must Find Deep Satisfaction in Christ" in *The Art and Craft of Biblical Preaching: A Comprehensive Resource for Today's Communicators*

IN MY EARLY DAYS OF MINISTRY, I SPENT HUGE AMOUNTS OF TIME absorbed in scripture and great spiritual writers. The Lord made it possible for me to spend whole days—without any issue of preparing for something or taking an examination—soaking up the scripture. I literally wore out the books of great spiritual writers. This focus was foundational to my spiritual journey, to finding satisfaction in Christ. Experiencing God in that way leads me to satisfaction in Christ and to speaking to others out of that satisfaction. There is no substitute for simple satisfaction in the word of God, in the presence of God. That affects all your actions.

CHARACTERISTICS OF DISSATISFACTION

Men and women in ministry who are not finding satisfaction in Christ are likely to demonstrate that with overexertion and over-preparation for speaking and with no peace about what they do after they do it. If we have not come to the place of resting in God, we will go back and think, "Oh, if I'd done this," or "Oh, I didn't do that." When you come to the place where you are drinking deeply from God and trusting him to act with you, there is peace about what you have communicated.

One of my great joys came when I got up from a chair to walk to the podium and the Lord said to me, "Now remember, it's what I do with the word between your lips and their hearts that matters." That is a tremendous lesson. If you do not trust God to do that, then he will let you do what you're going to do, and it's not going to come to much. But once you turn it loose and recognize we are always inad-equate but our inadequacy is not the issue, you are able to lay that burden down. Then the satisfaction you have in Christ spills over into everything you do.

The preacher who does not minister in that satisfaction is on dangerous ground. Those who experience moral failure are those who have failed to live a deeply satisfied life in Christ, almost with-out exception. I know my temptations come out of situations where I am dissatisfied, not content. I am worried about something or not feeling the sufficiency I know is there. If I have a strong temptation, it will be out of my dissatisfaction.

The moral failures of ministers are usually over one of three things: sex, money, or power. That always comes out of dissatisfac-tion. Ministers are reaching for something, and they begin to feel, "I deserve something better. I sacrifice so much and get so little. And so I'll do this." The surest guarantee against failure is to be so at peace and satisfied with God that when wrongdoing presents itself it isn't even interesting. That is how we stay out of temptation.

CHARACTERISTICS OF A SATISFIED SOUL

We are long on devices and programs. We have too many of them, and they get in the way. What we really need are preachers who can stand in simplicity to manifest and declare the richness of Christ in life. There isn't anything on earth that begins to compete with that for human benefit and human interest. When people hear preachers who are satisfied in this way, they sense that much more is coming from them than what they are saying. When I hear preachers like this, I sense something flowing from them. Preachers like that are at peace. They are not struggling to make something happen.

That is one of the biggest issues for ministers today because of the model of success that comes to us. We get the idea we are supposed to make something happen, and so we need our services to go just right. The concluding benediction has hardly ceased before those in charge are saying to one another, "How did it go?" or "It went really well." The truth is, we don't know how it went. From God's point of view, it will be eternity before we know how it went. These folks are not at peace if they are trying to manage outcomes in that way.

One mark of preachers who have attained deep satisfaction is they are at peace, and they love what they are doing. Peace comes from them. From such preachers I sense something coming to me that is deeper than the words. Hearers sense the message opening up possibilities for them to live. In the presence of this kind of preacher, people find ways of doing the good that is before their hearts.

That is the living water. Jesus brought people that "opening up" of possibilities. In John 8, when he said to the woman caught in adultery, "Go now and leave your life of sin," I don't think she felt, "I've got to do that." She experienced Jesus's words as, "That's really possible. I can do that." Such a response is one characteristic of preaching that comes from a satisfied life.

Another mark of satisfied preachers is they can listen. They can be silent in the presence of others because they are not always trying to make something happen. Such a person has the capacity to listen to people and come to an awareness of the needs that underlie the felt needs. We should be attentive to the felt needs of people, but we should know that the game is at a much deeper level of the soul.

A large part of what the pastor does in preaching and life is to listen and help people feel their real needs, not just superficial needs. The satisfied preacher speaks from a listening heart. Since people often do not know what they really need, such preaching can help them find out. This requires a spaciousness that only comes if your cup is running over because you are well cared for by God.

STEPS TOWARD FINDING SATISFACTION IN CHRIST

We can take steps to find this deep satisfaction and to preach from the well within us. I encourage pastors to have substantial times every week when they do nothing but enjoy God. That may mean walking by a stream, looking at a flower, listening to music, or watching your children or grandchildren play without your constantly trying to control them. Experience the fullness of God, think about the good things God has done for you, and realize he has done well by you. If there is a problem doing that, then work through the problem, because we cannot really serve him if we do not genuinely love him.

Henri Nouwen said the main obstacle to love for God is service for God. Service must come out of his strength and life flowing through us into receptive lives. Take an hour, sit in a comfortable place in silence, and do nothing but rest. If you go to sleep, that's okay. We have to stop trying too hard. There may be a few pastors for whom that is not the problem, but for most, it is. We need to do that not only for ourselves but to set an example for those to whom we speak.

There is a place for effort, but it never earns anything and must never take the place of God with us. Our efforts are to make room for him in our lives.

CHAPTER 38

Rules for Religious Leadership

This article addresses church leaders and pastors with wise counsel on best practices for teaching discipleship. Through a question-and-answer format and a list of ten essential techniques, Dallas offers clear insights and practical guidelines for ministers to follow.

First published in 1999 as "Becoming the Kinds of Leaders Who Can Do the Job" in *Cutting Edge* magazine, a publication of Vineyard USA

WE SAID, "TAKE THE GLOVES OFF, DALLAS. TELL US WHAT WE really need to hear." We had read all of Dallas's books and been deeply impacted by them—not least by his latest, *The Divine Conspiracy*. But Brian McLaren had just finished presenting some thoughts on new models of leadership—leaders marked not so much by conquest and technique, but by spiritual goodness and wisdom. And so we sat there, slumped pensively in our chairs, until someone finally said, "Dallas . . . please talk to us about how we become those kind of people." So, during a break, Dallas began listing some of his thoughts on a whiteboard. And then in his gracious, careful way, he challenged us to become the kind of leaders this world so desperately needs. The following is some of what he told us.

1. People are constantly looking for methods. God is looking for people. Methods are often temporary, but what God is looking

for is a life. God is far less interested in your results than the person you are becoming. Many people in our life have tried to substitute results for what they lacked: joy, relationship, character. This part of your existence is a very short part of all of it, and probably you will not be a pastor in the next part.

2. You must be a person who doesn't need this job, who finds his personal sufficiency in God. If you don't have this one down, you will drive yourself nuts. You will be torn between pleasing people and pleasing God. You will be torn between your own integrity and what people who don't understand are saying about you. You won't be able to lead like this. You will find yourself caught between two different driving forces, and your only resource is an internal sufficiency before the Lord.

3. In order to carry that out, you have to have a strategy for constant renewal. Start by looking at what has strengthened you in the past and cultivate that. Don't regard such activities as peripheral, but central. Of course, I've written a whole book on spiritual disciplines, but I think we all know what to do. Sometimes this will mean giving up sleep, and sometimes strengthening yourself may mean getting enough sleep.

4. You need things that are not directly a part of your ministry that give you a kind of rootedness. These could, of course, include things that would help you in your ministry. For example, if you love literature, your love of words will help you speak and write. Powerful language is one of the greatest benefits to a minister. I've watched for decades how ministers who can really use language will know how to say things in a way that people who are not as adept with words cannot. Part of that, of course, is knowing the language of the Bible. Memorize it. Soak it in. Make it a part of your whole life. That will be in itself a strategy for personal renewal.

5. Write. Not to publish, but write. Writing is one of the surest ways to hone your sense of what you are saying. You must be able to say things with force and clarity. Write out your sermons—

even if you don't use the manuscript. Write out your thoughts. Copy things out of books. One of your greatest assets in church planting is the power of your words. People are desperate to hear something good.

6. Know your Bible. Generally speaking, seminary training does not make people adept in working with the Bible. Your life and your Bible should start forming a seamless whole. Wear out your Bible. Read it in large stretches, and repeatedly. Read the New Testament in one go. Set aside time so that you can read through the New Testament five times in one week. Take notes, because you will get stuff that will be life-giving.

7. Don't pretend anything. Eliminate pretending from your repertoire. That will be wonderfully helpful in becoming the kinds of leaders the world desperately needs. We often pretend that we are interested in things we are not, for example, or that we know things we don't know. One of the lies commonly told in my university context is, "Oh, yes, I've read that book." We may pretend to have accomplished things we haven't accomplished. We can be evasive. To be "an Israelite in whom there is no guile" is a great strength in the battle of life. Actually, people will forgive you many things they might otherwise get mad at you about if you are guileless.

I have a three-step plan for humility:

1. Never pretend.
2. Never presume.
3. Never push.

Most of the things that we try to accomplish go according to the saying: "Things that can be pulled can't be pushed, and things that can be pushed can't be pulled." Most of what we're doing can't be pushed; it has to be drawn out at the appropriate time.

8. Listen to your critics. Proverbs says, "Rebuke a wise man and he'll love you for it." Listen not with the attitude "I don't deserve this, they're dead wrong." Lay it down and just listen; see what

you can learn. Practice walking off without reply. What goes along with this is: don't defend yourself. Now, sometimes you need to explain yourself. But this is a fine line. If you are actually doing this to help the person, you are not defending yourself. When we are in a ministry that is going through change, then we do need to help people. But to defend yourself is hopeless. You have a defender, and you let him do his job.

9. Grow in making distinctions for people. For example, I believe we should never be in a hurry. But sometimes we should act quickly. Acting quickly is a form of action. Being in a hurry is a state of mind. Another example: when talking about spiritual disciplines, one of my slogans that I use to help people with the difference between works and grace is: "Grace is not opposed to effort, it is opposed to earning. Earning is an attitude; effort is an action." It's very important to help people grasp these distinctions, and often once you state them for people, it can be like a flash of insight for them.

10. Identify what you admire, and stay with it. What do you think is really good in your work, and in others that you know? No matter what it is—and it will often be associated with someone who you think is really doing that particular thing well—stick with it. Vacillation hurts us very badly in relation to our success as ministers. Find what's good in your work and stick with it and make it better. For example, if you find some topic that is especially helpful, don't just take one shot at it and drop it. Develop it. Certainly that's true of much that I have written. I have never sought to publish a book; each book came about from people having heard what I've said. Richard Foster's and my work on disciplines all came out of a half-page outline that I did in the late 1960s, and we just started working on it.

Question: How would you balance that with Paul's admonition to teach the whole counsel of God?

I've seen churches built around just one or two things, and there's no balance or health there. What you do is look for the others in the church who contribute in the other areas, and you develop them. And you must develop a sense of who to bring in to balance things out. You order things so there is a range of teaching. Billy Graham has a real gift. But if you had to listen to Billy Graham preach every Sunday, you'd say, "This is not the best for the church."

Another thing we need to do consciously is talk about success. In another age it might have been enough for your people to know that you are devoted and that you are called of God. But we live in a world where this issue is enough to drive anyone nuts. You have people constantly surveying, "Is this a success?" I often imagine people handing out little questionnaires at the end of the Sermon on the Mount about whether or not it was a success. I would teach about this, especially in the midst of a process where many groups will misunderstand one another about how we reach a world such as this.

Question: Would *faithfulness* be a word that should replace *success*?

I don't think so. I think it's more complicated than that. I think success has to do with producing results. But what kind of results? I'm not big on the saying, "All God requires is that we be faithful." I'm sure that there's a lot to that, but it's not all. Faithfulness means more than just doing the same things over and over. I would say that, in our faithfulness, one of the things we do is change—and sometimes we need to change before God will respond to our efforts.

Question: So what do you think constitutes success for a pastor in the postmodern era?

I think in any era it must mean the spiritual growth of the people. We may understand that a little differently in a modern versus a postmodern context, but that has to be a given. I would suggest that you float the idea that a church could grow not by having more Christians but larger Christians. Of course, my view is that if you have larger Christians, you're going to have a lot more of them, too.

Question: What practices would you like to see in the churches for making disciples?

I'll tell you something very direct and very simple: preach on the kingdom of God. People just don't do it. My general counsel for making disciples—and something I follow as much as I have opportunity—is to preach what Jesus preached in the manner Jesus preached it.

What I mean is that Jesus preached the gospel in the style of manifesting and teaching about the kingdom of God. And, of course, manifesting will include signs and wonders. But I think if you dig into the Gospels and do your background studies, you will see how Jesus taught. He taught in a manner very much like what we've been doing here for these couple of days together. He didn't get up and put on a big production. Perhaps what we need to do is spend a lot of time sitting around talking to people in this same manner.

This would include having lots of occasions for lengthy talks of a conversational sort, responding to questions, bringing the approach Jesus uses in Matthew 13 into play—teaching about the kingdom in the context of our ordinary life. Most of Jesus's teachings about the reality of the kingdom come out of commonplace parables and stories from everyday life.

I think Jesus confused people a lot with the parables. I always feel like I've failed people if I haven't been completely clear, or if I engender controversy and conflict. Jesus seemed unconcerned with that. I'm trying to give myself permission—if I interact with people and they get into lively discussions after I leave—that it's okay.

You have done them a real favor. I claim that you cannot understand what Jesus taught until you understand how he taught. The precise point of it is that he did not teach by systematically laying things out. He taught by catching people in the flight of their assumptions and letting the air out of their balloons. And they didn't need a recorder or a pad to jot it down, because their heads were buzzing and probably they were blushing half the way home. Jesus does that constantly.

For example, whenever you see Jesus teaching, "Blessed are the poor," you have to see what assumption it is that he's letting the air out of. If you don't understand that, you'll decide that it's a good thing to be poor. And you'll say, "Jesus said it." Or, "Woe to you who laugh." You guys here in this room are in real trouble! He's not talking about laughing being a terrible thing. What he's getting at, if you read the "woes," is a list of precisely what we think of as being "on top of the world": rich, good reputation, good health, laughing it up. So you have to understand the issue Jesus is addressing.

We have to stop trying to systematically make sure that everybody "gets" everything. We shut their minds down when we do that. Some of you know that, in many parts of the world, if you do that to a person they will be insulted! They don't want you to grab them by the ears and stuff it down their throats and say, "Have you got it?" They want you to talk in a way that leaves them free to think and negotiate and come back. It's regarded as bad taste to lay it all out as though they were idiots. In our culture, our educational system has trained us to want it all laid out, because we've had to spit it all back on a test.

Question: How can we apply Jesus's method—which seems like a situational approach—to our preaching, where we speak to a wide range of people all coming from different places of maturity and mind-sets?

The main thing is to identify the assumptions your people are resting on that are holding them up. Charles Finney said that the main job of the minister is to study the assumptions of the people to whom he speaks. What are the assumptions that are impeding spiritual growth and progress? We must be alive to people's mental furniture.

Now, of course, we have to combine this with the realities of our situation. If you fail the expectations of your people too much, they won't hear a word you say. So teaching in this way requires great grace and wisdom. But I would say that, in general, even given the dynamics of speaking in a large auditorium, make it as conversational in style as possible, and give people time to think. Don't just rattle on. Literally pause.

Watch how Jesus teaches in the Gospels and you will see that he always discusses things in a way in which he does not state everything. Many times, he would put something "out there" and just leave it. So identify the assumptions in a loving, gentle, humorous way; ask them a question to which they're going to give the wrong answer, and then gently point out why the answer is wrong. (Of course, I will usually say, "Now don't answer this," because I don't want them to be embarrassed! I want them to have *thought* of the wrong answer.)

Question: Are there more things ministers can do, other strategies?

Do something incremental, something in your skills that keeps growing. For example, writing, or teaching, or praying. Something that keeps developing incrementally, and that doesn't depend on where you are living. Don't look for the great leap forward. It will probably not come. I don't know how much memorization of scripture you do, but it's one of the most renewing things I do. I love Colossians 3. Romans 8. The Psalms. To take that stuff in is to fill one's self with a literal life force. Make sure that you rest well. Enjoy your family. And be sure you have times when you don't have anything to do.

CHAPTER 39

Principles on Teaching Discipleship for Church Leaders

Dallas knew well what a crucial role well-trained church leaders played in assisting an individual's discipleship to Jesus. Because of this, he devoted many of his writings to advising professional ministers and church community leaders. He hoped to better facilitate a leader's faith journey while also encouraging and assisting the spiritual transformation of those in their congregation.

Written as "Leadership with Christ: Some First Principles" (previously unpublished)

COULD IT BE THAT, IN THIS DAY OF VAST SOPHISTICATION ABOUT group dynamics and managerial skills, the bedrock need of God's people is for leaders who are more "spiritual"? It could be, and it is. The finest personal talents, the most highly developed skills in management and personal relations, will do little to meet the needs now confronting the church, unless they are given substance by life manifestly "from above."

Those of us who exercise leadership for Christ must constantly look to him for power to accomplish what lies far beyond human strength and ingenuity. More deeply, we must find from him his character to bear his power. Especially as a Christian organization grows in size, the challenge to keep its inner quality Christlike while effectively advancing its mission becomes ever greater. Size and complexity easily defeat the best of intentions and managerial "techniques," and even lay us open to outright abuse of the power naturally radiating from leadership positions.

Our contemporary situation calls for Christian leaders and followers alike to plan for Christlikeness to the full through sensible use of disciplines for life from the Spirit. As with Jesus himself, periods of solitude and silence, study and worship, sacrifice and fellowship, make our lives accessible to our Father and open to us the resources of his kingdom. The great ones for Christ through the ages have known this, and with all their shortcomings have combined a high degree of inner Christlikeness with astonishing effectiveness in their missions. Today as never before, we require strength and insight to love and honor our role among Christ's people and to inspire the same in others. Let us think, then, about our individual plans for living our lives as Christ would live them within our leadership roles.

Christians understand spirituality by reference to Jesus Christ our leader. As the Son of God, he is the preeminently spiritual man. Judging simply from his effects on history, he was the greatest leader humanity has ever seen. The principles of leadership under God, so strikingly manifested in biblical figures such as Moses, David, and Nehemiah, are brought to completion in his example and teachings. Those same principles are validated in the lives of his great followers through the ages. Whatever leadership role one may have, however high or low in organizational structure, it will flourish under God as we follow Jesus in living out some key truths.

First, the leader with Christ knows that we do not exercise leadership for our own gratification. Power is not a prize. Position is not for personal gain in any respect. To get or hold onto position is simply not an objective. Leading is not something we need to make us okay. My self-esteem is not tied to success as a leader. In companionship with Jesus, I am abundantly cared for. Who leads is God's business. We even want others to lead if that would better promote the good that we serve, and we cheerfully seek for others who can do better than we. Fear of failing to keep our position does not cross our minds as we follow Jesus. We are entirely freed from what, in the world's way, everyone recognizes to be the number-one burden of leaders.

Paul's great "*kenosis*" passage in Philippians 2 lays out the path of the disciple of Jesus in leadership: "Leave no room for selfish ambition and vanity, but humbly reckon others better than yourselves." Jesus's own teaching in the Gospels was that his leaders must be "the slave of all, just as the Son of Man did not come to be served but to serve" (Matt. 20:28). The configuration of leadership is totally transformed by Jesus as we follow him into the kingdom of the heavens.

Second, the leader with Christ knows that power belongs to God (Ps. 62:11). She knows that advancement does not come from any place on earth, "from the east or the west," nor "out of the blue," but from God only (Ps. 75:6–7). As Jesus taught, "Any plant that is not of my heavenly Father's planting will be rooted up" (Matt. 15:13). Living in this confidence is how she submits herself to the mighty hand of God, who will exalt her "when the time is right" (1 Pet. 5:6). Accordingly, she will not manipulate by power that lies entirely in her own hand.

Jesus's temptations in the wilderness primarily relate to his role as leader. He rejected leadership by material reward, by appearance or "image," and by force (Matt. 4:3–10). He was content to wait upon the movement of his Father on the hearts of human beings— though no doubt he could have overwhelmed the world with his own greatness. When he knew that Peter would fail him, he simply said: "I have prayed for you, Peter, that your faith shall not fail" (Luke 22:32). Surely he could have just "fixed" Peter. But he would not use his power alone. He waited upon the Father's power to achieve the goal.

Third, the leader with Christ is competent in the reality of the Spirit. He is completely assured of the Spirit of God moving with him in life, thought, and action. He knows by experience "how vast are the resources of his power open to us who have faith, as seen at work when he raised Christ from the dead" (Eph. 1:19). He knows how to make things happen through prayer and how to act with God. He has seen ways opened when there was no way out, and confidently attempts and/or waits upon God for the attainment of what is humanly impossible.

For such a one, God's spiritual reality is not a hope beyond knowledge, but a familiar resource in ordinary as well as extraordinary events, a "very present help in trouble" (Ps. 46:1). Confidence is recognized by all to be indispensable in a leader, but the leader with Christ has confidence based on competence to deal with life from the infinite resources of God.

Fourth, the leader with Christ abounds in joy. How strange that Jesus is thought, even by many Christians, to be a rather gloomy and depressed individual! Miserable people make poor leaders. Before he left his little troop, he assured them of their abundant power in the abundant power of the Father. This he did that his joy might stay with them, filling them with joy to the brim (John 15:11). Those full of joy have no room for any more. And then he prayed to the Father that his joy might fill them to overflowing (17:13).

It may be that the most common weakness found in those of us who try to lead for Christ is lack of a joy appropriate to the confidence in God we profess. We are not speaking of the supercilious hilarity that is seen all too often. But Jesus's faith is inseparable from all-encompassing joy. Even our sorrow, our concern, our suffering is permeated by a quiet and boundless joy as we walk with Jesus. Angry, disappointed, and discouraged people who fail to find sufficiency of joy and peace in their lives with him cannot lead us as he intends. The well-known "moral failures" that occur in leaders come from the desperately needy condition of their inner life. Leaders with Jesus do not live desperately even though they may live in desperate circumstances.

Fifth, the leader with Christ knows and uses the techniques for sustaining the serene and powerful life in God. She knows that God's initiative opens the door to plans for Christlikeness. In one of his most desperate circumstances, where his own people were on the verge of stoning him, we read that "David encouraged or strengthened himself in the Lord his God" (1 Sam. 30:6). Paul, one of the greatest examples of leadership with Christ, speaks of his regular discipline in terms of the athlete in training: "I do not spare my body, but bring it under strict control, for fear that after preaching to others I should find myself disqualified" (1 Cor. 9:24–27). With Jesus we walk into his disciplines for life from above: solitude and silence, study and worship, secrecy and sacrifice, celebration and fellowship, and so forth. It is these practices that form the constant framework of our life, not the projects and efforts by which others may outwardly identify us. Confronting the loss of his life for his faith, Daniel "went to his house, which had windows open toward Jerusalem, and there he knelt down three times a day and offered prayers and praises to his God as was his custom" (Dan. 6:10).

We are saved by grace, not paralyzed by it. It is we who are given the task of putting off the old personality and putting on the new. The leader with Christ is one who, with utter confidence in the generosity and availability of God, assumes the responsibility for her own spiritual condition and employs the proven means for sustaining it at the very highest level. She does the things Jesus did in his life with his Father and thereby receives the power to lead as Jesus led.

These principles of leadership with Christ are not dreamy, mystical impracticalities. Unless they are implemented, our "successes" will seem so only by comparison to worse failures, and the awesome needs facing the church and the world will remain unmet. They are the heart of the true science of Christian leadership, the indispensable foundation for all further technique, for they are the heart of Jesus and of the life from above.

Reflections Focusing on Leadership as a Disciple

Questions to aid perception of what is and what could be:

1. Are there tensions between "doing the right thing" and "getting things done"? How do I experience them?

2. Are there manifestations of power beyond us, God's hand, in the ordinary process of life together here? Is this something we count on?

3. What is the level of "fruit of the spirit" (Gal. 5:22–23) here? Of "vain glory" (Gal. 5:26, Phil. 2:3)? Of "wisdom from above" (James 3:13–17) in my own life?

4. What is the quality of joint prayer and prayerfulness here (Matt. 18:19–20; Phil. 4:6–13; 1 Tim. 2:1–8)?

5. Are there ways of improving our life together as a beachhead of the kingdom of God? What activities and structures might help?

6. Personal resolutions.

CHAPTER 40

The Price and the Glory
of Intellectual Excellence
in the Christian University

As a philosophy professor, Dallas was keenly interested in
the decline of moral knowledge, moral philosophy in universities, and Western culture in general. He collaborated
with his academic peers and with higher-education admin-
istrators to keep moral knowledge relevant in higher education. He also believed that this was an essential part of
his own Christlike way of living, because in promoting moral
knowledge he could teach the indispensable knowledge
of God as well. These final two essays summarize Dallas's
vision for calling on Christian educators to continue this
mission.

Presentation given in 1984 at a meeting
of the BIOLA University faculty in Apple
Valley, CA (previously unpublished)

*I have filled him with the Spirit of God, with skill, ability and
knowledge in all kinds of crafts.* (Exod. 31:3, NIV)

RECENT YEARS HAVE SEEN AN INCREASING EMPHASIS UPON INTEL-
lectual, scientific, and artistic excellence as a primary goal in evangelical educational institutions. A number of the most prominent

leaders among evangelical Christians have given voice to this emphasis. Those of us who have had a long association with evangelical education cannot but see in this a very great change in its professed outlook and endeavor. Until quite recently, at least, none of the evangelical institutions that arose in reaction to the defections of the older American universities from substantial Christian faith thought of their work as creative, frontline research or development in the major areas of academic and cultural life. Reflecting the motives that gave them birth, they saw their task to be the preparation of men (and, unfortunately to a much lesser degree, of women) for the work of ministry, understood to be basically evangelistic, pastoral, and teaching activities. Beyond that, they took their function to be the negative one of not teaching, or of mentioning only to reject the views and attitudes that were opposed to, or thought to be subversive of, sound Christian faith and practice. They aided young people to gain an education without the risk of losing their faith at the hands of unbelievers or through a too serious examination of anti-Christian opinions and outlooks.

Now, without leaving the older goals aside, we hear a distinctively new note. Consider the words of Charles Malik, who is Greek Orthodox in tradition, but widely respected by evangelical leaders in this country. In his address on the occasion of the dedication of the Billy Graham Center at Wheaton in 1980 he warned: "Evangelicals cannot afford to keep on living on the periphery of responsible intellectual existence." He called his distinguished audience to achieve "under God and according to God's own pace the twofold miracle of evangelizing the great universities and intellectualizing the great evangelical movement." "The great universities control the mind of the world," he continued to say. "And how can evangelism evangelize the university if it cannot speak to the university? And how can it speak to the university if it is not itself already intellectualized?"[1]

The level of excellence that he sees as required for world evangelization is made clear by words from the booklet associated with his Wheaton address:

What I crave to see is an institution that will produce as many Nobel Prize winners as saints, an institution in which, while producing in every field the finest works of thought and learning in the world, Jesus Christ will at the same time find Himself perfectly at home.[2]

Now as we shall later see by reference to J. Gresham Machen, this aspiration is not something new to evangelical Christians. It simply calls us back to what was assumed as a matter of obvious course through most of the history of the church and by the most outstanding evangelical scholars and educators at the turn of the century. But it is a stunning departure from the recent evangelical past. It must be dealt with honestly and thoroughly if our renewed aspirations are to be translated into reality. A price will have to be paid. It must be paid by responsible leaders in pastoral and evangelistic ministry, and by the administrations and boards of our universities. But most of all it must be paid by those of us who stand in the ranks: the privates and corporals, the sergeants and lieutenants in the army of Christian educators, scientists, artists, and intellectuals. To aid in understanding the price of intellectual excellence in the Christian church and her institutions, I would like to pose a series of questions for us to consider as a way of illuminating past attitudes within Christian education. This will help to make clear what must be changed for the future. The answers may seem to be very obvious. I hope so. But they go to the heart of the most fundamental issues facing evangelical higher education today.

1. Do we, in our heart of hearts, believe that the Christian must be intellectually inferior, in ability or development, in order to be a fervent, orthodox follower of Christ because what the Christian believes may not stand up under the strictest intellectual scrutiny? And then what would we do? Or because only a sense of our inferiority can protect us from pride and keep us trusting in the Lord? "Knowledge puffs up," we recall.

2. Do we believe that intellectual or cultural attainments are all right in the Christian only if they come without great, sustained effort, as a gift of talent or grace? Are they therefore something that we should not make a primary goal of our endeavors? Do we accordingly expect God to make up for the intellectual short-comings of the Christian? "If it is His will?" (If you were going into brain surgery, would you be happy with a surgeon who did not think it compatible with humility and devotion to God to give "his utmost to be the best"? He piously counts on God to guide his fingers, perhaps. I know your answer. But should we think any differently about an individual who operates on minds and spirits by their teaching of world literature or biology or his-tory—or theology?)

3. Do we believe that the mission of Jesus Christ through his church—the full and effectual carrying out of the Great Commission—can be accomplished without the preparation of Christians to occupy leading positions of all areas of culture, intellect, research, business, government, and education through the excellence of their work?

4. Are we, as teachers in Christian institutions, prepared to accept or give expressions of Christian faith and piety as substitutes for the best efforts and end results of intellect? In ourselves? In others? Always? Sometimes? Never? Or do we, rather, see in piety the indispensable, firm foundation for efforts and results that outstrip even the best of human ability unaided by faith?

5. Do we believe that ignorance of certain things or theories—refusal to think about, recognize, seriously study, or even see them—is not only advisable on some occasions but is the only available protection for Christian faith? For the young? For those in special ministerial work? For all Christians?

6. When we hear the words "I am the way, the truth and the life," do we accept them as dealing only with matters usually marked out as religious but not with the binomial theorem, the laws of planetary motion, the regularities of production and exchange of

goods, or the principles and realities of poetry and music? Charles
Finney's statement was: "The very distinction between classical
and theological study is a curse to the church, and a curse to the
world."3 Does this make sense to us? Do we regard every work
to which God appoints us as equally important, equally sacred,
not requiring some further justification in terms of evangelistic
or missionary outreach, for example? Do we understand the
priesthood of the believer to mean that every believer who does
not engage in ministerial activities of the recognized variety is a
second-class citizen in the kingdom of God? Or does it mean that
the believer is—insofar as he or she has and lives in faith—by
that fact a priest in all they do?

These questions are meant to bring to light attitudes toward
full-hearted commitment to intellectual and artistic excellence, and
to suggest some fundamental changes in attitude that will most
certainly be a part of the price that must be paid by evangelical
institutions if they are to attain such excellence. But before dealing
with this price in more exact terms, let us clarify the nature of that
excellence of which we speak.

First, let us understand that *excellence* is not used here in any
absolute sense. We are not necessarily called upon to be better than
Newton or Einstein, than Beethoven or Debussy, Raphael or Monet,
Spurgeon or Billy Graham. The excellence sought merely means
for us to be among the leaders in our fields for our time and place.
When, for example, understanding of economic processes, computer
technology, the present state of the novel, or nineteenth-century
American history is sought, you will be one of those looked to in
your professional context. And perhaps you will be the one most
looked to. Your work will be illuminating and helpful to others
doing the creative work in your field. That is the excellence of which
we speak.

When the problems of education, or of the cultural institutions
in the community, or of government, or of evangelization or spiritual

growth and so forth, are earnestly dealt with, then you will have significant help to give, and will be sought out accordingly. They may not call you to Oslo, Harvard, Oxford, or the Sorbonne—of course, they also may—but within your community of concerns you will be an effectual leader over a significant range.

The signs or proofs of such attainment will vary somewhat from field to field and from person to person, and of course we must not set our minds and hearts on these. But for those of us on the scholarly or creative side, excellence will normally mean that we come in for a share of the awards and grants. Our writings will be published and used, the results of our creativity profited from and appreciated. We will play a role in determining and directing thought and experience in our field and our world. We may not break the established records, but we run to the front, pushing those who do win, and taking the "medals" and the "honorable mentions" with some frequency.

Thus do we "occupy 'til he comes." We do not "cumber the ground," but give light and life, are the light of the world, in our place: an outpost of heaven where the angels of grace come and go in the midst of the busy life of humanity where we are appointed.

To accomplish great things, we give our best, in confidence that he who appointed us to teach Spanish II and be a part of our scholarly or creative community of faith will also give his best. We undertake in his strength as well as ours. We will not be short of resources for the task to which he appoints us, if our faith sees it as his appointment and proceeds in a faithful, disciplined manner.

And this brings us to a more exact statement of the price of intellectual or academic excellence for the Christian university. I shall briefly speak of four of its aspects—very important aspects, I believe—but without any hope of treating the subject in systematic completeness. The price of intellectual excellence will involve:

1. A new attitude toward our work, a new vision of the intrinsic worth and holiness of intellectual and artistic endeavor without regard to any further ends.

The great work of the evangelist or soul-winning has, because of its obvious importance, often been made into the total end of the Christian life. All else, it is sometimes said, must be justified by advancing it. Those not engaged directly in it are then somehow second class. I recall a chapel service at my own undergraduate university, Tennessee Temple. Dr. Lee Roberson, president of the school, often spoke in chapel, and on this particular day he began by asking us to identify what the most important thing was in our service to God. One young man quickly and firmly responded: "To win souls!" Had he not said it, five hundred others would have, for that is an overwhelming emphasis of Tennessee Temple, as is well known. But to that young man's burning chagrin, and in a way that he alone could do it, Dr. Roberson said: "No, that is not right! The most important thing in our service to God is to love and worship him and his Son with all our hearts."

The love and worship of God and his Son is the center and foundation of our lives around which alone all else, including evangelism, safely revolves. Evangelism speedily reaches the point of diminishing returns, may even become self-defeating—and I believe that this is nowhere clearer than in our own nation at the present time—if it is not firmly held as but one of the essential functions of the total worshipful body of the risen Lord. To know, to teach, to create, are other essential functions of that body. That is the message of the Bible from beginning to end.

But these functions can never be brought to excellence until they are seen by those engaged in them as acts of service of equal importance in the overall economy of God to any "religious" activity. J. Gresham Machen, in his 1912 address, "Christianity and Culture," comments on a common misunderstanding of intellectual work among Christians:

> Very many pious men in the Church today admit that the Christian must have a part in human culture. But they regard such activity as a necessary evil—as a dangerous and unworthy task necessary to be gone through with under a stern sense of

duty in order that thereby the higher ends of the gospel may be attained. Such men can never engage in the arts and sciences with anything like enthusiasm—such enthusiasm they would regard as disloyalty to the gospel.[4]

The last sentence is the telling point for our purposes here. Machen himself points out that "such a position is really both illogical and unbiblical." What we must add is that it also makes impossible the attainment of excellence in the arts and sciences. Intellectual and creative work is extremely hard to do well. It is among the most difficult of human endeavors, and the difficulty simply cannot be sustained except by a strong sense of the intrinsic worth of and interest in the work that is being done.

Thought and art are, to the full of faith, just the contemplation and manifestation of that goodness and beauty that God himself remarked on after his periods of creation. As scholars, teachers, artists, and scientists, we are privileged to know and adore him in his works and, in that manifold knowledge, love and serve humanity to his glory. In this attitude alone can we attain to excellence in our fields.

2. But the price of intellectual excellence will also involve a commitment to arrange our lives in a way that is actually conducive to the attainment of excellence in our fields of work.

This will have dimensions that are personal as well as those that concern our family. It concerns serious financial planning, both by the individual and the university. It will require strong supervision and support by university administration, as well as the most extensive and intelligent of collegial cooperation.

Intellectual excellence has its specific conditions in reality just as much as does an excellent crop of corn or an excellent football team. Slogans and blind or sporadic efforts will not realize intellectual excellence; and grace will not substitute for a thoughtful, steadfast commitment at both the institutional and individual level, to an adequately detailed plan. This is true for any area of the spiritual life. We who are Christian educators will not be exempted from it just because we are working for the Lord.

3. And then our price will also include a testimony and a teaching that clearly proclaims that intellectual excellence is a part of our opportunity and duty as Christians and clearly explains why this is so.

These matters are not generally understood, and we must frankly face the fact that the message proclaimed in most of our evangelical congregations does not make them plain, nor even questions them. It will cost extensive time and effort on the part of evangelical educators and pastors to make them plain, and to show in what manner intellectual and creative excellence is a mandate of the gospel of Jesus Christ. This must be directly and thoroughly addressed.

Possibly we will have trying times when those who support us earnestly question our aspirations. Only the deepest insight into the Word and into life, the most tender ministries of the Spirit, and the most patient and yet courageous of leadership will suffice. But we must do full justice to the point that the relationship of intellectual excellence to the gospel is also a doctrinal matter, a division of soteriology, and one that is sadly underdeveloped in our evangelical world. A major effort will be required to develop and communicate the truth concerning it. It will not be easy.

4. Finally—and in many ways most importantly—the price for intellectual excellence in the evangelical university will be the enrichment and expansion of pastoral ministry to the intellectual, the artist, and the educator.

I will simply state here that the defection of the intellectual and the creative mind from sound Christianity, or the failure to be drawn to it, is, in my experience, rarely due to intellectual causes, or to these alone. Among the brightest and most creative people of past and present, a large percentage have maintained a most robust faith and devotion to God. This is a matter of history, and it demonstrates that it is factors other than intellectual excellence that are determinative of unbelief.

These factors are usually very human ones: fear of man, resentment because of injuries or failures of various kinds, lack of careful and thorough thought, ignorant and insensitive attempts on the part of those who endeavor to minister, and so forth. Too often the church and her ministers have made the mistake of treating intellectuals—even those in her own institutions—as if they were a different kind of human being. A terrible lack of understanding results on both sides. The intellectual or academic has most of the same personal and spiritual needs as any other person. These require an adequate pastoral approach, taking into consideration, of course, the conditions under which the intellectual works and lives.

Or sometimes the relation between intellectual work and normal church activities is wrongly approached. A. H. Strong was often visited by his concerned pastor to correct irregular church attendance in periods when he was deeply engaged in the writing of his masterful theological works. To visit was good, of course, but the understanding, encouragement, and prayerful assistance could have been of a better quality in this case, as in many similar ones.

I do not suggest that the Christian intellectual or artist should lack deep involvement with the local church. But on the other hand their work is not a nine-to-five occupation. There will be times of intense activity when business as usual must be interrupted and the fellowship must reach out in special ways to minister and sustain the brothers and sisters working in creative fields.

I am touching only the superficialities of this all-important area. The great fact is that the church in the modern period has not solved the problem of effectual ministry to intellectual and creative minds: a ministry that kindles and steadily fuels the flame of steadfast devotion to Jesus Christ above all. It has far too often found itself caught in an adversarial position with regard to this class of people. This is a grave problem of practical theology. Whatever the cost, it must be solved if we are to achieve and maintain intellectual excellence in the institutions of the evangelical church.

In conclusion, some final remarks about the glory of such excellence. There is first of all the glory of the testimony of Jesus in the place of power and influence. What rules the world is not material forces, but such forces under the control of ideas and attitudes. These latter, embodied in personal and social entities, are the true principalities and powers that must be brought into captivity to Christ. I quote once again from Machen:

> It should be ours to create, so far as we can, with the help of God, those favorable conditions for the reception of the gospel. False ideas are the greatest obstacles to the reception of the gospel. We may preach with all the fervor of a reformer and yet succeed only in winning a straggler here and there, if we permit the whole collective thought of the nation or the world to be controlled by ideas which by the resistless force of logic, prevent Christianity from being regarded as anything more than a harmless delusion. Under such circumstances what God desires us to do is to destroy the obstacle at its root. . . . What is today matter for academic speculation begins tomorrow to move armies and pull down empires. In that second stage it has gone too far to be combatted; the time to stop it was when it was still a matter of impassionate debate. So as Christians we should try to mold the thought of the world in such a way as to make the acceptance of Christianity something more than a logical absurdity. Thoughtful men are wondering why the students of our great Eastern universities no longer [this was 1912] enter the ministry or display any very vital interest in Christianity. . . . The real difficulty amounts to this—that the thought of the day, as it makes itself most strongly felt in the universities, but from them spreads inevitably to the masses of the people—is profoundly opposed to Christianity, or at least—what is nearly as bad—it is out of all connection with Christianity. The Church is unable either to combat it or to assimilate it, because the Church simply does not understand it. Under such circumstances, what more pressing duty than for those who have received the mighty experience of regeneration . . . to make themselves masters of the thought of the world in order to make it an instrument of truth instead of error.[5]

And yet again, Machen's resolve was:

> Instead of making our theological seminaries merely cen-
> ters of religious emotion, we shall make them battlegrounds of
> the faith, where helped a little by the experience of Christian
> teachers, men are taught to fight their own battle, where they
> come to appreciate the real strength of the adversary and in
> the hard school of intellectual struggle learn to substitute for
> the unthinking faith of childhood the profound convictions of
> full-grown men. Let us not fear the loss of spiritual power. The
> Church is perishing today through the lack of thinking, not
> through an excess of it.[6]

Although the theological is fundamental, these words must be extended to all arenas of art and intellect, and Machen so intended
them.

Then there is the glory of the effectual love of neighbor in the
attainment of good. The ideas and attitudes that rule the fallen world
do guarantee in manifold ways the perpetual misery of humanity.
When you look deeply into the problems of war and poverty, drugs
and sex, pollution and overpopulation, ignorance and crime, violence and mental illness, you see that only by a leadership of great
spirituality and intelligence can they even be understood, much less
resolved. To do good to all people, "especially unto them who are of
the household of faith," is a command that requires the best—and
grace-assisted—efforts in the realm of the intellect, as well as in
those of bodily endeavor and "special" spiritual work. In that realm
also we are to be all things to all men that we might by all means
save some. There above all, because of its vastly greater import, we
are to "let our light so shine before men that they may see our good
works, and glorify our Father which is in heaven." To exempt the
all-important realms of the intellect and the arts in our application
of these verses is not an act of faith, but is a thunderous declaration
of how little we believe in the grandeur and power of our God.

And at last there is the glory of the enjoyment and manifestation of God's companionship and of his presence in this world through the people who are his temple. It is the presence of God with us that allows us to maintain our identity in the world of science and learning, know who we are at all times, and assure all around us in our academic environment that he is indeed a very present help in time of trouble.

The destiny of God's ancient people was to be indwelt by him and so be the light of the world, showing the world how to live. Our destiny is the same today. The glory of effectual love and help for all of the human race is the natural outflow of the total life of the faithful—heart, soul, mind, and strength—being indwelt by God. From their innermost parts then flow the living waters. Here is the ultimate glory: humanity in dominion over the earth in union with God. The human intellect rises to its appointed excellence only in that union, and our aspiration to intellectual and creative excellence is, finally, an essential part of our hope for full life in God: "Low lie the bounding heart, the teeming brain, Till, sent from God, they mount to God again."[7]

How very much yet remains to be said about the price and glory of intellectual and artistic excellence in the evangelical university! Indeed, to say it all, to make it clear, is a major part of the task now facing the evangelical movement. But I hope to encourage us to believe that the price, while great, is fair, and that the glory is yet greater by far.

We face many uncertainties. On the one hand, the forces of evil are great, and our individual circumstances may be quite difficult. On the other hand, we know that at any moment our Lord may come and relieve us of our responsibilities here. But that is not our business, and can never serve as an excuse for the least slackening of our efforts. So with utmost faith and self-sacrifice in our appointed place and work, let us translate the words and thoughts of the poet William Blake into our country and our time and our understanding:

And did those feet in ancient time
Walk upon England's mountains green?
And was the holy Lamb of God
On England's pleasant pastures seen?

And did the Countenance Divine
Shine forth upon our clouded hills?
And was Jerusalem built here
Among these dark Satanic Mills?

Bring me my Bow of burning gold:
Bring me my Arrows of desire:
Bring me my Spear: O clouds unfold!
Bring me my Chariot of fire!

I will not cease from Mental Fight,
Nor shall my Sword sleep in my hand
Till we have built Jerusalem
In England's green and pleasant Land.

"And Did Those Feet in Ancient Time"

CHAPTER 41

Leading the Teachers of the Nations

In this essay, Dallas poses the question of whether or not the Christian church has been fulfilling its mission of providing a unique and influential truth to the world. Here Dallas begins with what have become well known as "The Four Great Questions" of philosophy and human life. He examines the ways in which the church has and has not succeeded in effective moral teachings and issues a call to action to Christians to further the church's mission of sharing the promise of truth revealed in the gospel of Jesus.

Remarks made at the 2004 annual U.S. Seminary
Presidents meeting (previously unpublished)

Affirmed: It is God's intent that the ministers of Christ and the people of Christ should be, in him, the light of the world, and should teach all people what reality is and how to live in it.

"It is too small a thing that you should be My Servant to raise up the tribes of Jacob, and to restore the preserved ones of Israel; I will also make you a light to the nations so that My salvation may reach to the end of the earth." (Isa. 49:6)

"Make disciples of all nations, submerge them in Trinitarian reality, and teach them to do all I have commanded you." (Matt. 28:19–20, PAR)

THE FOUR GREAT QUESTIONS OF LIFE, WHICH HUMANS CANNOT satisfactorily answer on their own and God must answer, are:

1.   What is reality? What do we have to deal with?

2.   Who is really well off, is "blessed," or has "the good life"?

3.   Who is a really good person? Who is the one for whom people are naturally grateful, who naturally calls forth affirmation and imitation?

4.   How does one become a really good person?

Now, what are the answers of Jesus Christ to these questions?

1.   Reality is God—a personal, self-sufficing being whose deepest nature is love (will to good)—and everything that comes from his action (his "kingdom").

2.   Those alive in the kingdom of the heavens are the ones who are truly well off or "blessed."

3.   The really good person is the one whose life is permeated with and animated by the kind of love that characterizes God (1 Cor. 13; 1 John 4; etc.).

4.   One becomes a "really good" person by placing their confidence in Jesus Christ and living as his apprentice in kingdom living.

Whoever the teacher or teachers of "the nation" and the nations may be, they will teach answers to these questions. If they do not do it in word and explicitly, they will do it in deed and example. In "open" societies, such as North America, there will be a tremendous struggle over the various "answers" because the "accepted" answers must serve as the basis of governmental and social policies and of individual life plans. In a closed society there is no such struggle. Policies based upon the answers "accepted" by power structures are simply enforced, and whatever "struggle" there might be is suppressed.

It is crucial for us to think about who the teachers are and what answers are taught in the Western, world, and U.S. society today, apart from the church. Think of the Eastern Bloc countries before the fall of the wall in 1989. Think of Islamic countries today. Think of our consumer-based society with its massive mental and physical health problems and drug dependency. The horrendous outcomes for human life from the human "answers" show us something very simple: human problems have, in general, no human solution. That is why we must all be taught by God (John 6:45). That is why the ministers of Christ with the people of Christ must be the light of the world and must teach the nations. That is why the Bible stands in the midst of human history as the single best source of information about the most important topics (the four questions, etc.).

Today I find that most pastors and teachers in the church are personally challenged and undermined in their confidence as "teachers of the nations." Indeed, many would find it very difficult to see themselves realistically in that role. They often are struggling just to hold themselves and their families together and deal with their "job." Often they are discouraged and sick at heart because "it" just doesn't work, or because what they have to do to "make" it work seems to be mere well-calculated human effort.

This is a great tragedy, not just for them, but for the world in which we live. The single most important thing happening in any community should be what is happening in the local gatherings of the disciples of Jesus. This has been true in the past, and surely it can be so today. Nothing essential has changed. Does humanity have any alternatives? Peter's question, "To whom shall we go?" (John 6:68), still stands unanswered. Nothing compares to Jesus as an answer to the basic questions of human life—and that is why even our secular culture cannot turn him loose, cannot stop dealing with him. But how shall we teach the teachers of the nations, those under our charge, in such a way that they are empowered to bring the eternal life of God flooding into lives of ordinary human beings, including themselves? Worldwide. How can we teach them to do this in such a way that the person and teachings of Jesus Christ are seen as the greatest treasure deposited in human history, and as the world's only valid hope?

The underlying issue today is whether or not the Christian minister actually is in possession of a body of unique and indispensable knowledge about life and reality that is more valuable to human beings—of far greater importance—than anything else one might seek to know. Does the Christian have an effective practical and moral teaching and direction, based on that unique knowledge, that far surpasses any other teaching in power to lead human beings, not only into eternity with God, but also into the good life and into being good persons now? As educators, do we know something others do not know, or are we just nicer?

How we can put those under our direction in possession of the knowledge and practice that does justice to Jesus Christ is the question that I wish to engage here. How shall ministers, leaders, and spokespersons, with well-grounded confidence, acquire that knowledge and practice? Are we doing it already? Really? I know these are not new questions to you. I believe they are questions to which you must have some answer just to get on with what you have to do as presidents of seminaries. I am sure it might be regarded as presumptuous on my part even to dare to think the answer to these questions is not in hand: in your hands. And yet, from where I stand at least, it seems we are not doing well with these questions today. And so I do dare to bring them up, with the hope that our times together here will bring better understanding of how we are to teach the teachers of the nations today.

It is perhaps needless to say that in approaching this question we are opening up difficult policy issues that concern our institutions, their traditions, faculties, and alumni, as well as our own sense of being right. We will need much grace, humility, and love to do the kind of "ground zero" planning that is surely required of us if we are to see the victory of Christ in our times, in an increasingly re-paganized world presided over by the highest levels of education and professional life.

GETTING THE MESSAGE RIGHT

What is the basic thing that we must say if we are to teach the nations? I believe it is that life in the kingdom of the heavens is available now to anyone who will place their confidence in Jesus Christ. It is that in Christ every provision has been made for anyone to enter right now into the eternal kind of life "which was with the Father and was manifested to us" (1 John 1:2). The message of Jesus, John says, is "that God is light, and in Him there is no darkness at all" (v. 5).

Surely we are to preach the "at-handedness" of the kingdom in the person of Christ: thus, to present what he presented in the manner he presented it—proclaiming, manifesting, and teaching (explaining) the presence of the kingdom. This is the same as "a personal relationship with Christ" and the "birth from above," where these phrases have any biblical sense; and we must never permit them to mean anything less than that kingdom connection.

It is to this message that the promises of the New Testament are attached. If we proclaim another message, it will not be prospered by God in the manner he intends. Perhaps it can be stated in various ways, but it is this message of available kingdom life that lays the foundation for life transformation through discipleship, and thereby for world transformation brought to completion when Christ returns.

A crucial question for us is always, Does the gospel I preach have a natural tendency to produce disciples of Jesus in kingdom living, resulting in people who actually live in the character and power of Christ? Or is discipleship—character transformation, routine obedience to Christ—something that is not a part of "the deal" we are offering, something we at most try to tack on as an option? There is no doubt how this matter stands in our churches generally at present. The transforming life is optional.

The resistance to this gospel of the available kingdom is very strong, and from within the "church visible" itself there are three major counter-gospels:

1. Forgiveness only: believe that Jesus died for your sins and your sins will be forgiven. Get your doctrine right and you will be accepted by God at death or judgment. Right belief, or profession of right belief, is the key issue.

2. Removal of "structural" evils: fight injustices. Jesus was killed by power. Resist such power. The "gospel of the left" favors justice above all. How justice is applied and for whom is the key issue.

3. Take care of your church and it will take care of you. Not said all that often, but in fact practiced much more widely than one might think.

While all three of these have an essential point, they are at best partial truths, and do not and cannot serve as the basis of a glorious redemptive community in the midst of the earth, which could teach the nations.

Much of the force lying back of these three partial "gospels" is a hermeneutic that says there must be two gospels in the New Testament: roughly, the one Jesus preached, and the one Paul preached. Jesus, it is said, proclaimed the nearness (the about-to-be-ness) of the kingdom as a political/social reality. He was disappointed. Paul preached a gospel of forgiveness of sins and heaven when you die. (I am of course oversimplifying these matters.) Simple Christians, some seem to think, cannot handle such matters, and just need to be faithful to their church.

I believe, to the contrary, that there is one and only one gospel in the New Testament, and that is the availability here and now of a life from "above" (from God / "the heavens") through confidence that Jesus is "the One"—the promised anointed one from God. It is the gospel of new life now in God's present kingdom or rule. It is the one Nicodemus had such trouble understanding (John 3).

This gospel is the one we see in action in the incidents in the Gospels (e.g., Matt. 8). We see Jesus's observations concerning the transition to it in Matthew 11:11–12 and Luke 16:16, and in Matthew 21:43. And we see how this gospel of the Gospels gradually melds with the gospel about Jesus in the book of Acts (1:3; 8:12; 14:22; 17:7; 19:8; 20:21, 25; 28:23, 31).

It is therefore quite natural for Paul to describe salvation as God "delivering us from the domain of darkness and transferring us into the kingdom of the Son of his love" (Col. 1:13), and for him to say that "the kingdom of God is not eating and drinking, but righteousness, peace and joy in the Holy Spirit" (Rom. 14:17). The gospel about Jesus and the gospel of the availability of the kingdom are not two gospels, but one; and Jesus without the kingdom and the kingdom without Jesus is simply no gospel at all.

The kingdom of God (and of the heavens) is simply God in action, God reigning. The kingdom of God is where what God wants done is done. He is a living God: that is, one who acts and incorporates us in his action. Thus: "He that has the Son has life." "He has given us life, and that life is in His Son." Salvation is a life that is of God and that makes us "partakers of divine nature" (2 Pet. 1:4). The good news to Zion is: "Your God reigns" (Isa. 52:7).

Those who would teach the nations must teach out of their experience of the reality of the present kingdom of the heavens: "The scribe who has become a disciple of the kingdom of the heavens is like a head of a household, who brings forth out of his treasure things new and old" (Matt. 13:52). By who they are they carry the kingdom of God within themselves and bring it near to others (Luke 10:9). To lead the teachers of the nations, we must lead them into such a life, make them competent practitioners of it, capable of passing it on to others. It is in the kingdom with Jesus that we become his disciples and learn from him in the "easy yoke" (Matt. 11:28–30). A disciple of course can be, and certainly is at the first, very imperfect. But life in the kingdom with Jesus is the process through which we develop his character and come to exercise the kind (though never the degree) of power that was in him. No doubt there is always room for improvement, but no doubt also the disciple is always improving.

The improvement in question will always be along very specific lines, such as those stated and explained by Jesus. For example, "Love your enemies, bless those who curse you," and so forth. It will be seen in the peace and power with which one lives one's life and does one's work. Discipleship and "spiritual formation" are a matter of becoming the kind of person for whom the deeds and power of Christ are increasingly "natural."

I believe that our first step in teaching the teachers of the nations is to help them to be comfortable and strong in preaching, manifesting, and teaching this salvation, which is eternal life in the kingdom of the heavens, through reliance upon Jesus Christ. We must, as teaching institutions and leaders, be sure that this is what we do. We dare not send our students out to preach and live a message that will not produce disciples of Jesus, living in the real world with others who so desperately need to see, to feel the influence of, the God who is here and who is love.

Can we uphold the news of Jesus the present king as the fundamental message of salvation? Dare we do it? Can we accept it? If not, how will other messages serve as a basis for the advance of Christ in our times? Will our institutions stand for the gospel of the kingdom? Will our faculties?

THE GOSPEL OF SECULARISM

Jesus and his gospel come to us saying: The ultimate reality is a spiritual (nonphysical), personal being, who is independent of all else, completely self-sufficing, completely in charge, and who is unlimited in power and goodness. And he tells us we are unceasing spiritual beings with eternal destinies in God's great universe. Moreover, this ultimate personal reality has planned on you from the beginning of creation. He has prepared a kingdom for you from the beginning (Matt. 25:34). He has made a place for you in history, along with every provision for your ultimate safety and well-being. As you place your confidence in Jesus Christ, and through him in God (1 Pet. 1:21), even this present world becomes a perfectly safe place for you to be (Luke 12:22–34).

Now, the most subtle and powerful contemporary opposition to the gospel of the availability of the kingdom in Jesus Christ is the secular picture of life (and the secular answer to the four great questions) that is sponsored by the academic establishment and its offshoots in professional life—even, to an astonishing extent, in the profession of the clergy. This outlook is quietly assumed in many ways as the truth, or at least as what it is right to endorse. And it is currently aggressively represented in books, like Owen Flanagan's *The Problem of the Soul*—the most recent in a long line of similar books going back through the last three centuries.[1]

Flanagan bluntly states: "Supernatural concepts have no philosophical warrant"—that is, nothing to support them. Hence, he argues there is no support "for beliefs in divine beings, miracles, or heavenly afterlives."[2] "There are no such things as souls, or nonphysical minds."[3] "There is no self that is constituted by an immortal soul, and God is something about which, if you have good sense, you will resist speaking, especially with an air of confidence. Nothing sensible can be said."[4] And so forth.

This is a very adequate statement of the secular view of life that is presented by the weight of course content and academic practice in the university system. The acceptable course content does not differ appreciably in Christian universities, and that is enforced by the professional organizations and standing therein for the faculty in those universities. (Of course there are rare individual exceptions.) It is the dead weight of what counts as "acceptable knowledge" that chokes off any confidence in the content of "standard" Christian teaching—"Mere Christianity," as C. S. Lewis called it. This weight undermines both the confidence of ministers and teachers, that they are imparting essential knowledge about life and reality when they proclaim and teach the New Testament message (the content of the Apostle's Creed, to put it concisely); and the confidence of those who hear them, that what they are hearing is a presentation of how things really are. That is, the rumor—it is no more than that—of what is "acceptable knowledge" buffers the content of Christian teaching from impacting the hearer (and often the speaker) as conveying hard facts that all must deal with and can count on.

Not as if this "acceptable knowledge" (often just called "science" though no science presents it as a result) had been actually established. It hasn't been. But the shift of sociological force, now in almost total control of the universities and their offshoots, does not require that in order for the secular picture to be "acceptable" and all else "unacceptable" for teachable course content and for practice.[5]

Rather, what has happened is that, through a historical process, in large part having to do with the disassociation of the educational establishment from the church, the very concept of what knowledge is has been changed. Indeed, knowledge itself has largely disappeared (along with truth) from the university scene and language, and has been replaced by "research." (You probably have never heard of a "knowledge university," but the title "research university" is greatly prized.) Julie Reuben has done a beautiful job of showing how this happened in her book *The Making of the Modern University*.[6] By careful analysis of the internal documents of the most well-known universities in America, she shows how knowledge (and then research) came to be identified with the physical or "natural" sciences, and how that inevitably put, first, the content of religious claims, and then that of morality outside of the limits of "acceptable knowledge," so far as university life was concerned.

Now, it is simply false—and this is something that is crucial for the teachers of the teachers of the nations to understand—that science has shown any of the teachings of "Mere Christianity" to be false or meaningless. I often challenge my students in classes (who have imbibed the myths about "science" from their surroundings) to find the widely used textbook or peer-reviewed article or book in a specific scientific field that teaches the nonexistence of God or the nonsurvival of the person beyond physical death. There are none. And of course there is no field of knowledge called science. "Science" is a cultural myth, an academic rumor, perpetuated mainly by certain philosophers or literary types. "Science" says nothing and has nothing to say. But it currently serves as a point of reference by which to define "acceptable knowledge" (and "research") and to brand religious and moral teachings as beyond the pale. Teachings of (the Christian) religion and of (traditional) morality are then marked out as dangerous enemies of the enlightened "scientific" or at least "secular" view, and the teachings of Christians are excluded from the classroom and lecture hall, even as something to be thoughtfully considered. This, then, is forcibly carried over to the wider society through the media, which are dominated by those who are governed—well meaning, no doubt—by the rumors of the academic ("research") world, which has now become the cultural authority in our society. That is, it has become the source of ideas "acceptable" as guides to life.

In the wider society, there are now three recognized accounts or "stories" of life and reality. These are:

1. The theistic story
2. The "scientific" / "physical universe only" story
3. The "Nirvana" (spiritualist / new age) story

These float about in odd mixtures, and you rarely find anyone who holds constantly and clearly to just one, though they are mutually inconsistent. Consistency and intellectual thoroughness are not regarded as essential virtues now; rather, the adeptness to shift one's weight from one story to another "as needed" is regarded as good. Flanagan, for example, a professor at Duke University and a well-known writer in the philosophy of mind, tries to use account 2 to refute account 1, and then turns to account 3 to find a way of, supposedly, overcoming the challenge to any significant morality and meaning in life if account 2 is all you have. Of course account 2 is just as inconsistent with account 3 as with 1, but Flanagan simply drops out of 3 whatever he is uncomfortable with, and redefines "Buddhism" so that he can claim to follow Buddhist practice without the obviously essential beliefs of the teachers of Buddhism through the ages.[7] Trying to align 2 and 3 together against 1 is increasingly adopted as a way of getting rid of God and still being "spiritual."

The adoption of "research" as the model of knowledge, and the shift over to a "nirvana" version of how to live, explains most of what constantly now comes down in the many attempted reinterpretations of Jesus that assail us in scholarly circles and in the popular press.[8] These interpretations all share the goals of (1) the elimination of the supernatural and (2) the undermining of traditional moral teachings (hence advancing "political correctness"). The despiritualization of God and of the human person (usually in the form of the reinterpretation of the spiritual) is central to attaining these goals, and the undermining of the scripture as a source of knowledge concerning God and the soul and the spiritual life is therefore required. But with that goes the basis for traditional morality (the Ten Commandments, etc.), and the way is opened for "human flourishing" defined in strictly human terms, to become the only point of reference in determining what we ought to do and who is a good or bad person—if we even dare to speak of that. God, the nature of the human person, the status of the Bible, and the content of moral goodness form the battlefield for those who would be "teachers of the nations."

Here we must explicitly, courageously, and thoroughly carry the case for Christ and his spiritual kingdom if we are going to teach all nations. If we do not do that, we must be prepared to hear that "the Christian religion, as organized in the churches, has been and still is the principle enemy of moral progress in the world." This is a statement by Bertrand Russell, but in many "learned" quarters today it is regarded as commonplace, and it has, for several centuries, been the steady drumbeat of supposedly enlightened persons who regard themselves as in the forefront of "research" or as "advanced thinkers."[9] (See John Lennon's "Imagine.") The vision of life-now-in-the-kingdom-of-God, and all that would naturally flow from that, is of course ruled out by the "research" vision; and to sustain the kingdom vision in the face of the "research" vision is impossible without substantial help in understanding and living it in confrontation with constant opposition from "authoritative sources." This help must be provided by those who would teach the teachers of the nation for Christ.

BEING DISCIPLES MAKING DISCIPLES

Those who would lead and teach the nations for Christ must be under the teaching of Christ, and must bring others under that teaching. They must, in other words, be disciples who make disciples. So must be those who teach the teachers. By the "teaching of Christ" we here mean not just what he taught, to be passed on through the ages—of course that, too, and that centrally—but we mean the ongoing engagement of individuals with the living Lord who now stands in personal interactive relationship to them. They are to be constantly taught in the Trinitarian community by the members of the Trinity.

If there is a body of Christian knowledge and practice ("Mere Christianity"), we can become students of it and learn it, just as is the case in other areas where there is knowledge. If there is not, then we cannot. Now, here is an unhappy truth: being a *disciple* of Jesus is not currently regarded as a natural part, much less an essential requirement, of being a Christian, and certainly not of being a Methodist, a Roman Catholic, a Presbyterian, Assembly of God, Baptist, and so forth.

I realize that there is considerable lack of clarity about the meanings of terms; but the long usage of *disciple* by what was, for many years of the late twentieth century, regarded as the premier "disciple making" para–church group, the Navigators, is surely a silent witness to the optional status of discipleship among Christians. The Navigators divided those with some allegiance to Christ into "Christians" (those with sins forgiven), "Disciples" (those who could make Christians), and "Workers" (those who could make disciples and train them to make Christians). This is not a secret, of course, and we have to take our hats off to Dawson Trotman and the Navigators, because they at least were serious about being and making disciples in a time when few were. But the point is that even for them you didn't have to be a disciple to be a Christian. And this is a model of life in Christ that still hangs over us. In fact, it is a many-faceted misunderstanding of soteriology, in my opinion, and a gross misreading of the scriptures and of what grace is and how it works.

You can easily see, I think, how nondiscipleship Christianity relates to the three versions of the gospel that were mentioned previously. Clearly these gospels leave it open to omit discipleship in any transformative sense. If mentioned at all, it will become a matter of getting conversions (gospel 1), of social activities (gospel 2), or faithfulness to church activities (gospel 3). But as it turns out, you don't really have to do any of these. That is an open secret, and the reason why, as someone recently said, American Christianity is three thousand miles wide and an inch deep. I think this inability to come to grips with discipleship is now also true of what would traditionally have been called the "Arminian" wing of the American church, which emphasized the essentiality of "works" to salvation. And we should ask ourselves, "In what sense, if any, do our institutions make discipleship to Jesus a natural part, or essential to, being a Christian, and especially to being a teacher of the nation and to the nations? What is the place of discipleship in our educational programs?"

Some interesting insight into the nature of New Testament discipleship comes from Jesus's teachings in the Gospel of John.

1. Disciples are those who abide (live in, practice) his words (John 8:31).
2. Disciples are those who come to manifest the quality of love among themselves that Jesus himself manifested (John 13:35).
3. Disciples are those who bear "much fruit" (John 15:5–8). And we can perhaps safely add on that:
4. The disciple of Jesus is one for whom the most important thing in the world is following him into his teachings and practices in the kingdom of the heavens (Luke 14:26–35; Matt. 6:33).

Now, it is important to understand that a disciple can be very green and imperfect and still be a disciple, a student, an apprentice. We certainly see that in Jesus's first disciples. And this is good to know, for most of us have a long way to go. Being an apprentice is a matter of one's intention and of the process in which one is caught up, though a certain progress is required. And it also is important to understand that one's efforts in discipleship are not a matter of earning anything. Rather, it is a matter of learning to appropriate something—namely, the gift of the eternal kind of life (1 John 5:20). Grace is opposed not to effort, but to earning. Effort is action; earning is attitude.

How then shall we characterize a disciple in a working definition? We can safely say that a disciple of Jesus is one who is with him, learning to be like him. That would be fitting as a general description of anyone who is learning from someone. We should add that, as a disciple of Jesus, I am learning from him how to lead my life as he would lead my life if he were I. Of course, I will be his disciple only if I have confidence in him, and if I have confidence in him I will do my best to do what he says and to learn how to do what he says where I do not know how to proceed.

So, for example, when he says, "Love your enemies and bless those who curse you," or even where he says that we should "love one another," I will say, "This is the very best thing for me to do. I will not be deprived and miserable if I do it. I don't know how to do it, and mere trying, I see, will not be enough. But I will learn from him how to do it. He will help me learn this, and he has made all provision for it."

There will be three main areas of learning or apprenticeship for the disciple:

1. The explicit statements of Jesus as to what I should do.
2. How to conduct the ordinary affairs of life in family, work, and community (including church).
3. How to exercise the power of Christ and his kingdom by prayer,

speaking, and acting "in the name of Christ" (Col. 3:17; remember Acts 8:12).

Practically speaking, there are three things required for spiritual growth in those three areas (indeed, for any purposive process of personal transformation). These are:

1. Vision of the goodness to be realized. (Life in the Kingdom with Jesus, in this case. That is why getting the message right is so important.)

2. Intention to realize the vision, to become that kind of person. Intention, of course, is incomplete without decision to bring the intention to pass. Many people have never decided to become disciples of Jesus, and may have never even been invited to do so.

3. Means to carry out the decision. What are the specific activities required to implement the intention to realize the vision? The test here is simple effectiveness. What will actually do the job?

This structure—call it the VIM structure—will be abundantly assisted by grace and will be lived out under the direction of our teacher, if we will simply step into it with confidence in him. So perhaps we can now say that we know who the disciple (apprentice) of Jesus is, what they do, and how they do it. The test of whether we are disciples of Jesus will simply be: Are we with him learning to be like him? And which of his commandments have I learned from him to do or am I now learning from him to do? Nondiscipleship is the root of nearly every evil we see in individuals and communities that profess to be trusting Christ.

How much time and energy do you spend dealing with issues that should not even be coming up among people who profess faith in Christ? But then, are our practices as Christians such as to lead people out of bondage to evil and into the "free indeed" life of the maturing apprentice to Jesus? Do our institutions foster such practices and people who can make those practices live in our local congregations?

CLAIMING THE LOCAL CONGREGATION FOR KINGDOM APPRENTICESHIP

Local congregations—generously conceived of as "where two or three are gathered in my name" (Matt. 18:20)—are the primary focus points for teaching the nation and the nations. In teaching the teachers of the nations, we are primarily growing them into people who are equipped to induct individuals in groups into powerful and holy living right in the midst of communities on the earth where they are located. We have noted that these local congregations are supposed to be groups of disciples of Jesus but that, unfortunately, this is not now generally the case with local congregations. Following upon this sad fact is another. You will rarely if ever find in an established group an effort, a sustained program, designed to teach people how to do the things Jesus and his New Testament followers said to do. Just as discipleship on any New Testament pattern is not now regarded as essential, neither is teaching and learning how to do the kinds of things Jesus said.

For example, he said that when we are insulted and persecuted and lied about because of our alignment with him, we should "rejoice and be glad, for your reward in the heavens is great, for so they persecuted the prophets who were before you" (Matt. 5:12). Or, how about just "blessing those who curse you"? Or "laying up for yourselves treasures in heaven"? And so on.

Now, you might think that an absolutely essential task for the disciples would be to teach those who become disciples "to observe all that I commanded you" (Matt. 28:20). At least that is what Jesus told us to do, and at many points both he and the Bible strongly emphasize the necessity of doing and not just hearing. Yet in fact, our local congregations do not do such teaching, and, as a result, they often seriously impede rather than further the call of Christ's people to be "Children of God above reproach in the midst of a crooked and perverse generation, among whom you shine as lights in the world, holding forth the word of life" (Phil. 2:15–16).

Can we deny that we are supposed to do such teaching and training? And can we imagine that it is not possible, if Christ has sent us to do it? Is it even possible that his provision for doing it is not contained in his statement "And look, I'm with you every minute, until the job is done even until [the end of the age]" (Matt. 28:20)? This is where the all-importance of *vision* comes in once again: but now at the group level. Our congregations must come to see this kind of teaching and training as something good and to be done. They do not seem to do so at present.

Of course if they are going to actually teach people how to do all that Jesus commanded, we ourselves must know how to do what he said. As disciples we must learn how to do it through a path of honest effort, inquiry, and growth. We must then be reflective about the process so we can intelligently instruct and help others. How did we come to the point of rejoicing when we are insulted for Christ's sake? As the leaders you are, you have probably had many opportunities to rejoice when insulted, even when those insulting you are professing Christians! And our studies have perhaps led us to see how others, from Jesus and Paul to John Paul II and Billy Graham, have learned to do it. Not through gritted teeth, of course, but from heartfelt and generous love of God and others.

If we are going to teach the teachers of the nation, we must come to understand the fine texture of spiritual growth. We will quickly learn, as we go along that path, that what are standardly prescribed as activities for "good Christians" in general are nowhere near enough. We have to go much deeper, searching out the Vision, Intention, and Means (VIM) that actually suffice to change us inwardly, so that the words and deeds of Jesus naturally and routinely flow from us. "The good tree cannot bring forth bad fruit," the teacher says (Luke 6:43). And then in our local congregations we must have programs of activities that enable those who intend to be apprentices to actually become adept at doing all "in the name of the Lord Jesus, giving thanks through Him to God the Father" (Col. 3:17).

Generally speaking, this will mean arranging for a life of "spiritual disciplines" into which disciples under our care can sensibly enter as reliable means for implementing their vision and intention of kingdom living. A discipline is something within our power that enables us to do what we cannot accomplish by just trying. Almost without exception the commands of Jesus are things we cannot do by just trying. We must have a plan for activities that lead to growth. Below is a look at what I call the "golden triangle" within which we put on the character of Christ may help us.

As an illustration of a spiritual discipline we might consider scripture memorization, which is a subactivity to study. This is one of the most beneficial things one can do to keep the true word of God before one and to become strongly inclined to do from the heart the things that Jesus said. As we memorize lengthy passages—say, 1 Corinthians 13, or Romans 8, or Ephesians 4—the beautiful order in these words will increasingly take possession of our whole being,

The Golden Triangle of Spiritual Growth

The Action of the Holy Spirit
John 3:5 • Rom. 8:10-13 • Gal. 5:22-26

**Centered in
the Mind of
Christ**

Phil 2:12-15
Rom. 13:14

**Ordinary Events of
Life: "Temptations"**

James 1:2-4
Rom. 5:1-5

**Planned Discipline to
Put on a New Heart**

Col. 3:12-17
2: Pet. 1:5-10

including our body and the depths of our soul. Thus, for example, when we are cursed by someone who would be happy to see us dead, it is blessing in us—not cursing—that is already there, on the tip of our tongue and the depths of our heart, ready to come forth. When we are persecuted, it is joy that is already there. And so forth. When Paul and Silas sang in jail at midnight, it was because of what was in them already. They were happy.

We cannot go into greater depth here, but each of the disciplines has a transforming effect on our internal condition—the "insides of the cup," in Jesus's terms. And now, perhaps, we can imagine a church that understands the process of growth in Christlikeness so well that it is prepared to put a sign out front, offering to teach all comers willing to rely on Christ how to live without domination by anger or lust, how to love their enemies—and even those who just "bug" them—and how to live in all the other beautiful teachings of Jesus, which the world usually respects even when it despises Christians and "church." This would certainly work, given all that we have said already, and without it nothing much works in the local congregation—at least, not as it should.

Charles Finney (a lawyer) used to say that the Christian minister is like a lawyer in court, who argues the case he is going to prove to the jury, calls his witness, and the witness contradicts everything he said. Perhaps that is an exaggeration, but there is too much truth in it for comfort, and it will not be the case if we simply do in our local congregations what Jesus told us to do. How to bring that about is a part of the task of those of us who must teach the teachers of the nations.[10]

Can we think of our seminaries and Christian universities as places where we teach leaders in our societies, along with pastors and teachers in our local congregations, how to lead their people into doing all things Jesus commanded?

Some things we might try to do in our universities and seminaries as teachers of the leaders and teachers of the nations are to:

1. Establish, through biblical and theological studies, the gospel as the good news about life with Christ in the kingdom now present (Col. 3:1–4).

2. Explicitly confront and effectively defeat the claims of "science" and secularism against the gospel of the kingdom. Make this a pastoral, not just an apologetic, matter.

3. Make active apprenticeship to Jesus the "normal Christian life" and the central "invitation" in our evangelization.

4. Make our local congregations centers of training and of enabling apprentices to do what Jesus said—not legalistically, but as a natural expression of who they have become in his presence.

I realize that these propositions may seem "untraditional," or even heretical, but certainly not "normal." Dare we do it? The real question surely is, Dare we not do it? We dare do nothing less if we are to fulfill the calling of God on our lives to be "a light to the nations, so that My salvation may reach to the end of the earth" (Isa. 49:6).

Notes

CHAPTER 1: Transformation of the Mind

1. A. W. Tozer, *The Knowledge of the Holy* (New York: Harper & Row, 1961), 8–10.
2. Roland Herbert Bainton, *Here I Stand: A Life of Martin Luther*, Abingdon Classics (Nashville, TN: Abingdon Press, 1990), 182.
3. Isaac Watts, *Logic; Or, the Right Use of Reason, in the Inquiry After Truth* (London: Crosby and Co., 1802).
4. Watts, *Logic*, vi.
5. Thomas Watson, *The Complete Works of Thomas Watson (1556–1592)*, ed. Dana Ferrin Sutton (Lewiston, NY: Edwin Mellen Press, 1997).

CHAPTER 2: Living a Transformed Life

1. William Wordsworth, "Lines Composed a Few Miles Above Tintern Abbey, on Revisiting the Banks of the Wye During a Tour. July 13, 1798," in *The Complete Poetical Works of William Wordsworth*, ed. John Morley (New York: Macmillan and Co., 1903), 98.
2. Mary Seraphim, *Clare: Her Light and Her Song* (Chicago: Franciscan Herald Press, 1984), chap. 24.
3. Ernest Gilliat-Smith, *Saint Claire of Assisi: Her Life and Legislation* (London: J. M. Dent and Sons, 1914), 114.
4. William Law, *A Serious Call to a Devout and Holy Life* (London: J. M. Dent and Sons, 1931).
5. Law, *A Serious Call*, 10–17.
6. William Wilberforce, *A Practical View of the Prevailing Religious System of Professed Christians in the Higher and Middle Classes in This Country, Contrasted with Real Christianity* (New York: American Tract Society, 1820).
7. J. F. Webb, *Lives of the Saints* (Baltimore: Penguin Books, 1965), 18.
8. Blaise Pascal, *Pensées* (Mineola, NY: Dover Publications, 2003), 39.
9. Samuel Taylor Coleridge and Henry Nelson Coleridge, *The Friend:*

A Series of Essays to Aid in the Formation of Fixed Principles in Politics,
Morals, and Religion. With Literary Amusements Interspersed (London:
Edward Moxon and Co., 1863), 166.

10. William James, *Talks to Teachers on Psychology and to Students on Some of*
    Life's Ideals (New York: H. Holt and Company, 1899), 64.

11. Albert Schweitzer, *The Quest of the Historical Jesus: A Critical Study of Its*
    Progress from Reimarus to Wrede, trans. W. Montgomery (London: Adam
    and Charles Black, 1910), 410.

CHAPTER 3: Flesh and Spirit

1. All scripture references in this chapter are from the New American Standard Bible unless otherwise noted.

2. Aristotle, *The Nicomachean Ethics,* ed. J. A. K. Thomson (London: Allen
   & Unwin, 1953).

3. William M. Ramsay, *The Cities of St. Paul: Their Influence on His Life*
   and Thought (New York: Hodder & Stoughton, 1907), 4.

4. James S. Stewart, *A Man in Christ* (New York: Harper, 1935), 21.

5. This is a Victor Herbert song. "I Want What I Want When I Want It"
   from his 1905 operetta *Mlle. Modiste.*

6. Paul gave much thought and expression to the dreadful chaos of the
   sinful life. See his lists in Romans 1:29–32 and 3:10–18, as well as
   2 Timothy 3:2–7.

CHAPTER 4: Beyond Pornography

1. These statistics can be found in Amy Frykholm's helpful article "Pastors
   and Pornography: Addictive Behavior," *Christian Century* (September 4,
   2007), 20–22.

2. It turns out that feeling alive is a major problem for human beings, es-
   pecially in a highly regimented and organized culture. See, for instance,
   Sigmund Freud, *Civilization and Its Discontents* (New York: W. W.
   Norton & Co., 2010).

3. A depressed person is typically one who has little or no desire and "doesn't
   want anything." When people get locked into that, it is extremely hard to
   do anything that is helpful for them. Sometimes just getting them physi-
   cally active will help, but it is very hard to pull them out.

4. See chapter 5 of *Renovation of the Heart* (Colorado Springs, CO: Nav-
   Press, 2012), 77–92.

5. Frykholm, "Pastors and Pornography," 21.
6. For more on this, see William James's chapter on "Will" in *The Principles of Psychology* (New York: Dover Publications, 1950), 486–592.
7. A very effective DVD on breaking the grip of pornography is *Somebody's Daughter: A Journey of Freedom from Pornography*. Directed by John Evans and released September 18, 2008.

CHAPTER 6: Spirituality for Smarties

1. A good study of the range of these terms is found in the introduction to Peter H. Van Ness, ed., *Spirituality and the Secular Quest* (Norwich, UK: SCM Press, 1996), 1–17.
2. Sharon Janis, *Spirituality for Dummies*, 2nd ed. (Hoboken, NJ: Wiley John, 2008).
3. George Herbert Palmer, *The Field of Ethics* (New York: Houghton Mifflin Company, 1901).
4. The magical, but not usually the spiritual, is thought to involve some element of illusion, or at least of bizarre causation (hurting you by sticking a pin in an effigy of you, etc.), whereas this is not associated with the spiritual, except by those suspicious of it or hostile to it.
5. Jo L. Long, *Employing Spirituality in the Workplace* (Lincoln, NE: Writers Club Press, 2000).
6. Tahir Shah, *Sorcerer's Apprentice* (New York: Penguin Books, 1998).
7. Cornelia Dean, "Scientists Speak Up on Mix of God and Science," *Wall Street Journal*, August 23, 2005.
8. William B. Provine, *Origins Research* 16, no. 1 (1994), 9. Also quoted by Roger Patterson in *Evolution Exposed* (Hebron, KY: Answers in Genesis, 2006), 82.
9. In *From Max Weber: Essays in Sociology*, ed. H. H. Gerth and C. Wright Mills (New York: Oxford Univ. Press, 1946), 150.

CHAPTER 7: When God Moves In

1. J. Gilchrist Lawson, *Deeper Experiences of Famous Christians: Gleaned From Their Biographies, Autobiographies and Writings* (Chicago, IL: Glad Tidings Publishing, 1911).
2. Lawson, *Deeper Experiences of Famous Christians*.
3. Lawson, *Deeper Experiences of Famous Christians*, 133.

4. Thomas à Kempis and William C. Creasy, *The Imitation of Christ* (Macon, GA: Mercer University Press, 1990).

5. John Wesley, *Sermons on Several Occasions* (New York, NY: published by T. Mason and G. Lane for the Methodist Episcopal church, 1800), and John Wesley, *The Journal of the Reverend John Wesley: September 6, 1750* (New York, NY: T. Mason and G. Lane, 1837).

6. William Law, *A Serious Call to a Devout and Holy Life* (London, UK: J. M. Dent and Sons, 1931).

7. Jeremy Taylor, *Holy Living and Dying: With Prayers; Containing the Whole Duty of a Christian, and the Parts of Devotion Fitted to All Occasions and Furnished for All Necessities* (London, UK: G. Bell and Sons, 1897).

8. Charles G. Finney, *Lectures on Revivals of Religion* (New York, NY: Leavitt, Lord & Co., 1835), and Charles G. Finney, *Charles G. Finney. An Autobiography* (Westwood, NJ: Fleming H. Revell Co., 1876).

9. Jean Calvin, *Institutes of the Christian Religion*, trans. John Allen, vol. III (Philadelphia, PA: Nicklin and Howe, 1816).

10. Dietrich Bonhoeffer, *The Cost of Discipleship* (London: SCM Press, 1959), 43–44.

CHAPTER 8: Apologetics in the Manner of Jesus

1. ταπεινοφροσύνη *(tapeinophrosúnē),* "lowminded," "base," which is from tapeinós, "lowly," "humble." Humility, lowliness of mind, the esteeming of ourselves small, inasmuch as we are so, the correct estimate of ourselves (Acts 20:19; Eph. 4:2; Phil. 2:3; Col. 2:18, 23; 3:12; 1 Pet. 5:5). For the sinner *tapeinophrosúnē* involves the confession of his sin and a deep realization of his unworthiness to receive God's marvelous grace. See Spiros Zodhiates (#5012) in *The Complete Word Study Dictionary: New Testament* (Chattanooga, TN: AMG Publishers, 2000).

2. See Walter Grundmann's article in *Theological Dictionary of the New Testament,* ed. Gerhard Kittel, Gerhard Friedrich, and Geoffrey W. Bromiley (Grand Rapids, MI: Eerdmans, 1964), 21–22.

CHAPTER 9: A History of Asceticism and the Formation of a Christlike Character

1. Aristotle, *Nicomachean Ethics,* 1105b, 10–12; 1103b, 27–30.

2. Alasdair C. MacIntyre, *After Virtue* (London: Gerald Duckworth & Co., 1981).

3. Gerhard Kittel, Gerhard Friedrich, and Geoffrey W. Bromiley, eds., *Theological Dictionary of the New Testament* (Grand Rapids, MI: Eerdmans, 1985).

4. Otto Zöckler, *Askese und Mönchtum* (Frankfurt, Germany: Heyder und Simmer, 1897).

5. David Hume, *Essays and Treatises on Several Subjects,* new ed., vol. 3 (Edinburgh: Bell & Bradfute, 1817), 339.

6. David Hume, *An Enquiry Concerning the Principles of Morals,* ed. L. A. Selby-Bigge (Oxford: Oxford Univ. Press, 1957), 270.

7. George F. Thomas, *Christian Ethics and Moral Philosophy* (New York: Scribner, 1955), quoted in Richard B. Brandt, *Value and Obligation: Systematic Readings in Ethics* (New York: Harcourt, Brace & World, 1961), 315.

8. See Albert Rabil, *Merleau-Ponty: Existentialist of the Social World* (New York: Columbia Univ. Press, 1967), 24–39.

9. *Solfeggio* is an Italian term that refers to a form of music education that teaches sight-reading of music notes and relative pitch.

10. William James, *The Principles of Psychology* (New York: Henry Holt and Co., 1890), 105.

11. Reinhold Niebuhr, *An Interpretation of Christian Ethics* (San Francisco: Harper & Row, 1963), 226.

12. Niebuhr, *An Interpretation of Christian Ethics,* 228.

13. Niebuhr, *An Interpretation of Christian Ethics,* 230.

14. Quoted in Richard Watson, *A Collection of Theological Tracts,* vol. 4 (London: J. Nichols, 1785), 147.

CHAPTER 11: Reflections on *Renovation of the Heart*

1. This description can be found on their website at https://renovare.org/about/overview.

2. Editor's note: It is important to note that this comment regarding an "Oprah" form of spirituality should not be taken as a critique or slight on the person of Oprah Winfrey. Dallas and I spoke of this specifically when working on *The Divine Conspiracy Continued.* Rather, Dallas is suggesting that those who are often guests that use that program as a platform for their spiritual worldviews is what Dallas is critiquing. See Gary Black Jr., *The Theology of Dallas Willard: Discovering Protoevangelical Faith* (Eugene, OR: Pickwick Publications, 2013), 94–95.

3. Neale Donald Walsch, *Questions and Answers on Conversations with God* (Charlottesville, VA: Hampton Roads Pub., 1999), and Helen Schucman, *A Course in Miracles: Original Edition* (Omaha, NE: Course in Miracles Society, 1993).

CHAPTER 16: Spiritual Disciplines in a Postmodern World

1. Lily Tomlin in Jane Wagner's book *The Search for Signs of Intelligent Life in the Universe* (New York: Harper & Row, 1986), 18.

CHAPTER 17: Getting the Elephant Out of the Sanctuary

1. *The Divine Conspiracy,* 37–38.

CHAPTER 18: The Gospel of the Kingdom

1. In 2005, Keith Giles conducted an interview that was intended for the second issue of *Noise* magazine. However, a second issue never materialized. The interview instead appeared on Giles's blog (www.KeithGiles.com) and was later published by Giles in *Subversive Interviews Volume 1: Subversive Underground.*
2. The *Left Behind* books Dallas refers to are a set of 16 best-selling biblio-fiction novels written by Tim LaHaye and Jerry B. Jenkins. They articulate a Christian dispensationalist view of the end times (eschatology) which includes certain views of a pretribulation, premillennial rapture theory read into an interpretation of the New Testament book of Revelation.

CHAPTER 21: The Evolution of Discipleship

1. This threefold scheme is laid out in LeRoy Eims, *The Lost Art of Disciple-Making* (Grand Rapids, MI: Zondervan, 1978), which long served as an unofficial guide for the work of Navigators.
2. See Betty Lee Skinner, *Daws: A Man Who Trusted God* (Colorado Springs, CO: NavPress, 1974).
3. There are, of course, many individuals among evangelicals today who would not accept this. Charismatics and heirs of the various "holiness" traditions would find it hard to swallow. But then, what is emphasized by them is still not discipleship.
4. Keswick is a town in the district of Allerdale, Cumbria—in the "Lake District" of England, a center of tourism for centuries. Keswick

became the venue for an annual Christian Convention beginning in 1875 and continuing today. It was a well-known source of "higher life" teachings for more than a century, and has been influential around the world.

5. Hannah Whitall Smith, *The Christian's Secret of a Happy Life* (Grand Rapids, MI: Chosen Books, 1984).

6. Rosalind Rinker, *Prayer: Conversing with God* (Grand Rapids, MI: Zondervan, 1959).

7. Thomas à Kempis and William C. Creasy, *The Imitation of Christ* (Macon, GA: Mercer Univ. Press, 1990); Brother Lawrence, *The Practice of the Presence of God*, ed. Robert J. Edmonson and Hal McElwaine Helms (Brewster, MA: Paraclete Press, 2010).

8. The work of Richard Foster and his Renovaré ministry was highly influential in this direction.

9. On this, consult Charles G. Finney, *Lectures on Revivals of Religion* (New York: Leavitt, Lord & Co., 1835), along with the works of Jonathan Edwards.

10. See the careful study of the history of the "disciple" in the world of the New Testament provided in Michael J. Wilkins, *The Concept of Disciple in Matthew's Gospel, as Reflected in the Use of the Term* Μαθητής (Leiden: E. J. Brill, 1988).

11. John McClintock and James Strong, eds., *Cyclopaedia of Biblical, Theological, and Ecclesiastical Literature*, vol. 8 (New York: Harper and Brothers, 1894), 870.

CHAPTER 22: Discipleship How-To

1. Brother Lawrence, *Practice of the Presence of God*, 17.

2. William Law, *A Serious Call to a Devout and Holy Life* (London: J. M. Dent & Sons, 1931). 8.

3. Law, *A Serious Call*, 8.

4. Law, *A Serious Call*, 11.

5. Law, *A Serious Call*, 12.

CHAPTER 23: How to Live One Day with Jesus

1. Jeremy Taylor, *The Rule and Exercises of Holy Living* (Romford, UK: Langford Press, 1970).

CHAPTER 25: The Disciple's Solidarity with the Poor

1. John Wesley, *The Journal of the Reverend John Wesley*, vol. 2, entry for September 6, 1750 (New York: T. Mason and G. Lane, 1837), 208.
2. John Wesley, *The Works of John Wesley*, sermon 120, vol. 2 (New York: J. Emory and B. Waugh, 1831), 441.
3. Wesley, *Works*, 441.
4. Wesley, *Works*, 445.
5. Law, *A Serious Call*, 1.
6. Law, *A Serious Call*, 1.

CHAPTER 26: Spiritual Formation as a Natural Part of Salvation

1. *The Divine Conspiracy*, chaps. 1 and 2.
2. See works cited in the "For Further Reading" section at the end of this chapter.
3. I have tried to outline some of the basic changes in chapters 12 and 13 of *Renovation of the Heart*.
4. Richard Foster, *Life with God* (San Francisco: HarperOne, 2008).

CHAPTER 27: The Faith of Unbelief

1. William K. Clifford, "The Ethics of Belief," in *Lectures and Essays*, ed. Leslie Stephen and Frederick Pollock (London: Macmillan and Co., 1886).
2. William James, *The Will to Believe, and Other Essays in Popular Philosophy* (New York, NY: Longmans, Green, and Co. 1897), 11.
3. See his *Pensées*, subsections 233–41.
4. Rudolph Binion, *After Christianity: Christian Survivals in Post-Christian Culture* (Durango, CO: Longbridge-Rhodes, 1986), 9–10.

CHAPTER 29: The Foundations of Moral Realization

1. Paul L. Holmer, David Jay Gouwens, and Lee C. Barrett, *Thinking the Faith With Passion: Selected Essays* (Eugene, OR: Cascade Books, 2012), 313.
2. Søren Kierkegaard, *Attack upon "Christendom"* (Boston: Beacon Press, 1959), 110–11.
3. William K. Frankena, *Ethics*, 2nd ed. (Englewood Cliffs, NJ: Prentice-Hall, 1973), 6.

4. Aristotle, *Nicomachean Ethics*, bk. 2, chap. 4.

5. Immanuel Kant and Thomas Kingsmill Abbott, *Fundamental Principles of the Metaphysics of Morals* (Mineola, NY: Dover Publications, 2005), sec. 1.

6. Aristotle, *Nicomachean Ethics*, 1097b 3–5.

7. Nicolai Hartmann, *Ethics*, trans. Stanton Coit, 3 vols. (London: Allen and Unwin, 1932), 2:167–68.

8. Kant, *Fundamental Principles*, opening paragraph of section 1. By contrast, one of Hume's statements of the nature of virtue is that it is "a quality of the mind agreeable to or approved of by every one who considers or contemplates it." In David Hume, *An Enquiry Concerning the Principles of Morals*, ed. L. A. Selby-Bigge (Oxford: Clarendon Press, 1902), 261n.

9. Henry Sidgwick, *The Methods of Ethics* (New York: Dover Publications, 1966), 111. Recall Dewey's concept of the good as the satisfactory.

10. Aristotle, *Nicomachean Ethics*, 1106a 25–1106b 10.

11. Hume, *Principles of Morals*, 289.

12. Hume, *Principles of Morals*, 268, 277.

13. Aristotle, R. C. Jebb, and John Edwin Sandys, *The Rhetoric of Aristotle* (Cambridge, UK: The University Press, 1908), 1366b, 1–3.

14. Hume, *Principles of Morals*, 277–78.

15. Hartmann, *Ethics*, 2:226.

16. Henry Sidgwick, *Outlines of the History of Ethics* (Boston: Beacon Press, 1968), 131, 143.

17. Robert Merrihew Adams, "Saints," *Journal of Philosophy* 81, no. 7 (July 1984), 396.

18. Albert Schweitzer, *Civilization and Ethics* (London: Unwin Books/A. & C. Black, 1961), 42.

19. Lin Yutang, *The Wisdom of China and India* (New York: Random House, 1942), 364.

20. Lin Yutang, *Wisdom of China and India*, 345

21. Lin Yutang, *Wisdom of China and India*, 109.

CHAPTER 30: The Problem of Evil

1. Significant portions of this chapter also appear in the introduction to Dallas Willard's *The Allure of Gentleness* (San Francisco, CA: Harper-One, 2015).

CHAPTER 32: **Truth in Fire**

1. C. S. Lewis, *Mere Christianity: A Revised and Amplified Edition of the Three Books: "Broadcast Talks," "Christian Behaviour," and "Beyond Personality"* (London: G. Bles, 1952), 13.

2. Lewis, *Mere Christianity*, 58.

3. Lewis, *Mere Christianity*, 121.

4. Lewis, *Mere Christianity*, 11. Also see C. S. Lewis, *The Abolition of Man* (London: Oxford Univ. Press, 1943), 27–29.

5. David Hume, *An Enquiry Concerning Human Understanding, and Other Essays*, ed. Anthony Flew (Peru, IL: Carus Publishing, 1988), 195.

6. Christopher Norris, *What's Wrong with Postmodernism: Critical Theory and the Ends of Philosophy* (Baltimore: Johns Hopkins Univ. Press, 1990), 168.

7. Norris, *What's Wrong with Postmodernism*, 167.

8. Norris, *What's Wrong with Postmodernism*, 168.

9. C. S. Lewis, *The Screwtape Letters* (New York: Harper Collins, 1996), 1–2.

10. Lewis, *The Screwtape Letters*.

11. Bertrand Russell, *The Philosophy of Logical Atomism and Other Essays, 1914–19*, ed. John G. Slater (Boston: Allen & Unwin, 1986), 1st lecture.

12. W. V. Quine, *From a Logical Point of View; 9 Logico-Philosophical Essays* (Cambridge, MA: Harvard Univ. Press, 1953), 161.

13. See Lewis, *The Abolition of Man*, 81, for what he understands as "Natural."

14. See C. S. Lewis, "Religions Without Dogma," *Socratic Digest* 4 (1948), 87–88; and C. S. Lewis, "Is Theology Poetry?" *Socratic Digest* 3 (1945), 25–35. See also chapter 3 of *The Abolition of Man* and chapter 3 of C. S. Lewis, *Miracles: A Preliminary Study* (New York: Macmillan, 1978).

15. See the exhaustive treatment of this point in Edmund Husserl, *The Crisis of European Sciences and Transcendental Phenomenology: An Introduction to Phenomenological Philosophy* (Evanston, IL: Northwestern Univ. Press, 1970).

16. J. Richard Middleton and Brian J. Walsh, *Truth Is Stranger Than It Used to Be: Biblical Faith in a Postmodern Age* (Downers Grove, IL: InterVarsity Press, 1995).

17. Lewis, "Is Theology Poetry?"

18. Ronald Grigor Suny, *Los Angeles Times*, June 28, 1998, "Book Review" section, 6.

19. Thomas Aquinas, "Knowledge in God: 1a. 16,2," in *Summa Theologiae*, vol. 4, ed. Thomas Gornall (Cambridge: Cambridge Univ. Press, 1969), 80.

20. Immanuel Kant, *Critique of Pure Reason*, ed. Max F. Muller (London: Macmillan and Co, 1882), 51, 83.

21. Lewis, *Abolition of Man*, 27–29.

22. Edward O. Wilson, *Consilience: The Unity of Knowledge* (New York: Knopf, 1998), is the latest popular statement of this view.

23. Richard Taylor, *Metaphysics* (Englewood Cliffs, NJ: Prentice-Hall, 1983); John R. Searle, *The Rediscovery of the Mind* (Cambridge, MA: MIT Press, 1992).

24. The Wittgensteinian emphasis upon the centrality of what is "public" in the understanding of language and mind comes out to much the same thing.

25. Jean-Paul Sartre, "Intentionality: A Fundamental Idea of Husserl's Phenomenology," *Journal of the British Society for Phenomenology* 1 (1970), 4–5.

26. John Hick, "On Religious Experience," in *Faith, Skepticism, and Personal Identity*, ed. J. J. MacIntosh and H. A. Meynell (Calgary: Univ. of Calgary Press, 1994).

27. See Lewis's discussion of Ratio and Intellectus in chapter 7, subsection D, of C. S. Lewis, *The Discarded Image: An Introduction to Medieval and Renaissance Literature* (Cambridge: Cambridge Univ. Press, 1994).

CHAPTER 33: Postmodernism and the Christian Faith

1. Charles William Banister, "Twelve Psalms & Hymn Tunes," in *With One Heart and One Voice: A Core Repertory of Hymn Tunes Published for Use in the Methodist Episcopal Church, 1808–1878*, by Fred Kimball Graham (Oxford: Scarecrow Press, 2004), 45.

2. Richard Rorty, *Philosophy and the Mirror of Nature* (Princeton, NJ: Princeton Univ. Press, 1979).

3. Jean-François Lyotard, *The Postmodern Condition: A Report on Knowledge* (Minneapolis: Univ. of Minnesota Press, 1984).

CHAPTER 34: The Failure of Evangelical Politics

1. David Wells, *Above All Earthly Powers: Christ in a Postmodern World* (Grand Rapids, MI: Inter-Varsity Press, 2005).
2. Dallas Willard, *Renovation of the Heart: Putting on the Character of Christ* (Colorado Springs, CO: NavPress, 2002), 49.
3. This process has been carefully studied by Julie Ruben in *The Making of the Modern University: Intellectual Transformation and the Marginalization of Morality* (Chicago: Univ. of Chicago Press, 1991).
4. Thomas Hill Green, *Lectures on the Principles of Political Obligation* (London: Longmans, Green, 1895).
5. Green, *Lectures on the Principles of Political Obligation*, 207.
6. William Wilberforce, *A Practical View of the Prevailing Religious System of Professed Christians, in the Higher and Middle Classes, Contrasted with Real Christianity* (New York: American Tract Society, 1832). Read it together with William Law, *A Serious Call to a Devout and Holy Life* (London: J. M. Dent & Sons, 1931).
7. The Evangelical Manifesto can be found at www.anevangelicalmanifesto.com. Dallas was a member of the Steering Committee.

CHAPTER 35: Hermeneutical Occasionalism

1. Kevin Vanhoozer, "The Spirit of Understanding: Special Revelation and General Hermeneutics," in *Disciplining Hermeneutics: Interpretation in Christian Perspective,* ed. Roger Lundin (Grand Rapids, MI: Eerdmans, 1997), 131–66. All parenthetical notations refer to this work.
2. Augustine of Hippo, *Against the Academicians; the Teacher*, ed. Peter King (Indianapolis, IN: Hackett Publishing Co., 1995).
3. I have tried to be helpful at a popular, nonscholarly level on these matters with my book *In Search of Guidance: Developing a Conversational Relationship with God* (San Francisco: Harper & Row, 1993).

CHAPTER 40: The Price and the Glory of Intellectual Excellence in the Christian University

1. Charles Malik, "The Other Side of Evangelism," *Christianity Today,* November 7, 1980, 40.
2. Charles Malik, *The Two Tasks* (Wheaton, IL: Cornerstone Books, 1980), 28.
3. Charles Finney, "How to Preach the Gospel," in *The Christian Treasury:*

*Containing Contributions from Ministers and Members of Various Evangel-
ical Denominations* (Edinburgh: Johnstone, Hunter, 1846), 523.

4. John Gresham Machen, *What Is Christianity and Other Addresses*, ed.
   New B. Stonehouse (Grand Rapids, MI: Erdmans, 1951), 159.

5. Machen, *What Is Christianity,* 162–63.

6. Machen, *What Is Christianity,* 168–69.

7. Hymn, "Lift Up Your Hearts," by Henry Montague Butler.

CHAPTER 41: Leading the Teachers of the Nations

1. Owen J. Flanagan, *The Problem of the Soul: Two Visions of Mind and
   How to Reconcile Them* (New York: Basic Books, 2002).

2. Flanagan, *The Problem of the Soul,* xiii.

3. Flanagan, *The Problem of the Soul,* 3.

4. Flanagan, *The Problem of the Soul,* 212.

5. See Max Picard, *The Flight from God* (London: Harvill Press, 1951).
   Picard discusses the great sociological reversal in the Western world since
   the 1930s.

6. Julie A. Reuben, *The Making of the Modern University: Intellectual
   Transformation and the Marginalization of Morality* (Chicago: Univ. of
   Chicago Press, 1996).

7. Flanagan, *The Problem of the Soul,* 24–26, 208ff.

8. See David Van Biema, "The Lost Gospels," *Time,* December 22, 2003,
   for a beautiful illustration.

9. Bertrand Russell, *Why I Am Not a Christian and Other Essays on Religion
   and Related Subjects* (New York: Touchstone, 1957), 21.

10. For further discussion of the local congregation, see the final chapter
    of *Renovation of the Heart: Putting on the Character of Christ* (Colorado
    Springs, CO: NavPress, 2002).

Permissions

GRATEFUL ACKNOWLEDGMENT IS GIVEN TO THE FOLLOWING FOR the use of their work in this publication.

(p. 3)   Some content taken from *Renovation of the Heart*, by Dallas Willard. Copyright © 2002. Used by permission of NavPress. All rights reserved. Represented by Tyndale House Publishers, Inc.

(p. 11)   Dallas Willard, "Living a Transformed Life Adequate to Our Calling." Reprinted with permission of the Augustine Group, Washington, DC.

(p. 54)   Dallas Willard, "Spiritual Formation and the Warfare Between the Flesh and the Human Spirit," *Journal of Spiritual Formation and Soul Care* 1, no. 1 (Spring 2008), 79–87.

(p. 66)   Dallas Willard, "Beyond Pornography: Spiritual Formation Studied in a Particular Case," transcribed by Paul Rheingans and edited by Steve Porter, *Journal of Spiritual Formation and Soul Care* 9, no. 1 (2016), 5–17.

(p. 84)   Image from page 38 of *Renovation of the Heart* by Dallas Willard. Copyright © 2012. Used by permission of NavPress. All rights reserved. Represented by Tyndale House Publishers, Inc.

(p. 85)   Image from page 40 of *Renovation of the Heart* by Dallas Willard. Copyright © 2012. Used by permission of NavPress. All rights reserved. Represented by Tyndale House Publishers, Inc.

(p. 105) Dallas Willard, "When God Moves In: My Experience with *Deeper Experiences of Famous Christians*," chap. 6 in *Indelible Ink: 22 Prominent Christian Leaders Discuss the Books That Shape Their Faith*, edited by Scott Larsen (Colorado Springs, CO: WaterBrook Press, 2003), 49–56.

(p. 137) Lyle SmithGraybeal, "A Conversation with Dallas Willard About *Renovation of the Heart*," *Perspective* 12, no. 4 (October 2002), 3–5.

(p. 146) Dallas Willard, "A New Age of Ancient Christian Spirituality," transcribed by Scott Sevier on July 18, 2002, and published in two parts in *Steadfast* (October and December 2002.)

(p. 154) John Ortberg, "What Makes Spirituality Christian?," *Christianity Today* (March 6, 1995), 16–17.

(p. 158) Dallas Willard, "Gray Matter and the Soul," *Christianity Today* (November 18, 2002), 74.

(p. 161) Hope McPherson, "Going Deeper," *Response* (Winter 2000). Copyright ©
          2000 University Communications, Seattle Pacific University, Seattle, WA.

(p. 172) Luci Shaw, "Spiritual Disciplines in a Postmodern World," *Radix* 27, no. 2
          (Spring 2000), 4–7 and 26–31.

(p. 191) Gary Moon, "Getting the Elephant Out of the Sanctuary," *Conversations
          Journal* 8, no.1, (Spring/Summer 2010).

(p. 212) Keith Giles, "The Gospel of the Kingdom: A Conversation with Dallas
          Willard," in *Subversive Interviews: Volume 1* (Orange, CA: Subversive Un-
          derground, 2011), 67–82.

(p. 228) Andy Peck, "Kingdom Living," *Christianity + Renewal* (May 2002), 18-21.

(p. 237) Dallas Willard, "Your Place in This World," in *The Graduate's Bible*, tran-
          scribed and edited by Steve Bond (Nashville, TN: B&H Publishing Group,
          2005), 1117–22. Copyright © Dallas Willard, 2004.

(p. 246) Dallas Willard, "Discipleship," in *The Oxford Handbook of Evangelical The-
          ology*, edited by Gerald McDermott (Oxford: Oxford Univ. Press, 2010),
          236–46. Used by permission of Oxford University Press, USA.

(p. 261) Dallas Willard, "How to Be a Disciple," excerpts from pp. 281–99 (as
          adapted in the April 22–29, 1998, issue of *The Christian Century* maga-
          zine) from *The Divine Conspiracy* by Dallas Willard. Copyright © 1998 by
          Dallas Willard. Reprinted by permission of HarperCollins Publishers.

(p. 280) Dallas Willard, "How Does a Disciple Live?" *Radix* 34, no. 3 (Spring
          2009), 12–14.

(p. 301) Dallas Willard, "Spiritual Formation as a Natural Part of Salvation," in *Life
          in the Spirit: Spiritual Formation in Theological Perspective*, edited by Jeffrey
          P. Greenman and George Kalantzis (Downers Grove, IL: IVP Academic,
          2010), 45–61. Copyright © 2010 by Jeffrey P. Greenmand and George Ka-
          lantzis. Used by permission of InterVarsity Press, P.O. Box 1400, Downers
          Grove, IL 60615, USA. www.ivpress.com.

(p. 325) Dallas Willard, "Jesus," chap. 6 in *Dictionary of Christian Spirituality*,
          edited by Glen G. Scorgie with Simon Chan, Gordon T. Smith, and James
          D. Smith III (Grand Rapids, MI: Zondervan, 2011), 58-63. Copyright ©
          2011 by Glen G. Scorgie, Simon Chan, Gordon T. Smith, and James D.
          Smith III. Used by permission of Zondervan. www.zondervan.com.

(p. 358) Dallas Willard, "How Can Jesus Be the Son of God?" *The Student*
          (March 1988), 16–17. Reprinted and used by permission.

(p. 361) Dallas Willard, "C. S. Lewis and the Pursuit of Truth Today," *Sacred His-
          tory* (December 2005), 69–73 and 111–15.

(p. 390) Dallas Willard, "The Failure of Evangelical Political Involvement (in the
          Area of Moral Transformation)," *God and Governing: Reflections on Ethics,
          Virtue, and Statesmanship*, ed. Roger N. Overton (Eugene, OR: Pickwick
          Publications, 2009), 74–91.

(p. 411) Dallas Willard, "Hermeneutical Occasionalism," in *Disciplining Hermeneu-*

tics: Interpretation in Christian Perspective, edited by Roger Lundin (Grand Rapids, MI: Wm. B. Eerdmans Publishing Co., 1997), 167–72. Reprinted by permission of the publisher; all rights reserved.

(p. 421) Dallas Willard, "The Roles of Women in Ministry Leadership," foreword to *How I Changed My Mind About Women in Leadership*, by Alan F. Johnson (Grand Rapids, MI: Zondervan, 2010), 9–11.

(p. 425) Dallas Willard, "A Cup Running Over," in *The Art and Craft of Biblical Preaching: A Comprehensive Resource for Today's Communicators*, ed. Craig Brian Larson and Haddon Robinson (Grand Rapids, MI: Zondervan, 2005), 71–73. Copyright © 2005 by Christianity Today International. Used by permission of Zondervan. www.zondervan.com.

(p. 429) Dallas Willard, "Becoming the Kinds of Leaders Who Can Do the Job," *Cutting Edge* magazine, a publication of Vineyard USA (Summer 1999), 13–15.

(p. 475) Image © Rebecca Willard Heatley, 2001.

Bible quotations reflect the translations used in the original work. **PAR** refers to the author's paraphrase.

Scripture Index

Subject Index

God (*cont.*)
  Matthew Arnold's description of,
    101; means to growth in grace, 283;
    in occasionalism, 414–16; paradox
    of guidance and, 176–77; paths for
    being with without transformation,
    304; personal engagement and,
    64–65; plan of, 206–7; practice of
    the presence of, 330–31; principles of
    leadership under, 438; problem of evil
    and, 353–57; redeeming the time and,
    50–51; revealing himself, 189–90;
    role of worship and, 43; satisfaction/
    penal substitutionary theory, 193–94;
    scientist belief in, 99; sight of, 188;
    spiritual disciplines for objective of
    loving, 40; terrible images of, 208;
    thinking and, 8; view life from God's
    point of view, 278
going without sleep, 116
good, 342
"the good life", 118
good persons, 341–42, 406–7
Good Samaritan parable, 129–30
"good will", 341
Gordon, A. J., 107
gospels: of the atonement, 212–14;
    dwelling in word of Jesus, 272–73;
    forgiveness in, 148–49; four great
    questions of life and, 110–11; getting
    the message right, 461–64; heaven,
    186–87; of the kingdom, 212–13;
    life and, 149; in mind of disciple, 25;
    of secularism, 464–69
grace: as abundance, 183; action and,
    432; beauty as manifestation of, 185;
    discipline in spiritual life and, 311;
    divine grace, 12, 31; forgiveness and,
    218; as God acting in our life, 315–
    16; grace for abundance, 296–97; in-
    creasing, 315–16; inductive study of,
    219; living by, 39; means to growth

in, 31–32; means to growth in grace,
    283, 408; natural desires and, 64;
    salvation by, 108, 305, 441
grading, 87
Graham, Billy, 223, 247, 433, 447
gratification, 58, 72, 76
Great Commission, 143, 388
Green, Thomas Hill, 401
guidance, 176–77

habit, 72, 80
harm, 346
Hartmann, Nicolai, 341, 342
Hauptman, Herbert A., 99
Havergal, Frances Ridley, 107
"head knowledge", 405
Hearing God (Willard), 138, 177
heart, 46
heaven, 186, 213, 218, 288
hedonism, 173
Hegel, Georg Wilhelm Friedrich, 378
Heidegger, Martin, 370, 378
hell, 207
Hempel, Carl, 381
hermeneutical occasionalism, 411–18
Hick, John, 381
Hinduism, 101, 349
In His Steps (Sheldon), 165
Hobbes, Thomas, 372
Hobhouse, L. T., 99
holiness, 249, 252
Holy Living and Holy Dying (Taylor), 110
Holy Spirit, 64, 101, 106–7
hope, 344–45, 350–52
How I Changed My Mind About Women in Leadership (Johnson), 421
Huguenots, 403
human authority, 329
human relationships, 47
"humbleness of mind", 113
Hume, David, 118, 119, 342–43,
    363–64, 366

unhappy marriages, 76
University of Southern California,
102–3, 162–63

"vampire Christian", 310
Vanhoozer, Kevin, 411–18
VIM pattern: claiming local congregation for kingdom apprenticeship
and, 474–75; general pattern of,
15–16; ideal outcome of process of,
44–48; pornography and, 73–80;
quick survey of, 16–22; *Renovation of
the Heart* (Willard), 139; requirements for spiritual growth in, 472;
scriptural high points for, 48–49; in
spiritual formation, 16, 148; vision
of life in the kingdom, 17–18
Vineyard Church, 231–32
Virgin Birth, 157
Virgin Mary, 220
virtues: Aristotle on choosing, 341;
Aristotle on forms of, 343; bodily
behavior and, 123; cardinal virtues,
121; Christian virtues, 344–50; discipleship and, 265, 314–15; found in
monasticism, 334; generosity toward
enemies and others, 346–49; Hartmann on, 344; Hume on, 343–44;
intention in spiritual formation
and, 31, 119; monkish virtues, 118;
"Platonic" virtues, 344; temptation
to assume poverty and, 293
vision: of disciple of Jesus, 22–23;
disciple's solidarity with the poor
and, 297–98; of life in the kingdom,
17–18; pornography and, 73–80;
prurient, 75–76; *Renovation of the
Heart* (Willard), 139; as requirement
for spiritual growth in personal
transformation, 472; in spiritual
formation, 16, 148
vital knowledge, 405

vital will, 59
voluntary exile, 33
vulgarity, 274
walk, 297–98

Wallis, Jim, 224
watchfulness, 61–62
watching, 35, 116
Watson, Thomas, 10
Watts, Alan, 96
Watts, Isaac, 9, 242
Weatherhead, Leslie, 198
Weber, Max, 104
well-being, 286–87, 330, 332
Wells, David, 391
Wesley, John, xi, 9, 31, 103, 107, 110, 163,
229, 251–52, 254, 273, 294–95, 401–2
What Would Jesus Do (WWJD) movement, 233
Whitefield, George, 107, 251
Wiccan spirituality, 93, 101
Wilberforce, William, 31, 401
will: for child of light, 46; desire and,
69; distinguishing soul from,
141–42; embodied will, 61–62;
enslavement by desire, 73; impulsive
will, 59; power of choice and, 59;
reflective will, 60; Schopenhauer's
doctrine of the body as, 122–23;
vital will, 59; weakness of, 56–57,
58; will-to-good, 59
willful decisions, 276
Williams, Michael, 381
will power, 78
will-to-good, 59
Wimber, John, 231–32, 234
Winfrey, Oprah, 138
wisdom, 44, 50–51, 121
Wittgenstein, Ludwig, 371, 381
Wolf, Susan, 348
women, 421–24
Women at the Well group, 178

Also by Dallas Willard

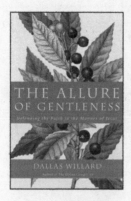
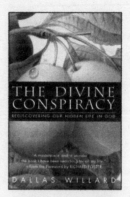
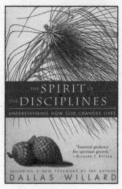